JOHN HALL
and his Patients

D0376401

For Charles

Stratford-upon-Avon
July 19, 1998
John Hall's house

Margarita Kay
(520) 296-8882

JOHN HALL
and his Patients

The Medical Practice of Shakespeare's Son-in-Law

JOAN LANE

Medical Commentary by
MELVIN EARLES

The Shakespeare Birthplace Trust

First published in the United Kingdom in 1996
The Shakespeare Birthplace Trust
The Shakespeare Centre · Stratford-upon-Avon

British Library Cataloguing in Publication Data

A catalogue record for this book is available from the British Library.

ISBN 0-7509-1095-X

Typeset in 11/12 pt Baskerville.
Typesetting and origination by
Alan Sutton Publishing Limited.
Printed in Great Britain by
Ebenezer Baylis, Worcester.

CONTENTS

General Editors' Preface   vi
Preface   viii
List of Figures and Illustrations   x
List of Abbreviations   xi
Introduction   xiii
A note on case numbers   xli
A note on the facsimile   xli
Select Observations and Commentary   1
Appendices:
    1. John Hall's will   350
    2. Chronology of John Hall's cases   351
    3. Concordance   353
Bibliographies:
    A History   357
    B Medicine   360
Indices:
    Drugs and preparations   362
    Medical conditions and related terms   367
    Persons   369
    Places   376

GENERAL EDITORS' PREFACE

The objects of The Shakespeare Birthplace Trust, as defined by the Act of Parliament under which it operates, are:

a) to promote in every part of the world the appreciation and study of the plays and other works of William Shakespeare and the general advancement of Shakespearian knowledge;
b) to maintain and preserve the Shakespeare birthplace properties for the benefit of the nation;
c) to provide and maintain for the benefit of the nation a museum and a library of books, manuscripts, records of historic interest, pictures, photographs and objects of antiquity with particular but not exclusive reference to William Shakespeare, his life, works and times.

It is from these objectives that the series of publications, of which this volume is part, derives. The central focus of the series is Shakespeare: his plays and their performance, his life, and the environment, historical, topographical, and domestic, in which he lived; and the raw material for volumes in the series is derived largely from the rich Shakespearian holdings of the Trust's Library and Records Office, in the form of printed books and archival and pictorial material relating to Shakespeare's life in Stratford, to the history of the town, to scholarship and criticism on his writings, and to the performance history of his plays. Such a collection of volumes, covering a wide range of topics – theatrical, literary and historical – cannot, of course, observe rigid editorial uniformity. To a considerable extent, therefore, treatment and approach from volume to volume are determined by the aims and needs of individual authors and editors. Within this rather broad scope, however, we seek to produce a series of volumes that will be of interest to the general reader while maintaining a high standard of scholarship in the furtherance of that basic objective of The Shakespeare Birthplace Trust, the general advancement of Shakespearian knowledge.

Robert Bearman
Robert Smallwood

Publications of
The Shakespeare Birthplace Trust
in association with
Alan Sutton Publishing

Robert Bearman
Shakespeare in the Stratford Records
1994

Joan Lane
John Hall and his Patients:
The Medical Practice of Shakespeare's Son-in-Law
1996

Philip Tennant
The Civil War in Stratford-upon-Avon:
Conflict and Community in South Warwickshire 1642–1646
1996

Jeanne Jones
Family Life in Shakespeare's England:
Stratford-upon-Avon 1570–1630
Forthcoming

PREFACE

When research makes the historian use a variety of different provincial record repositories, an interesting comparison emerges. All provide records and reference titles; the majority of the offices I have approached have provided photocopied material. However, some have been helpful well beyond any call of duty, looking up obscure details, checking material, suggesting further sources in my pursuit of Hall's patients and in the last two years many debts have been incurred. I would like to acknowledge my gratitude to the following record offices and libraries, especially the individuals who have provided information:

Bedfordshire, Mr Kevin Ward; Berkshire, Miss S.J.A. Flynn; British Library Manuscript Room; Buckinghamshire, Mr Hugh Hanley; Cambridgeshire, Mrs E. Staziker; College of Arms, Mr R.C. Yorke; Cornwall, Mr R. Petre; Derbyshire, Mrs M. O'Sullivan; Devon, Mr B. Carpenter; Durham, Miss J. Gill; Durham University, Mrs J.L. Drury; Glamorgan, Mrs A.M. Burton; Guy's Hospital Medical School Library; Hampshire, Mrs M. Cooke; Harrow, Mr R.W. Thompson; Leicestershire, Mr R.P. Jenkins; Northamptonshire, Miss R. Watson; Oxfordshire, Mr M. Priddy; Shropshire, Miss S.J. Acton; Surrey, Ms J. Pillay; Wellcome Institute Library, London; West Sussex, Mr R.J. Childs; Worcestershire, Mr R. Whittaker; York, The Borthwick Institute, Dr D. Smith.

Most of the research on the biographies, however, was carried out in Warwickshire, at the County Record Office and at The Shakespeare Birthplace Trust Records Office, Stratford-upon-Avon. I would particularly like to thank Miss Monica Ory and Mr Richard Chamberlaine-Brothers at Warwick for their unfailing help and Mr Andrew Snell for his willing assistance. At Stratford Mr Roger Pringle, the Birthplace Trust's Director, has enthusiastically supported the project and the joint general editors, Dr Robert Smallwood and Dr Robert Bearman, have provided valuable editorial advice and encouragement.

Not all records are in public offices, however, and many family pedigrees and archives reside with the present-day descendants of Hall's patients. I am obliged to Mr M. Fetherston-Dilke, Lady Hamilton, Mr A.V. Izod, Canon I. MacKenzie, the Marquess of Northampton, Sir Richard Hyde Parker, Captain N.C. Pease, Lord Sandys and Lord Saye and Sele for the considerable interest they have shown in the project.

I am grateful also to colleagues and friends who have suggested sources and allowed me to talk to them about Hall, particularly Professor B.C. Capp, Dr Robin Clifton, Dr Richard Cust, Dr Ann Hughes, Mrs Anne Tarver and Dr Philip Tennant. Dr Nita Burnby kindly helped to get me started; Dr Bill Allen at Warwick County Museum and Miss Wendy Hefford at the Victoria & Albert Museum provided advice on the Sheldon tapestries. My family have endured regular bulletins on my struggles with identifying Hall's patients and visited places associated with them. My son, Dr Charles Lane, heroically produced a graph from my Stratford parish register statistics and Mrs Anne Tarver provided the map of Hall's practice area. The pharmacological part of the work would not have been possible without Dr Melvin Earles's patient scholarship.

Joan Lane
Leamington Spa
February 1996

LIST OF FIGURES AND ILLUSTRATIONS

Figures
 1. Long-lived patients   xix
 2. Baptisms, marriages and burials, 1600–35,
    Stratford-upon-Avon   xxiv
 3. Map of Hall's practice area   xlii

Illustrations
 1. A page from Hall's manuscript case book   20
 2. William Compton, first Earl of Northampton   28
 3. Michael Drayton   36
 4. Huddington Court, Worcestershire, the home of
    John and Margaret Winter   88
 5. Part of the Sheldon tapestry map of Warwickshire   94
 6. The tomb of Mary and Richard Murden in
    Moreton Morrell church   106
 7. Westwood Park, Worcestershire, the home of Sir
    John Pakington   112
 8. The tomb of Sir Henry Rainsford and Anne his
    wife in Clifford Chambers church   116
 9. Warwick Priory, the home of Sir Thomas and
    Lady Puckering   168
10. Southam, Gloucestershire, the home of Margaret
    Delabere   206
11. Conway pedigree, showing the family of
    Katherine, Lady Hunks   224
12. Spencer Compton, second Earl of Northampton   252
13. Weston House, the Sheldon family home   258
14. John Trapp, schoolmaster of Stratford-upon-Avon   289
15. The tomb of John Thornborough in Worcester
    Cathedral   296

LIST OF ABBREVIATIONS

BL	British Library
Brinkworth	E.R.C. Brinkworth, *Shakespeare and the Bawdy Court of Stratford*, Chichester, 1972
Chamberlain	N.E. McClure (ed.), *The Letters of John Chamberlain*, Philadelphia, 1939
Chester	Joseph Foster (ed.), *Colonel Chester's London Marriage Licences, 1521–1869*, 1887
CL	*Country Life*
CSPD	*Calendar of State Papers, Domestic*
DNB	*Dictionary of National Biography*
Dugdale	William Dugdale, *The Antiquities of Warwickshire*, 1730
Fogg	Nicholas Fogg, *Stratford-upon-Avon, Portrait of a Town*, Chichester, 1986
Foster	Joseph Foster (ed.), *Alumni Oxoniensis; The Members of the University of Oxford, 1500–1714*, Oxford, 1891
Fripp	E.I. Fripp, *Shakespeare, Man and Artist*, Oxford, 1938
Grazebrook	H. Sydney Grazebrook, *The Heraldry of Worcestershire*, 1873
Hamper	William Hamper (ed.), *The Life, Diary and Correspondence of Sir William Dugdale*, 1827
HMC	Historical Manuscripts Commission
Hughes	Ann Hughes, *Politics, Society and Civil War in Warwickshire, 1620–1660*, Cambridge, 1987
Hughes, *MH*	Ann Hughes, 'Religion and Society in Stratford-upon-Avon, 1619–1638', *Midland History*, XIX, 1994, pp. 58–84
HV	*Heralds' Visitations*
(H)WRO	Hereford and Worcester Record Office, Worcester
Joseph	Harriet Joseph (ed.), *John Hall, Man and Physician*, New York, 1964
Lewis	B. Roland Lewis, *The Shakespeare Documents*, Stanford, 1941
Life	S. Schoenbaum, *William Shakespeare, A Documentary Life*, Oxford, 1975
LJRO	Lichfield Joint Record Office

Mins & Accts	Levi Fox (ed.), *Minutes and Accounts of the Corporation of Stratford-upon-Avon*, 1593–1598, Dugdale Society, XXXV, 1990
Morgan	Paul Morgan, 'The Subscription Books of the Diocese of Worcester and Class Structure under the Later Stuarts', Univ. of Birmingham MA, 1952
Nash	T.R. Nash, *Collections for the History of Worcestershire*, 1781–2
NRO	Northamptonshire Record Office
Pevsner	Nikolaus Pevsner, *The Buildings of England*
PRO	Public Record Office
QSOB	S.C. Ratcliff and H.C. Johnson (eds), *Warwick County Records: Quarter Sessions Order Books*, Warwick, 1935–64
RAMT	H.A.C. Burgess (ed.), *Register of Admissions to the Middle Temple*, 1949
SBTRO	Shakespeare Birthplace Trust Records Office, Stratford-upon-Avon
Shaw	William A. Shaw, *The Knights of England*, 1971
Symonds	C.E. Long (ed.), *Diary of the Marches of the Royal Army*, Camden Society, 1st series, LXXIV, 1859
VCH	*Victoria County History*
Venn	J. and J.A. Venn (comps), *Alumni Cantabrigiensis*, part 1, Cambridge, 1922–7
WCRO	Warwickshire County Record Office
WoQS	J.W. Willis Bund (ed.), *Worcestershire County Records: Calendar of the Quarter Sessions Papers, 1591–1643*, Worcester, 1900
Worthies	F.L. Colvile, *The Worthies of Warwickshire*, 1869

INTRODUCTION

Dr John Hall and his patients

Even if their author had not been William Shakespeare's son-in-law, the early seventeenth-century case notes kept by John Hall, covering a quarter of a century of provincial medical practice, would be of unique importance. The very scarcity of such a source for this period and its survival for well over three centuries make it an unrivalled record of social and medical history, especially for the Midlands. Hall's fame, however, has rested on the Shakespearian connection, for many scholars have questioned whether he was the source of the poet's scientific (especially medical) knowledge, whether he was the model for Lord Cerimon and, above all, whether he treated his father-in-law in his last illness. Other aspects of the casebook have been largely ignored, although the brief appearance of Michael Drayton among the patients has usually warranted comment.

The historical importance of Hall's case notes, however, extends beyond an interest in the county's most famous inhabitant, a significance recognised by their first editor, James Cooke, a Warwick surgeon, in 1657. Three centuries later, it is impossible to know how commonly practitioners kept case notes; they must have had medical and financial records of some kind, if only to be able to render accounts to patients. The survival rate of their papers, however, is very poor for the early seventeenth century, although after the Restoration they are slightly more common. With the grandest of patients, Sir Theodore Mayerne (1573–1655) filled twenty-three volumes. Case notes of provincial physicians in print, such as those of Napier or Symcotts,[1] show a remarkable similarity to Hall's in range of patients, treatments and geographical area served. John Hall's patients came from every social class and held widely contrasting religious views. They were of all ages and suffered many distressing physical afflictions; females predominated. Most

---

1. Michael MacDonald, *Mystical Bedlam: madness, anxiety and healing in seventeenth-century England* (Cambridge, 1981); F.N.L. Poynter and W.J. Bishop, *A Seventeenth-century Doctor and his Patients: John Symcotts, 1592(?)–1662*, Beds. Hist. Rec. Soc., XXXI, 1951.

lived within a 15 mile radius of Stratford (see map p. xlii) and they either consulted Hall in his dispensary or he made domiciliary visits. For a small minority of patients, all of very considerable status, Hall took his 'surgeon's box' and travelled long distances to their homes, to Worcester to treat the Bishop, to Ludlow to attend the Earl of Northampton and to Ombersley to see Lady Sandys. The difficulties of travel can be clearly imagined from John Speed's maps of 1610; many roads were impassable in the winter months, dusty in the summer and often hazardous. John Aubrey recalled how Dr William Harvey (1578–1657) 'rode on horseback . . . to visitt his Patients, his man following on foote, as the fashion then was'.[2]

The first problem in considering Hall's career is in attempting to discover when and why he began practising in Stratford. Research has shown that he came from Bedfordshire, one of the eleven children of a physician, William Hall of Carlton. John Hall must have been baptised about 1575, for he wrote that in 1632 he was aged about fifty-seven. With his brother he attended Cambridge (1589–93), becoming a Master of Arts in 1597. The next ten years of his life are a mystery. It has been suggested that he went to a continental university, perhaps Montpellier, favoured by Protestants, for further medical training and James Cooke, who edited and 'Englished' the notes from Hall's original Latin, was convinced that he had gone to France for this purpose. Hall's first indisputable appearance in Stratford, however, was in 1607, when he married Susanna Shakespeare on 5 June of that year. At the time of their marriage, she was, at twenty-four, eight years younger than her husband. Their only child, Elizabeth, was baptised on 21 February 1608, thirty-seven and a half weeks after the wedding. Shakespeare gave a hundred and five acres of land with Susanna when the marriage was arranged.[3]

What encouraged Hall to settle in Stratford in the early years of the seventeenth century cannot be established. At this period the town, with some three hundred houses, 'reasonably

2. John Aubrey, *Brief Lives* (1972), p. 291.

3. Mairi Macdonald, 'A New Discovery about Shakespeare's Estate in Old Stratford', *Shakespeare Quarterly*, vol. 45, no. 1 (Spring 1994), pp. 87–9.

well buylded of tymbar', had endured two serious fires (in 1594 and 1595). It relied on malting as its main industry but was a general market town for the surrounding farms and villages. Its river was an important asset for trade and transport. Hall may have come to Stratford through an acquaintanceship with Abraham Sturley, a Worcester man, who left Cambridge about 1580 to be a legal agent for Sir Thomas Lucy of Charlecote who had a Bedfordshire estate at Pavenham, the neighbouring village to Carlton. Sturley certainly knew Shakespeare, and their daughters were almost the same age. Dr William Hall's assistant, Matthew Morris, was bequeathed four pounds and all his master's astrology and astronomy books in 1607, to teach these skills to John Hall in due course (Appendix 1). It appears that Morris followed John Hall to Stratford; in 1613 he married Elizabeth Rogers and settled there. He may also have had local connections, for in 1597 Alice Morice had married John Court in the town and, a decade before, Mr Richard Morris and John Morris had also been residents.

In the seventeenth century qualified medical practitioners were clearly divided into three categories, the physician, the surgeon (with the barber-surgeon) and the apothecary. Of these, the physician was educated at Oxford, Cambridge, or the Scottish or European universities, and held the qualification of MD; surgeons and apothecaries were apprenticed, usually for seven years. Surgeons carried out practical procedures, such as amputations, blood-letting, setting fractures and lancing abcesses. In the early seventeenth century the Stratford parish register names nine surgeons or barber-surgeons in the town, two of whom, John Johnson and Arthur Rawson, died in 1609 and 1610 respectively. There were also apothecaries who sold medicines in their shops and made up prescriptions. Physicians, however, were essentially the consultants of their day and practised in only a minority of communities. In Hall's day, for example, there were physicians in Coventry, Warwick, Sutton Coldfield and Worcester.[4] When Hall was himself very ill, his wife summoned two unnamed physicians, his friends, to attend him. At the beginning of the

4. J.H. Raach, *A Directory of English Country Physicians, 1603–43* (1962), p. 117.

century there was no physician living in Stratford and the opportunity to set up in practice with a prosperous local bride must have been considerable. Scandal was to touch them in 1613, when Susanna Hall sued John Lane, a young Alveston gentleman, for defamation; he had said she suffered from a venereal infection as a result of having 'bin naught[y] with Rafe Smith', a hatter. Lane was summoned to the Worcester consistory court to answer the slander and was excommunicated for not attending; the case was closed.[5] Later that year Hall treated John Lane's aunt, Joan Lane of Alveston, in her last illness.

The earliest of Hall's cases has always been cited as the Earl of Northampton's, whom he treated in 1617, and this is, indeed, the first year that he gave an actual date with a patient's name. However, internal evidence in two patients' notes indicates that the earliest case dates from at least six years before. As he attended Elizabeth Boughton at the age of thirty-six and she had been born in 1575, Hall must have treated her in 1611; patients' ages have been found to be an extremely accurate category in the case notes. The probate inventory of another patient, Joan Lane, was made on 11 October 1613 and Hall attended her in her final illness. Two other patients, Sir Thomas Beaufou (about 1614) and Lady Rous (1616), were also certainly treated before the year 1617.

At whatever date Hall arrived in Stratford before his marriage to Susanna Shakespeare in 1607, he would have found a town with a decided puritan element and an opposing papist group. Their quarrels ran through all aspects of community life, especially the Corporation's affairs, with increasing bitterness, sometimes exacerbated by national politics as well as local grudges.[6] It is therefore all the more surprising that, alongside staunchly protestant patients, Hall, a known Puritan, also attended Catholics of various categories – papists, recusants and church-papists (who attended minimally to avoid prosecution) – especially as his knowledge of their views might well have been dangerous. The accusation that

---

5. *Life*, p. 237 shows a photograph of the entry in the court books.
6. Hughes, *MH*, pp. 58–84.

his wife was 'popishly affected' in 1606 may, of course, have influenced this sector of society.[7]

Hall noted that seven of his patients were Catholics. Apart from Browne, a priest, this annotation was given to one man, Nicholas Fortescue of Cookhill, and five women, Clare Peers, Elizabeth Richardson, Lady Smith, Mary Talbot and Margaret Winter. Such descriptions would have been widely acknowledged, for all belonged to intransigent recusant families, most of whom had suffered very considerably for their faith. Religious conformity, especially as a measure of trustworthiness, rather than crime, became the main preoccupation of the county magistracy in the years up to 1642. The whole region of south-west Warwickshire and across the border into Worcestershire was an area of old religious loyalties, as demonstrated by the families involved in the Gunpowder Plot of 1605. It was furthermore a locality of remote houses, such as Huddington or Grafton, where secrecy was possible. In 1596 the Bishop of Worcester, Dr Bilson, could write despairingly to Sir Henry Cecil that the diocese was 'as dangerous as any place that I know' for recusancy[8] and matters were to change little in the next decades. Hall also attended patients who belonged to other known Catholic families, such as the Throckmortons and the Sheldons, whose religion he did not record. He had a striking number of patients living in the folk-rhyme area of 'papist Wixford'. The general fear of papists was such that they were not allowed to bear arms in 1613.[9]

Just as the region was divided in religious terms, there were also distinct political factions, each with aristocratic and gentry leadership, and there seems to have been a decided political wariness across the county. Dugdale had noted this sense of a 'changing' society, reflected, for example, in the loss of local wakes.[10] Warwickshire's links to the court were weak, with the worst success rate of any county in collecting Ship Money for Charles I, as the sheriff and constables refused to act or name defaulters. Many from these families were also Hall's patients. Thus he attended loyal protestant gentry and

7. Brinkworth, p. 132.
8. *VCH Worcs.*, III, p. 57.
9. Chamberlain, I, p. 411.
10. Dugdale, II, p. 682.

aristocracy (Sir Thomas Puckering, the Earl of Northampton), as well as the most extreme puritan preachers and their supporters (John Rogers, Thomas Wilson, George Quiney, Lady Browne, Lady Rous, Mary Murden). Even though Hall had died before war broke out, his personal allegiance was firmly held and we know, for example, that he travelled to Warwick a month before his death in 1635 in the company of John Trapp to visit Thomas Dugard, a noted Puritan.[11]

It is apparent that Hall frequently treated several members of a family, many with widespread kin connections. This is especially so among females, so that mothers and daughters, aunts, cousins and more distant relations by marriage in a family would in turn be attended by Hall. Some women he treated both before and after marriage, and several examples of this have been traced. In addition to his wife and daughter, it is also striking that ninety-three of the 155 patients selected for the 'Observations' (60 per cent) were females, irrespective of status and age, though since these came from a much larger total, it is difficult to know what weight may be placed on the proportion. Hall recorded only a small number of children, eight boys aged from six months to fifteen years and six girls between nine and seventeen. His young patients were primarily in wealthy families, sometimes a precious heir or only child (George Talbot, Thomas Underhill, Sarah Harington), but he also treated Stratford children such as Lydia Trapp, Margaret Baker and Edward Rawlins. Contemporaries believed that the cure of children should be left to nature.

The oldest of his patients were John Thornborough, the Bishop of Worcester, who was eighty-three, Sir Thomas Beaufou (seventy), Lady Hunks (sixty-nine) and Francis Harvey (sixty-five). Several outlived Hall, attaining a great age; Lady Sandys survived to ninety-three, Thornborough to ninety, Beaufou to eighty-six, Lady Clark to eighty-four and Lady Hunks to about eighty-five. Ten patients lived into their seventies and twenty-two into their sixties (Fig. 1). Clearly, prosperity was likely to extend a patient's life expectancy, and recent research has shown that at twenty-one the heirs of Jacobean squires and above could look forward to reaching

11. BL 23146.

the age of sixty-three, although average male life expectancy for the years 1601–31 was only 38.7 years.[12] The prospect for married females was noticeably worse, for in the years 1558–1641, 45 per cent of aristocratic wives died before the age of fifty, a quarter from childbirth and its complications. Indeed, childbed deaths at this period (1600–50) were 125 to 158 per thousand.[13] In spite of such figures, Francis Bacon was able to comment that in 1623 he saw at least one person over sixty in every village.

Figure 1: Long-lived patients

Age at death   Age at death

93	Lady Sandys	66	Lady Browne
90	John Thornborough		Susanna Hall
86	Sir Thomas Beaufou	64	Sir Stephen Harvey
85	Lady Hunks		Elizabeth Sheldon (Petre)
84	Lady Clark	*c.* 64	Michael Drayton
82	George Underhill		Henry Izod
79	Susanna Vernon	62	William, Earl of
	Thomas Underhill		Northampton
78	Julian West		Mary Nash
76	Elizabeth Richardson	61	Francis Bassett
75	Isabel Sadler		Robert Hanslap
	Simon Underhill	60+	Leonard Kempson
74	William Barnes		John Symons
	Frances Fiennes		Elizabeth Sheldon
73	Sir Simon Clark		Henry Parker
72	Thomas Fawcet		Lady Underhill
68	Mary Combe		Margaret Sheldon
	Lady Jenkinson		Lady Carrington (Smith)
	John Trapp		Countess Compton
	Sir Edward Underhill		

Often Hall precisely recorded patients' ages, status and, usually, their place of residence. Only rarely was an

12. Peter Laslett, *The World we have Lost – further explored* (1983), p. 108.
13. Lawrence Stone, *The Crisis of the Aristocracy, 1558–1641* (Oxford, 1967), p. 283.

occupation stated, and then presumably to avoid confusion with another person of the same name. Clerics, several of whose children Hall treated, were noted as a form of status, as were knights, gentlemen and ladies. A number of females were identified only in their relationship to the head of a family, 'wife to the Lord Say's eldest son' or 'Mrs Sheldon, wife to the Son'. At the other end of society, however, some patients were noted without a title, by only a surname (Austin, Lynes, Rogers), their gender indicated by the Latin text and, sometimes, by symptoms. Only three patients were intentionally difficult to identify, well-to-do males with urino-genital conditions, 'one of Northampton', William Clavell and 'Mr Psamire', although the first two cases seem to have been censored by Cooke rather than disguised by Hall.

As well as treating prosperous patients, Hall also attended members of their households, usually identified as such, the fees presumably paid by their employers, as shown in the Compton family's surviving household accounts. Thus Hall's Casebook includes notes on patients in the households of Mrs Iremonger, Mrs Sheldon, Mr Broad, Lady Puckering and the Countess of Northampton, and also on well-born companions, Edward Pennell, Lord Northampton's gentleman, Elizabeth Stoker and Fulca Swift. Predictably, the very poorest were least often his patients, although Hudson and Roberts were in this category at a time when about a quarter of Stratford's inhabitants were paupers. Hall also treated humble patients such as the wife of a small farmer (Elinor Sheffield), one apothecary's wife, another's daughter and an inn servant (Joseph Jelfes), but they were all local inhabitants with whom he had personal links.

The question of whether Hall attended William Shakespeare in his last illness in 1616 has long intrigued scholars and, if he did, why the details were not given in the Casebook, especially as Hall included notes on his wife's, his daughter's and his own ailments. There is no doubt that Hall was practising in Stratford in 1616 and that Shakespeare died there, with no suggestion that the relationship between the two men was other than amicable. Several members from the widespread Shakespeare family were certainly Hall's patients and it may be that Cooke's interest in the manuscripts stemmed at least partly from the Shakespearian connection.

However, Cooke referred to there being a thousand cases originally in Hall's notes and such a number could feasibly have been a total in some twenty-five years of practice. He seems to have described only cases of medical significance and almost exclusively those with a successful outcome. He recorded few deaths among his patients. We know too the names of other patients than those chosen as 'observations', because they are mentioned in passing or in other sources, Mrs Savage, Mr Ferriman, Sidrak Davenport, William Colemore, Lady Temple, Lady Tyrrell and the Countess of Leicester, for example.

The year of Shakespeare's death, however, was one of several when the mortality rate rose exceptionally, both in the whole year and in certain months, not only in Stratford but in Warwickshire and England.[14] Although not the worst of early seventeenth-century epidemics in the town (a distinction given to that of 1624), the one that occurred in 1616 is notable for its extended character (1617–19 also had high death rates) and the slow return to normality achieved by 1620 before the next and far worse outbreak of 1624–5. To assess the dramatic nature of such epidemics, it is clear from the town's burial registers that, in the early years of the century when Hall arrived in Stratford, between forty-five and seventy-five (average sixty-five) inhabitants a year were buried. With annual baptisms always above this total (Fig. 2), the population level remained stable. However, in years with dramatically increased burial rates (1604, 1608, 1616–18, 1624–5), deaths exceeded births very noticeably, resulting in a decline in population that was slow to reverse. In overall terms, the cause of death and type of epidemic may not seem important, but infections selected different inhabitants. Thus, the relatively high rate of child/infant deaths from the increased total of April and May 1604 is annotated in the Stratford register as *de peste*, meaning an epidemic, not necessarily bubonic plague as such. This mortality pattern suggests diphtheria as the cause, while the greater number of warm-weather (May–July) burials in 1608, with adults and children equally affected, indicates a smallpox epidemic. Hall occasionally noted that a patient had had smallpox (the sons

14. C. Creighton, *A History of Epidemics in Britain* (Cambridge, 1894), I, p. 537.

of Mr Bishop and Mr Holyoak) and Mr Farman was unable to leave Lady Beaufou's house at Emscote for this reason. The months widely acknowledged for bubonic plague were August, September and October, as Stratford had experienced in such years as 1558, 1564 and 1581, and the south Midlands, especially Worcestershire, was very badly infected with plague in both 1604 and 1608–10.[15]

By 1616, however, a far more severe affliction, a typhus epidemic, appeared and was noted by Hall as 'the new fever' when he attended Lady Beaufou near Warwick in July 1617. It had a high morbidity rate and attacked even the wealthiest. General immunity in the population was lacking to this relatively new disease, which was originally known as 'ship-fever' and came inland after 1588. Prince Henry, James I's heir, had died of it in November 1612 in London. As typhus is louse-borne it naturally spread best in the colder weather when people huddled together for warmth in unventilated living conditions, although typhus was unusual in rarely killing very young children. It was an infection of medical interest and Sir Theodore Mayerne, later to treat Sir Thomas Puckering of Warwick, wrote a clinical treatise after he had attended Prince Henry, *Ad Febrem Purpuream*. In 1616 and 1617 death rates had increased not only in Stratford but also in the surrounding hamlets of Shottery, Luddington and Bishopton, and there were three or four strangers a year recorded in the town's burial register, perhaps as carriers or victims of typhus.

In 1624–5 a more dramatic picture emerges from parish registers, not only in Warwickshire, as spotted fever (typhus), again called the 'new disease', struck across the whole country, aggravated in some parishes by particularly virulent plague. Preceded as it was by a severe drought, the 1624 outbreak was undoubtedly far worse than that of 1616. Parliament did not meet from 4 September 1623 until 15 February 1624 and was then again adjourned, while in Warwickshire all wakes, bear-baiting, fairs and May games were forbidden for fear of infection.[16] Even remote villages were affected. Death was often very sudden: the Duke of Lennox, for example, died

15. J.F.D. Shrewsbury, *A History of Bubonic Plague in the British Isles* (Cambridge, 1970), pp. 276–7.
16. QSOB, I, p. 35.

only three days after being taken ill and many patients succumbed to heart failure before the distinctive typhus rash appeared. The Stratford statistics, with over a hundred burials, tell the same story (Fig. 2), including some seventeen deaths in Shottery alone. Although not always in agreement with Holy Trinity's vicar, Thomas Wilson, the Corporation was so impressed with his 'learned sermons . . . in the tyme of the late visitation and sickness of the plague' that they raised his stipend in January 1627 from £40 to £60 a year.[17]

The 1624–5 typhus epidemic was exacerbated by an overlapping new, virulent strain of plague (*Pasteurella pestis*) across the south Midlands and, in Worcestershire, some parishes were so badly afflicted that money to relieve victims was raised in the county.[18] Fear of infection was understandably general: Thomas Hobson of Cambridge, whose daughter, Hall's patient, had married Sir Simon Clark, wrote of his concern that sending letters spread infection from one area to another. The high sickness and death rates were seen as a portent of disaster at the beginning of Charles I's reign and his unpopular marriage. As labour became scarce and travel was feared, trade and the economy suffered, while reports of civil disorder and looting increased. A bad harvest and wet spring worsened poverty generally. The godly could depict such a combination of events as divine punishment, and many must have found the afflictive hand of God hard to endure.

For the rest of Hall's career there was no year of extremely high deaths in Stratford, although he noted in 1630 that the nine-year-old Margaret Baker had just recovered from smallpox and the rise in the town's burials for 1630–1 may well have been because of this disease; Birmingham had an outbreak of plague at this time. The cause of Hall's own death in November 1635 at the age of sixty is not known, although two of his neighbours were also buried in the same month and he made his will orally a day before burial, which suggests sudden and mortal illness. He did die, however, in the period leading to February 1636, a month with an exceptionally high rate of twenty-one burials. John Hall's entry in the register for

17. Hughes, *MH*, pp. 58–84.
18. Shrewsbury, p. 301.

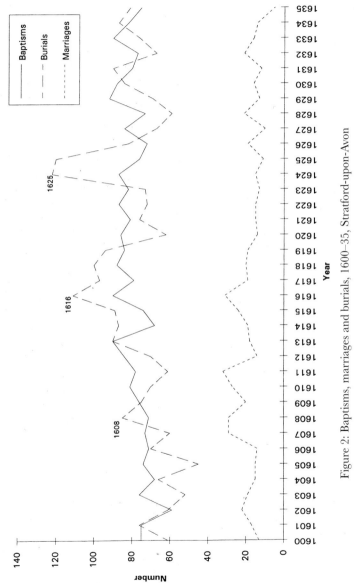

Figure 2: Baptisms, marriages and burials, 1600–35, Stratford-upon-Avon

26 November 1635 noted him as *medicus peritissimus* (a most skilful physician), the only medical practitioner thus distinguished.

Hall's role as an inhabitant of Stratford has been explored by many scholars during the last hundred years and it is clear that he was a significant local figure.[19] His marriage and his professional activities made him well known. He participated to a limited extent in civic affairs, although always trying to avoid greater involvement in Corporation matters. He was fined £10 rather than be knighted by Charles I in 1626. He did act as churchwarden, but only for a single year, 1628, whereas most men served for several, as a sidesman (1629) and as vicar's warden (1633). He twice pleaded his medical duties as the reason for not participating in Stratford's affairs, but, obliged to be elected as a burgess in 1632, he responded by not attending. He was, however, actively involved in the bitter struggles over appointing incumbents to Holy Trinity Church. With Bishop Thornborough's support he won an unseemly wrangle to change his family pew to near the Clopton tomb in the church and was accused of using 'abusive speech' against the Bailiff. On a later occasion he was expelled from the Council for 'wilful breach of language . . . and continued disturbances'. In 1629 he presented a carved pulpit to the parish church, a fitting gift for a man of puritan sympathies. Primarily medical practice must have made Hall anxious to be seen as neutral while civic duties, for which he had a great distaste, interfered with his professional obligations. He was, however, clearly a man of decided convictions who did not shrink from debate and confrontation. Hall's commitment to Thomas Wilson, the puritan cleric, may be judged from the use of his house for a special session of the peculiar court, with Wilson presiding.[20]

After over three centuries, a practitioner's relationship with his patient is hardest of all to evaluate, largely from lack of evidence, but one of Hall's gentry patients, Sidrak Davenport, wrote to him reporting symptoms, discussing the obligations of professional attention and Hall's borough duties.[21]

19. Researchers such as Wheler and Fripp.
20. Hughes, *MH*, pp. 58–84.
21. SBTRO, ER1/1/94.

Good Mr Hall

I sent my boy to you this morning to carrie my water &
acquaint you with what daunger & extremitie I am faullen
into in respect my shortness of breath & obstructions of my
liver, that I cannot sleep nor take anie rest, and although I
have more need of yr presence this daie than to stay untill
to morrow yet in regard of the multitude of yr affairs being
ye Markett daie yet I well hoped you would not have failed
me to morrow morning being fridaie at 7 of the clock in the
morning, for I will not eat or drink untill I see you. My
owne Servante is not yet returned from Stratford, but about
dynner time this daie I received a note from you howe that
you cannot be here at Bushwood with me to morrow in
respect of some private meeting at yr hall concerning the
affairs of yr Towne you saie you are warned to be there & if
you be absent you are threatened to be fined, I did not
expect to receive such a kinde of excuse from you,
considering the daungerous estate I am in, as maie appear
bie my water, & the relation of my servant whome I sent to
you this morning of purpose, & therefore I think it is not
anie Town business, that can hinder you but rather that you
have promised some other patient & would put me off with
this excuse: And if it were so indeed that you are sommoned
& warned to appear as you wright & for not appearance to
be fined, it is verie strange to me, & unheard off that a
Phisitian should be incorporated of anie Towne or made a
Member of anie corporation, not onlie to interupt his
Studies, hinder his practice but also to indaunger the liefe
of his patient for want of his presence, because in a tedious
& daungerous disease his presence is to be preferred before
his private occasions, for what cannot a daie bring fourth &
a little error causeth a relapse wch is worse than the disease,
I know my disease is p[ar]lous & procrastination is
daungerous. I have relied on you I trust you will not faile
me now, I know you cannot be fined for visiting yr patients.
Neither the Towne so barren of able men, nor the
Magistrates so indiscreet to lay this burthen uppon you
whose profession is to be most abroad & cannot be effected
by an apprentice as theirs maie, & for you to be vexed with
Towne buissenes whose calling is out of Towne it would

seem a great folly in you & more mallice in them to requier. Therefore I councell you as a friend never be bounde as long as you may be free you shall but derogat from yr selfe, heap a great deale of troubles uppon you distract you from yr Studie wch deserveth the whole employment of anie Man, had he a 100 yeres to lyve longer: Therefore I pray you all excuses set apart that you wilbe here to morrow morning by 7 of ye clock for I will fast untill ye come, and I know you cannot incurr anie daunger having so lawfull a calling. Thus with my best wishes & hartie love remembered to yr self & ye rest of my good friendes with you I commit you to Gods holie protection & ever remain

Yor trewly loving friend & Servant
Sid Davenport

My Brother Colemores Phisick is ended & all is taken he staieth at home purposely to speak with you tomorrow morning for further directions.
Bushwood. thursdaie 5 July 1632

Davenport lived at Bushwood Hall, some 12 miles from Stratford; unmarried, he was the brother-in-law of the Puritan William Colemore, whom Hall obviously also attended. In 1618 Davenport had bought land from Sir Thomas Beaufou (no. 74), to whom he was related.[22] The letter reveals some significant details of Hall's practice methods, in that he had written to Davenport to defer a promised visit, that he was expected to set out very early in the morning to arrive at Bushwood by seven o'clock and he had already received a urine sample delivered by Davenport's servant.

Davenport stressed that a physician should undertake domiciliary visits and that it was not acceptable to send an apprentice, as craftsmen might. He knew something of medical practice, for his cousin was the London barber-surgeon John Woodall,[23] and he was aware that Hall would expect him to have starved before the consultation. Davenport suspected that another patient's condition was regarded as

22. J.W. Ryland, *The Records of Rowington* (Oxford, 1922), II, p. 191.
23. PRO, Prob 11/162.

more serious than his, and yet the letter shows a touching confidence that Hall would treat him. Davenport had made his will on 30 April 1632 and his fears for his own health were well founded, for he was dead by late October, only three months after writing to Hall. The Corporation minutes indicate that Hall performed his civic duty and also attended to his practice during these July days.

Although Hall's monument in Holy Trinity Church predictably praises his skills and character, perhaps the best assessment of his professional standards can be found in his own words, *Qui sine via et methodo Medicinam facit est sine clavo at remis navigit* (he who practises medicine without course and method, sails without rudder and oars).

Hall died in November 1635 a wealthy man, with goods worth some £2,000, including £600 or £700 in ready cash. After his death, the widowed Susanna seems to have lived at New Place, which had been Shakespeare's home. John Hall left his wife his London house (uncertainly identified), with half his money and goods; his daughter, Elizabeth Nash, inherited the family property, 'Butlers' in Acton, meadow-land near Stratford and the rest of his money and goods. Hall requested his son-in-law, Thomas Nash, to dispose of both books and manuscripts, the latter of which Nash might burn if he so wished (Appendix 1). Susanna survived John Hall by fourteen years; she died on 11 July 1649 and was buried five days later, at the age of sixty-six, next to her husband in Holy Trinity. Their only daughter, widowed in 1647, later remarried; Elizabeth's second husband was Sir John Barnard of Abington (Northants.), an elderly widower. She died in 1670 and he four years later: the marriage was childless.

The casebook

The early history of the case notes was described by James Cooke (1614–88) in his preface to the first edition of *Select Observations*, which appeared in 1657. In 1644 Cooke had been attending some soldiers in Stratford and visited Susanna Hall, from whom he bought two manuscript volumes in John Hall's handwriting. Cooke considered that they were 'both intended for the Presse'. He added that these Observations had been selected by Hall 'as choysest' from at least a thousand, as 'fittest for publique view'. These original notes were translated by Cooke from Hall's Latin and the first volume of cases was published. The so-called second volume has disappeared, as have Hall's other papers. Cooke was not new to medical authorship, for in 1648 his *Mellificium Chirurgiae* (*The Marrow of Surgery*) had been published. Cooke loyally dedicated the *Select Observations* to Fulke, Lord Brooke of Beauchamp Court, near Alcester, whose parents and brothers he had treated.

Select Observations went into two more editions, in 1679 and 1683 and it is the second (1679) edition, closer to Hall's Latin notes than the first, that is here reproduced. Cooke's preface to the second edition is dated 25 March 1675. His personal editorial role can occasionally be discerned, for both as a local man and as a practitioner he added some minor material of his own. Thus, he noted that the young John Emes lived at Alcester (no. 12 in this edition) and identified which Southam was intended for one patient (no. 9). As a practitioner, he also added his own preferred treatment for some patients (as for no. 49) and substantial comments from famous medical authors (nos 68, 90, 155, 160). Conversely, he often omitted, presumably as no longer relevant or politically acceptable, some of Hall's notes on his patients' characters. He disguised some patients from his readership (nos 113, 114, 143), although their identity was clear in Hall's notes. The issue of patient confidentiality was clearly not significant. In the introduction to the 1657 edition, Dr John Bird commented that Hall had not wished the work to be published until after his own death, but more to guard his medical secrets (as in no. 114) than to protect patients' privacy. Indeed, those of Hall's patients who did reach a great age, such as Lady Sandys, Thomas Underhill and Mary Combe, were still alive in 1679 when the second edition was published; their reactions are not known. By the second edition, however, the title page added that the Observations were 'of Eminent Persons in desperate Diseases' and surviving patients may have felt flattered to have been included.

Cooke's editing only rarely confused identification of patients, but in some cases a serious mistranslation or misunderstanding can be found. Thus Mary Hunt (no. 15) was given the wrong gender, and the slightly unclear entry headed

'Wife' (no. 133) was misunderstood by Cooke who wrongly thought the preceding patient was male, when the Latin case notes indicated it was a woman being treated. Cooke is misleading, however, in his labels of status. Hall's use of *Generosus/Generosa* (gentleman/woman) and *Oppidanus/Oppidana* (townsman/woman of Stratford) were clear and accurate, but not easy to translate into English and so Cooke relied on 'Mr/Mrs' and 'Goodwife'. Sometimes, however, he calls a patient 'Mrs' although Hall had noted her as *Domina*, as in the case of Lady Sandys (no. 37). Occasionally, Cooke mistranslated and so later editions have wrongly identified patients, for example, Mary Talbot (no. 60) or Sarah Harington (no. 145). Cooke's most misleading identifications to the modern reader, however, are of the personal companions, members of grand households, whom he always described as 'maid', 'waiting maid' or 'servant'. Hall used the term *pedisequa* (companion) for Elizabeth Stoker, Alice Collins and Mrs Wincoll, while William Broad's family tutor, whom Hall noted as *pedagogus* (schoolmaster), Cooke also described as 'servant'.

Although ninety-seven of Hall's cases were either dated in his notes or can be calculated from details he provided (53 per cent), we do not know exactly how or when he wrote them up, though in some instances it was well after the treatment had been given. The observations were not arranged by date, but Hall continued to describe cases in the year of his own death. We can only conclude that the last months of his life were spent in preparing them for publication (Appendix 2). For some patients he added a note suggesting continued contact many years after treatment (no. 48) and several of his female patients he attended as girls, young mothers and mature women. Hall does not seem to have had a particular system for arranging his observations; they were not grouped chronologically, geographically or by diseases, but he cross-referenced on many occasions for similar medications or symptoms. Hall's criteria for choosing certain cases are unclear, although curing or relieving a patient was an obvious factor and sufferers of substantial status predominated.

The *Observations* went into a third edition in 1683. The original manuscript casebook was owned in the eighteenth century by David Garrick and later by Edmond Malone, before being bought on 10 October 1868 by the British

Museum from the Edinburgh bookseller, William Paterson of Princes Street, to become part of the Egerton MSS. Scholars have long been intrigued by the Casebook and endeavoured to identify the patients. For example, R.B. Wheler owned an interleaved copy of the *Observations* where he recorded his identifications and Edgar Fripp kept substantial notes on likely candidates who could be the patients. More recently Harriet Joseph prepared her edition of *Shakespeare's Son-in-Law: John Hall, Man and Physician* (1964), based on the second edition of *Select Observations*. This new edition has concentrated on identifying the patients Hall attended and interpretation and explanation of Hall's treatment in the context of medical practice in his time. The majority (125) of his patients have been positively identified, suggestions can be made for a further sixteen, and for only fifteen is no identification feasible.

Hall's prescriptions

The system of therapy practised by John Hall had its origins in early Greek medicine and was based on a concept of four cardinal humours: blood, associated with the heart, phlegm, associated with the brain, yellow bile or choler, the humour of the liver, and black bile or melancholy, the humour of the spleen. Galen of Pergamon (*c.* AD 130–200) associated each humour with the four elements of Greek philosophy and their abstract qualities. Blood (air) was warm and moist, phlegm (water) cold and moist, yellow bile (fire) warm and dry, black bile (earth) cold and dry.

Each individual and each part of the body had a natural combination of humours. In this system there was an interaction between physical and mental processes, and the dominant humour determined both physical constitution and temperament. Where blood was dominant the person exhibited a sanguine constitution and temperament, characterised by a full habit of body, ruddy complexion and a courageous, hopeful outlook on life. A thin frame, dark complexion and meditative disposition indicated a melancholic constitution where black bile was the dominant humour. A preponderance of phlegm and yellow bile resulted in phlegmatic and choleric constitutions respectively.

Ill-health was the result of a perturbation of the balance of the humours, when the humour in dominance created a predisposition to certain forms of bodily or mental illness. Climate, diet, insomnia, lack of exercise, emotional disturbance and, in the opinion of some physicians, astrological influences, could all affect the state of the humours. Illness was believed to be caused by one or more humours upsetting the natural balance (*dyscrasia*) or if the humours became unhealthy and depraved (*cacochymia*). It followed that because each person had a unique normal or healthy humoral composition any change in the humours resulted in an illness peculiar to the patient. Thus a prerequisite to therapy was a knowledge of the normal humoral constitution of the patient. In some of Hall's observations he makes a diagnosis that appears to agree with the modern ontological concept of disease as a separate and classifiable entity distinct from the individual. Nevertheless, it is obvious that the thrust of his therapy was not primarily to attack a 'disease' but to restore his patient's humoral balance.

Symptoms were caused by the condition or movement of the humours. An excess of phlegm moving down from the head to the bowels resulted in a dysentery. If it lodged in the abdomen it caused dropsy and in the lungs a cough and other pulmonary symptoms. Boils were associated with the condition of the blood, erysipelas with yellow bile and oedema with phlegm. A malignant ulcerating cancer was caused by acrid black bile, a non-ulcerating tumour by a milder form of black bile. Fevers were attributed to a malignant accumulation of the humours causing putrefaction and excessive heat. A morbid condition of the blood resulted in a continuous fever. The intermittent fevers were related to other humours. These malarial-type fevers are characterised by a paroxysm of fever occurring at regular intervals, now known to be governed by the reproductive cycle of the invading parasite. A quotidian fever, where the fits of fever occurred daily, was attributed to an excess of phlegm. Yellow bile or choler was associated with the tertian fever, where the fits came every third day. A quartan fever, with fits every fourth day, was the fever of black bile.

Before treating a patient the physician had to determine the state of the humours and to do this he looked for certain recognisable signs. Redness of the skin, swollen veins, high pulse and headaches were among the signs that blood was in excess. A running nose, bad digestion, slow pulse, languor and loss of appetite indicated an excess or morbidity of phlegm. A yellow skin was a clear indication of an excess of yellow bile and peccant or excessive black bile revealed itself in many ways, including mental disturbances such as nightmares, fear and dementia. The symptoms indicated the state of the humours and the physician had to decide which humours were in excess or in a morbid state. He had to determine if the humours were in a natural or unnatural form. Black bile, for example, could be in the form of natural melancholy, which was cold and dry, or in the adust or burnt form, which was hot and dry.[24] Therapy followed on logically from the pathology. Humours in excess must be expelled to restore the *krasis* or humoral balance; distempered humours must be tempered.

To correct a humour, medicines having qualities opposite to those of the offending humour were used. As an example, a hot/dry drug was deemed best to treat a cold/moist or phlegmatic illness. Thus Katherine in *The Taming of the Shrew* would have been regarded as having an excessively choleric (yellow bile) temperament and when Petruchio forced her to leave the wedding feast and brought her tired and wet into his cold house, he went some way to quench her hot/dry choleric humour.[25]

Galen classified medicines according to the four qualities and subdivided them into degrees. A medicine hot in the first degree caused the patient to sweat and reduced pain. To cut compacted humours it was necessary to employ a medicine hot in the third degree. A medicine hot in the fourth degree raised a blister on the skin. The principle was extended to foodstuffs, so that lettuce and other salad vegetables were believed to be cold and moist in the second degree and helped temper unnatural body heat in the summer months.[26] A

24. Robert Burton, *The Anatomy of Melancholy* (2nd edn, Oxford, 1624), p. 32.

25. J. Draper, 'Humoral Pathology in Shakespeare's Plays', *Bull. Hist. Med.*, 35 (1961), p. 319.

26. Nicholas Culpeper, 'A Key to Galen's Method of Physick' in *Pharmacopoeia Londinensis or, the London Dispensatory* (6th edn, 1659), p. 345.

medicine had to be selected with the correct qualities and in the right degree. It was also important to prescribe a drug that was appropriate to the part of the body affected. Nicholas Culpeper (1616–54) observed that 'if the head be distempered by heat and you give such medicines as cool the heart or liver, you will bring another disease and not cure the former'.[27]

Various methods were adopted to expel the offending humours. Venesection, the technique of removing blood by cutting a vein, was extensively practised, although by the early seventeenth century this was becoming controversial, with some physicians opposed to it.[28] Hall, from the evidence of the *Select Observations*, was a moderate in the use of blood-letting. In the cases where venesection was prescribed he directed the removal of from four to ten fluid ounces of blood. It was taken by cutting either the cephalic vein of the arm (no. 29) or from the liver vein, the old name for the basilic vein of the right arm (no. 101). In the case of William Broad (no. 104), blood was taken from under the tongue. It was also removed by means of leeches (no. 31) and by cupping over scarified skin (no. 154).

John Hall's favoured method for expelling putrescent or excessive humours was the purge. The majority of his treatments began with a purgative preparation and the report often gives an explicit record of its effects. Purgation, which was at times extreme in its application (no. 173), was avoided where the patient was pregnant, had recently given birth (nos 66, 149) or was aged and weak (no. 169). Purgative drugs and preparations varied from the fierce to the mildly laxative. Some were recommended to expel a specific humour, for example, agaric for phlegm, while scammony purged yellow bile.[29] Senna was thought to expel all humours and when used in the case of Julian West (no. 49), it 'emptied her Body from ill humours'. If the afflicting humour was in the bowels, a liquid medicine was the most efficient. If it had to be drawn from remote parts, such as the head or limbs, a pill was

27. Ibid., p. 348.
28. E.H. Ackerknecht, 'Aspects of the History of Therapeutics', *Bull. Hist. Med.*, 36 (1962), p. 394.
29. O. Tempkin, 'On the Specificity of Cathartic Drugs' in A. Debus (ed.), *Science, Medicine and Society in the Renaissance* (1972), vol. I, p. 61.

believed to be of more value because 'it stops longer in the body and [is] better able to perform its office'.[30]

Other methods for expelling humours were emetics (which caused vomiting), diaphoretics and sudorifics (which caused the patient to sweat, seen as nature's own method to expel febrile humours), diuretics (to increase the flow of urine) and clysters or enemas. There was also the fontanelle (small fountain), where a cut was made in the skin and kept open by inserting a pea or some other small round foreign body. This was said to give ease by carrying off acrid humours.[31] Medicines to expel humours were supplemented by attenuating ones to thin the humour. Alterative medicines were used to bring about changes in the humour by heating, cooling and drying. Incising medicines were intended to cut and divide phlegm and resolvents were prescribed to loosen and disperse humours.[32]

Medicines were made and administered in a variety of ways: decoctions, syrups, pills, powders (also called species), electuaries (species mixed with honey or syrup), ointments, plasters, enemas and other pharmaceutical forms. A common feature of all preparations was the large number of ingredients used. This was the polypharmaceutical tradition of Galen which required the administration of a mixture of numerous drugs allowing the body to select those it needed.[33] Pharmaceutical preparations for use in prescriptions often had from fifty to over a hundred ingredients. In the sixteenth century guilds of physicians and apothecaries began to establish standard formularies for these complex medicines and 'official' pharmacopoeias were established for Florence, Nuremberg and Augsburg, as well as for other cities and city-states. The London College of Physicians in 1618 published the *Pharmacopoeia Londinensis*, which became the first national pharmacopoeia by virtue of a proclamation of James I charging apothecaries within 'this our Realme of England or

---

30. Culpeper, p. 377.

31. W. Brockbank, *Ancient Therapeutic Arts* (1954), p. 117.

32. Nicholas Culpeper, 'A Physicall Dictionary' in Lazarus Riviere (Riverius), *The Practice of Physick* (trans. Nicholas Culpeper, Abdiah Cole and William Rowland, 1655).

33. E.H. Ackerknecht, 'Aspects', *Bull. Hist. Med.*, 36 (1962), p. 392.

the dominions thereof' to prepare medicines after the manner and form set down in the *Pharmacopoeia*. A large number of the preparations prescribed by Hall are to be found in the London formulary.[34]

The *materia medica* used in Hall's time was an extensive collection of drugs from centuries of medical practice. It originated from a wide variety of sources, which include the writings of the Hippocratic School (fifth century BC), the herbal of Pedanius Dioscorides (first century AD), the works of Galen (second century), Al-Razi (Rhazes, ninth century) and Ibn Sina (Avicenna, tenth century), the formularies attributed to the physicians of Salerno (twelfth to thirteenth centuries) and the European physician who wrote under the name of Mesue (thirteenth century). In the sixteenth century the *materia medica* had been augmented by drugs imported from the New World and the Far East. Another new source was the chemical remedies of the school of Theophrastus Bombast von Hohenheim, who was known as Paracelsus (1490–1541). The Galenists were in bitter contention with the Paracelsians but there were physicians who adopted an eclectic view either by attempting to reconcile the two doctrines or, as in the case of many English physicians, by prescribing chemical remedies but not subscribing wholly to Paracelsian theories. Hall was one of those who occasionally prescribed the new medicines.

The *Pharmacopoeia Londinensis* of 1618 in its *Catalogus Simplicium* listed 1,190 simples or crude drugs, a collection supported by centuries of medical tradition, superstition and credulity. They were arranged under the headings: roots, barks, woods, leaves, flowers, fruits, seeds, gums, juices, plant excrements (for example, tree fungi), whole animals, animal parts and excrements, marina (things belonging to the sea), and salts, metals and minerals (which included precious stones). In practice the range of drugs prescribed by the

---

34. There were two issues of the *Pharmacopoeia*. The first, published in May 1618, was replaced by an extended edition the following December. The two issues are compared by G. Urdang in an introduction to the facsimile edition of the May issue published in Madison in 1944. The reasons for the suppression of the May issue are discussed by M.P. Earles, *The London Pharmacopoeia Perfected*, Thomas Harriot Seminar Occasional paper No. 3 (Durham, 1985).

physicians and stocked by the apothecaries tended to be smaller in number than the pharmacopoeial lists. John Hall, in this selection of his cases, used just under 300 vegetable drugs, thirty-nine animal drugs and thirty-eight mineral items.

In the introduction to the first edition of the *Select Observations* (1657), Cooke wrote that he had made his translation being 'somewhat acquainted with the Author's conciseness, especially in the Receipts [prescriptions], having had some intimacy with his Apothecary', whom he did not name. That apothecary, John Court, had died in 1639 before Cooke acquired the manuscript. Earlier editors assumed from Cooke's statement that the apothecary helped him with the translation, but there is no reference to such assistance. Cooke refers only to 'having had' some intimacy with an apothecary familiar with the nature and presentation of the prescriptions written by Hall. There are errors and omissions in transcription and translation (for example, nos 31, 36, 159).

There are also considerable variations in nomenclature. Cooke, who was writing before a systematic nomenclature for botany and chemistry had been established, used both English common names for plants and the Latin names from contemporary herbals. Scurvy-grass is sometimes referred to as *cochlearia*, wormwood as *absinthium* and so on. Chemical names were based on alchemical sources. *Crocus martis* was the name for iron oxide, Litharge of gold for the yellow crystalline form of lead oxide, while zinc sulphate was referred to as white vitriol in one observation and as white copperas in another. The identification of the drugs is made more complicated by variations in spelling and abbreviations, while the names themselves are sometimes misleading. *Mercurious vitae* is not a mercurial but a mixture of antimony salts; nightshade or *solanum* could mean any one of three species that went under that name.

The prescriptions in Cooke's editions were printed in italic and began with the traditional ℞ for *recipe* (take). The drugs and preparations were listed with the quantities given in the troy system of weights used by goldsmiths, silversmiths and apothecaries. In this system the unit was the grain defined by Philip Barrough in *The Method of Phisick* (London, 1601) as 'a barley corne taken from the middle of the eare'. The standardised grain was equivalent to 65 mgms.[35] There were 480 grains to the ounce and 12 ounces to the troy pound. The ounce was subdivided into scruples (20 grains) and drachms (60 grains). These weights and the corresponding symbols are given in the table of characters printed opposite page 1 of the *Select Observations.*

Each prescription was followed by directions for administration. Liquid medicines were often prepared to be taken in a single dose or simply as a drink. Solid medicines were made into pills, which could be counted out as a dose, as a single-dose electuary (known as a bole), or as an electuary which could be divided up according to a simple domestic measure, for example, in the size of a filbert or a nutmeg.

The prescription would have been made up by the apothecary *secundem artem*, 'according to the [pharmaceutical] art'. It was not unusual at that time for the apothecary to attend a patient to administer the medicine. The cost of the drugs and the combined fees of the physician and apothecary contributed to the high cost of medical care, putting it beyond the purse of the poor man and his family, something that Cooke referred to in his Preface to the *Select Observations.*

The remedies employed by Hall included some, the effective use of which had been empirically determined: for example, the narcotic opium and wormseed *semen santonicum*, which contains santonin, a constituent effective against roundworm. Many of the other vegetable drugs prescribed also have medicinal properties but other items, animal and mineral drugs in particular, were of little or no medicinal value and employed only on the strength of tradition, superstition, credulity and a belief in 'hidden virtues'.

The presence of active drugs in the *materia medica* does not mean that they were always used effectively. There was no concept of dose in the modern sense and the polypharmaceutical habit meant that effective drugs were diluted with numerous inert ingredients. The preparation of the medicine was often detrimental to the activity of the drug. The scorbutic drugs, scurvy-grass, brooklime and water-cress, offer an example of this. These herbs contain vitamin C and

35. D. Vangroenweghe and T. Geldof, *Pondera Medicinalia* (Brugge, 1989), p. 58.

are therefore of value in the treatment of the vitamin-deficiency disease, scurvy. It is believed that physicians were made acquainted with the antiscorbutic qualities of these herbs through their use by the common people, who would have used the fresh plant.[36] Hall, however, rarely prescribed the fresh herbs for the treatment of scurvy. He employed them in multi-ingredient diet drinks and in medicated beers prepared by infusion and concentration by heating, a process that destroyed the vitamin content.[37]

'Rational' drugs and preparations in Hall's system of medicine were not those containing stabilised and correctly measured active constituents, as in modern pharmacology, but the purges and emetics to expel morbid humours and those drugs with hot, cold, dry or moist qualities that could be used to temper the humours. The patients, believing their illness was caused by humoral changes within their bodies, would have been comforted by cooling drinks, welcomed hot spicy remedies and accepted scouring, purging regimes intended to temper and restore the humoral constitution. Because of this the reported success of these treatments is often attributed to a placebo effect, when an inert substance given as a medicine to satisfy the patient has a beneficial effect. This explanation may apply to some of Hall's patients but common sense indicates that it cannot account for all the cures claimed by Hall.

The statement 'thus he [or she] was cured' occurs regularly as a coda to Hall's reports on his patients with variations such as 'thus he was delivered' and 'thus she was freed' (from her symptoms). The term 'cure', meaning a totally successful outcome and a return to full health, requires some qualification when considering Hall's case histories. John Rogers (no. 76) was suffering from a swelling of the tonsils and could hardly swallow or breathe. Hall claimed that as a result of his treatment 'in a nights space he was cured', but this must surely refer only to the fact that the patient's problem with swallowing had been relieved. A successful cure for Hall was

36. K.J. Carpenter, *A History of Scurvy and Vitamin C* (Cambridge, 1988), p. 35.

37. R. Elwyn Hughes. 'The Rise and Fall of the "Antiscorbutics"', *Med. Hist.*, 34 (1990), p. 61.

the freedom from symptoms and in most cases the patient's history ends at this point. William Clavell (no. 80) was 'altogether cured of his Gonorrhea' meaning that the purulent urethral discharge had cleared up, but the account of Francis Harvey (no. 143) indicates that, in all probability, Clavell's problems were far from over. In some cases the cure was short-lived. The consumptive Mary Wilson (no. 21) died within the year and Hall's 'thus she was cured' means nothing more than 'thus she was treated'. Another patient, aged thirty-eight and a great drinker (no. 173), exhibiting the serious symptoms of jaundice and dropsy, was 'perfectly cured' within six weeks, yet died in the same year.

The records do not say to what extent Hall examined his patients beyond noting their symptoms (often reported to him) and inspecting their urine. We know he was prepared to prescribe without seeing the patient (no. 54). Descriptions of his patients' conditions are varied and there is only an occasional reference to future health. What is consistent throughout, however, is a statement relating to the success of the treatment. This is because the collection of case notes is not a random sample but a selection. Hall in his manuscript presented those patients whose symptoms were relieved or modified and where there was a recovery, either permanent or only temporary. For these reasons, although the *Select Observations on English Bodies* is an interesting and valuable source of information on the nature of seventeenth-century therapy in general and Hall's methods in particular, it cannot be considered an exact representation of his medical practice as a whole or of the overall success of his treatments.

A NOTE ON CASE NUMBERS

Hall's original manuscript was composed of 178 cases, written in abbreviated Latin, with prescriptions making up the bulk of the text. Cooke divided the collection into two groups, called First Century and Second Century, substituting Roman numerals for Hall's Arabic. He also added some observations of his own, bringing the total to 182. As a result of these additions, or the occasional splitting of Hall's cases, after Observation 49 the numbers in Cooke's text no longer correspond to those of Hall's original manuscript. A concordance is therefore given as Appendix 3. Cooke's cumbersome system of numbering cases after 100 – as 1 to 82 under the heading Second Century – has also been simplified in this commentary, giving a continuous series 1 to 182 in Arabic numerals.

A NOTE ON THE FACSIMILE

The facsimile which follows is taken from a copy of the third edition of *Select Observations* (identical with the second edition except for the title page) held by The Shakespeare Birthplace Trust, but slightly enlarged (by approximately 25 per cent) and omitting the nineteen pages of the preliminaries which contain an unhelpful index. The title page (p. xliii) is reprinted, with grateful thanks, from the copy of the second edition at Yale Library, Harvey Cushing/John Hay Whitney Medical Library.

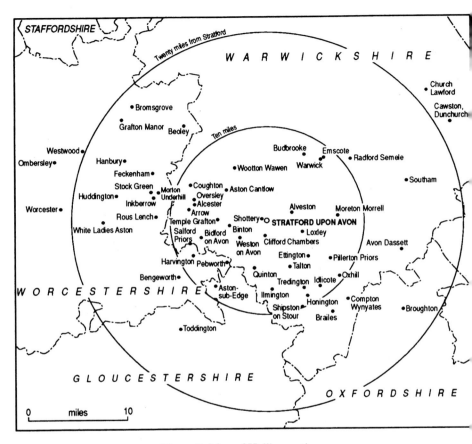

Figure 3: Map of Hall's practice area

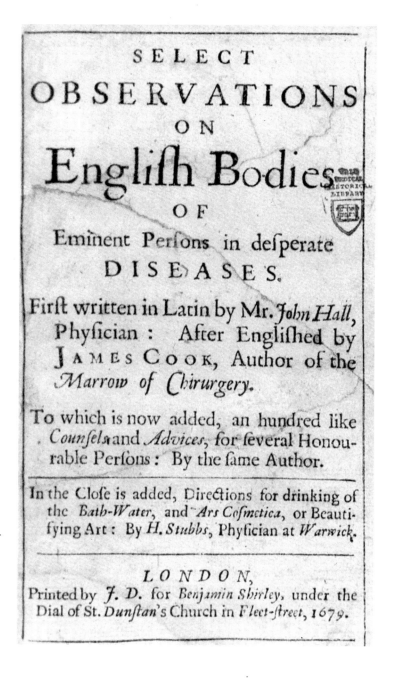

SELECT
OBSERVATIONS
ON
Englifh Bodies
OF
Eminent Perfons in defperate
DISEASES.

Firft written in Latin by Mr. *John Hall*,
Phyfician : After Englifhed by
JAMES COOK, Author of the
Marrow of Chirurgery.

To which is now added, an hundred like
. *Counfels* and *Advices*, for feveral Honourable Perfons : By the fame Author.

In the Clofe is added, Directions for drinking of
the *Bath-Water*, and *Ars Cofmetica*, or Beauti-
fying Art : By *H. Stubbs*, Phyfician at *Warwick*.

LONDON,
Printed by *J. D.* for *Benjamin Shirley*, under the
Dial of St. *Dunftan's* Church in *Fleet-ftreet*, 1679.

TO THE

Right Honourable,

FULK, Lord Brook,

Baron BROOK

OF

Beauchamp-Court,

Right Honourable,

HE great and undeſer-
ved Favours for many
years conferred on me
by your noble Ance-
ſtors, with thoſe which I
ſtill receive from your ſelf, and o-
her their Survivors, encourage me

A 3   to

to prefent to your Lordfhip this Piece, now called to be made public a fecond time ; humbly begging your acceptance and protection of what I tender in acknowledgment of my Duty and Service. The Part formerly printed, and what is added thereto, are moft fit to be laid at your Honour's Feet, having received allowance from your Honourable Family to be made public, and moft of it practifed among them, for the fpecial ufe of thofe Noble Perfons, who are now gone from us ; and for whofe memory I could not tranfcribe with dry eyes. What their Lofs vvas to the Public, is vvell known, and no lefs lamented ; and fo great to me, that I can never forget it.

The Right Honourable, your Father, was pleafed to fhew me greater Favour than I do pretend

to deſerve. Your Right Honourable Mother was ſeldom ill at home
or abroad, without commanding
my attendance: The ſame have the
Right Honourable your Brothers and
your Lordſhip done. By whom
ſcarce any thing was taken without
my thoughts, from the moſt eminent
Phyſicians, till they became acquainted with their Bodies. In all
which Services it pleaſed God, I ſo
ordered my ſelf, that I have had
from your Phyſicians, not only thanks
but commendation. Which I have
always looked on as proceeding more
from the Favour of your Honour's
Family, than my Deſerts.

These Obligations under which I
lie, have given your Lordſhip the
trouble of this Dedication, and this
poor Piece, which I here preſent with
my hearty and humble Prayers for all
and each of your Honourable Family,

that

that they may receive the greatest of God's Favours here, and the full enjoyment of Himself in Bliss hereafter: Which is and shall be the continued Petitions of,

My Lord,

Your Honour's most

humble Servant

in all Duty,

Warwick,

March 25.

1679.

J AMES COOK, Sen.

THE

THE
PREFACE
TO THE
READER.

Courteous Readers,

 *O you it is that I now address my self, to give you some small account of what is added in this Impression. To the Select Observations on English Bodies, you have an hundred* Counsels and Advices, *by very eminent Physicians, on several Honourable Persons, and others of no inferior Rank and Repute in this and other Counties. The Honourable Family which I have attended, and do still, hath always commanded me, as to receive all Prescriptions, so to see them made up in several places*

where

The Preface

where I have attended, both to see them taken, and to observe their Success. Their favourable allowance I have for what is done. Their Honours, when Physicians were with them, were always ready to engage them to be helpful to their sick Neighbours; the Advices for such being for most part entrusted in my hands. I hope what is made publick can be no wrong to any of those Physicians, having for their Pains, Prescriptions, and Directions, received generous Pay and noble Entertainment. If there necessarily occur any thing concerning those living, I humbly beg their Pardon, and if I had not feared giving offence, I had named them as well as those dead: But this is not all, for as I have a due remembrance of those deceased, (whose freeness I always found in communicating to me what they kept private from most) so I give hearty thanks to those living, who have been like minded, and by whose Directions I have received no small advantage. Something there is intermixed, and something also in the Close, of Dr. Stubbs's, whose Civilities and Openness I cannot but remember. He was not a Person greedy of Gain. Not many months before he died, he said to me, "We must "study all ways possible to find out and appoint "Medicines of cheap rate, and effectual; for "Money is scarce, and Country-People poor:.

To

to the Reader.

*To which I answered, That it had been, and
should be my constant Course as long as I lived.
I have heard it was said by one, over whom none
is supreme in these Nations, (whom God preserve and continue here, and crown with Himself in Glory hereafter) That if* Dr. Stubbs
had but some of Saturn *to poize his* Mercurial
Brain, *he would make a good Statesman. And
not a few famous Practitioners have said the
like of him, as a* Physician. *But he is gone,
and I cannot but say, Seldom comes a better.
But to pass this, I hope my Service in this Im-
pression will be civilly accepted, which is all,
save to crave leave to subscribe my self always a
Friend to the Friendly, and an Enemy to
none of* Mankind.

JAMES COOK, Sen.

Warwick,
March 25.
1679.

An

Characters for brevity used herein.

℔	a pound.	M.	an handful.
℥	an ounce.	ß.	half.
ʒ	a dram.	*q.ſ.*	quantity sufficient.
℈	a scruple.	*quar.*	a quart.
gr.	a grain.	*f.*	make.
p.	as much as may be held between the Thumb and two first Fingers.	*pul.*	a pouder.
		ā	each.
		Misc.	Mix.
		C.C.	Harts-horn.

Twenty grains
Three scruples
Eight drams
Twelve ounces
} make {
a scruple.
a dram.
an ounce.
a pound.

Health

Select Observations
and
Commentary

Health is from the L O R D.

CURES Historical and Empirical, experienced on Eminent Persons in several Places.

OBSERV. I.

THE Countess of *Northampton*, aged 44. on *March* the 6th, 1622. as she was walking in her Bed-chamber, suddenly fell into a swoon, without either sense or motion for half an hour; she fell with her face on the frame of a Table, which caused a Wound with contusion, whence arose Inflammation, as also a great and troublesom Flux of Rheum, which distilling from her eyes, excoriated the whole face with exulcerations; the habit of her Body was Scorbutick and Cacochymick: her residence then was at *Ludlow-Castle*: To whom being called, I cured perfectly, by God's assistance, with

B   the

1: ELIZABETH, COUNTESS OF NORTHAMPTON

Elizabeth Spencer was aged twenty-one when she ran away to marry William Compton, later first Earl of Northampton, on 18 April 1599. An only daughter and heiress, she was an excellent choice for this Warwickshire nobleman, who was twice her age. In his Latin notes, Hall described her as 'pious, beautiful, chaste, richly-endowed and excellently-mannered but *non bono ingenio*', suggesting low intelligence. At his death in 1610, her father, Sir John Spencer, reputedly left £300,000 to William Compton.[1]

When Hall had attended Lady Northampton on 6 March 1620 at Ludlow (no. 99) and again on this occasion, 6 March 1622, she was past her child-bearing years; she had three children, two daughters and a son. The heir was Spencer, born in May 1601.

Although little is known about Lady Northampton, she accompanied her husband on his travels to Ludlow (Salop.) and entertained royalty at both Compton Wynyates and Castle Ashby (Northants.), where there were eighty-three in her household.[2] However, a long and detailed letter survives, written to her husband, describing how she wished part of her father's wealth to be spent on her personal requirements. She addressed the letter to 'my Sweet Life' shortly before 1618 and in expectation of his enhanced status. She said she required £1,600 a year for clothes and a further £600 for charitable works; she was to have three horses, two gentlewomen to attend her, each with her own mount, and two coaches (one velvet-lined for herself). Her gentleman usher was also to have his own horse. As well as laundresses and chambermaids, her servants were to include two coachmen and two footmen. Her husband was to defray all these charges. He was also to pay for twenty gowns (six of excellent quality), £2,000 and a further '£200 for my purse', £6,000 for buying jewels and £400 for 'a pearle chain'. He was to be responsible for the children's clothes, education and all her servants' wages. She added that, as she had 'been and (am) so reasonable unto you', she expected her demands to be met at present and increased when he was ennobled, by a further £1,000 allowance and double the charges for attendance.[3] She became the Countess of Northampton in August 1618.

Widowed in 1630, she died on 8 May 1632 aged fifty-four;[4] mourning for her funeral cost £45 7s. 4d.[5] She was buried at Compton Wynyates next to her husband.

John Hall, who had treated the Countess two years earlier for edema

---

1. William Compton, *History of the Comptons of Compton Wynyates* (1930), pp. 51–3.
2. Castle Ashby accounts, FD 1084(5).
3. Compton, *History*, pp. 54–6.
4. Ibid., p. 63.
5. Castle Ashby accounts, FD 1084(5).

the fol'owing Medicines. She was purged with the following, ℞ *Sena* ℥j. *Agarick* ℥ iij. *Rubarb* ℥ii. *Cinnamon* ℥iß. *Infuse them all for twelve hours in three pints of White-wine on warm embers, after it was strained through an Ippocras bag, six or seven times, and sweetned with half a pound of Sugar.* Dose ℥v. twice a day, *viz.* in the morning fasting, and at four a clock in the afternoon. This gave five or six stools a day without gripings, it was continued four days. Her face was anointed with *white Ointment camphorated,* which cured it in four days. The Body being not sufficiently emptied, the following Pills were used, ℞ *Pil. Ruffin. & Succin. Crato.* of each equal parts ; of ℥i, were made seven Pills, three of which she took when she went to bed, the next day she had six or seven stools. But this was observable, that instead of swallowing the Pills, she chewed them, and so let them down, saying she could not swallow them, though never so little ; withal, that she thought it the best way. She took of these twice a week. Those days she took not the Pills, I administred the following : ℞ *Elect. Chalyb. Crat. mixed with the salts of Scurvygraß, Wormwood and Coral.* In her Broth was boiled these Scorbutick Herbs, viz. *Scurvy-graß, Water-Cresses,* and *Brook-lime.* After all, she took this Scorbutick Beer, ℞ *Scurvy-graß* M iv. *Watercresses, Brook-lime, each* M ii. *Wormwood, Fumitory, and Germander, each* M. j. *Roots of Fennel, Borage, Succory, each* ℥i. *Root of Elicampany* ℥ß. *Liquoris* ℥i. *Flowers of Borag. Bugloße, Rosemary, each* p ii. *Boyl them all in five gallons of Beer, till one be wasted. After having the following Ingredients in a bag,* viz. *Sarsaparilla, Calamus aromaticus, Cinnamon, Mace,*
Seeds

(no. 99), attributed the symptoms on this occasion to her body being scorbutic and cacochymic. Cacochymia was the term used to describe a depraved state of the body humours and to rectify this a purgative infusion of senna leaves, rhubarb root and agaric was prescribed.[1] Her body 'being not sufficiently emptied', a second purge was administered composed of *Pilula Ruffi* and *Pilula de Succino Crat[o]*, both preparations containing the purgative resin from Aloes vera.[2]

Scorbutic symptoms are those of scurvy, caused by an insufficiency of vitamin C and this scourge of sixteenth- and seventeenth-century mariners was endemic inland. Fresh fruit was available only in season, fresh vegetables often in short supply in the winter, while the contemporary habit of cooking fruit and vegetables to a mush destroyed much of the vitamin content.[3]

There are twenty-three observations in which Hall describes the symptoms as scorbutic but it does not follow that all were cases of true scurvy. The principal symptoms of the disease are putrid gums, purple haemorrhagic blotches on the skin and ulceration. Medical works known to Hall listed numerous other symptoms for the disease with the result that conditions unrelated to true scurvy were often described as scorbutic.[4] The case of Lady Browne (no. 110) is an example. The Countess was treated with medicated beer and diet drinks containing three scorbutic herbs: scurvy-grass *Cochlearia officinalis*, brooklime *Veronica beccabunga* and water-cress *Rorippa nasturtium aquaticum*. Gerard, in his *Herball* of 1597, gives a history of the use of scurvy-grass in beer for the treatment of scurvy and refers to water-cress as having similar virtues.[5] Cooke in the Preface to the first edition of the *Select Observations* (1657) makes the claim that Hall led the way to the practice of adding these well-established scorbutic herbs to most remedies.

1. (i) The purgative action of rhubarb and senna was sufficiently well known for Shakespeare to refer to them in *Macbeth* (V, iii, 57). The First Folio reads 'rhubarb, cyme' and there is some controversy over the meaning of cyme (one of the names for cumin). The usual emendation to 'senna' assumes that 'cyme' is a misprint for an early spelling of the drug. Textual problems apart, rhubarb and senna fit the scouring, purgative image of Macbeth's speech. (ii) Agaric is a purgative tree fungus growing on the larch; that imported from the Levant was considered to be the best. (iii) An Ippocras (or Hippocras) bag used in the preparation of the infusion was a pyramid-shaped woollen filter.

2. *Pilula de Succino* were amber pills. Amber *Succinum* had many uses in medicine and, combined with wormwood and aloes, it was reputed to amend the evil state of a woman's body. Crato refers to Crato von Krafftheim (1519–85), the author of the formula for the pill. The name of the physician who devised the formula was regularly attached to the name of the preparation. Hall invariably abbreviated the name (Mes. for Mesue and Forest. for Forestus).

3. *Nutritional History Notes* No. 13 (1982), pp. 1–5.

4. S. Eugalenus, *De scorbuto* (Bremen, 1588); D. Senertus, *De scorbuto tractatus* (Wittenberg, 1624); Observation no. 117.

5. J. Gerard, *The Herball or, generall historie of plantes* (1597), pp. 324–5.

Seeds of Anis and Fennel, each ℥ß. *Juniper-berries*
℥ viii. *Let them be infused in the hot liquor, well covered till it be cold, after put it up, hanging the bag in
it.* After fifteen days ſhe drank of it, uſing no
other; this ſhe drank in *April.* Till it was ready,ſhe
took the following; ℞ *Sarſaparila* ℥ ii. *Guaicum*
℥i. *Saſſafras roots* ℥ii. *Slice aud bruiſe them, after infuſe them in* ℔ xv. *of Spring-water for twelve hours.
After add Scurvy-graſſ* Mij. *Brook-lime, Water-
creſſes, each* M i. *Betony, Agrimony, each* Mß. *Currants* ℥ii. *Boyl them all till* v ℔ *be waſted; after take
it from the fire, adding preſently of Cinnamon bruiſed*
℥i. *after let it paſs through an Hippocras bag.* Doſe
℥ vi. taken hot, being in bed, compoſing the Body
to ſweat gently; cover the Head and Neck with
hot linnen clothes: after ſweating, the ſweat was
rubbed of gently with fine dry warm linnen. An
ordinary Drink was made of the ſecond Decoction, which was uſed in thoſe days ſhe did not
ſweat, with which was taken the juice of Scurvy-
graſs rightly prepared, ſix ſpoonfuls in one
Draught; in her Broths was uſed the Salt of the
ſame. By the bleſſing of the Almighty, ſhe was
by theſe Remedies perfectly cured, beyond the expectation of her Lord and Friends.

OBSERV. II.

WIlliam, Earle of *Northampton,* labouring of
the heat of Urine, *April* 4. 1622. was
cured as followeth. ℞ *Caſſia new drawn* ℥i. *Terbentine waſht* ℥i. *Rubarb* Ði. *Liquoris powdered* Ðß.

2: WILLIAM COMPTON,
FIRST EARL OF NORTHAMPTON

Power and influence came to the Comptons through royal friendships and, from Henry VII onwards, various members of the family were confidants of both Tudor and Stuart monarchs, who rewarded such loyalty with enhanced titles and positions at court.[1] Their Warwickshire seat was at Compton Wynyates, originally built in 1460, but this large moated house was too old-fashioned for Henry, first Lord Compton, who began building a grand new family home in 1574 at Castle Ashby (Northants.). Compton Wynyates, however, was to become an important royalist stronghold in the Civil War, ringed round by parliamentary forces at Banbury, Warwick and Broughton. It was finally captured in June 1642 after a two-day siege. The family estates were sequestrated and restored only on payment of a £20,000 fine.[2]

As any great family with land and tenants, the Comptons employed agents and stewards to manage their affairs. For the years 1629–35 the disbursements of the steward, William Goodman, included payments for medical attention, alongside such services as farriery and the purchase of provisions and wine:

30 Dec 1631–24 Mar 1632	Phisitians and Chirurgeons and books	£16 7s 6d
Michs 1631–25 Mar 1632	Docters & Apothicaires Bill	£ 9 0s 2d[3]

By his marriage on 18 April 1599 to Elizabeth Spencer, daughter of Sir John, a former Lord Mayor of London, William Compton spectacularly enhanced the family fortunes. A contemporary noted that they married against her father's wishes, and Sir John was put in the Fleet prison for beating and abusing his daughter. A marriage portion of £10,000 was rumoured for Elizabeth, 'a warm catch'. Although 'the hardhead her father relents nere a whit', a reconciliation was finally effected by Queen Elizabeth I, who was god-mother to their first-born son.[4] William Compton was a friend of Sir Walter Raleigh, in whose house he stayed at Christmas 1602.[5] However, having married a fortune, he also knew how to spend it, so that, by the year of his death (1630), although his annual income was over £6,000, he had debts of £10,000.[6] At Castle Ashby, for example, where he

1. The present Marquess of Northampton kindly verified many family details.
2. Philip Tennant, *Edgehill and Beyond: the People's War in the South Midlands, 1642–1645* (Stroud, 1992), pp. 75–6.
3. WCRO, DR 556/274.
4. Chamberlain, I, p. 124.
5. Ibid., p. 179.
6. Compton, pp. 50–63.

4. *Select Observations*

make them in a bole with Sugar. The next day and the following he took this, ℞ *Malloes* Mi. *Liquoris* ʒi. *Boil them in a quart of Milk, after strain it, and add Syrup of French Mallowes* ʒvi. Dose ʒ iv. or v. every morning; at night when he went to bed, he took ʒß. of *Cyprus Terbentine*, in the form of a Pill in a rosted Apple. Thus was he presently and perfectly cured, being at *Ludlow*, at that time being President of *Wales*, and Councellor to the King.

OBSERV. III.

Mrs. *Smith* of *Stratford* upon *Avon*, aged 54, being miserably afflicted with a hot Distillation in her Eyes, so that she could not open them in the morning, was cured thus. First there was administred for four nights together when she went to bed, ʒß. of *Pil. de Succin. Craton.* made in three Pills. These gave five or six stools without pain the following days. In the interim, to the Eyes was applied the following, ℞ of the *Juyce of Housleek* a spoonful, *White-wine* two spoonfuls, *mix them together* : Of which there was dropt one or two drops into the Eyes, laying upon them all night a double linnen Rag wet in the same; this mitigated the heat. After I commanded to distill one or two drops of the following into the eyes twice or thrice a day :

Collyrium for the Eyes. ℞ *Sarcocol* wash'd. ʒ iij. *Prepared Tutty* ʒij. *Aloes* ʒi. *White Sugar-candy* ʒiß. *Saffron* gr. iv. *Rosewater* ʒ iv.

entertained James I three times, for the 1616 visit there were eighty-three household servants, four chaplains and three musicians in attendance.[1] He and his son both served as Lords Lieutenant of Warwickshire.

William Compton was President of the Council of the Marches of Wales from 1613 and Lord President of Wales from November 1617. This appointment explains why John Hall left his Stratford practice and made a round trip of nearly 100 miles to Ludlow Castle, the administrative centre of the Council, where the Comptons often lived for months. Hall remained in Ludlow for extended periods to treat both the family and two other patients, Mr Powell (no. 7) and Mrs Bettes (no. 5). Hall's description of him in Latin as 'most illustrious hero' was omitted by Cooke. A contemporary reported that he had had an attack of colic when, climbing out of a boat on the Thames, he stood in water 'but to the knees'. He died suddenly in London a few days later aged sixty-two on 24 June 1630.[2] He was buried at Compton Wynyates.

Heat of the urine is a symptom of an inflammation of the urethra; treatment began with a mixture of two purgatives, cassia and rhubarb, with turpentine as a diuretic to increase urination and cleanse the urinary passages.[3] These were mixed with liquorice powder and sugar to make a bole, a large soft pill. This was followed by a mucilaginous mixture, with mallow as the main ingredient, to be taken in the morning.[4] At night the Earl was to have a dose of Cyprus turpentine made palatable in a roasted apple. Hall treated the Earl again (no. 72) for this condition.

3: ANN SMITH

Described by Hall as a Stratford inhabitant, Ann was the youngest daughter of Ann and Raph Shaw and had been baptised in the town on 21 December 1580. Her father was a prosperous wool merchant who lived in Henley Street. Ann married Henry Smith, two years her senior, on 22 September 1596. They had four or five children, but their offspring are difficult to identify from the many of this surname in the town, a problem that defeated even Wheler.[5] Ann Smith's elder brother was July Shaw (b. 1571), who served as a churchwarden, was made an alderman in 1613

1. Castle Ashby accounts, FD 1084(5).
2. Dugdale, I, p. 549; Compton, p. 63.
3. Turpentine *Terebintha* is a clear resin taken from the conifer; its nature varies with the source. Hall specified the product imported from Cyprus, *Terebintha chia*, which had the consistency of thick honey and a more agreeable smell than other turpentines.
4. Marsh mallow *Althea officinalis* was used to treat irritation of the intestinal and urinary tracts.
5. SBTRO, Wheler's interleaved and annotated copy of Hall's *Observations* (1657).

℥ iv.   Mix them, letting them ftand a day, fhaking them oft. By thefe fhe was cured.

OBSERV. IV.

MR. *Wilfon*, Minifter of the faid Town, aged
40. being grievoufly vexed with a Rheum
in his Eyes, was cured by the following Medicines.
℞ *Pil.Succin.* ℨi. *Aurear.* ℨß. *Troch. agar.* ℈i. *cum
Syr. betonic.* f. *Pil.* N° 10, He took five of thefe
when he went to bed, which gave him the next
day fix ftools; the other five he took the following night.   Outwardly was applied to the forehead and Temples the following Plafter, ℞ *Bole
Armoniack* ℨß. *Gypfum* ℨiii. *Dragons blood, Acaciæ,*
each ℨii. *Pomgranate-Pills, Galls,* each ℨi. *Pouder
them all, and with the whites of Eggs, and a little
Vinegar make a Plafter.*   Behind the Ears was laid
Bole and *Gypfum*, framed into a Plafter as the former.   Upon the Eyes were applied *Whites of Eggs
well beaten with Rofewater and Womans milk.*   Into
the Eyes were dropp'd twice or thrice a day fome
of our *Opthalmick Collyrium,* prefcribed in the former Obfervation.   This is remarkable, that a
while after it was ufed, he found the tafte of the
Sarcocol on his Palat.   By thefe Remedies he was
cured, bleffed be God.

and was one of the witnesses to the will of William Shakespeare, his neighbour in Chapel Street.[1]

As Hall noted Ann Smith's age as fifty-four he must have been treating her in 1634 shortly before her death; she was buried on 12 May 1635, survived by her husband. Her funeral was the occasion of an incident that brought about an enquiry by the Vicar-General, Nathaniel Brent, for Wilson, the vicar of Holy Trinity, had sat on the pulpit stairs to prevent Simon Trapp from preaching the sermon.[2]

Ann Smith's ophthalmia in the context of humoral pathology was caused by the distillation or falling down of humours from the brain.[3] Although a local condition, it was seen as the result of a perturbation of the body humours and therefore to be treated initially with a purgative pill to help restore the *krasis* or humoral balance. For a local application Hall employed a preparation of the houseleek or sengreen *Sempervivum tectorum*, which was said to be cold in the third degree and to cool hot rheums in the eyes.[4] The second local application was a collyrium, the name for eye medications derived from the Greek, meaning to check a defluxion or falling down of a humour.[5]

4: THOMAS WILSON, VICAR OF STRATFORD-UPON-AVON

Thomas Wilson replaced John Rogers as vicar of Stratford on 22 May 1619. The appointment was furiously opposed by John Lane of Alveston, whose papist sympathies were well known, and warmly promoted by John Hall. Later in 1633 Hall supported Wilson's claim to be paid a higher stipend,[6] a sensitive topic for some years. Wilson, 'a learned Minister' and 'a very good Scolar', was the son of Thomas, Dean of Worcester; he graduated from Oxford (BA in 1588, MA in 1591) as had his brother, Robert (b. 1572).[7]

1. *Life*, p. 53.
2. Hughes, *MH*, pp. 80–1.
3. Culpeper, 'A Physical Dictionary' in Riviere.
4. Culpeper, *A Physicall Directory*, p. 29.
5. Sarcocol in the collyrium is a soluble gum imported from the Middle East. Tutty or *tutia* is an impure form of zinc oxide. Its use in a collyrium required it to be finely divided and diffused in the vehicle, illustrating the requirement that prescriptions of this nature had to be prepared *secundem artem*, or after the [pharmaceutical] art by the apothecary. Rose-water used as the vehicle was one of several preparations of roses used in the seventeenth century. White, red and damask roses were all listed in the London *Pharmacopoeia* of 1618. (The shop of the penurious apothecary in *Romeo and Juliet* contained 'old cakes of roses', V, i, 47.)
6. SBTRO, BRU 15/13/81.
7. Foster, p. 1657.

OBSERV. V.

Mrs. *Beats* of *Ludlow*, aged 50, who being
troubled with a great Cough, *Asthma*, and
grievous Pain in the Side, was thus cured. First,
I administred this Electuary, ℞ *Conserve of red Roses* ℥ij. *Raisins of the Sun stoned, Sugar-candy, each*
℥i. *make them into an Electuary: To which was added
Oil of Vitriol, and Sulphur, sufficient to make it sharp.*
Dose morning and night the quantity of a Nutmeg. For a Fume was prescribed the following ;
℞ *Frankinsence, Mastich , each* ℥iss. *Brimstone* ℥iiss.
Juniper ℈ii. *Storax* ℈i. *Terbentine sufficient to make
a Past, which frame into what figure pleaseth.* Some
of which being cast on some embers, the Fume
was received into her Mouth by a tunnel, her
Head being covered ; this dried up the superflous
humidities of the Brain. For a pain in her Stomach, I applied the following; ℞ *Labdanum* ℥i.
Wax ℥ii. *Species Aromatic. rosat.* ℥iii. *Caranna* a
little, make a Plaister *S. A.* spred upon Leather.
For the Pain of her Side I used this, ℞ *Ung. Dialthæa* ℥ii. *Oil of sweet Almonds* ℥ii. Mix them, and
with it anoint the Part pained, hot ; upon it I
laid a linnen Cloth dipped in Butter, hot ; this
gave her some ease. For a long time following
she used this Drink : ℞ *of the Water distilled from
Coltsfoot, Ground-Ivy, Mullin, Speedwel, Elicampany, Knapwood, Scabious, Hyssop, Herb Trinity,
Great Figwort, both Maiden-hairs, Horehound, the
cordial*

Thomas Wilson had a family of a girl and six boys, all born at Stratford during the period 1621 to 1638. Two of the children had died young. His fifth child, baptised on 9 June 1630, was named Grindal after Queen Elizabeth's evangelical archbishop. Dugdale noted that Anne Wilson was buried in the chancel of the parish church on 27 October 1642.[1]

Wilson was clearly a controversial figure in the town, where his advanced puritan activities produced riots and offended many traditionalists. He would not, for example, use a wedding ring in the marriage ceremony, make the sign of the cross in baptisms or permit communicants to kneel. Wilson was accused of profanity in allowing children to play in consecrated premises and of 'suffering his poultry to roost, and his hoggs to lodge in the chancell' of the Gild Chapel.[2] He came to clash with the Corporation more frequently and Bishop Thornborough considered him 'conformable in nothing'. At one stage, in June 1635, he was suspended from duty for three months. He witnessed John Hall's will on 5 November 1635.[3] Thomas Wilson died in October 1638 and the living remained vacant while the right of presentation was disputed. His successor was Henry Twitchet, appointed by the Crown in 1640.

Rheum was the term used to describe a pernicious humour in the eyes and this treatment was similar to Ann Smith's in the preceding observation. Hall prescribed a purgative of aloes and agaric, with a soothing application for the eyes composed of egg-whites mixed with rose-water and woman's milk,[4] as well as a collyrium. Astringent plasters were applied to the forehead, temples and behind the ears.[5]

5: MISTRESS BETTES OF LUDLOW, SHROPSHIRE

Presumably because of the Compton family's long-standing official connection with Ludlow, Hall also treated a handful of other people there, among whom was this patient noted by Hall as M^ris Bettes. She must have been born in the period 1561 to 1585, and died after 1612. It is possible

1. Dugdale, II, p. 689.
2. SBTRO, ER1/1/97; Hughes, *MH*, pp. 58–84.
3. Appendix 1.
4. Human milk *Lac mulieris* was included in the London *Pharmacopoeia* of 1618 under the heading *Animalium partes*.
5. *Bole Armoniack* in the plaster was an astringent pale red clay from Armenia. Boles were earths or clays coloured red or yellow due to the presence of iron oxide. Dragon's blood *Sanguis draconis* was the name given to a resin from trees growing in the East Indies. It was reputed to be astringent as were the pomegranate pills or seeds and oak galls. Acacia was also known as Gum Arabic and listed in the London *Pharmacopoeia* under the heading *Lachrimae* (tears). ('Drops tears as fast as the Arabian trees/Their medicinal gum.' *Othello*, V, ii, 359.)

cordial Flowers, *Roots of* Oris, Angelica, Sopewort, *and* Water-Betony, ℔xij. Guaiacum ℥xij. Sarſaparila ℔ſſ. *Oris roots* ℥ij. China *ſliced* ℥iij. Elicampany *roots* ℥iij. Maiden-hair, Speedwel, *each* M i. Liquoris ℥ij. Aniſeed ℥i. Raiſins *of the Sun ſtoned* ℥vi. *Boyl them in a double* Veſſel *well ſtopt, after ſtrain and clarify it.* Doſe two or three good Draughts every day. Each night I gave at Bed time the quantity of a walnut of this℞: ℞ Conſerve Roſes ℥i. *Bole* ℈i. mix them. She alſo took of the following Julep oft in a day. ℞ prepared *Snails* ℔i. *Pieces of white Bread* ℔ſſ. Whites *of Eggs* 30. Cream ℔ iv. Cinnamon ℥ii. Beſt Sugar ℔ij. Muſcadine ℔ij. *Diſtil them all in* B. M. It was drunk with *Manus Chriſti perlat.* (now called *Sacchar. Tabuli perlat.*) and ſometime with the following Lohoch. ℞ Loh. San. & *expert* ℥ii. Penidies ℥ij. Syrup *of Maiden-hair,* Hyſſop, Liquoris, *and* Coltsfoot, *each* ℥i. *Roots of An-gelica and* Elicamp. *candied, each* ℥ſſ. *Roots of Oris* ℥i. mix them ; *to* ℥iv *of which add* Flower of Brimſtone ℥ii. Theſe in the ſpace of five weeks cured her ; afterward ſhe died, but of what Diſeaſe I know not.

O B S E R V. VI.

A Servant of Mr. *Naſhes*, lying at the Bear in *Stratford* upon *Avon*, aged 28, having the Yellow Jaundice, with a Tertian Ague, was thus cured℞: ℞ *Wine of Squils* ℥ſſ. Oxymel *of the ſame* ℥i. *Our emetick* Infuſion ℥ſſ. mix them. This exhibited gave ſeven Vomits. After I purged him with this, ℞ Rubarb *powdered* ℥i. Elect. Diaphæn. ℥iij. Pul.

that, from her status, she had been a companion to Lady Northampton and a member of the household, but she was not described as '*Generosa*'. Cooke seems to have amended her surname to 'Beats'.

However, among the Comptons' Castle Ashby retinue in 1616 was Mr George Betts,[1] who later sold cattle at Ludlow in 1631 and paid £227 7s. 2d. into the estate accounts.[2] A man of this name was buried at Long Compton on 12 May 1662. Betts does not seem to have been a Shropshire surname at this period. She was one of the few patients whose subsequent death Hall recorded.

The 'great cough', *Asthma* (meaning to breathe with difficulty), and the pain in the side indicate that this patient was suffering from an acute pulmonary infection. In Hall's terms this was caused by superfluous humidities of the brain (phlegm) descending and lodging in the lungs. Hall claimed to have cured her after treatment lasting for five weeks but observes that afterwards she died.

Treatment began with a demulcent, soothing electuary, a mixture of drugs formed into a soft mass with syrups or honey and divided up for administration.[3] A 'fume' or vapour was prescribed composed of resinous drugs mixed with juniper, sulphur and turpentine, which was thrown on to hot coals and the vapour directed into the mouth of the patient. A plaster was applied to the stomach[4] and for the pain in the side a hot application of oil of almonds with *Unguentum Dialtheae*, marsh mallow ointment, was used. For a drink Hall prescribed a distillate of a mixture of drugs which included horehound, hyssop, liquorice and aniseed, all items recommended for pulmonary complaints. The other drugs in the distillate were of a cordial and restorative nature.

A second distillate prepared on a B.M. (*Balneum Maris*) or water bath, formed a julep, which is a sweetened drink. This included snails, considered to be a remedy for consumptions.[5] The julep was taken with a solid medicine known as *Manus Christi* or Hand of Christ.[6] Finally a soothing, mucilaginous *Lohoch* or linctus was prescribed.[7]

1. Castle Ashby accounts, FD 1085(5).

2. WCRO, CR 555/274.

3. Oil of vitriol or sulphuric acid was added to the electuary. Hall frequently adds a few drops of the acid to a preparation in order to sharpen it and give it a 'pleasant and grateful taste'.

4. *Species Aromaticum Rosatum* used in the plaster was a mixture of red roses and spices. The formula was standardised in the London *Pharmacopoeia* of 1618.

5. Snails, *Limaces terrestres*, were among the whole animals listed in the London *Pharmacopoeia* of 1618.

6. *Manus Christi* was a restorative medicine prepared from a liquor made from damask roses, concentrated with sugar and poured onto marble. When solidified it was cut into tablets. *Manus Christi perlatum* contained powdered pearls and gold leaf. As Hall indicated, the name had been changed to *Saccharum Tabuli perlatum*.

7. *Lohoch Sanum et Expertum* in the final linctus included hyssop, liquorice and other drugs used for treatment of coughs. Penidies or *penidium* was clarified barley sugar.

8 *Select Observations*

Sen. lax. ʒß. *Syrup of the Juice of Roses* ʒi. *Celendine water* ʒiij. *mix them.* It gave him eight stools for four mornings. After I administred to him fasting the following; ℞ *of the inner Rind of the Barbery Tree, Turmerick, Shavings of Ivory and Hartshorn, of each alike quantity. Saffron half the quantity of one of them: make a Powder of all.* Dose ʒi, in a rear Egg. These cured him perfectly, although the Jaundice was very much all over his Body.

Observ. VII.

MR. *Powel* of *Ludlow*, aged 50, havingan *Opthalmia*, accompanied with a continual Defluxion, so that his whole face was excoriated, neither could he endure to see the light, was cured as followeth. There was given him ʒß. of *Amber Pills of Crato's*, made in three Pills four nights together; the first three gave him six stools the next day. Outwardly was applied the following, ℞ *Mastick, Frankinsence, Myrrh, each* ʒiß. *Dragons blood* ʒi. *Bole, Bean-meal, each* ʒß. *Saffron* Ði. *with White of Eggs, Oil of Roses, and a little Vinegar, make a Frontal,* which was applied. Into the Eye was distilled the following Collyrium. ℞ *prepared Tutty* ʒiß. *Camphire, Saffron, each* gr. xij. *Tie them up together in a fine Rag, and hang them in Rose water and White-wine, each* ʒiß. Of this there was dropt into his Eyes, he lying on his back, two or three drops three or four times a day. Whiles this was doing, was used the Decoction of *Sarsaparilla, and Guaiacum,* &c. without the Herbs prescribed,

Observ

6: [JOSEPH JELFES OF STRATFORD-UPON-AVON]

In 1622 Anthony Nash bequeathed the Bear in Bridge Street to his son, Thomas, later to become John Hall's son-in-law. Among other minor bequests was one of £10 to his servant, Joseph Jelfes, who may therefore be the patient in this case. The will was witnessed by a relative, Thomas Jelfes, who died in Stratford in June 1631: the inventory of his possessions shows that he owned basic furniture and clothes, but also a crop of corn (worth £2) and a horse (£2 10s.). In all, his goods were valued at £30 5s. Two members of his family, John and William, made their marks on the documents.[1]

Joseph Jelfes was suffering from yellow jaundice, the result of absorption of bile into the blood[2] and tertian ague, an intermittent fever where the paroxysms of fever occur every forty-eight hours. A yellow discolouration of the skin is among the symptoms of a serious chronic malarial infection.

The initial treatment was an emetic infusion mixed with a wine of squill *Scilla maritima* and an oxymel, which is a mixture of vinegar and honey. This was followed by a purge.

Finally various drugs were prescribed to be administered in a rear (rare or partially cooked) egg. The drugs included shavings of ivory *Ebur* or *Dens Elephantis*, often given in cases of jaundice, hartshorn *Cornu cervi*, which was frequently prescribed by Hall for the treatment of fevers, and saffron *Crocus sativus*. All parts of the crocus were used in medicine and it had many uses. Gerard refers to it as a drug to be used 'against stoppings of the liver, and gall, and against the yellow jaundice'.[3]

7: [MR] POWELL OF LUDLOW, SHROPSHIRE

The fact that this patient was recorded as a Ludlow inhabitant suggests that he was treated through Hall's links with the Compton family, who spent periods of residence in an official capacity in this Shropshire market town.

Unfortunately, the scant details that Powell was *Generosus* in status and born in the period 1561 to 1585, make him impossible to identify. Powell does not appear in any capacity in the Compton estate ledger (1629–35), where others of the household are mentioned.

This case of ophthalmia accompanied by an outbreak of ulcers on the face was attributed to a continuous defluxion of humours. Hall's treatment

1. (H)WRO, class 008.7 1632/145.

2. For an account of Galen's theories on the cause of jaundice see E.R. Long, *A History of Pathology* (New York, 1965), p. 20.

3. Gerard, *The Herball*, p. 124.

Obferv. 1. And fo in twenty days he was cured beyond all expectation.

Observ. VIII.

Mrs. *Chandler* of *Stratford* upon *Avon*, aged 34, after long Sicknefs, and a great Flux of her Courfes, falling into an ill habit of Body, was cured thus; Firft, fhe took the Decoction of *Sena*, &c. prefcribed *Obferv.* 1. for five days; after being let blood, her Courfes ftayed to admiration, and fhe became well. Three years after being extremely weakned with the like Flux in the time of her lying in, fo that Death was expected, fhe was cured by bleeding.

Observ. IX.

CHriftian *Bafs* of *Southam* in the County of *Warwick*, aged 29, was miferably tormented with Wind and Phlegm in the Stomach, which although by the taking of *Aqua Vitæ* fhe was for prefent eafed, yet it prefently returned with more violence, yea almoft to ftrangling; after which followed the Cholick. She was cured as follows, R Emetick Wine ℥v. *Wine of Squils* ℥ſſ. *mix them.* This given wrought very well by Vomits and Stools. The next day I gave this, R *Laurel prepared with Vinegar, the weight of 6 d. with Syrup of Violets, and Poffet-drink, make a Potion.* It gave
feven

was similar to that used in Observations 3 and 4; first a purgative amber pill, a plaster applied to the forehead, known as a frontal, and a collyrium into the eyes.

A decoction of sarsaparilla *Smilax* and guaiacum *Guaiacum officinale* (also known as *Lignum vitae*) were prescribed. These were drugs introduced into Europe from the West Indies by the Spaniards in the sixteenth century. They were recommended for the treatment of syphilis and other venereal diseases (no. 80). By Hall's time their use had been extended to the treatment of cutaneous diseases. In his treatment of the Countess of Northampton (no. 1) Hall also employed Sassafras *Sassafras albidum*. This too was introduced to Europe in the sixteenth century as a reputed anti-syphilitic. The first imports were from Florida and later from Virginia by Raleigh's colonists.

8: [MRS] CHANDLER OF STRATFORD-UPON-AVON

William Chandler (b. 1577) and his second wife, who was Hall's patient, lived in Ely Street. He was a prosperous mercer and had earlier married Elizabeth (b. 1582), eldest of Richard Quiney's ten children, on 8 November 1603. She was buried on 22 May 1615; there were three children of the marriage, only one of whom survived. In 1614 Chandler, as an alderman and commoner, became involved in a bitter dispute with William Combe, described in detail by Thomas Greene, town clerk of Stratford, when attempts were made to enclose common land at Welcombe.[1] Chandler was Greene's step-son.

Chandler remarried very soon after the death of his first wife, for on 1 July 1616 his son, Francis, was baptised, the eldest of eight children christened in Stratford between 1616 and 1639. Mrs Chandler's maiden name has not been traced. Hall attended her again (no. 28) two years later, when she had serious post-parturient symptoms. In her thirties, she was old by contemporary standards for repeated pregnancies. However, only one of her children died young. By 1635 William Chandler was living at Milcote but no record has been found of either his or his wife's burial.

On this occasion Hall was attending Mrs Chandler for a uterine haemorrhage and he treated her as a case of cacochymia, an 'ill habit of body', resulting from a long illness. Treatment involved the purgative decoction he prescribed for the Countess of Northampton (no. 1) and bleeding. Unlike other observations where venesection was used, Hall gave no details of which vein was opened or of the volume of blood taken.

---

1. SBTRO, BRU 15/13/26a–29.

seven ftools. The Body thus emptied, I prefcribed this, ℞ *London-Treacle, Mithridate, each* ʒi.
Conferve of Wormwood ʒiii. *mix them.* For three
mornings fhe drunk the Decoction of Mints and
Balm in fteeled Water. And fo fhe was perfectly
cured, for which fhe gave me many thanks, and
never was molefted with the like pain.

OBSERV. X.

Mrs. *Wincol*, the Countefs of *Northampton's*
Chamber-maid, aged about 48, afflicted
with a *Tenefmus*, and falling out of the Fundament,
was cured as follows: ℞ *Camomel* Mi. *Sack* ℔iſſ.
infufe them on hot coals for an hour or two: After
with linnen Clothes doubled, the *Anus* was fomented as hot as could be endured. After the Fundament was put up with ones finger, and a Spunge
dipt in the faid Decoction, and wrung out, was
applied thereto, on which fhe fate. Note, the
Flowers of *Camomel* are much better. Thus was
fhe delivered from both the aforefaid Evils.
After the fame manner was cured a Servant of
Mr. *Broads*.

OBSERV.

9: CHRISTIAN BASSE OF SOUTHAM

This patient cannot be identified with certainty from the details in Hall's notes. He gave her place of residence as *Southã* and Cooke added the Warwickshire location, possibly to distinguish it from Southam near Gloucester where Margaret Delabere lived (no. 115). No social status was recorded, and she was not noted as a gentlewoman.

There were only two girls baptised in Southam named Christian in the period 1582–1606 who could have been Hall's twenty-nine-year-old patient. Of these, neither was called Basse as a surname, but the young woman might have been Christian Bate, baptised at Southam on 15 March 1601/2, the eldest of the seven children of Thomas and Sara (née Jackson), married there on 12 November 1599. Christian Bate married into a family that Hall was later to attend (no. 39) when, on 18 April 1626, she became the bride of Thomas Judkin (b. 1600). This would not be the only occasion when Hall recorded a married woman he had known earlier by her maiden name. If Christian Judkin were his patient, he attended her in 1630 between her second and third pregnancies. Christian Bate was buried at Southam on 23 December 1657.

The patient had taken *Aqua Vitae*,[1] a spirit distilled from grain, to ease her stomach pains but gained only temporary relief. Hall began by ejecting phlegm from the stomach with an emetic medicine followed by a purgative of laurel, possibly spurge laurel *Daphne laureola*, which Gerard, quoting Dioscorides, recommended as a purge for phlegmatic humours.[2] The laurel was administered with syrup of violets in a posset (hot milk curdled with wine or ale).

After the patient had been purged, a mixture of the panaceas Treacle and Mithridate[3] was prescribed, mixed with wormwood.[4] This was followed by a stomachic drink containing mints and balm *Melissa officinalis* in steeled water,[5] designed to act as a stimulant to the stomach.

1. *Aqua vitae* is noted as a 'hot infusion' in *The Winter's Tale*, IV, iv, 787.

2. Gerard, *The Herball*, p. 938.

3. Treacles or *Theriacs* were electuaries composed of many ingredients including opium. They date from classical times. They originated as antidotes against the venom of serpents, then evolved as medicines to be used for protection against all poisons. Mithridate was a theriac based on the formula believed to have been composed by Mithridates, King of Pontus (132 to 63 BC), who feared death by poison. Hall prescribed London treacle *Theriaca Londinensis*, made to the formula of the London *Pharmacopoeia*. In the early seventeenth century these complex formulae were regarded as preservers of health and panaceas against all ills. See G. Watson, *Theriac and Mithridatum: A Study in Therapeutics* (1966).

4. Wormwood *Artemisia absinthium* is a bitter herb described by Dioscorides as good for wind and griping pains of the stomach. It was also used to wean infants as described in *Romeo and Juliet*, I, iii, 25.

5. Water in which steel had been quenched (no. 85) or containing an iron salt (nos 42, 152).

A page from Hall's manuscript case book (by kind permission of the British Library, Egerton MS 2065)

10: MRS WINCOLL, COMPANION TO
THE COUNTESS OF NORTHAMPTON

When the Earl of Northampton died suddenly on 24 June 1630, his steward, William Goodman, must have been exceptionally busy, to judge from the surviving estate account book for the years 1629 to 1635. Apart from the considerable funeral expenses, bills had to be settled and bequests made.

Mrs Wincoll appears regularly in these accounts as the recipient of an annuity of £5. She was entered in the accounts as 'M^ris', a definite indication of her status that matches Hall's description as *Generosa*. He also called her *pedissequa*, clearly a personal companion rather than 'chambermaid', and may well have been one of the two gentlewomen that the Countess demanded from her husband as part of her own household at his expense (no. 1). The Countess of Northampton, whom Mrs Wincoll attended, was to die two years after the Earl. The two entries in the ledger that were undeniably for medical services (£16 7s. 6d. and £9 0s. 2d.) at this period, 1632, could presumably have covered Mrs Wincoll's treatment as well as that of the Earl and Countess.[1]

It is not possible to identify Mrs Wincoll precisely and her surname is not common in the Midlands.

'Falling out of the fundament' probably means a prolapsed haemorrhoid. *Tenesmus* is the term for rectal pain. The condition was corrected by manual manipulation and the use of a fomentation prepared from a handful (*manipulus*) of the heat-retaining chamomile flowers in sack (either sherry or canary wine). For Mr Broad's 'servant', also treated by this method, see Observation 104.

11: ANNE HANBURY OF WORCESTER

Anne Hanbury (spelled, correctly, thus in Hall's manuscript notes) was the daughter of a Worcester alderman, John Hanbury, a royalist who lost his civic status when the city was captured by the parliamentary forces. A gentlewoman, Anne was married to the Bishop of Worcester's great-nephew, John Thornborough,[2] who was probably born at Suckley (Worcs.) in 1622 and died there in 1648 aged only twenty-six. By her father's will, she inherited £500 and £4 for a mourning gown.[3] He died on 1 December 1643 and after this date Anne married. She had one son, also John, born in 1646, who was still living at Suckley in 1670.

1. WCRO, CR 556/274.
2. *HV Worcs.*, 1682–3, p. 92.
3. (H)WRO, class 008.7 1644/57.

OBSERV. XI.

Mrs. *Hamberry* was cured of her Face that was
full of Puftles, Itch, and Excoriations,
and deformed as a Leper, with the following
Medicines. I purged her Body with *Amber-Pills*
ʒi. given when fhe went to bed, at twice; ufing
to her Face *Aq. Mercurial. Penot.* with the Emulfion of white Poppy-feeds, Borax, and white Sugar-candy.

OBSERV. XII.

JOhn *Emes* of *Alcefter*, aged 15. was cured of
piffing in bed thus, ℞ *the Windpipe of a Cock*
dried, and made into powder, and with Crocus Martis
given in a rear Egg every morning.

OBSERV. XIII.

Mrs. *Anne Gibs*, aged 19, cured of an Apoftem
in the Stomach. After its breaking, firft I
prefcribed her this Linéture, ℞ *Syrup of Hyffop,*
and Coltsfoot, each ʒi. *Vinegar of Squils* ʒi. *make*
a Linéture: Of which with a Liquoris ftick fhe
licked often. After fhe was purged with this;
℞ *Caffia new drawn with Endive water* ʒi. *Ruharb*
                                                powdered

Hall treated Anne again at her home in Worcester before her marriage (no. 91). She died on 18 September 1648, the same year as her husband, and is commemorated, along with her mother, in St Martin's Church, Worcester. Her age was cited then as thirty-four, and she was in fact baptised at St Swithin's, Worcester, on 31 July 1614.

The patient's severe cutaneous affliction was treated with a purgative amber pill (p. 3, note 2) and then with a lotion prepared from a water formed from the herb mercury *Chenopodium bonus-henricus*, poppy seeds, borax and sugar. Mercury was one of the herbs recommended for the treatment of skin diseases, its leaves applied by the common people to wounds and sores.[1]

12: JOHN EMES OF ALCESTER

This is one of Hall's cases where presumably Cooke added to the text from his own knowledge, for in the original Latin version the youth's place of residence was not recorded.

He was the son of John Emes, gentleman (1573–1655), who married Elizabeth Bellers on 29 May 1600; she died in 1627 and their monument, noted by Dugdale, can be seen in Alcester church. John Emes, junior, was baptised on 3 April 1608 and therefore was attended by Hall in 1623. He and his wife, Amy, had a son, also John, who was baptised on 1 April 1637, but was buried a month later. Emes made his living as a mercer and in 1629 he sold mill tithes to Robert Throckmorton.[2] In 1636 he was one of the overseers of the will of John Bovey of Alcester,[3] whose wife Hall attended (no. 166).

Joseph Emes, apparently John's nephew (baptised 15 October 1646), later became a medical practitioner, and was licensed as a surgeon by the Bishop of Worcester in August 1670.[4]

In this case the habit of bed-wetting (*enuresis*) was treated with a powder formed from the dried windpipe of a cock, and *Crocus martis* or iron oxide[5] administered in a 'rear' or partially cooked egg. Dioscorides refers to the crop of a fowl when dried being of help against immoderate evacuations.[6]

1. William Lewis, *An Experimental History of the Materia Medica* (2nd edn, 1768), p. 146.
2. *VCH Warws.*, III, p. 113.
3. (H)WRO, class 008.7 1636/30.
4. Morgan, no. 1340.
5. *Crocus martis* is an alchemical term, derived from the association between iron and the planet Mars.
6. R.T. Gunter (ed.), *The Greek Herbal of Dioscorides* (Englished by J. Goodyer 1655, Oxford, 1934), p. 104.

powdered ʒi. *Scabious Water* ʒiv. *Syrup of Chichory with Rubarb* ʒi. *make a Potion.* This gave eight Stools. To the Stomach I outwardly applied this hot. ℞ *Wormwood, Roſes, Bugloſſe, each a ſufficient quantity ; which make into a Pultis with the Oil of Roſes, Maſtick and Violets.* Laſt of all I' uſed this, ℞ *Roots of Flower-deluce, and Lillies,* each ʒi. Boil them in a Pint of White-wine to the half. Doſe ʒiv. in the morning. Thus ſhe became well, and of a good colour.

Observ. XIV.

FRances *Reyland* of *Quenton*, taking cold in the time of her Courſes, there aroſe Tumours both in her hands and feet, ſo that ſhe could not move her ſelf. She was cured as followeth ; firſt, ſhe received this. ℞ *Elect. Caryccoſtin.* ʒ iii. *Cryſtal. Tartar.* Ɔi. *cum Sacch. f. Bol.* It gave her ſix ſtinking Stools. After I cauſed a Vein to be opened, and ſo ſhe was freed.

Twenty days after ſhe relapſed, then I cauſed her to be purged with Laurel prepared, and after uſed the following Potion. ℞ *Guaiacum* ℔ſſ. *A-grimony, Brook-lime, Water-creſſes, Sage, Betony, Roſemary, each* Mi. *Boil them in* ℔ viii. *of Spring-water, till half waſted. In the end of the boyling, add Cinnamon and Anniſeed, each* ʒii. *after ſtrain them.* Doſe ʒviij in the morning, which procured ſweat. At her going to bed ſhe uſed this Bath. ℞ *Oak leaves* Mxx. *Camomel, Sage, Rhue, each* Mii. *Salt* ℔ii. *Allum* ℔i. *Quick Brimſtone* ʒ iv. *Boyl them*

13: ANNE GIBBS

Anne Gibbs is one of Hall's patients for whom very few details and no place of residence are given. Harriet Joseph suggested that Anne could have been related to George Gibbes, a borough overseer who knew the Shakespeare family. Alternatively, Wheler thought she may have been the daughter of Mr John Gibbs, alderman and thrice Bailiff of Stratford, who was buried on 12 December 1625. A more recent researcher considers she might be this man's second wife, who inherited his substantial wealth.[1]

Hall's original notes identified Anne as *Generosa* but not where she lived. She must have been born after 1592, although not baptised in Stratford, and she is possibly the Mrs Anne Gibbs who married Mr Thomas Cowper in the town on 30 October 1628, and therefore was born about 1607 and attended by Hall not long before her marriage. Only rarely was the bride's status title given in the registers, as, for example, when Hall's daughter married Thomas Nash, although the groom's was invariably noted. Thomas Cowper has proved equally elusive. The few facts known about her do not fit any other Anne Gibbs in the Stratford registers.

In this case Hall did not record the symptoms but stated that Anne had an *apostem* or abscess of the stomach which had broken.[2] Treatment began with a lincture, a term derived from the Latin *lingere*, to lick. These medicines were designed to be licked from a spoon or, as in this case, from a piece of liquorice root. Hyssop *Hysoppus officinalis*, coltsfoot *Tussilago farfara*[3] and squill were all expectorant drugs.

A purgative preparation containing cassia[4] and rhubarb was administered and a poultice applied containing wormwood which, when used externally, was believed to heat and strengthen the stomach. The decoction of the roots of lilies and Flower-deluce or common iris in white wine was another medicine with cathartic properties.

---

1. Jeanne Jones, *Family Life in Shakespeare's England: Stratford-upon-Avon 1570–1630*, forthcoming.

2. An *apostema* was defined as a 'hot impostume' or ulcer that speedily heals after it has broken. The symptoms were severe pain with a fever. Christoph Wirsung, *Praxis Medicinae Universalis or, a generall practise of physicke* (trans. Jacob Mosan, 1598), p. 374.

3. Coltsfoot was one of the principal pectoral herbs. Its Latin name was derived from *tussis*, a cough.

4. Cassia may be assumed to refer to the purgative pulp of the fruit of the tree *Cassia fistula*. References to this drug occur in the writings of the Arabic physicians, Avicenna and Mesue. The pulp deteriorates on removal from the fruit and had to be used 'new drawn'.

them all in a *ſufficient water for a Bath.* Often the
Member was anointed with this : ℞ *Vnguent.*
Martiat. ʒi. *Ol.Lumbric. & Terebinth.*ana ℨſſ. *miſc.*
Thus ſhe was perfectly cured.

Observ. XV.

MR. *Hunt* of *Stock-green,* aged about 46. labouring of a grievous Scab and Itch, was
thus helpt : ℞ *Fumitory, Borage, Bugloſs, Scabious,*
Wormwood, of each a like quantity, as much as you
pleaſe ; draw out the Juyces, of which take ℔ii.
boyling it in Whey to the Conſumption of the Whey,
always ſcumming of it ; after it is boyled ſuffer it to
ſettle. Drink every day a good draught of it cold
with Sugar. This is the *Syr. Scabious. Joh. Anglici,*
and a Secret by which hecured many of the Scab,
with which I have cured many alſo.

Observ. XVI.

MR. *Diſon,* who was grievouſly tormented with
a Pain at the mouth of the Stomach (uſu-
ally called the Heart-ach), fainting, as alſo Ill-
neſs in a morning till he eat, was cured thus : ℞
Pil. Ruffi. de Succin. Stomac. Hier. ſimpl. ana ℈i.
f. Pil. 7. Theſe purged freely. After I gave him
the following every morning : ℞ *Conſerv. Roſar. &*
Mithrid. ã ℨi. *Conſerv. Abſynth.* ℥iii. *Theriac. Lond.*
℥vi. *Miſc.* Doſe ℨiſſ. By theſe he was wholly freed.

OBSERV.

14: FRANCES RILAND OF QUINTON

Although he recorded her name and place of residence, Hall noted neither status nor age for this patient. She was most likely the wife of Thomas or Richard Riland of Quinton, on the Gloucestershire border with Warwickshire. Thomas Riland (b. 1580), who was churchwarden there in 1629, had eleven children, including a set of twins, born in the years 1606 to 1624. Richard Riland's six children were baptised in the period 1614 to 1624, but unfortunately neither man's marriage has been traced. The Rilands seem to have been of modest status and Frances was not noted as *Generosa*, a detail that Hall regularly recorded.

Frances Riland was suffering from tumours or swellings of the hands and feet which Hall attributed to taking cold during her menstruation. The first object of treatment was to deal with the disturbance of the humours by the administration of a purgative electuary[1] and by bleeding. When she relapsed after twenty days, Hall prescribed a purge of laurel and, to make her sweat, a potion containing guaiacum, scorbutics and other herbs. He also recommended a bath prepared from herbs, sulphur and two astringent drugs, alum and oak galls. The patient's hands and feet were rubbed with *Unguentum Martiatum* or Soldier's ointment[2] mixed with turpentine and oil of earthworms.[3]

15: MARY HUNT OF STOCK GREEN, WORCESTERSHIRE

In Hall's Latin version this patient was entered as *Generosa Hunt*, a female of genteel birth, rather than as a male, as in Cooke's edition. Earlier commentaries, such as Fripp's, identify the patient, because of gender confusion, as Simon Hunt, a Stratford schoolmaster between the years 1571 and 1575, who may indeed have taught Shakespeare. However, this suggestion cannot be sustained as the patient was female and lived at Stock Green (Worcs.), just off the main Alcester–Worcester road.

Mary was the daughter of Richard Russell (d. 1617) of Flyford Flavell (Worcs.) and she married Henry Hunt of nearby Bradley in about 1612.[4]

1. *Electuarium Carycostinum* contained the purgative resin scammony. Crystal tartar is the purified deposit thrown off during the fermentation of wine. Very fine crystals obtained by a modification of the purification process was known as cream of tartar.

2. The formula for Soldier's ointment was attributed to the Byzantine physician, Nicolaus Myrepsus or Alexandrinus, who lived in the second half of the thirteenth century. It had over seventy ingredients, mostly herbs, but also some animal medicines such as marrow of a stag bone *Medulla cervi* and grease of bear *Adeps ursi*.

3. Oil of earthworms *Oleum lumbricorum* was prepared by digesting earthworms in olive oil and wine (no. 108).

4. *HV Worcs.*, 1682–3, p. 64 and 1634, p. 50.

William Compton, first Earl of Northampton
(by kind permission of the Marquess of Northampton)

Her sister, Jane, married George Simonds of White Ladies Aston in 1628 and Mary Hunt was thus the aunt of another Hall patient in the locality, Isabel Simonds (no. 48). The Hunts were substantial farmers in the Crowle area.[1]

Mary Hunt was widowed by the time she made a will on 18 November 1647, her husband having died in about 1635 aged over fifty; her inventory was written a week later.[2] She made money bequests ($£2$ to $£10$) to three sons and two daughters, all married, and to her nine grandchildren; the daughters also received small pieces of furniture. The inventory shows that she was worth $£80$ 13s. 4d., comprising the usual modest household goods, livestock and apparel, but also, unexpectedly, $£70$ owed to her in bills and bonds.

To treat her skin condition a drink was prepared from the juice of herbs mixed with whey and sugar. Of the herbs, fumitory *Fumaria officinalis* was recommended for scorbutic and cutaneous maladies, and the flowers of scabious *Scabiosa arvensis* were said to be hot and dry in nature and of use in leprous conditions.[3] Hall attributed the formula to *Johannes Anglicus* or John of Gaddesden (*c.* 1280–1361), physician to Edward II. His *Rosa Anglica Practica Medicinae* was the first medical work by an Englishman to be printed (in Pavia by J.A. Birreta in 1492).

16: THOMAS DYSON OF MORTON UNDERHILL, WORCESTERSHIRE

In 1545 Robert Dyson of Inkberrow acquired substantial Worcestershire lands at the Dissolution and Hall's patient, Thomas Dyson, was his great-great-nephew. The family continued to live in the parish into the eighteenth century.

Hall was attending a number of other families in the area, and this patient appears to be Thomas Dyson, the eldest of the twelve children of Thomas and Margaret (née Hanway). He bought part of the manor of Morton Underhill,[4] a hamlet close to Inkberrow, in 1624–5 and married Elizabeth Manning of Weybridge (Surrey) in about 1628. Dyson kept turkeys and poultry on the Worcestershire border.[5] He had seven children.[6] The heir, Thomas, was born in 1629, but, by the time his father's will was

1. Nash, App., p. 100.

2. (H)WRO, class 008.7 1648/85.

3. Culpeper, *The London Dispensatory*, p. 35. Scabious was derived from *scabies* scab, mange or itch. Scabies is the name now given to the condition caused by the itch mite *Sarcoptes scabiei*, first described by Giovanni Bonomo in 1687.

4. *VCH Worcs.*, II, p. 424.

5. WoQS, pp. 392, 536.

6. *HV Worcs.*, 1634, pp. 32–3.

OBSERV. XVII.

MAry Heath of *Libington*, aged 34, being cruelly vexed with a *Dysentery Catarrh*, Pain in the Back, Worms, casting out a thick stinking matter by Urine, having been before fat, but now grown lean, was thus cured ; ℞ *Rubarb* powdered ʒiſs. *Syrup of Roses solutive* ʒi. *Borage Water* ʒiij. *make a Potion.* This was given in the morning. Afterward this Clyster was cast in : ℞ the *Decoction of torrified Barly* ℔i. *Oil of Roses* ʒiii. *two Yolks of Eggs,* red *Sugar* ʒiſs. *make a Clyster.* After the Clyster this was exhibited, ℞ *Yellow Wax* ʒſs. *Crocus Martis* ʒi. *Make of them a Ball like a Nutmeg, after put it into the midst of an Apple, the Core taken out ; after roast the Apple under hot Ashes, so that they may be melted into the substance of the Apple ;* and so she eat it fasting. Her Drink was steeled, her Diet was *Panados*, made of French Barly dried, and Crums of Bread, with steeled Water and Sugar. With these Remedies she was perfectly cured. *I have also cured many with Wax so prepared.*

made in 1651, he had left home and the estate was promised to his younger brother, Francis. There had clearly been bitterness between father and son, for Thomas junior was left £200 'if he come again to Morton Hall', forfeit if he caused a disturbance trying to claim the manor for himself.[1] Thomas Dyson's two surviving daughters were unmarried. His baptism has not been traced as the parish registers are too late and the transcripts are defective.

The Catholic Fortescues were neighbours and in 1636 Thomas Dyson signed as an appraiser of the inventoried goods of William Ballard of Inkberrow.[2] A monument in Inkberrow church porch, where he wished to be buried, recorded Dyson's death in 1651. His will was proved on 22 September 1653.

Hall treated this case of heart-ache or heartburn with a purgative pill composed of the formulae of three preparations: amber pills, *Pilulae stomachicae*[3] and *Hiera picra*,[4] all three containing aloes. This was followed by a stomachic electuary containing the panaceas Mithridate, Theriac and a conserve made with the bitter absinthium or wormwood. Bitters were traditional remedies for loss of appetite and digestive problems. In the original manuscript Hall added comments on concoction or digestion (no. 116).

17: MARY HEATH OF 'LIBINGTON'

This patient cannot be identified with any certainty but her lack of title suggests a humble social status. Furthermore, Libington, as written by Hall, is not a known place-name. If she were born in the period 1577 to 1601 she could be Mary Edley, the wife of John Heath, a Stratford labourer's eldest son, whom she married on 8 January 1623, and the eldest daughter of John Edley and Mary Spearpoint (m. 1603).

Tracing the Heath family is confused by the use of the alias Swanne by some members and if Mary's husband were also known by this surname, then they had two daughters baptised in Stratford. The place 'Libington' has been presumed to be Luddington, some 2 miles south-west of Stratford, although this would be a strange mistake for Hall to have made.

1. PRO, Prob 11/229.

2. (H)WRO, class 008.7 1641/14.

3. *Pilulae stomachicae* had a relatively simple formula composed of aloes, mastic and red roses mixed with syrup of wormwood. It was attributed in the London *Pharmacopoeia* to Mesue, an anonymous thirteenth-century Latin author known as Mesue junior to distinguish him from Mesue (777–857), the Nestorian Christian who wrote in Arabic. See G. Urdang, 'History of the Pharmacopoeia Londinensis' in *Pharmacopoeia Londinensis*, 1618 (1944), p. 7.

4. The formulae for *Hiera picra* was attributed to Galen. *Hiera* was the name given to an electuary containing aloes.

OBSERV. XVIII.

Mrs. *Lain* of *Auſon,* aged 49, much troubled with Pain in her Breaſt, and great difficulty of breathing, was cured as followeth : ℞ *Troches of Agarick* ℈ii, *with Honey of Roſes, and Syrup of preſerved Ginger, make a Bole.* This was taken for three days ; the firſt day it gave four Stools, the ſecond day ſix, and third three. The fourth day was taken a Spoonful of the following, as often as difficulty of breathing required, ſwallowing it by degrees. ℞ *Raiſins* ℥ ſs. *Hyſſop, Origanum, Horehound, Penny-royal, Speedwel, Germander, Scabious, Coltsfoot, Carduus benedictus, Nettles, each* Mſs. *Oris Roots ſliced, Calamus Aromaticus, each* ℥i. *Agarick* ʒiij. *Sena* ℥ii. *Ginger* ʒii. *Of theſe make a Decoction in* ℔ij. *of Wine-Vinegar, pouring in a third part of Water, and boil it to the third part. After ſtraining, add of the beſt Honey* ℥xii. *after boyl it to the thickneſs of an Oxymel.* You may hang in it afterward theſe things following in a little fine Rag, viz. *Cinnamon, Cloves, Calamus Aromaticus,* all powdered, Doſe a ſpoonful at a time. This is excellent, and worth Gold.

Mary Heath suffered from worms (no. 40) and a dysentery with a mucous discharge. Treatment began with a rhubarb potion, followed by a clyster or enema prepared using torrified or roasted barley. The principal medicament was what Hall calls a 'wax'. *Crocus martis* or iron oxide was mixed with yellow beeswax and placed inside an apple, which was roasted so that the wax penetrated the substance of the apple.

Hall noted that the patient had grown lean and his final treatment was of a dietary nature. Her drink was to be steeled, that is, to contain iron (no. 9), and she was to eat *panados*, a bread made with French barley and boiled to a pap with steeled water and sugar.

18: JOAN LANE OF ALVESTON

Joan Lane, a gentlewoman, was the wife of Richard Lane of Bridgetown, Stratford-upon-Avon. He was the younger son of Nicholas Lane of Stratford, gentleman (d. 26 July 1595), whose effigy stands in the old church at Alveston,[1] locally pronounced 'Auson' and spelled phonetically by Hall, as in his notes on Clare Peers (no. 127).

Richard Lane bought Alveston manor in 1603. He married Joan, the daughter of Henry Whitney of Mitcham, Surrey, in about 1588.[2] Whitney was sufficiently loyal to guard an important Worcestershire recusant prisoner, John Talbot of Grafton, who lodged at Mitcham in 1587.[3] Joan Lane's eldest son, Edward (1589–1625), married Mary Combe of Old Stratford, whose mother, Katherine (née Boughton), and sister, Mary, were also Hall's patients (nos 134, 144).

Newly widowed, Joan Lane died in 1613, and Hall was presumably attending her in her last illness; if she were aged forty-nine, she must have been born in 1564. Hers is thus the second earliest case in his notes, for Elizabeth Boughton was attended in 1611 (no. 73). Joan Lane's inventory, now damaged, was made on 11 October 1613; of the total value (a little more than £47) her clothes were worth £13 6s. 4d. and she had £3 13s. 6d. cash in her purse. Among her personal goods was a supply of rose-water, presumably as prescribed by Hall. Her possessions in all were valued at £26 3s. 6d. and she also had money due to her from fourteen local inhabitants to a total of some £23. William Chandler was an appraiser.[4]

Joan Lane was suffering from a pulmonary illness with difficulty of breathing. Treatment began with the customary purge, this time using a

1. Pevsner, *Warws.*, p. 65.
2. *HV Warws.*, 1619, p. 307.
3. John Humphreys, *Studies in Worcestershire History* (Birmingham, 1938), p. 180.
4. (H)WRO, class 008.7 1613/208a.

Observ. XIX.

Mrs. *Hall* of *Stratford*, my Wife, being miſerably tormented with the Cholick, was cured as followeth. ℞ *Diaphœn. Diacatholic.* ana ℥i. *Pul. Holand* ℨii. *Ol. Rutæ* ℥i. *Lact. q. ſ. f. Clyſt.* This injected gave her two Stools, yet the Pain continued, being but little mitigated; therefore I appointed to inject a Pint of Sack made hot. This preſently brought forth a great deal of Wind, and freed her from all Pain. To her Stomach was applied a Plaiſter *de Labd. Crat. cum Caran. & Spec. Aromat. roſat. & Ol. Macis.* With one of theſe Clyſters I delivered the Earle of *Northampton* from a grievous Cholick.

Observ. XX.

Mrs. *Herbert*, miſerably vexed with a Pain of her Side, was thus eaſed: ℞ *of Spirit of Wine, or Aqua Vitæ* (which is next hand) ℥vi. *Camphire* ℥i. *boyl them a little till the Camphire be diſſolved, adding whilſt hot, red Saunders pulverized* ℨiſſ. A Cloth was wet in this Liquor, and applied.

preparation of agaric.[1] She was then prescribed a decoction of pectoral drugs, cathartics and other herbs made into an oxymel by heating with honey. Among the herbs used were nettle *Urtica dioica*, which had many uses, horehound *Marrubium vulgare*, which was recommended for humoral asthma, and carduus benedictus or holy-thistle *Cnicus benedictus*, a bitter, astringent herb reputed to be hot and dry in the second degree.[2] The oxymel was to be taken as often as difficulty of breathing required and Hall's acknowledgement of its excellent qualities referred to its soothing nature and the fact that it afforded some temporary relief in what appears to have been a final illness.

19: SUSANNA HALL OF STRATFORD-UPON-AVON

John Hall's wife, Susanna, was Shakespeare's eldest daughter, baptised on 26 May 1583, six months after her parents' marriage, when her father was only eighteen but her mother eight years older. Nearly two years later Susanna acquired a brother and sister when the twins, Hamnet and Judith, were born. Susanna was an uncommon Christian name, first appearing among Stratford baptisms in 1574.

How Susanna Shakespeare came to marry John Hall in 1607 has not been discovered. She must, however, have been an acceptable bride, for by early 1598 the Shakespeares had moved into New Place, the town's second largest house. She became wealthy at her father's death in 1616, inheriting New Place, two houses in Henley Street, Stratford, and a London property at Blackfriars. John and Susanna Hall were executors of the poet's will.[3] Elizabeth Hall was the only child of their marriage.

During Shakespeare's lifetime, however, and when Hall was a well-regarded Stratford resident, a case of slander concerning Susanna burst upon the town. It must have been an irresistible topic of conversation when John Lane, junior, was sued in the Worcester consistory court for claiming that Susanna 'had the runinge of the raynes [a venereal infection] & had bin naught [had committed adultery] with Rafe Smith at John Palmer[s]'.[4] The assertion was clearly very serious and Susanna must have felt it so to seek redress in the church court. Rafe Smith (b. 1577) was a prominent hatter in the town. The reasons why the young John Lane, aged only twenty-three, was moved to make the accusation are unknown. He was the

---

1. Troches of Agaric *Agaricus Trochiscatus* were lozenges of agaric and listed in the London *Pharmacopoeia* of 1618 under the heading *Trochisci Purgantes*.
2. Carduus benedictus was widely prescribed and sufficiently well known to be used as a pun on the name Benedick in *Much Ado About Nothing*, III, iv, 68.
3. *Life*, pp. 236–7.
4. Ibid., p. 237.

Michael Drayton, from an engraving in his *Poly-Olbion*, 1619

second son of John Lane of Alveston manor and later in the same year, 1613, Hall was treating his aunt, Joan, in her last illness (no. 18). However, as Lane failed to attend the Worcester court, the case was closed and he was excommunicated.

Susanna was widowed in 1635. She inherited Hall's house in London[1] but continued to live at New Place and is believed to have been hostess to Queen Henrietta Maria there in July 1643. She died on 11 July 1649 and was buried five days later aged sixty-six. Her epitaph (noted by Dugdale) was damaged, but later reinstated:

> Witty above her sex, but that's not all,
> Wife to salvation was good Mistress Hall
> Something of Shakespeare was in that, but this
> Wholy of him with whom she's now in blisse,
> Then Passenger ha'st ne're a teare,
> To weep with her that wept with all;
> That wept, yet set her selfe to chere
> Them up with comforts cordial.
> Her love shall live, her mercy spread,
> When thou ha'st ner'e a teare to shed.[2]

Hall treated his wife's colic with two purgative electuaries, *Diaphoenicon* and *Diacatholicon*,[3] and a purgative powder *Pulvis Rodolphi Holland laxitivus*, all three represented in the London *Pharmacopoeia* of 1618. In this case they were mixed with oil of rue and milk to form a clyster or enema. A second enema composed of hot sack appears to have been more successful in relieving the patient. Hall informed his readers that with one of these enemas he cured the Earl of Northampton of colic, but for some reason does not say which one.

It was usual in cases of stomach pains to prescribe a plaster to be applied over the stomach. In this case Hall used a plaster devised by Crato containing labdanum, a resin from a shrub grown in Crete. To this formula Hall added Caranna, a tree resin imported from South America, *Species aromaticum rosatum* and oil of mace.

1. Appendix 1.
2. Dugdale, II, p. 686.
3. *Diaphoenicon* contains the purgative gum-resin *diagrydium* or scammony. The prefix *dia* is from the Greek meaning 'made from'. The formula for *Diacatholicon* included cassia, tamarind, senna and rhubarb. *Catholicon* was a name given to a preparation intended to purge all humours.

OBSERV. XXI.

MAry *Wilfon* aged 22, afflicted with a Hectick Feaver, with a Cough, Obftructions of her Courfes, and Weaknefs, was thus cured : There were appointed Meats boiled, as Veal, Hens, Capons, fed either with Barley, or crammed with Paft made of Barly Meal ; Frogs, Snails, and River-Crabs were alfo exhibited ; by this fhe got Flefh. Our Reftorative was a Caudle made of the yolks of Eggs, Wine, and Sugar. She alfo ufed the following Panatella ; R *Crums of Bread moiftned with Milk, and after mixed with Almond Milk, Rofe-water,* and *Sugar.* A *Ptyfan,* or Cream of Barly was thus prepared : R *Barly* ℥ii. *Purflain, Borage,* each M℥. Boil *them in* ℔x *of Water, till a fourth part be wafted ; after ftrain it, and drink of it.* She frequently ufed Sugar of Rofes. For a Clyfter this was ufed : R *Chicken-broth* ℥x. *in which was boyled Seeds of Poppies, Flowers of Water-Lillies, Violets, Lettice, Mallowes,* each M℥. *Being ftrained, there was added Oil of Violets* ℥iß. *White Sugar* ℥ii. *Honey of Violets* ℥iß. *Common Salt* ℥iß. *the Yolk of one Egg ; mix them.* She fucked Womens Milk, nourifhed with cooling and moiftning Diet, as Lettice. A year after this fhe died.

C OBSERV.

20: MRS HERBERT

Although this patient was recorded in Hall's original case notes as M^ris Harbert' (Herbert was Cooke's version), no further information is given to make identification possible. She does not appear to be of Stratford and she is one of the few females to whom he gives the title 'Mistress'.

The pain in the side was relieved by the application of a hot fomentation. Hall prescribed camphor dissolved in spirit of wine or *aqua vitae* (whichever was available)[1] and powdered red saunders wood *Pterocarpus santalinus*. This wood, imported from the East Indies, was used as an astringent and for the deep red colour it imparted to spiritous preparations.

21: MARY WILSON

Although Mary Wilson must have been born in the period 1589 to 1613 and died between 1612 and 1635, she has not been identified. Hall did not note this young woman as *Generosa* or as a Stratford inhabitant, and indeed there is no one of this very common mix of names in the parish registers of Warwickshire and Worcestershire who could be positively identified as Hall's patient.

The symptoms[2] and the treatment prescribed indicate that Mary Wilson was suffering from tuberculosis. Hall advised a diet of light meats which included snails, frogs and river crabs *cancri fluviales* (crayfish), all cooling in their nature. In addition he recommended a caudle (a warm sweetened drink), a *ptysan* (a barley drink), including the restorative and cordial purslane *Portulaca oleracea* and borage *Borago officinalis*, a *panatella* (similar in its nature to a *panados* described in Observation 17) and an enema with chicken broth and cooling herbs. Finally he reported that she sucked woman's milk[3] and kept to a cooling moistening diet. This was the regime for a consumptive patient, a prescribed diet that would reduce the acrimony of the humours, of a restorative, cooling nature and easy to digest.

Hall reported that Mary Wilson died the following year. In the manuscript he added 'she sleeps with God'.

1. Comparable to choosing between brandy and whisky.

2. A hectic fever is one where the patient's temperature rises during the day and falls in the early hours.

3. Woman's milk for this purpose was recommended long after Hall's time. In 1772 William Buchan wrote that it had performed extraordinary cures in consumptive cases: *Domestic Medicine* (2nd edn, 1772), p. 225.

Observ. XXII.

MR. *Drayton,* an excellent Poet, labouring of a Tertian, was cured by the following : Rx *the Emetick Infusion ʒi. Syrup of Violets a spoonful : mix them.* This given, wrought very well both upwards and downwards.

Observ. XXIII.

GOod-Wife *Betis,* aged 40, who once a month (yea sometimes twice or thrice) was grievously pained on the right side of her Head, which often ended with vomiting, and in her Fit could neither walk nor stand : was cured thus : First, she took this Vomit : Rx *the vomiting Infusion ʒi.* This wrought six times. For the next day was provided the following Pills : Rx *Pil. de Succin. ʒii. Cephal. Fernel. ʒi. f. Pil.* Nº xv. She took three of them before supper, every day till they were spent. After I caused a Vein to be opened to ʒvi. After she took this Decoction : Rx *Sarsaparilla ʒiv. Water ℔x. being sliced, let them infuse for twenty four hours, after boyl them till half be wasted, strain it.* Dose a draught morning and night, when she went to bed. For ordinary Drink, she took the second Decoction, which was made of the same Wood, adding ℔xv of Water, boyling it without infusion till the third part be wasted.

OBSERV.

22: MICHAEL DRAYTON, POET

The best-known of Hall's patients today is the poet Michael Drayton, Shakespeare's contemporary, born at Hartshill in north Warwickshire in 1563 (or 1567 by his own account in 1627).[1] He has been described as 'very temperate in life, slow in speech and inoffensive in company'.[2] He came to be treated by Hall through Anne, Lady Rainsford, second daughter of Sir Henry Goodere of Polesworth, whom Drayton had served as a page. Drayton's role in the household may be judged from his witnessing Sir Henry's will (1595) and also participating in a land transaction in 1618 with two members of the Goodere family.[3] He depicted Anne Goodere as 'Idea' and dedicated to her the sixty-four sonnets he published in 1594, including 'Since there's no help, come let us kiss and part'.[4]

After Anne Goodere (no. 168) had married Henry Rainsford of Clifford Chambers in 1596, the poet seems to have been a regular visitor, for two or three months every summer, at her new home. He described 'dear' Clifford in his topographical *Polyolbion* (completed in 1622) as a 'place of health and sport' in the fourteenth song, printed in 1612. The work also noted the medicinal plants growing in the area and the Warwickshire section begins with words of praise for a pious and learned practitioner, generally presumed to be John Hall:

> His happy time he spends the works of God to see,
> In those so sundry herbs which there in plenty growe.

Although the occasion is not dated and the patient's age omitted, Hall must have been treating Drayton for fever when he was a visitor at Clifford Chambers. Drayton certainly wrote to William Drummond of Hawthornden from Clifford on 14 July 1631, with less than six months to live. Drayton died at his lodgings in London in December 1631; the inventory of his goods showed a value of only £24 8s. 2d.[5] He was buried in Westminster Abbey, his black marble monument by Edward Marshall, whose work he may have seen at Holy Trinity, Stratford, commemorating the Earl of Totnes (1629). Michael Drayton never married and the night before he died wrote, presumably to his 'Idea':

> Soe well I love thee, as without thee I
> Love Nothing: yf I might Chuse, I'd rather dye
> Then bee on[e] day debarde thy Companye . . .[6]

1. Professor B.C. Capp kindly provided advice and help with Drayton.
2. Cited in Fogg, p. 58.
3. *VCH Warws.*, IV, p. 189.
4. Bernard H. Newdigate, *Michael Drayton and his Circle* (Oxford, 1941), pp. 40–55.
5. Ibid., p. 222.
6. Ibid., p. 54.

Observ. XXIV.

Mrs. *Boughton*, being with Child, and troubled with Vomiting, and a Flux of the Belly, was thus freed: ℞ *Sack* ℥vi. *Oil of Vitriol fix drops.* She took an Ounce of it every morning fafting as long as it lafted. Her *Stomach* was anointed with the following: ℞ *Oil of Wormwood, and Mace, each* ℥ß. *Spec. aromatic. rofat.* ℈ß. *mix them, and make an Ointment.* As fhe pleafed fhe took of this Julep: ℞ *Syrup of Poppies* ℥iii. *Waters of Scabious and Mints, each* ℥ii. *of Borage* ℥vi. *Oil of Vitriol to fharpen it for tafte: mix them, and make a Julep.* Thus fhe was cured, praifed be God.

Observ. XXV.

MR. *Randulph*, aged 35, troubled with Pain of the Head, great Diftillation, and continual Spitting, with coldnefs of his Head, fo that he was conftrained to wear three Caps, was delivered from all in feven days by the following: ℞ *the Emetick Infufion* ℥i. This gave fix Vomits, and three Stools. The next morning were taken the following Pills. ℞ *Pil. Coch.* ℈i. *Aurear.* ℈ß. *Troch. Alhand.* gr. vi. *cum Syr. Betonic.* f. *Pill.* 7. Thus purged, there was taken away ℥vi of Blood. Afterward there was taken morning and evening ℥i of the following Powder: ℞ *Powder of Sena* ℥vi.

Rocket

With the exception of Mrs Barnes, who was pregnant (no. 66), Hall treated all cases of tertian fever with an emetic infusion mixed either with oxymel or, as in Drayton's case, with the gently laxative syrup of violets.

23: MRS BETTES

The most difficult of all patients to identify after over three centuries are women such as this, whose only personal detail is her age. She must have been born in the period 1571 to 1595. In the original Latin notes Hall spelled her name and that of Mrs Bettes of Ludlow (no. 5) identically and they may be the same woman. She was recorded here by Hall as 'mulier' or wife. In the Compton family account ledger there was a male servant, William Betts, regularly paid wages for household expenses in the 1630s, to whom she could have been related.[1]

The migraine-like symptoms experienced by the patient were treated first with an emetic infusion to remove peccant humours from the stomach and then with a pill made from the ingredients for amber pills mixed with a cephalic composed by the French physician Jean Fernel (1497–1558). *Cephalica* were remedies for the cure of disorders of the head. Among the cephalic drugs were amber, musk, clove, cinnamon, camphor, betony, rosemary and sage.[2]

Hall ordered Mrs Bettes to be bled and six fluid ounces of blood to be removed from a vein. The sarsaparilla decoction was intended to cause sweating and purify the humours. Hall claimed to have cured his patient.

24: JOYCE BOUGHTON OF CAWSTON, DUNCHURCH

Joyce Boughton was baptised on 10 May 1593 at Stratford-upon-Avon, the third child of Thomas and Mary Combe; her elder brother was William, who married Katherine Boughton of Lawford (no. 134), one of the several links between the two families. Joyce Combe married Edward Boughton of Cawston, grandson of another Edward (d. 1589), who had built Cawston House, Dunchurch, much praised by Dugdale.[3] She bore five sons and four daughters in sixteen years; the eldest two, Edward and William, died as infants. Her other children were Francis (baptised on 7 September 1619), Elizabeth (17 October 1620), Anne (28 April 1622), Bridget (1625), Thomas (1627), Richard and Mary.

1. WCRO, CR 556/274.
2. A list of cephalic drugs is given in Renodoeus (J. Renou), *A Medicinal Dispensatory* (Englished and revised by Richard Tomlinson of London, Apothecary, 1657).
3. Dugdale, I, p. 287.

Rocket Seed ʒſſ. Long Pepper ʒiſſ. *Make a Powder of these.* After the taking of it ſeven days he became altogether well.

OBSERV. XXVI.

Mrs. *Boughton* of *Cauſon*, aged 28, three days after Miſcarriage in the fifth month, fell into a Feaver, accompanied with abundance of After-fluxes, Vomiting, Loathing, Thirſt, Swooning, and in danger of Death, was ſpeedily helped as follows : ℞ *burnt Hartſhorn finely powdered* ʒi. *Boyl it in three quarts of Spring water, till a quart be waſted, then remove it from the Fire; after add Syrup of Limons* ʒii. *Roſewater* ʒiv. *Sugar a ſufficient quantity.* This ſhe drank conſtantly inſtead of Drink, which gave great eaſe. The following Decoction was given morning and evening, which did cleanſe, cut, caſt out, and extinguiſh Thirſt. ℞ *French Barly* Miv. *Violets* p. ii. *Liquoris* ʒſſ. *Jujebs* ʒi. *Sebeſtens* ʒii. *Carduus benedictus* M i ſſ. *Make a Decoction in a ſufficient quantity of Water to* ℔xij. *To the ſtraining add Sugar of Violets* ʒiv. *and make a Drink.* By theſe Medicines alone ſhe was cured beyond all expectation, praiſed be God.

Joyce Boughton's husband died in October 1642, when she was forty-nine years old. No record of her burial has been found and Cawston parish register carries a note in a contemporary hand that 'From the year 1648 to ye year 52 ye Register is defective during the troubles of Cromwell'.[1]

Mrs Boughton suffered from vomiting and flux of the belly (diarrhoea) and Hall treated her with ounce doses of sack (sherry or canary wine), acidified with oil of vitriol (sulphuric acid). She was instructed to take, when required, a julep containing the narcotic syrup of poppies mixed with water made from mints, scabious and the cordial borage. The ointment prescribed contained oil of wormwood, which, when applied externally, was believed to heat and strengthen the stomach.

25: FERRERS RANDOLPH OF WOOD BEVINGTON, SALFORD PRIORS

Ferrers Randolph was baptised at Salford Priors on 14 October 1584, heir to property at Bevington. He inherited at his father's death in 1626, but was soon in financial difficulties. In 1630 he began mortgaging parts of the estate and in 1636 sold the whole to St John's College, Oxford, for £3,633 13s. 4d. and an annual rent of £200 to become the College's tenant on a 300-year lease.[2] By 1637 he had also incurred a substantial debt to Edward Ferrers of Baddesley Clinton. He served Warwickshire as a County Treasurer in 1633.[3]

Ferrers Randolph was fined in 1640 at Quarter Sessions for not maintaining the section of the Stratford–Worcester road that was his responsibility. He complained that he suffered particularly in the Civil War from the depredations of both sides, since his estate was sited in between important military towns.[4] Dugdale noted him as a royalist in 1642.[5]

He married Elizabeth (no. 65) in about 1619, the year he was attended by Hall. His younger brother, Edward, married Dorothy Izod of Stanton (Glos.), whose father Hall also treated (no. 121). Ferrers's son and heir, Thomas, was born in 1620. His daughter, Elizabeth, was Edward's god-daughter and was bequeathed £2 and a piece of black plush by her uncle in 1651. By this time Ferrers was dead,[6] although the exact date of his death has not been traced.

1. WCRO, DR 73/1.
2. *VCH Warws.*, III, p. 160.
3. QSOB, I, p. 175.
4. Ibid., VI, pp. 54, 56.
5. NRO, Finch-Hatton 4284.
6. H.S. Gunn, *Wood Bevington: a history of the old manor house of Wood Bevington* (1912), p. xvii.

OBSERV. XXVII.

CAptain *Baſſet*, aged about 50, afflicted with a Tertian, was thus cured: ℞ *Emetick Infuſion* ʒv. *Wine of Squils* ʒii. *Syrup of Violets a ſpoonful*; *mix them.* This was given an hour before the Fit, which wrought by vomit and ſtool ſufficiently. At the end of vomiting he took this: ℞ *Elect. de Gem. frigid.* Ɖii. *Diaſcord.* ʒſſ. *Syr. Papav. erratic.* ℥i. *Aq. Scabioſ.* ℥iii. *Miſc.* The next day he was free from his Fit, he took the following: ℞ *Diaphænic. Diacathol.* ā ʒii. *Rhab. Pul. Pul. Sen. laxat. Ruland.* ā ʒſſ. *Pul. Holand* ʒi. *Syr. Cochl.* ℥i. *Aq. Card. benedict. & betonic.* ā ℥ii. *Miſc.* This purged and cured him.

Three months after he fell into a Dropſy, with a ſwelling in his feet, which was removed by the following: ℞ *the Emetick Infuſion* ℥ſſ. *Wine of Squils* ʒii. *Barly water, and Syrup of Violets, each* ℥ſſ. *mix them.* This gave ſeven Vomits, and three Stools. The next day, and for three mornings, he took the following: ℞ *Leaves of Succory, Borage, Bugloſs, Violets, Strawberries, each* M i. *Seeds of Anis and Caraway, each* ʒi. *Roots of Smalage and Sharpdock, each* ℥i. *Flowers of Borage, Bugloſs, Violets and Roſes, each* p. i. *Boyl them in a quart of Water to* ℥xij. *Of the ſtraining thereof,* ℞ ℥iiij. *in which infuſe Troches of Agarick, Rubarb, each* ʒi. *Mecoachan* Ɖii. *Ginger* Ɖiſſ. *Spicknard* gr. iv. *Cinnamon* ʒſſ. *In the morning ſtrain them again, to which Expreſſion add Syrup of Roſes* ℥iſſ. *Manna* ℥ſſ. *Mix*

C 3

them

Randolph's great distillation (of phlegm) made him so sensitive to cold that he needed to wear three caps. Although the information given is sparse it is possible that the patient had a bad cold with catarrh extending into the sinuses and causing pain. Treatment was particularly severe: first an emetic, then a strong purgative pill[1] followed by bleeding. The prescribed powder, to be taken morning and evening, was designed to remove and temper the cold wet phlegm. It contained senna, one of the drugs reputed to purge phlegm, and two califactive or hot spices, long pepper and rocket seed, which resembles mustard.

26: JOYCE BOUGHTON OF CAWSTON, DUNCHURCH

On this occasion Hall recorded his patient's age, which he had not done when he described her condition earlier in the Casebook (no. 24). Unusually, he made an alteration in the manuscript, changing her place of residence from Lawford to Cawston, for he also treated Elizabeth Boughton of Lawford (no. 73), her daughter and grand-daughter (nos 134, 144).

Hall attended her when she miscarried in the fifth month of her pregnancy, which would have been in the spring of 1621, between the births of Elizabeth and Anne, the fourth and fifth of her nine children.

Joyce was suffering from a fever, faintness, thirst and 'loathing', a distaste for food. In all cases involving pregnancy Hall avoided purgative and emetic regimes. In this case the treatment consisted of a sweetened decoction of burnt hartshorn[2] and a thirst-quenching, restorative drink which included two plum-like fruits, jujubes and sebestens.

27: CAPTAIN FRANCIS BASSETT OF DEVONSHIRE

Francis Bassett, who was presumably visiting the south Midlands, was baptised at Atherington (Devon) on 19 May 1584.[3] He was the fourth of the five sons of Sir Arthur Bassett (1528–86), who had married Eleanor, Sir

1. *Pilulae Cochiae* and *Pilulae Aureae* were strong purgative pills containing aloes and scammony. They also contained the drastic and bitter colocynth, which was included in *Trochisci Alhandell.* Colocynth was the pulp of the fruit of *Citrullus colocynthus.* Its synonym, Coloquintida, is mentioned in *Othello,* 'bitter as coloquintida', I, iii, 349.

2. Burnt hartshorn *Cornu cervi ustum* was obtained by calcination of the antlers of deer. The product was a mixture of calcium carbonate and phosphates and was regarded as a medicine to restrain fluxes and cure fevers. At the end of Observation 33 Hall remarked that he had cured fevers in a short time with hartshorn. He also used shavings of hartshorn and 'prepared' hartshorn, made by pulverising the antler after boiling to remove the gelatinous matter (no. 59).

3. Devon Record Office, 1562 A/PR1.

them for one Dose, and *so for four mornings.* This being done, there was adminiſtred the following Pills: ℞ *Pil. aggregat.* ℈i. *Gambog.* gr. v. *Ol. Aniſ.* gut. v. *Syr. Cichor. cum Rhab. q. ſ. f. Pill.* ii. Theſe gave ſeven Stools, the next day one Pill gave five Stools, and with happy event, for thereby he could both better breath and walk. After he took this ſweating Potion: ℞ *Sarſapar.* ʒii. *Saſſafras* ʒi. *Bul. in Aq. fontan.* ℔viij. *ad Conſumpt. dimid.* (this muſt be after they have been infuſed 24 hours). *Towards the end of the boyling was added bruiſed Cinnamon* ʒii. *Seeds of Anis, Carraway, Coriand.* ā ʒſ. Doſe ʒvi. in a morning taken hot. After he uſed this laxative Drink: ℞ *Sarſaparilla* ʒii. *China* ʒi. *Saſſafras* ʒvi. *Guaiacum* ʒii. *Sena* ʒiiſſ. *Rubarb* ʒi. *Agarick* ʒiii. *Mecoachan* ʒi. *Shavings of Ivory and Hartshorn, each* ʒſ. *Seeds of Fennel, Nutmegs, Cloves, each* ʒii. *Leaves of Violets, Roſemary, Fumatory,* ā M i. *put them into a Bag, and hang them in* 3 *gall. of Beer.* Theſe perfectly cured him. In *Auguſt* he laboured of an Hypocondriack Melancholy, with Pain of the Head, for which was uſed the following: ℞ *Pill. de Succin.* ʒii. *Spec. Hier. ſimp.* ℈ii. *cum. Syr. Chicor. cum Rheo. f. Pil.* N xi). He took three of theſe at the hour of Sleep, theſe eaſed him of his Head-ach. After which was uſed *Pil. aggregat. cum Cambog.* &c. as before; only they were made up with the Syrup of Apples into two Pills, which gave eight Stools with a great deal of eaſe. After to the Stomach was applied this: ℞ *Origanum, Wormwood, Mints, each* Mſ. *Seeds of Milium, Anis* toſted, *each* ʒſ. *Flowers of Camomel, Roſemary, and Coltsfoot, each* p. i. *Bay-berries* ʒi. *Nutmegs* ʒſ.

John Chichester's daughter, about 1570.[1] Eleanor's brother, Arthur, was an important political figure of his day, who in 1604 became Lord Deputy of Ireland and eight years later Baron Chichester of Belfast. He was sufficiently trusted by Charles I to be sent to meet the daughter of the King of Spain, the royal bride, at Southampton in 1623; he was in contact with another loyal servant of the king, Secretary Conway.[2] At his death, childless, early in 1625, Chichester's estates passed to his younger brother, Edward (d. 1648).

The Bassett house was at Umberleigh (Devon). Francis's mother was buried on 10 July 1585 when he was only a year old, two weeks after the birth of his younger brother. His father and his uncle, Sir John Chichester, both died in a severe epidemic of gaol fever (typhus) after the Black Assizes at Exeter;[3] Sir Arthur was buried on 2 April 1586. Like his brothers, the young Francis was bequeathed £10 a year by his father until he reached the age of fourteen, when the amount increased to £20;[4] he also had lands in Heanton Punchardon (Devon), where the parish church has a Bassett chapel. Lord Chichester wrote to Viscount Conway recommending his nephew, Francis, for a captaincy in 1624 under Count Mansfeldt, and this was granted. In December 1624 Bassett was handling conduct money in Berkshire.[5] Hall must have treated him in about 1634. The link with Hall may be through the Conways of Ragley or the Hunks family's connection with both Ireland and the Conways (no. 138). He is not to be confused with his more famous namesake, his cousin, Sir Francis Bassett of Tehidy (Cornwall), but further details of his life have proved elusive. He was not buried at Atherington.

The lengthy observation devoted to Captain Bassett described a sequence of three illnesses: a tertian fever, a dropsy with swelling of the feet, which occurred three months after the fever, and then an attack of hypochondriac melancholy. Hall closed the observation by stating that his patient, whose age was given as about fifty, was perfectly cured, and continued so for a long time. Observation 34, however, states that Bassett, still aged fifty, suffered from hypochondriac melancholy and swollen ankles. There are two possible explanations for this. Either he was not cured perfectly and suffered a relapse or Observation 34 is Hall's first encounter with the captain and it is this observation that records the relapse.

The treatment of the tertian fever is described here in greater detail than in similar cases. The emetic mixture was given one hour before the onset of the fever fit which, in a tertian, occurred every forty-eight hours. When the

1. J.L. Vivian, *The Visitations of the County of Devon* (Exeter, 1895), p. 47.
2. Chamberlain, II, p. 501.
3. Creighton, *A History of Epidemics*, I, p. 385.
4. PRO, Prob 11/69.
5. *CSPD, 1623–5*, p. 409; *1624*, p. 375.

ʒſ. *make a grofs Pouder of them all, and ſtitch them
in Sarſanet, and make a Bag in form of the Stomach,
which was befprinkled with Sack, and applied and
reiterated as oft as there was occaſion.* Thus he was
perfectly cured, and continued ſo for a long time.

Observ. XXVIII.

Mrs. *Chandler*, of *Stratford* upon *Avon*, aged 36,
five days after Labour, fell into an Erratick
Feaver, with horror, heat, and ſhaking often day
and night, was thus cured : ℞ the Decoct. of *Hartshorn* (as *Obſ. 26.*) ℔iij. Of this ſhe drank continually, ſhaking the Glaſs as ſhe was to take it. After ſhe
took the following : ℞ *Hartshorn prepared* ʒiij.
Rain water ℔ſſ. *Boyl them to* ʒiv. *After add Syrup
of red Poppies* ʒii. *Roſe water* ʒi. *Spirit of Vitriol
ſufficient to make it acid :* It was for two doſes :
After which ſhe was very well.

Observ. XXIX.

MR. *Forteſcue*, aged 20, was troubled with
the Falling-ſickneſs, by conſent from the
Stomach, as alſo Hypochondriack Melancholy,
with a depravation of both Senſe and Motion of
the two middle Fingers of the Right-hand ;
his Urine was much clear, like Spring-water, and
heavy. Being called to him, I thus proceeded :
The fifth of *June* 1623. were adminiſtred theſe
Pills :

patient had finished vomiting he was given an opiate or narcotic mixture.[1] The day following, when he was free from the paroxysms of fever, he was dosed with a purgative.

The patient's swelling of the feet was treated with a drastic regime of evacuant preparations. An emetic-purge was followed by a decoction of drugs into which were infused the purgatives, agaric, rhubarb and mechoacan.[2] A strong purgative pill followed[3] and then a diaphoretic or sweating medicine involving sarsaparilla and sassafras.[4] Treatment ended with a laxative beer.

28: [MRS] CHANDLER OF STRATFORD-UPON-AVON

Five days after childbirth Mrs Chandler suffered an erratic fever and 'horror', a term meaning shuddering or shivering. Treatment involved hartshorn and was similar to that of Joyce Boughton (no. 26).

This was the second recorded visit by Hall to Mrs Chandler (no. 8).

29: WILLIAM FORTESCUE OF COOKHILL, WORCESTERSHIRE

William Fortescue, attended by John Hall in 1623, was born in 1602, the eldest of the seven children of Sir Nicholas and heir to the Cookhill estate near Inkberrow (Worcs.). In about 1621 he married Jane, younger daughter of Thomas Wylde (d. 1599) of Glaseley (Salop.) and of Kempsey (Worcs.).

Fortescue was a noted papist and in 1642 both he and Jane, as well as his brother, John, were presented to Worcestershire Quarter Sessions as recusants. Fortescue was so trusted a royalist supporter that Charles I slept at Cookhill on Saturday 10 May 1645, before moving on 9 miles to

1. In the opiate the electuary *Gemmis frigidi* included crushed pearl and coral which, when given together, were believed to resist fever. *Syrupus papavere erratico* was syrup of wild poppies. *Diascordium*, named for the herb scordium or water-germander, contained opium and was listed in the London *Pharmacopoeia* of 1618 under the heading *Opiata*. The formula was attributed to Gerolamo Fracastoro or Fracastorius (1478–1553).

2. Mechoacan was the root of an American convolvulus coming from a province of Mexico of the same name. It was imported into Europe in the early sixteenth century, as was China root, which Hall used in the laxative beer (no. 70).

3. *Pilulae Aggregativae* was a powerful purgative containing agaric, aloes, colocynth and rhubarb. *Syrupus Cichorio cum Rhubarbaro* was the pharmacopoeial name for syrup of chicory with rhubarb.

4. The abbreviated Latin for the preparation of the sweating potion (*Bul. in Aq. fontan. lb viii. ad consumpt. dimid.*) is translated as 'boil in eight pounds of spring water until half is evaporated'.

24   *Select Observations*

Pills: ℞ *Pil. fine quibus* ʒi. *Fœtid.* ∋ii. *Caftor* ∋i.
Aq. Borag. q. f. f. Pil. 7. Thefe exhibited gave
three Stools. At the conclufion of its working,
the Senfe and Motion of the Fingers were returned. The fixth day there was drawn ʒviii of
Blood from the Cephalick Vein ; the fame night
at bed-time was given *Pil. Succin.* Nº iii ; the fe-
venth day he had three Stools. The eighth day
the following was prefcribed : ℞ *Caftor. opt. Affæ
fœtid.* ā ʒſs. *Rad. Pæon. fubtilif. pul.* ʒi. *Aromat.
rofat.* ʒii. *Mifc. cum Syr. de Menth. f. Pil.* 7. He
took one of them when he entred his Bed. The
next morning was given the quantity of a Nutmeg of the following : ℞ *Conferv. Buglof. Borag. Anthos,* ā ʒiſs. *Confect. Alkerm.* ʒii. *Lætific.
Gal. & de Gem.* ā ʒſs. *Pul. Rad. Pæon. Ariftol.* ā ∋i.
Rafur. Ebor. C. C. Coral. ā ∋ii. *cum Syr. de Hyffop.
q. f. f. Opiat.* In the very inftant of the Fit the
following Fume was ufed : ℞ *Benzoin. Mum. Pic.
nigr.* ā ∋i. *Mifce cum Succ. Rut. f. Suffit.* You may
alfo anoint the Nofe with the fame more liquid.
Obferve that in the morning before the *Opiat,* was
ufed this neezing Powder : ℞ *Pyreth. Rad. Pæon.*
ā ∋ii. *Hell. nigr.* ∋ſs. *f. Pul. fubtilif.* By thefe
means, through the mercy of God, he was in a
fhort time cured ; and now ten years from the
time afflicted he hath been very well.

OBSERV

Worcester.[1] The family later suffered severely for this loyalty. In 1765 a portrait of the king was discovered hidden behind panelling in a bedroom at Cookhill Priory.[2]

William Fortescue died in 1649 and, for not following the Catholic faith, disinherited the eldest of his four children, John (b. 1622), in favour of Francis, the second son (b. 1625).[3] A priest, Valentine Harcourt, was noted as living at Cookhill as late as 1665.[4]

William Fortescue had suffered an epileptiform disorder which left him with a temporary paralysis of two fingers of the right hand. The seizure was said to have occurred 'by consent from the stomach' or by sympathy with the stomach, when the cause was 'some other part with which the part offended hath a fellow feeling'.[5]

The patient was also in a state of hypochondriac melancholy, a form of melancholy[6] where the primary affliction is in the hypochondrium, the part of the body immediately under the ribs on each side of the abdomen. In this condition the patient exhibits a morbid preoccupation with ill health.

Hall began his treatment with a pill composed of *Pilulae sine quibus esse nolo* mixed with two antispasmodic drugs, castor and *foetid* or asafoetida.[7] *Pil. sine quibus esse nolo* ('pills I do not wish to be without') were attributed to Nicolaus Myrepsus and, containing aloes, senna, scammony, agaric and rhubarb, were to purge phlegm, choler and black bile or melancholy from the head.

Six days after beginning treatment Hall had eight fluid ounces of blood taken from the anterior vein of Fortescue's arm, called the cephalic vein, in the belief that to open it relieved the head. This was followed by another purgative pill and then one containing the two antispasmodic drugs used earlier mixed with *Rad. poen. subtilis pul.*, (abbreviated Latin for finely powdered paeony root), an ancient remedy for falling sickness or epilepsy (no. 35). A sneezing powder or snuff containing paeony and *Helleborus niger* or black hellebore was commonly used in the treatment of melancholy (no. 31).

An opiate in the form of an electuary was also prescribed.[8] In Hall's time

1. Symonds, p. 166; WoQS, p. 699.

2. *VCH Worcs.*, III, p. 420.

3. *VCH Warws.*, III, p. 188.

4. Godfrey Anstruther, *The Seminary Priests*, p. 144.

5. Culpeper, 'A Physical Dictionary' in Riviere.

6. See Observation 31 for a discussion of melancholy.

7. Asafoetida is an evil-smelling gum resin which was used as an antispasmodic and in cases of hysteria (no. 127). *Castorum* was made from the dried inguinal glands of the beaver. Used from classical times, it was recommended for the treatment of spasmodic diseases such as epilepsy and hysteria.

8. In the opiate, *Laetific Gal. & de Gem.* is abbreviated Latin for *Species Laetificans Galen* and *Species Electuarii de Gemmis*. Both formulae are given in the London *Pharmacopoeia* of 1618. Species were powders usually composed of numerous ingredients and intended to be mixed with syrup or honey to form an electuary.

OBSERV. XXX.

Mrs. *Nash*, aged 62, having of a long time laboured of a Consumption, and now afflicted with Wind of the Stomach, as also Heat thereof, with sweating from the Pit of the Stomach to the Crown of the Head, having great Pain of the Head, especially after Meat, was thus cured: ℞ Loaf-sugar ℥iv. *Cubebs, Grains of Paradise, Galangal, Ginger,* each ℥i. *Long Pepper* ℥ß. *Cinnamon* ℥iii. *White-wine* ℔ii. *Let them stand to infuse for twenty four hours, after strain them through a Bag, and make a Drink commonly called Hippocras:* Of which she took ℥iii in a morning. There was used a Clyster of Linseed Oil with good success. Lastly she took ℥iii of the following Syrup: ℞ *Cinnamon grosly beaten* ℥iij. *Calamus Aromaticus* ℥i. *Infuse them in* ℔ii *of Sack for three days in a Glass Vessel, near the gentle heat of the Fire. To the straining add Sugar* ℔iß. *Boyl them gently, and make a Syrup, S. A.* These freed her from Wind, and she was able to eat, and said she was very well for a long time after.

the term opiate was applied to any medicine, with or without opium, that was intended to induce sleep. At the onset of a fit the patient was made to inhale a vapour formed by burning a mixture of the aromatic resin benzoin, powdered mummy,[1] black pitch and juice of rue.

30: MARY NASH OF STRATFORD-UPON-AVON

Mary Nash, a gentlewoman, was one of the ten children of Rowland and Mary Baugh of Twyning (Glos.) and was born in about 1565; one of her six brothers, Stephen, died with Drake off the West Indies.[2] She had not married by 15 May 1589, the date of her grandmother's will, under which she inherited a flock bed and a pair of flaxen (linen) sheets.[3] She must have married Anthony Nash, a substantial gentleman of Welcombe, near Stratford, later that year. They had a household of twelve.[4] In the years 1615 to 1615 two children born to Mary's youngest brother, Rowland, were baptised in Stratford. Greene noted in his diary for 1615 that Mary Nash received £30 as part of a total £50 from Thomas Combe in the Welcombe enclosure affair.[5]

Mary Nash had four children born in the years 1590 to 1598, two daughters and two sons, the elder of whom, Thomas (1594–1647), on 22 April 1626 married Elizabeth, John Hall's only daughter and Shakespeare's grand-daughter. Anthony Nash had been a friend of Shakespeare, who had bequeathed him 28s. 6d. to buy a memorial ring.[6] Nash died in November 1622, leaving Mary £600 in his will.[7] The Bear Inn, in Bridge Street, which he had also owned, was bequeathed to his son, Thomas, who, although he had been a student at Lincoln's Inn, never practised law. Mary Nash was an aunt by marriage to William Broad of Bidford (no. 104), also a patient of Hall. Hall must have treated Mary in about 1627. The date of her death has not been found, but she was not buried at Stratford in the years for which the registers are complete.

Hall was treating the consumptive Mary Nash for flatulence. The first remedy was a carminative spiced wine or Hippocras. The drugs infused in the wine included cubebs, a warm pungent spice, the hot peppery grains of paradise and galangal, an aromatic, bitter root from China and the East Indies. The infusion was strained through an Hippocras bag (no. 1).

A clyster or enema was prescribed followed by a syrup to be prepared

1. See Observation 113 for information on the use of mummy in medicine.
2. *HV Worcs.*, 1682–3, pp. 10–11.
3. SBTRO, DR 194/10.
4. *Mins & Accts*, V, p. 66.
5. SBTRO, BRU/15/13/26a–29.
6. *Life*, pp. 242–5.
7. SBTRO, DR 194/5.

Observ. XXXI.

MR. *Kempson*, aged 60, oppreſſed with Melancholy, and a Feaver with extraordinary heat, very ſleepy, ſo that he had no ſence of his Sickneſs, was cured as followeth : ℞ *Leaves of Mallowes, Beets, Violets, Mercury, Hops, each* M iſs. *Borage* M ii. *Epithymum* ʒſs. *Peny-royal* p. ii. *Rhue, Wormwood, Cammomel, each* Mſs. *Seeds of Anis, Rhue, Carraway, Cummin, Fennel, Nettles, Bay-berries, each* ʒſs. *Polypod.* ʒiſs. *Sena* ʒi. *Bark of black Ellebore* ʒi. *Boyl them all in* ℔iii *of Whey, till half be waſted. Of this ſtrained, take* ʒx. *Confect. Hamech, Diaphænic. each* ʒv. *Salt* ʒi. *Mix them, and make a Clyſter.* This brought away two Stools with a great deal of Wind ; it was given in the morning, and again at night. After theſe there were applied to the Soals of his Feet, *Radiſhes ſliced, beſprinkled with Vinegar and Salt,* renewed every third hour. This hindred the Recourſe of Vapours, and drew them back, and ſo he ſlept far more quietly, without ſtarting and fear. The following was prepared for his ordinary drink , ℞ *Spring water* ℔iv. *Syrup of Limons* ʒi. *Julep of Roſes* ʒiſs. *Hartshorn burnt and powdered finely* Ɔiv. *Spirit of Vitriol, ſo many drops as ſufficed to make it tart.* After the Leeches being applied to the Anus, there was drawn forth ʒviii of Blood. After which was exhibited this : ℞ *Lap. Bezoar.* gr. v. *Tinct. Coral.* gr. iv. *mix them* ; it *was given in Poſſet-drink.* After this the Urine was very frothy,
with

S.A. *secundum artem* (no. 3). The ingredients for the syrup were cinnamon bark and Calamus aromaticus, the dried root of the sweet-scented flag *Acorus calamus*, which was described as a warm stomachic remedy.

31: LEONARD KEMPSON OF STRATFORD-UPON-AVON

Leonard Kempson was the second son of Edward Kempson of Ardens Grafton, who had married a local heiress, Frances Swift. She was left a considerable estate there of over 1,000 acres as a child.[1] George (d. 1635), Leonard's elder brother, inherited the Grafton property. They were both interrogated by the Star Chamber in 1601 for taking money from local men who wished to avoid muster-duty,[2] a scene of which there is an irresistible echo in Justice Shallow's garden (*2 Henry IV*).

Kempson married Margaret (b. 1589), daughter of John Sadler of Stratford, but not apparently in the town. They seem to have had no surviving children. Kempson became established in the life of the community, and was appointed Taster in 1619 and Constable a year later.[3] He was overseer of his father-in-law's will and from him inherited a municipal robe, 'furred with foins' (beech marten's fur).[4]

Leonard Kempson was buried at Stratford on 26 August 1625, nine weeks after his father-in-law. Included in his inventory were music books, virginals, two viols, a cittern, recorder and flute. Of the total value of £22 10s., his clothes were worth £3.[5] Described by Hall as a gentleman, Kempson must have been born about 1550, although his baptism has not been found. Hall noted that Kempson 'lived for many years' after being treated at the age of sixty. His widow remarried soon after his death.

Kempson was suffering from a fever and oppressed with melancholy. The term 'melancholia' referring to a depressive mental disorder occurs in the Hippocratic writings of the fifth century BC. The word 'melancholy' is derived from the Greek term for black bile. A disturbance in the humoral composition caused by black bile resulted in a melancholic illness where the mind is affected as well as the body. Galen described the condition as a chronic non-febrile disorder and Hall's contemporary, Robert Burton, discussed it at great length in his *Anatomy of Melancholy*, published in 1621.

1. Dugdale, II, p. 722.

2. SBTRO, DR 362/26.

3. Richard Savage (ed.), *Minutes and Accounts of the Corporation of Stratford-upon-Avon 1553–1620* (III, Dugdale Society, V, 1926), pp. 61–2.

4. (H)WRO, class 008.7 1627/138.

5. SBTRO, BRU 15/1/50.

with a great fediment, and he was much better.
The Clyfter, Drink, and Powder was repeated
with defired Event. To remove Sleepinefs, he
ufed to neeze only with Tobacco. The *Reftora-*
tive of Quercitanus, fol. 187. *of his Diæteti. poly-*
chreft. fect. 4. chap. 8. was ufed. But yet his
Stomach being ill, I gave him this; ℞ *Emetick*
Infufion ʒvi. *Syr. Violets* ʒii. *Oxymel of Squils* ʒi.
This gave four Vomits and nine Stools: After
which he was well for five days, and then relap-
fing into a fhaking Ague, a Clyfter being injected,
he became well, bidding farewell to Phyfick, and
fo was cured beyond all expectation, and lived
for many years.

Observ. XXXII.

Mrs. *Garner* of *Shipfon,* aged 22, miferably
weakned with the Whites, was cured as
followeth : ℞ *Caffia newly drawn with Parfley wa-*
ter ʒvi. *Terbentine wafhed in Parfley water* ʒii. *Gum*
of Guaiacum ʒii. *With Sugar make a Bole.* The
next day this Plafter was applied; ℞ *Ung. Comi-*
tif. ʒi. *Gypf. Bol. Arm.* ã ʒfs. *cum Alb. Ovi f. Empl.*
It was applied to the Back. After I prefcribed the
following : ℞ *Coriander Seeds prepared, Seeds of*
Sorrel, Plantain, and de Agn. Caft. each ʒi. *Sealed*
Earth, and Bole Arm. each ʒfs. *Spec. Diatrag. frig.*
ʒi. *Make a very fine Powder, and with Sugar diffol-*
ved in Plantain water make Rouls or Tablets (add
Gum Tragac.) weighing ʒii. Of thefe fhe eat one
before dinner and fupper, and prefently after
drank

The melancholic patient was said to experience fear and sorrow without cause, was misanthropic, discontented, restless, weary of life and in extreme cases suffered from delusions and paranoia (no. 180). Hypochondriac melancholy occurred when the digestive organs were primarily affected.[1]

Kempson appears to have been in a feverish, comatose state and initially he was unable to take medicines by mouth. A clyster or enema was prescribed. Among its many ingredients was 'black Ellebore', *Helleborus niger* or Christmas rose. This drug was considered hot and dry in the third degree and used for purging black bile. Pomet observed that 'Authors have held it a Specifick to cure all diseases proceeding from melancholy'.[2]

Radishes soaked in vinegar and salt were applied to the soles of the patient's feet to hinder the rising of the vapours, which were believed to be exhalations developed within the body responsible for causing such ills as depression, fainting and convulsions. Culpeper described them as steams ascending to the head like the steams we see from a mess of hot broth.[3] Vapours were particularly associated with hysteria in women (no. 42).

Other items of the regime of treatment were a drink containing hartshorn for the fever, blood-letting by the application of leeches and opening of a vein to remove eight fluid ounces of blood, with a posset-drink containing *Lap. Bezoar* or Bezoar stone and tincture of coral prepared by the calcination of coral.[4] To treat Kempson's tendency to sleep he was made to sneeze with tobacco.

A restorative medicine was prescribed,[5] an indication that Hall considered his patient to be near recovery. There was, however, a relapse with stomach illness and fever before Kempson could, in Hall's words 'bid farewell to Physick'.

1. S.W. Jackson, 'Melancholia and the waning of the humoral theory', *J. Hist. Med.*, 33 (1978), pp. 367–76.

2. Pierre Pomet, *A Compleat History of Drugs, with Observations by Lemery and Tournefort* (1712), p. 38.

3. Culpeper, 'A Physical Dictionary' in Riviere.

4. Bezoar stone *Lapis Bezoar orientalis* is a small stone taken from the stomach of a goat which inhabited the mountainous parts of Persia. The name comes from the Arabic *pa-zaha* meaning destroyer of poisons. Culpeper observed that it acted by a 'hidden property'.

5. Quercitanus, whose restorative Hall prescribed, was Joseph du Chesne (1544–1609). His treatises, in addition to the older remedies, described the new chemical remedies of Paracelsus. The restorative was from his *Diaeteticon Polyhistoricon* (1606). In the manuscript Hall had written *Diaeteti polyhist* not *polycrest* as in Cooke's transcript.

28   *Select Observations*

drank a spoonful of red Wine. This is admirable in Uterine Fluxes. By these she was healed.

Observ. XXXIII.

BRown, a Romish Priest, labouring of an *Ungarick Feaver*, in danger of Death, was cured as followeth: ℞ the *Emetick Infusion* ℥vi. *Syrup of Violets* ℥ii. *Oxymel of Squils* ℥i. *mix them.* Being given, it gave five Vomits, and four Stools. The next day there was removed ℥vi of Blood. After which was prescribed the following : ℞ *Spring-water* ℔iij. *Syrup of Pomgranats, Julep of Roses,* each ℥ſs. *Hartshorn prepared* ℥iii. *Spirit of Vitriol, as much as will make it a little tart.* In Broths he took *Tinct. of Coral* ℈i. And at Bed time there was a Clyster injected, made of emollient Herbs, *Pul. Sen. lax.* and course Sugar, it gave three stools. In the day and night was taken the quantity of a Walnut of the following, often : ℞ *Rob. rib. Conser. Rosar. Conser. Car. citrior.* ā ℥i. *Cortic. Citr. condit.* ℥ſs. *Aurant. condit. Spe. liberant.* ā ℈ii. *C. C. præp.* ℈ iv. *Lap. Smaragd. rub. Hyacinth. præp.* ana gr. vi. *Flor. Sulphur.* ℥i. *Coral. rub. præp.* ℈i. *Succ. Granat.* ℥ſs. *Syr. acetoſ. Citr. q. ſ. f. Elect. liquid.* This I have used with happy succeſs without the precious Stones, to corroborate the Heart. I gave the following at thrice : ℞ *Conserve of Roses* ℥i. *Tincture of Coral* ℈ii. *C. C. præp.* ℥i. *Diaſcord.* ℥ſs. *Flor. Sulphur.* ℈ii. *mix them.* The following was prescribed to quench thirst : ℞ *Barly* ℥ii. *Liquoris* ℥ſs. *Borage, Succory,* each M i. *Boyl them*

32: [ELIZABETH] GARDNER OF
SHIPSTON-ON-STOUR

Hall noted this young female patient as *Generosa* but the parish registers of Shipston-on-Stour contain no family named Garner in the seventeenth century. However, the surname Gardner was often recorded as a variant and in the relevant years, 1591–1613, Elizabeth Gardner was baptised in the town on 1 March 1593; her parentage was not recorded. She would have been treated by Hall in 1615.

Whites or leucorrhoea are terms referring to a uterine discharge, a symptom of many diseases peculiar to women.

Hall's treatment in this case consisted of a bole (a single dose electuary) containing the diuretic turpentine, the laxative cassia and the resin extracted from guaiacum. A plaster made from an ointment *Unguentum Comitissae*, gypsum (hydrated calcium sulphate), Armenian bole (no. 4) and white of egg was applied to the back.

The last prescription was for a moulded round tablet known as a *roul* and claimed by Hall to be admirable in uterine fluxes. It was composed of the seeds of coriander, sorrel, plantain,[1] and the shrub *Agnus castus* mixed with Armenian bole, Sealed Earth and powder known as *Diatragacanthum*.[2]

33: BROWNE, A ROMISH PRIEST

Wheler thought that the priest was George Browne, because the word 'papist' was added to an entry in the Stratford register for 7 May 1613, when Frances Browne, his wife, was buried.[3] Certainly, George Browne can be traced through Stratford's records as a recusant, as, for example, not attending church.[4] Hall noted this patient as *sacerdos roman^s*.

However, the description 'Romish' suggests that he was European-trained, perhaps at Douai, and marriage would not have been a choice for such a man. There is no evidence in addition that the Romish priest was in Stratford and many such men were known by various aliases to protect

1. Plantain *Plantago major*, a common perennial herb, had many uses in medicine. The whole herb, used to treat minor wounds, had styptic properties. In *Romeo and Juliet* it is mentioned as a treatment for a broken shin, I, ii, 50; there is a similar reference in *Love's Labour's Lost*, III, i, 70.

2. Sealed Earth or *Terra Sigillatae*: earths or clays from Armenia, Lemnos, Bohemia and elsewhere were often made up into little flat cakes and stamped with a seal, for example, the half moon of the Turk. The name 'Sealed Earth' comes from this practice. *Diatragacanthum* contained tragacanth gum, gum arabic and starch. The term *roul* is thought to have come from *rouleau*, meaning a cylinder of coins.

3. SBTRO, Wheler's interleaved copy of 1657 edition of *Select Observations*.

4. Brinkworth, pp. 138, 168.

them in ℔iii of *Water* to ℔ii. *Add Sal. Prunel.* ℥ß.
Burnt Hartshorn ℥iii. *after boyl them a little.* He
took of this thrice a day. His Meat was besprinkled with this Cardiac and Alexipharmic Powder : ℞ *prepared Pearl, prepared Coral, burnt Hartshorn, prepared Granats, each* gr.viij. *The Fragments
of Jacynt. Smardines and Rubies, each* gr. iij. *One
leaf of Leaf-Gold ; mix them, and make a Powder.*
The former Julep being spent, this was used : ℞
Spring water ℔ii. *Burnt Hartshorn, and Crude, each*
℥iii. *Species liberant.* ℈iv. *Boyl them to the consumption of half a pint, add the Juyce of Limons, a sufficient quantity to make it tart, boyl them again, scum
it, and clarify it with Whites of Eggs.* He took of
this thrice a day. By these beyond all expectation
the Catholick was cured, especially with the Decoction of Hartshorn, with which I have cured
these and other Feavers in a short time, very many.

Observ. XXXIV.

CAptain *Basset,* aged 50. afflicted with Hypochondriac Melancholy, with trembling
and pricking of the Heart, as also with Pain in
the Head, and tumour about the Ancles, was cured as followeth : ℞ *the Leaves of Succory, Borage,
Buglofs, Violets, Strawberries, each* M i. *Root of
black Ellebore* ℥ii. *Liquoris, Polypody, each* ℥ii. *Citron
seeds* ℥iß. *Seeds of Anis and Caraway, each* ℥ß. *of
all the Myrobalans each* ℥ii. *Beat them all grosly, and
rub them with your hands with Oil of sweet Almonds,*
After infuse them *for twenty four hours in* ℔ß *of*
Fumitory

themselves and the recusants they served. If Browne were attached to a prosperous household where Hall already had patients, the expensive medication would be charged to the family's account. The rumour that the Fortescue children from Cookhill (no. 173) had a Catholic priest as a tutor may link this otherwise unexplained patient to Hall.

In his index to the *Select Observations* James Cooke listed this case under camp fever, one of the names given to the louse-borne typhus fever (no. 77).

Hall began his treatment with the emetic he employed in cases of tertian fever, followed by bleeding and the removal from a vein of six fluid ounces of blood. The ensuing treatment involving six prescriptions had, as its prominent features, the use of hartshorn (commonly used for fevers) and precious stones.

Numerous beneficial properties were attributed to gemstones.[1] As a group they were regarded as corroborant or strengthening medicines to be employed in cordials and alexipharmics (preparations that have the nature of an antidote to poison). In the cordial electuary to be given day and night in the quantity of a walnut, Hall prescribed *smaragdus* or emerald and *hyacinthus* or sapphire.[2] In the alexipharmic powder to be sprinkled on food, pearl, coral, hartshorn, granats or garnets, jacynth, *smardine* (emerald), rubies and gold were prescribed.

This would appear to have been a very costly treatment. The ingredients, however, were not as difficult to provide as might at first appear. Apothecaries at that time were prepared for such prescriptions, as shown by the inventory of Thomas Baskerville of Exeter, dated 1596, which listed among the contents of the shop 'fragments of precious stones and ragges of pearl [value] 4s. 0d'.[3]

34: CAPTAIN FRANCIS BASSETT OF DEVONSHIRE

This is the second observation reporting the illness of Captain Bassett. In both cases the patient was suffering swollen ankles and hypochondriac melancholy. In Observation 27 Hall prescribed an *epitheme* or stomach-shaped bag, filled with powdered drugs, which was moistened with sack before being applied to the abdominal region. In this second observation a purgative syrup was prescribed including in its many ingredients black hellebore, the specific for melancholy (no. 31).

1. For the properties attributed to individual gems see Pomet, *A Compleat History of Drugs*, pp. 400–2.

2. *Succ. granat.* in the electuary is not to be confused with granats or garnets. It means the juice of *granata* or pomegranate.

3. M. Rowe and G.E. Trease, 'Thomas Baskerville, Elizabethan Apothecary of Exeter', *Trans Br. Soc. Hist. Pharmacy*, I (1970), p. 19.

30   *Select Observations*

*Fumitory water. After take Roots of Parſly, Bugloſs,
each* ℥i. *Flowers of Borag. Bugloſs, Violets, Roſes,
each* Mi. *Boyl them all in five pints of Water, till
two pints be waſted ; ſtrain it, and add Sena, Epithymum, Tamarisk, each* ℥ii. *Boyl them again to
two Pints. In the ſtraining, infuſe for a night Troches
of Agarick, Rubarb, Mechoacan, each* ℨii. *Ginger*
Эiv. *Spikenard* ℨſs. *Cinnamon* ℨi. *Strain it again,
and boyl it with Sugar to the conſiſtence of a Syrup ;
to which add Syrup of Roſes ſolutive* ℥iv. *Manna*
℥ii. *and reſerve it for four Doſes.* This purged
well, with happy event. At the end of purging,
he took for a whole week one of the following
Morſels, morning and evening, two hours before
meat : ℞ *Spec. Lætiſican. Gal. Diamoſch. dulc. A-
romat. roſ. ana* ℨi. *Cinnamon* ℨſs. *Piſtach. mund.* ℨſs.
*Confect. Alker. Croc. oſſ. de Cord. Cervi, Coral. rub.
margarit. ana* Эi. *Chalyb. præp.* ℨii. *Sacch. diſſol.
in Aq. Cinam. q. ſ. f. Morſul. pond.* ℨiiſs. On the region of the Stomach this was applied ; ℞ *Labd.*
℥ii. *Ceræ* ℥ſs. *Ol. Macis* ℨii. *Spec. aromat. roſ.* Эii.
miſc. f. Emplaſt. It is to be ſpread on Leather. I
uſed a Clyſter framed of Emollients and Carminatives with Sugar. After meat he uſed the following : ℞ *Coriander ſeed prepared* ℨii. *Seeds of Fennel
and Anis, each* ℨi. *of Carraway* ℨſs. *Liquoris* ℥ſs.
Ginger ℨii. *Galangal, Nutmegs, Cinnamon, Cloves,
each* ℨi. Make a groſs Powder, or they may be
made into Tablets with Sugar diſſolved in Roſewater. Thus he was well cured, and thanked
me.

OBSERV.

The purgative was followed by a cordial, strengthening morsul (a form of lozenge), containing among other things red coral and *margarita* or pearl which, when given together, were believed to strengthen the heart. A plaster was applied, an enema injected and finally a prescription for a carminative powder to be moulded into tablets with sugar dissolved in rose-water.

35: JOHN WALKER OF ILMINGTON

The child suffering from convulsions was John Walker, the son of Thomas and the grandson of Augustine Walker (1558–1631), who had become Rector of Ilmington in 1586. Thomas Walker was born in 1596 and, having graduated at Oxford in 1623, became his father's curate in 1631.[1]

John Walker was baptised at Ilmington on 6 October 1633 and therefore attended by Hall in the spring of 1634, when the infant was probably teething. However, the Rector had made his will on 7 November 1631 and he died later in the same month.[2] After his father's death, Thomas Walker left Ilmington, to become Vicar of Leamington Priors by January 1633, where two more of his children were later baptised (1640–3).[3]

Galen was the authority for the use of paeony root in the treatment of falling sickness or epilepsy. Children suffering from spasmodic and epileptic illnesses had thin slices of the root hung about the neck as an amulet. In this case Hall extended its use to dusting the child's hair with the powdered root.

The pungent juice of rue applied to the child's nose at the time of the fit was used for its antispasmodic effect. The theriac (no. 9) mixed with powdered paeony root and applied to the region of the heart was commonly called Venice Treacle. Venice was one of the centres for the manufacture of theriac and the sixteenth-century physicians there endeavoured to identify and use the ingredients of the classical formula for theriac.[4]

1. Foster, p. 1657.

2. (H)WRO, class 008.7 1632/250.

3. T.R. Dudley, *A Complete History of Royal Leamington Spa* (Leamington Spa, 1896), p. 106.

4. R. Palmer, 'Pharmacy in the Republic of Venice', in A. Wear, R.K. French and I.M. Lonie (eds), *The Medical Renaissance of the Sixteenth Century* (Cambridge, 1985), pp. 108–10.

OBSERV. XXXV.

A Child of Mr. *Walkers* of *Ilmington*, Minister, aged six months, afflicted with the Falling-sickness, by consent was thus freed : First, I caused round pieces of Piony roots to be hanged about the Neck. When the Fit afflicted, I commanded to be applied with a spunge to the Nostrils the Juyce of Rhue mixed with White-wine-vinegar ; by the use of which it was presently recovered ; and falling into the Fit again, it was removed in the same manner. To the Region of the Heart was applied the following ; ℞ *Theriac. ven. ℨii. Rad. Pæon. pul. ℨſſ. Miſc.* The Hair was powdered with the powder of the Roots of Piony. And thus the Child was delivered from all its Fits.

OBSERV. XXXVI.

E *Lizabeth Hall*, my only Daughter, was vexed with *Tortura Oris*, or the Convulſion of the Mouth, and was happily cured as followeth: First, I exhibited these Pills: ℞ *Pil. Coch. & Aurear.* ana ℨi. *f. Pil.* 10. She took five the firſt day, which gave her seven Stools ; the next day with the other five ſhe had five ſtools. I fomented the part with *Theriac. Andromac.* and *Aq. Vitæ.* To the Neck was used this: ℞ *Unguent. Martiat.*

Martiat. magn. ℥i. *Ol. Laurin. Petrolei, Castor. &*
Terebinth. ana ℥ß. *de lateribus* ℥ß. *Misc.* By this
she had great advantage, her Courses being ob-
structed. Thus I purged her: ℞ *Pil. fœtid.* ℥i.
Castor. ℥i. *de Succin. Rhab. agaric.* ana ℈iß. *f.*
Mass. She took of this five Pills in the morning,
of the bigness of Pease; they gave eight stools.
The next day she took *Aq. Ophthalm.* see *Obser. 3.*
as ℞ *Tutiæ*, &c. her Courses flowed. For an
Ophthalmia, of which she laboured, I used our
Ophthalmick Water, dropping two or three drops
into her Eye. Her Courses staying again, I gave the
following Sudorific Decoct. ℞ *Lign. Vitæ* ℥ii. *Saf-*
safras ℥ß. *Sassap.* ℥i. *Chin.* ℥vi. *macerat. per 24 hor. in*
Aq. fontan. ℔ viii. *After boyl them to* ℔iv. After the
use of these, the former form of her Mouth and
Face was restored (there was not omitted *Ol.*
Sarsap. which was above all to anoint the Neck)
Jan. 5. 1624.

In the beginning of *April* she went to *London*,
and returning homewards, the 22d of the said
Month, she took cold, and fell into the said Dis-
temper on the contrary side of the Face; before
it was on the left side, now on the right; and
although she was grievously afflicted with it, yet
by the blessing of God she was cured in sixteen
days, as followeth: ℞ *Pil. de Succin.* ℥ß. *Aurear.*
℈i. *f. Pil.* v. She took them when she went to
bed. The same night her Neck was anointed
with Oil of *Sassafr.* In the morning I gave ℥ß
of *Pil. Ruffi.* and again used the said Oil with
Aqua Vitæ, and dropped into her Eye the Ophthalmick Water. The aforesaid Oil being
wanting, I used the following: ℞ *Pul. Castor.*
Myrrh.

Myrrh. Nuc. Moſch. Croci. ā ℈i. *Ol. Rutæ, Laurin. Petrol. Tereb.* ā ʒii. *Ungu. martiat.* ʒſſ. *Ol. Coſtin. de Peper.* ā ʒi. *Miſc.* But firſt the Neck was fomented with *Aqua Vitæ,* in which was infuſed *Nutmegs, Cinnamon, Cloves, Pepper.* She eat Nutmegs often. To the Noſtrils, and top of the Head was uſed the Oil of Amber. She chewed on the ſound ſide, Pellitory of *Spain,* and was often purged with the following Pills : ℞ *Pill. fœtid.* ℈i. *Caſtor pul.* ℈ſſ. *Pil. Ruffi. & de Succin.* ā ℈i. *f. Pil.* N° v. And thus ſhe was reſtored.

In the ſame year, *May* 24. ſhe was afflicted with an Erratick Feaver ; ſometimes ſhe was hot, and by and by ſweating, again cold, all in the ſpace of half an hour, and thus ſhe was vexed oft in a day. Thus I purged her : ℞ *the Roots of Parſly, Fennel, each* Mſſ. *Elder Bark* M ii. *Roots of the vulgar Oris, of Madder, each* M i. *Roots of Sparagus* M ii. *Boyl them in ſufficient quantity of Water to ſix pints. To the ſtraining, add Rubarb, Agarick, each* ʒſſ. *Sena* ʒvi. *Mechoacan* ʒii. *Calamus Aromaticus* ʒi. *Aniſeeds* ʒi. *Cinnamon* ʒſſ. *Infuſe them in a Veſſel well ſtopt according to art : ſtrain it again, and to the ſtraining, add Sugar ſufficient to make a Syrup. of this take* ʒiv. *Rubarb infuſed in* ʒv *of Cichory water* ʒii. *Mix them, and give ſeven ſpoonfuls every day faſting.* It gave ſeven or eight ſtools without pain. ℞ *Sarſap.* ʒi. *Saſſafr.* ʒii. *Guaiac.* ʒi. *Liquoris* ʒſſ. *Herb of Succory, Sage, Roſemary, each* Mſſ. *Boyl them in ten pints of Water till half be waſted.* Of which ſhe took a draught hot in the morning. The following was uſed to anoint the Spine : ℞ *Gum. Galban. Bdel. diſſol. in Aq. Vit.* ā ʒſſ. *Benzoin.* ʒi. *Styrac. liquid.* ʒi. *Fol. Rut. Chamæpith.*

D

36: ELIZABETH HALL OF STRATFORD-UPON-AVON

Elizabeth Hall was baptised at Holy Trinity on 21 February 1608, thirty-seven weeks after her parents had married. She was Hall's only child and Shakespeare's grand-daughter. The case notes suggest her father's great anxiety at her illness when she was aged seventeen and his relief when she recovered. We know that she travelled to London in April 1625 and, although the reason is not given, the celebrations for Charles I's coronation seem likely. On her return to Stratford she was very ill.

A year later, on 2 April 1626, aged only eighteen, she married. Her wealthy spouse, Thomas Nash, was a member of a prominent local family, whose mother, Mary Nash, Hall later treated in about 1627 (no. 30). At thirty-three, Thomas Nash was nearly twice Elizabeth Hall's age; their marriage was childless.

Elizabeth Hall received a small bequest and plate at Shakespeare's death in 1616 (when she was aged only eight),[1] but when her father died in 1635 she inherited his Acton (Middx) house and his lands near Stratford, as well as sharing the cash and goods equally with her mother.[2] Thomas Nash died in 1647, aged fifty-three, and was buried on 5 April. In his will he left his mother-in-law, Susanna Hall, a bequest of £50, as well as smaller sums to his wife's Hathaway cousins.

Elizabeth Nash remarried after fourteen months of widowhood when she was thirty-nine. Her mother died a month later. Her second husband was a royalist Northamptonshire gentleman, John Barnard of Abington, whose wife had died in 1641 three weeks after childbirth. Elizabeth became step-mother to the five of his eight children who had survived.[3] The second marriage on 5 June 1649 took place at Billesley manor, the family home of Anne Mary Lee, later Lady Jenkinson, Hall's patient (no. 124). This marriage was childless. John Barnard was created a baronet in 1661 for his civil war efforts. Elizabeth seems to have lived chiefly at Abington and was buried there on 17 February 1670 aged sixty-two. Sir John was buried on 5 March 1674.

This long observation was concerned with Hall's treatment of his daughter during the first half of 1624. He described her condition in January as a *Tortura Oris*, or convulsion of the mouth. Subsequent comments indicated that the side of her face, including the eye, were also affected, first on the left side and three months later on the right. Harriet Joseph suggested that Elizabeth was suffering from a *torticollis*, a nervous disorder involving the muscles on the side of the neck.[4] During the first attack she

1. *Life*, pp. 242–5.
2. Appendix 1.
3. *Life*, p. 261.
4. Joseph, p. 59.

34   *Select Observations*

mæpith. Flor. Stæchad. Lavendula, ā ʒii. *Rad.costi.*
ʒſſ. *Castorei* Əi. *infund. misc. & pulverisat. in Aq.
Vitæ.* It is to be infused in some hot place for
some days. Before it was used, the Spine was
rubb'd. An hour after it was used, all the Symptoms remitted daily till she was well. Thus was
she delivered from Death, and deadly Diseases,
and was well for many years. To God be praise.

OBSERV. XXXVII.

Mrs. *Sands* after her Purification was miserably afflicted with a Tumor, and pain of the
Hemorrhoids. I appointed they should first be
anointed with *Ung. Populeon.* After there was
applied the *Yolk of an Egg,* well beaten with Oil
of Roses, and added a little Saffron powdered.
In Winter may be used *Oil of sweet Almonds,* &c.
This mollified their hardness, and removed their
pain.

OBSERV. XXXVIII.

MR. *Queeny,* labouring of a grievous Cough,
with vomiting abundance of Phlegm and
Meat, having a gentle Feaver, being very weak,
and had red Urine without sediment, was thus
cured : ℞ *Troches of Agarick* ʒiſſ. *Olibanum, Mastic.*
each ʒſſ. *Terbentine sufficient to make a Mass of* ʒi,
make five Pills. These he took at Bed-time. In
his

also suffered *amenorrhoea*, or, in Hall's terms, an obstruction of her courses (menstruation).

Treatment began with a strong purgative, the first of four purgations over the two episodes. A sudorific or sweat-promoting decoction was also prescribed. Local treatment involved an *Aquae Vitae* fomentation to the neck, the first containing *Theriaca Andromachi* (no. 39) and the second four hot spices, nutmeg, cinnamon, cloves and pepper. The neck was also anointed with oils mixed with Soldier's ointment[1] and a collyrium (no. 3) to treat the ophthalmia.[2]

At the end of the second attack, oil of amber was applied to the nostrils and head, while the patient was told to chew Pellitory of Spain or pyrethrum root. Amber and pyrethrum were both drugs recommended for use in paralytic disorders. She was also to eat nutmeg, which Hall regarded as a medicine against facial convulsions.

The erratic fever which afflicted Elizabeth in May 1624 was treated with a purgative infusion and a sweating draught which, like the earlier sudorific prescription, contained sarsaparilla, sassafras and guaiacum. Treatment ended with a mixture of drugs infused in *Aquae Vitae* and applied to the spine.[3]

37: PENELOPE, LADY SANDYS OF OMBERSLEY, WORCESTERSHIRE

John Hall attended Penelope, Lady Sandys, after childbirth. She was born in 1587, daughter of Sir Richard Bulkeley of Beaumaris (Anglesey). In Hall's original Latin text he noted her rank as *Domina*, or Lady. She married Edwin Sandys of Ombersley, the heir of Sir Samuel (1560–1623), and they had four children, Samuel (1615–85), Richard (1616–42), Edwin (1617) and Martin, born posthumously in 1624, when she was Hall's patient.[4]

Sir Edwin died on 25 September 1623, having succeeded his father only a month before, on 25 August. They are buried in adjacent tombs at Wickhamford church, near Evesham.[5] Lady Sandys endured the loss of her

1. *Ol. de lateribus*, one of the oils used with Soldier's ointment, was oil of bricks also known as Philosopher's oil. Bricks were soaked in an oil, powdered then heated to release the oil.

2. Cooke's translation of the manuscript is confused here. He suggested the patient 'took' ophthalmic water and her courses flowed. The manuscript reads that after taking the purgative pills 'next day her courses flowed, for an ophthalmia of which she laboured . . .'

3. In the spinal application *Gum Galban. Bdel* means the resins Galbanum and Bdellium. *Fol. Rut. Chamoepith* means leaves of rue and ground pine *Ajuga chamaepitys*.

4. *HV Worcs.*, 1619, pp. 123–4.

5. Pevsner, *Worcs.*, p. 290.

his Sauces he ufed Saffron, becaufe profitable for the Breaft; and he eat Muftard and Honey, which caufed fpitting in abundance. ℞ *Hydromel fimplex, newly prepared with the beft Honey* ℔ß. add *Raifins of the Sun ftoned* ℥i. Figs 10. *Oris Roots, Calamus Aromaticus,* each ℥i. *Boyl them altogether, after ftrain them, to which add Sugar-candy and Penidies,* each ℥iii. *Cinamon bruifed* ℥ß. *So make an Hydromel.* He took of this morning and evening ℥viij or ix. To the Head I applied this : ℞ *Roots of Oris, Ga-langal, Ciperus, Angelica,* each ℥ii. *Roots of Pelli-tory of Spain, Agarick, Rubarb, Squils,* each ℥i. *Sena* ℥ii. *Marjoram* ℥i. *Coriander feeds, Bay ber-ries, Cloves, Nutmegs, Mace,* each ℥i. *Gith feeds, Muftard feeds,* each ℥ß. *Benjamin, Storax,* each ℥iii. *Chalcanth. alb.* ℥ß. *Lapis Calaminaris* ℥ii. *Alum* ℥i. *Oyl of Nutmegs fome drops, Oil of Marjoram and Sage diftilled, Rofin and Wax fufficient to make a Plafter.* The Head was firft fhaved. The days he refted, in the morning I gave the following in White-wine : ℞ *Saffron* Əj. *Musk* gr. i. For his hoarfnefs I gave the following : ℞ *the Juyce of Liquoris* ℥i. *Myrrh.* ℥ß. *Gum Tragacanth* Əi. *Su-gar-Candy, and Penidies,* each ℥ß. *of which make Morfels.* Hold one of them in your Mouth, lying on your back, to the end it may diffolve of it felf. There was alfo given an *Emulfion,* or *Milk of Al-monds, Pine-nuts, and fome new Goard-feeds,* ex-preffed to ℥iv. *in it was diffolved Sugar of Rofes* ℥ii. And it was drunk every other morning warm, fafting; it was continued fourteen days. Being not wholly freed from it, he fell into it again the next year, and all Remedies proving fuc-cefslefs, he died. He was a Man of a good
D 2 wit,

second son at Edgehill in 1642, but she lived on through the Civil War and the Restoration, not dying until 1680 at the remarkable age of ninety-three.[1]

Following childbirth Lady Sandys suffered from painful haemorrhoids (piles). Hall recommended *Unguentum Populeon*, which takes its name from *Oculi populi*, the young buds of the black poplar tree which yields a balsamic juice. The ingredients for the ointment also included *mandragora* or mandrake, a legendary drug due to the imagined resemblance of its root to the human form. It was believed to have narcotic powers comparable with those of opium.[2]

38: [GEORGE] QUINEY
[OF STRATFORD-UPON-AVON]

This patient was identified by Hall only with the title 'Mr'; no place of residence is given. However, the family was well known in Stratford and this young man, whose death Hall noted, appears to be George Quiney, one of the eleven children of Richard (d. 1602), a mercer who served as Bailiff in 1592 and in 1602.[3] George's parents married in 1592 and his mother was Elizabeth, the heiress of William Philips, a mercer; she died in October 1632. His brother, Thomas, married Judith Shakespeare and his sister, Elizabeth, was William Chandler's first wife (nos 8, 28).

Baptised on 9 April 1600, George Quiney took his degree at Balliol College and returned to Stratford to be the curate at Holy Trinity and an usher at the grammar school. In 1622 the Corporation, apparently encouraged by Daniel Baker, attempted to replace him with their own nominee, John Trapp.[4] George Quiney seems to have died of tuberculosis ('tussis' was noted by Hall), aged only twenty-four, in April 1624, and Hall must have been treating him in 1623.

The principal features of Hall's treatment were to expel and temper the morbid phlegmatic humour and to soothe and relieve the grievous cough; an agaric purge was prescribed. A plaster that included a number of hot, dry drugs was applied to the shaved head, the seat of the cold, moist, phlegmatic humour. A wine containing saffron and musk[5] was prescribed, together with a hydromel or honey drink, a soothing morsul or lozenge and an emollient emulsion.

1. Nash, II, p. 220.
2. The powers of mandragora are aligned with those of opium in *Othello*, III.iii.334; Cleopatra asks for mandragora to 'sleep out' the time that Antony is away, I. v. 4
3. Brinkworth, p. 28.
4. Fogg, p. 57.
5. Musk *Moschus* comes from the musk sac in the genitalia of the deer-like animal *Moschus moschiferus*. It was regarded as an antispasmodic and cordial. The fragrant Asiatic drug was very expensive; in London in 1604 it cost £1 6s. 8d. an ounce, while opium was 6s. 8d. a pound. See R.S. Roberts, 'The early history of the import of drugs into Britain' in F.N.L. Poynter (ed.), *The Evolution of Pharmacy in Britain* (1965), p. 179.

Wit, expert in Tongues, and very learned.

Observ. XXXIX.

JOan *Chidkin* of *Southam*, aged 50, being troubled with trembling of the Arms and Thighs, after felt Vapours ascend to the Heart, thence to the Throat, and after thought her self suffocated, was thus cured: ℞ *Merc. vitæ* gr. v. *Diaphœnic.* ʒſs. *Misc.* This exhibited, gave two Vomits and two Stools. After she took *Theriac. Andromac.* ʒi. in Posset-drink. I purged her with the former again, only adding one grain of the *Mercury,* which gave four Stools. After which she had the forciner *Theriac.* with the shavings of *Hartshorn,* for four days. By which she was helped miraculously, all Symptoms vanishing.

Observ. XL.

MR. *Winter,* aged 44, cruelly tormented with the Worms and Feaver, was cured as followeth: He first had a Suppository made of Honey, drank the Decoction of prepared and crude Hartshorn, had an Emplaster applied to the Navil against the Worms. I purged him with ʒſs of *Manna dissolved in Broth*; with which there came forth many dead Worms, with stinking Excrements. He also took in his Drink and Meat the following Powder: ℞ *Coral* gr. viii. *Pearl, Hartshorn,*

39: JOAN JUDKIN OF SOUTHAM

Joan Twigge was baptised at Southam on 7 May 1584, one of the three daughters of four-times-married Henry Twigge to be thus christened. On 27 July 1609 she married a local man, Robert Judkin, considerably older than herself (b. 1563). Their daughter, Sara, was born in 1610. The phonetic spelling of the surname 'Judkin' as 'Chidkin' accounts for Hall's and Cooke's entries; the name Judkin was common in Southam parish registers. John Hall must have attended her in 1634, six years after she was widowed. She may have been related by marriage to another of Hall's patients in the town, Christian Basse (no. 9). She was not apparently buried in Southam.

Hall's treatment of this illness, attributed to vapours (nos 31, 42) was a combination of galenic and paracelsian remedies. *Mercurius vitae*, recommended by the followers of Paracelsus, was a mixture of antimony oxychloride and antimony oxide.[1] It was a strong emetic and by modern standards highly toxic. It was prescribed with *Diaphoenicum*, a galenical purgative electuary containing scammony. *Theriaca Andromachi*[2] and hartshorn completed the treatment.

40: JOHN WINTER OF HUDDINGTON, WORCESTERSHIRE

John Winter of Huddington was the eldest child of the Gunpowder Plotter Robert Winter (1567–1606). He had three sisters, the eldest of whom, Helen (d. 1671), unmarried, was a considerable benefactor to the Jesuits.[3] This identification is strengthened by Hall's description of a Mrs Winter (no. 123) as Catholic.

The property Winter inherited has been described as 'the most picturesque house in Worcestershire' and its situation, even today, is as remote as any fugitive could wish (illustrated, p. 88). It had a moat from an earlier period, but the house was improved in the late sixteenth century and two priest-holes were provided. The Winters never undertook even temporary conformity and, with ironworking and land for income, were wealthy enough to survive recusancy fines. In 1650 the house had ten rooms on the ground floor and a further twelve above.[4] The whole area was noted for the numbers of

1. The name *Mercurius vitae* for a mixture of antimony salts is misleading. It arose from the fact that a mercurial salt was employed in the preparation of the mixture.
2. *Theriaca Andromachi* was one of the theriacs in the London *Pharmacopoeia* of 1618. It was named after Andromachus, a physician of the first century AD. It was made up of sixty-four ingredients, which included viper flesh and opium.
3. *HV Worcs.*, 1569, pp. 147–9; Grazebrook, pp. 638–9; Nash, I, p. 591–2.
4. Pevsner, *Worcs.*, p. 200; *VCH Worcs.*, III, pp. 408–12.

horn, *Granats*, all *prepared*, gr. viij. *Fragments of Jacinth*, *Smardine*, *Rubies*, each gr. iii. *one leaf of Gold: mix them for use.* For his Cough he used *Syrup of Poppies*, *with Syrup of Maiden-hair.* By these, with God's blessing, he was cured in three days.

OBSERV. XLI.

Mrs. *Fortescue*, aged 12, having a most vehement Cough, and cruelly troubled with the Worms, was thus cured : First there was used a Suppository of Honey ; to the Navil was applied the Emplaster against Worms. For her Cough this was used : ℞ *Flos Sulphur.* ℥ß. *Benzoin. vel Assæ Odorat.* ℈ß. Make them into very fine Pouder, and divide it into twelve parts : there was given every morning one part , and at night *Hartshorn*, with which the Cure was perfected.

OBSERV. XLII.

Mrs. *Throgmorton*, aged 35, being afflicted with pain at her Stomach, Melancholy, and the Mother, was thus cured : She first took the following Purge : ℞ *Rubarb* ℥i. *Agarick* ℈ii. *Sena* ℥ß. *Cinamon a little. Make an Infusion in* ℔ß *of Wormwood wine, to* ℥vi. *strain it.* Of this she took six spoonfuls, with two spoonfuls of the Syrup of Succory, with Rubarb, and so for three days,
D 3 which

Catholic gentry and the Worcester diocese had been described to Sir Henry Cecil as 'as dangerous as any place I know' by the Bishop. The region was not entirely safe for papists, however, for there were leading puritan families such as the Rouses and the Simondses living nearby. In one bedroom window-pane at Huddington, the words 'Past cark [pains], past care' were incised, appropriate for so persecuted a family.[1]

Hall, unusually, was unsure about Winter's age, noting it only as '4–' in his manuscript; Cooke later recorded it as forty in his first edition and later as forty-four. John Winter was born about 1581 and in 1616–18 married Margaret Russell, also Hall's patient, a young widow at his death in 1622 (no. 123). Their third son, George, succeeded and, a loyal supporter of the king, was created a baronet in 1642. In St James's church, Huddington, there is a small plain monument to John Winter and his mother, Gertrude Talbot, daughter of Sir John of Grafton. The estate later passed to the Earls of Shrewsbury.

In the early seventeenth century physicians followed Aristotle in believing that lower forms of animal life were spontaneously generated under the influence of heat, moisture and putrefaction. To doubt that mites were generated from cheese and maggots from a decaying corpse was to deny the evidence of the senses. In 1598 Christoph Wirsung wrote, 'There is not anything more certain, than that in a man's body, like as in all stinking kennels, in cheese, and in stinking flesh, wormes do growe, and that out of putrified matter'.[2]

The cure was to expel the worms along with the stinking corrupt matter that brought them into being. For John Winter, Hall prescribed manna, the sweet juice of certain trees, such as the ash trees of Sicily and Calabria, used as a gentle laxative. Complementary therapy involved a suppository, and a plaster applied to the navel. Plasters and ointments against worms usually contained rue, savin, wormwood, tormentil and aloes. Hall also recommended a restorative cardiac medicine which was identical to that prescribed for another Catholic patient, the priest Browne (no. 33).[3]

41: MARTHA FORTESCUE OF COOKHILL, WORCESTERSHIRE

Martha was the sixth of seven children of the recusant Nicholas Fortescue (no. 173) and, born about 1611, must have been treated by Hall in about 1623. Her eldest brother was William, also a patient (no. 29). Hall noted her status as gentlewoman. He was to treat her again, as Martha Lewis, after her marriage in about 1630 (no. 158).

1. John Bossy, *The English Catholic Community, 1570–1850* (1975), p. 103; Humphreys, *Studies*, p. 129; *CL*, cxxxvi, 1936, pp. 116–22.
2. Wirsung, *Praxis Medicinae Universalis*, p. 433.
3. See also Observations 153 and 166.

38   *Select Observations*

which gave fix ftools a day. The third night fhe
had a greater *Flux* of her Courfes than in many years
before, and fo for that time I was difmifs'd in *March.*
She fent again the firft of *April,* I purged her with
thefe Pills : ℞ *Pil. fine quib. & Ruffi.* ā ʒi. *f. Pil.*
9. She took three at a time when fhe went to
fleep. The Body being purged, there was given
of the following fteeled Wine two fpoonfuls, and
fo to four and fix, increafing it by degrees. ℞ *pre-*
pared Steel ʒi. *the middle Bark of Afh, Tamaris,*
Roots of Cappars, each ʒſ. *Saffafras, Juniper,* each
ʒvi. *roots of Elicampana, Angelica, Galangal, Ca-*
lamus aromaticus, each ʒii. *Shavings of Hartshorn,*
and Ivory, yellow Sanders, each ʒiii. *Fol. Wormwood,*
Ground-Pine, Spleenwort, Dodder, Balm, Germander, ā
p.ii. *Flowers of Bugl. Borag. Scab. Broom,* ā p.i. *Cinam.*
ʒſ. *Cloves, Ginger, Mace, Nutmegs,* ā ʒii. *Beat them*
very grofly, and mix them by degrees *in four pints of*
White-wine, and infufe them in Bal. Mar. *in a Veffel well*
ftopt for 3 or 4 *days ; after ftrain them through an Ippo-*
cras bag. After it is exhibited, exercife is to be ufed.
After meat fhe ufed this Pouder : ℞ *Coriander feeds*
prepared ʒi. *Seeds of Anis, Fennel,* ā ʒſ. *Carraway,*
Ɔi. *Cordial Flowers,* each ʒi. *Marjoram* ʒſ. *Liquor.*
Elicamp. Ginger, each ʒi. *Galangal, Nutwegs, Cloves,*
each ʒſ. *Beat them into grofs Pouder, adding Sugar,*
make a Pouder. The Stomach and Sides were anointed with the following, thrice a week. ℞ *Oil of Dil.*
Nard. Cap ars, each ʒſ. *Vinegar of Squils* ʒi. *Boyl*
them to the wafting of the Vinegar, add Gum. Amma-
niacum *diffolved in Vinegar* ʒii. *Roots of Afarabacca*
ʒi. *Gith feeds* ʒſ. *Saffron* Ɔi. *Wax fufficient to make*
a Liniment. Thus in the fpace of little more than
twenty days fhe was cured.

OBSERV.

Hall treated young Martha Fortescue for worms by prescribing a suppository and the worm plaster he employed in the case of John Winter in the previous observation.

Her cough was treated with a fine powder composed of *Flos Sulphur* or flowers of sulphur, mixed with *Benzoin vel* [or] *Assae Odorat*. Sulphur was among the drugs recommended for disorders of the breast. The imported aromatic tree-resin benzoin, which also went under the names of benjamin, *Assae odorat* and *asa dulcis*, was prescribed to remove obstructions of the lungs and promote expectoration.

42: MARY THROCKMORTON OF COUGHTON

In 1615 Robert Throckmorton succeeded his grandfather, Thomas, and then married his second wife, Mary (b. 1590–1600), the second daughter of Sir Francis Smith (d. 1629) of Ashby Folville (Leics.), where a grand four-poster tomb indicates the status of this Catholic family. Mary Smith's brother, Charles (later Viscount Carrington), of Wootton Wawen, was married to another of John Hall's patients (no. 122), and Mary was thus connected to such families as the Dormers, Winters and Giffards. Robert Throckmorton's first wife was Dorothy, the daughter of Sir John Fortescue of Salden (Bucks.); she had died childless on 4 November 1617. The Throckmortons were substantial Catholics and from their house, Coughton Court, near Alcester, were directly involved in the Gunpowder Plot. A prolific family, they were connected by marriage to many other Warwickshire gentry, not all of whom were recusants.[1]

Mary became Lady Throckmorton in 1642, when her husband was knighted. Sir Robert died on 16 January 1651 at Weston Underwood (Bucks.), where his young family had been brought up; his monument is in Coughton church.[2] They had two surviving children, Francis (b. 1640) and Anne, as well as three sons who died in infancy. By Sir Robert's will, Mary was entitled to the use of all the house contents; Anne had a dowry of £1,500.[3] The young Sir Francis married on 7 June 1659 and shortly afterwards Mary Throckmorton remarried. Her second husband was a near neighbour in Bedfordshire, Lewis Mordaunt of Turvey, who had witnessed Sir Robert's will; he was the second son of Henry, Lord Mordaunt, and the younger brother of the Earl of Peterborough. After their marriage, they moved to the Mordaunt estate at Walton in Warwickshire.[4] The date of her death has not been found.

1. *HV Warws.*, 1619, pp. 87–9.
2. Dugdale, II, p. 755.
3. WCRO, CR 1998, Box 73 (1).
4. E.A.B. Barnard, *A Seventeenth Century Country Gentleman, Sir Francis Throckmorton, 1640–80* (Cambridge, 1944), p. 61.

OBSERV. XLIII.

A*Uftin*, a Maid, had her Face full of red fpots, with red Puftles, very ill favoured, although otherwife very comely, and of an excellent wit, was thus cured: Firft, fhe was thus purged: ℞ *Elect. Diacathol.* ʒv. *Confect. Hamech.* ʒii. *Aq. fumariæ* ʒiii. *Syr. Cichorii cum Rhab.* ʒvi. *f. pot.* It purged her very well. The following day fhe took thefe Pills: ℞ *Pil. fœtid. de Hermod.* ã ʒſ. *Aurear.* ℈ii. *Mifc.* Thefe emptied plentifully. The Body thus purged, her Face was anointed with the following Liquor: ℞ *Litharge of Gold powdered* ʒi. *Alum* ʒi. *Borax* ʒiii. *Ceruß* ʒſ. *Vinegar* ʒii. *Rofewater, and Plantain water, each* ʒiii. *Boyl them to the wafting of the third part, after ftrain them, and add the Juyce of Limons* ʒſ. Before the ufe of this fhe was let blood. I advifed her morning and night (the Puftles opened, broken, and crufhed) fhe fhould wafh the Puftles daily with the faid Water, which fhe continued, and was wholly delivered from them in few days, and became well coloured.

The patient was reported to be suffering from stomach pains, melancholy and the 'Mother', the contemporary term for hysteria, a disease of women attributed to various uterine and sexual problems. The symptoms were believed to be caused by toxic humours and vapours rising from putrified menstrual blood. The many symptoms included respiratory distress, sometimes leading to a sensation of suffocation, palpitations, flatulence, dyspepsia, stomach cramps, pains in the limbs and various mental disturbances. It has been pointed out there was a similarity between the numerous scorbutic symptoms (no. 1) and those of the 'Mother', but the appearance of livid spots on the skin was the critical distinguishing feature between the two conditions.[1]

Hall's initial prescription was for a purgative infusion, which had a satisfactory outcome when the patient menstruated. Shortly afterwards she relapsed and Hall replaced the purgative infusion with a pill, more efficient in drawing peccant humours from the remote parts of the body.

The purgation was followed by a regime of increasing doses of a wine containing prepared steel[2] and numerous other ingredients, principally cordial and stomachic drugs. A carminative powder was prescribed to be taken after meat (food) and a liniment to rub on her stomach.

43: ALICE AUSTIN

One of his three female cases whom Hall described in his manuscript as *virgo intacta*, she was Alice Austin, whom he treated before she became the daughter-in-law of another patient, Elinor Sheffield (no. 86).

Alice, not apparently born in Stratford, married Thomas Sheffield (baptised 8 May 1603), the sixth of the ten children of John and Elinor, on 30 October 1627. Alice later had four daughters in the period 1628 to 1636, but all were to die, together with Alice and her husband, within ten days in August and September 1638. The first of the thirty-six local plague deaths was noted in the parish burial register on 9 June 1638, with nine more in July and a further seventeen in August. The epidemic was over by 5 September, the Sheffields virtually its final victims and Alice the last of the young family to be buried.

Alice Austin, whose comeliness and wit impressed Hall sufficiently to be recorded, was treated for a cutaneous affliction to her face. Treatment began with a purgative potion which featured the herb fumaria in the form

1. K.E. Williams, 'Hysteria in the seventeenth century', *History of Psychiatry*, I (1990), p. 382.

2. Prepared steel *Chalybs Praeparata* was rust. To prepare it iron or steel filings were moistened with vinegar and exposed to the air until they turned to rust, which was then separated. The use of rust of iron was described by Dioscorides, who observed that it was binding and controlled the menses (Gunter, *Greek Herbal*, p. 631).

Observ. XLIV.

ELizabeth *Kenton* of *Hunington*, aged 50, troubled with a Flux of Blood from her Mouth,
was thus cured : ℞ *Syrup of red Poppies* ℥ii. *Scabious water* ℥iii. *Rosewater a little: mix them.* She
took one half in the morning, the other at night.
℞ *Conserve of Roses* ℥i. *Bole Armoniack., Blood-stone,
red Coral, sealed Earth, each* ℈i. *make a mixture
with Syrup of Poppies.* She took of this the quantity of a Bean after the Julep, and so she was
cured.

Observ. XLV.

SImons of *Knowle*, a Vein being broken, vomited Blood, aged 40, was cured thus : ℞ *Rubarb powdered* ℥ii. *Syrup of Maiden-hair* ℥i. *Succory water* ℥iv. *mix them.* This he took. After
there was taken this : ℞ *Philon. Persic.* ℈i. *Syrup of
Myrtles* ℥i. *Plantain water* ℥iv. *mix them.* There
was also drunk Goats milk with Sugar. And at
night going to bed was given Conserve of Roses
℥i. By these few Medicines the Cure was performed quickly, safely, and pleasantly.

of a water and also included in the formula for the confection *Confectio Hamech*. Fumaria or fumitory was used to treat skin maladies (no. 15). A purgative pill was also prescribed. Local application to the face was in the form of a lotion containing lead salts, alum and borax.[1] This was of an astringent nature and would have been painful when applied to the 'broken, and crushed' pustules.

44: ELIZABETH KINGTON OF HONINGTON

Hall had a number of patients in the village of Honington. Elizabeth Kington (pronounced 'Kenton') was given no status title in Hall's case notes, but her husband's will indicates that he was a day-labourer.

Elizabeth (née Warde) married John Kington in Honington on 22 June 1612 and their daughter, Anne, was born a year later. However, Elizabeth Kington was soon widowed and when an inventory was made of John Kington's possessions in 1619, they were worth £26 6s. Even from this modest sum, he bequeathed 4s. to the parishioners of Honington. He left £10 and some household goods to his daughter and all the rest to his widow, also appointed his executrix.[2] Elizabeth Kington's burial at Honington has not been found.

Hall recorded that the patient was bleeding from the mouth but assigned no cause for the haemorrhage. The two prescriptions were for a julep and an electuary, both containing syrup of red poppies, which was included in the London *Pharmacopoeia* of 1618 under the title *Syrupus de papavere erratico*. It was made from the flowers of the wild red poppy or corn-poppy and recommended in cases of coughs and spitting of blood. The electuary included two ingredients recommended to stay fluxes of blood. They were red coral and haematite, a native iron oxide known as bloodstone. There was in this case the suggestion of an association between the illness and the colour of the preparations used to treat it.

45: JOHN SYMONS OF OVERSLEY

If 'Simons' lived in an area where Hall already had a number of other patients, his place of residence was probably the Knowle in Oversley, a hamlet in the parish of Arrow, close to Alcester. A non-gentry patient, John Symons's four children were baptised in Arrow in the years 1605 to 1612; he must have been born about 1580 and was not buried in Arrow before 1641, when the registers fail.

1. The lead salts were litharge of gold, the name for the yellow semi-vitrified scales of lead oxide, and *cerrusa* or lead carbonate, also known as white lead.
2. (H)WRO, class 008.7 1619/60.

Observ. XLVI.

COOper *Marit* of *Pebworth*, aged 48, perceived Vapours or Wind afcending from her Feet into the Stomach, and fo ill, that fhe could fcarce be kept from fwooning, was cured as followeth : R Pil. *Fœtid.* Rufft. ā Ӡiv. *mifc. f.* Pil. N. 9. She took three at the hour of Sleep. Afterward the following Powder was given after meals : R *Shavings of Hartshorn and Ivory, each* Ӡi. Spec. *Aromat.* Rof. *Gabriel.* Ӡfs. *Seeds of Coriander, Fennel, Anis, each* Ӡi. Carraway Ӡfs. *Cordial Flowers* Ӡi. *Marjoram* Ӡfs. *Roots of Liquoris, and Elicampane, each* Ӡi. *Ginger, Galangal, Nutmegs, Cloves, each* Ӡfs. *Saffron* Ӡi. *beat them grofly, and add Sugar of Rofes the weight of all.* Dofe half a fpoonful. She faid it was worth Gold. On the Stomach was applied a Plafter of *Labdanum, Wax, Caranna, Spec. Aromat. rof.* and *Oil of Mace.* By thefe alone fhe was delivered from all the Symptoms, and cured.

Observ. XLVII.

Mrs. *Wagftaff* of *Warwick*, aged 46, afflicted with Hypochondriac Melancholy, the Scurvy, beating of the Heart, Pain of the Head and Joynts, Ophthalmia, Vertigo, Morpheu, was cured as followeth, although they were Chronic, and

As in the former observation, the patient was experiencing haemorrhage from the mouth. In this case Hall diagnosed a broken vein. His treatment began with a laxative containing rhubarb, the syrup of the mucilaginous maiden-hair *Adiantum capillus-veneris* and the aperient succory or chicory *Cichorium intybus*. This was followed by an electuary having opiate and astringent properties. *Philonium persicum* was a preparation containing opium, the narcotic white henbane *Hyoscyamus albus* and bloodstone. Mixed with this were syrup of myrtle, deemed to have astringent properties, and plantain water, the many uses of which included the treatment of fluxes of blood.

In the manuscript Hall ended by observing that the cure was effected *cito, tuto et jucunde*, quickly, safely and pleasantly, an ancient axiom for therapy.

46: MARY COOPER OF PEBWORTH, GLOUCESTERSHIRE

In the original Latin notes, this patient was clearly described as 'Marita', indicating that she was married. She was almost certainly Mary or Maria Martin. Although the Pebworth (Glos.) registers are not early enough to record her baptism, Maria Martin was married on 8 June 1611 to Thomas Cooper in the parish church there. Two of her family name had served as church wardens in the 1620s.[1]

Thomas and Mary Cooper had three children baptised at Pebworth in the years 1614 to 1617 and Mary Cooper was buried in the parish on 9 June 1641; she must have been born during the period 1563 to 1587, and lived on for some years after Hall's treatment.

Hall's treatment of this case of vapours or wind began with a purgative pill composed of the ingredients of *Pilula Ruffi* and *Pilula Foetidae* or 'stinking pills'. This pill contained the purgatives colocynth, aloes and scammony, along with sagapenum and opopanax, two gum resins which gave the pill its disagreeable name. Other medicines were a stomach plaster and a carminative powder to be taken after meals. Carminatives were medicines described by Nicholas Culpeper as 'such as do break wind'.[2]

47: ELIZABETH WAGSTAFFE OF WARWICK

Elizabeth Wagstaffe was twice recorded by Hall as a patient; on the second occasion he noted she was a widow (no. 177). Her husband was Timothy Wagstaffe of the Middle Temple, a local magistrate and son of Thomas of

1. SBTRO, DR 41/65.
2. Culpeper, 'A Physical Dictionary' in Riviere.

and she almost wasted with them. Her Urine
was one day clear as Spring-water, otherwhile
thick and filthy, often changing, a discovery she
laboured of a Scurvy, with livid and purple spots
scattered on the Arms, &c. ℞ *Roots of Succory,
Buglos, each ʒi. Fennel, Oris, Bark of Tamaris,
each ʒß. Elicampana, Worwwood, each ʒiii. Marjoram, ground Pine, Germander, Fumatory, each ʒii.
Cordial Flowers, each ʒi. Seeds of Anis, Fennel,
Parsly, each ʒiß. Sena ʒiß. Carthamus bruised ʒi.
beat them, and put them into a quart of Whitewine,
boyl them to a pint; to the straining, add Syrup against
the Scurvy by* Forestus *ʒiii. It is to be used for five
days.* Dose ʒiv. with which she had six, sometimes
seven, eight stools. And thus she was freed from
the Heart-beating. The Body rightly purged, I
advised the Wine following: ℞ *the opening Roots
each ʒß. Worwwood ʒii. Marjoram ʒiß. Cordial
Flowers, each p. i. Bark of Tamaris, and Capars,
each ʒi. Seeds of Fennel, Anis, each ʒii. Carraway
seeds ʒi. Spike Ɔi. Tops of Centaury ʒiß. Steel
prepared ʒiii. put them in a quart of White-wine.*
Take of it three hours before meat, and an hour
after dinner take the Juyce of Scurvy grass prepared in Wine, Dose four or five spoonfuls twice or
thrice if need be. To keep the Belly always
open, take a Dose of the following Pills: ℞
*Aloes ʒii. Myrrh. ʒß. Gum. Ammoniac. in Acet. dissol.
Ɔi. Agarick, Rhab. ā ʒiß. Rad. Asari. Gentian.
ā ʒß. Mastic. Ɔi. Spicæ, Sem. Petroselin. ā Ɔß.
cum Succ. Absynth. instar extract. inspiss. f. mas.*
She took ʒß once a week or oftner, two hours before dinner. If you would have them work better,
mix them with *Pil. aggregat.* For after meat, use
the

Warwick. They had married in January 1605 and he was called to the bar six months later. Timothy Wagstaffe died in December 1625, leaving his widow with six children, the youngest aged five; the heir, Thomas (b. 1615), was made a royal ward.[1] In 1632 both Thomas and his younger brother, Timothy, entered the Middle Temple.[2]

Elizabeth Wagstaffe, a gentlewoman, was the daughter of Nicholas Fuller of Christchurch, London, a puritan barrister of Gray's Inn.[3] Aged twenty, she married on 2 January 1604/5 at Highgate (Middx).[4] As a widow she continued to manage the family estates and in the early 1630s was twice indicted at Warwickshire Quarter Sessions on parish matters.[5] She died in 1637 and was buried at Bishops Tachbrook on 2 May. Elizabeth Wagstaffe was related to the Combe and Rous families whom Hall also treated (nos 144, 79).

The appearance of scattered livid and purple spots confirmed that Elizabeth Wagstaffe was suffering from scurvy. 'Morpheu' in the list of symptoms was the name given to a 'leprous' or scurfy irruption of the skin.

Hall's lengthy treatment began with a purgative decoction of drugs in white wine, to which was added a syrup devised by Petrus Forestus.[6] This was followed by a stomachic, cordial steeled wine[7] to be taken before meals, with juice of scurvy-grass after meals. Pills were prescribed 'to keep the belly always open' and the patient was bled by means of leeches applied to the haemorrhoidal or anal veins.

The other prescriptions were to treat the variety of symptoms listed at the opening of the observation. A carminative powder and a liniment[8] to be rubbed over the heart region were followed by a cordial, stomachic tablet.[9] The morpheu was treated with a medicated soap.[10] Ophthalmic water (no. 3) was used on the eyes and an astringent plaster applied to the temples.

1. *VCH Warws.*, V, p. 161.

2. *RAMT*, p. 127.

3. Chamberlain, I, p. 248.

4. Chester, col. 1394.

5. QSOB, I, p. 776; II, p. 5.

6. Pieter van Foreest (1522–97) of Delft and Leiden.

7. The 'opening roots' in the steeled wine were five in number (*Quinque radices aperientes*) and were asparagus, butcher's broom, fennel, parsley and smallage.

8. *Succ. Cardiacae* in the liniment is the juice of motherwort *Leonurus cardiaca*.

9. *Diacydonium* in the tablet was a preparation of quince. *Nux Moschata* was the name for nutmeg and *Fol. Euphrasia* refers to the leaves of eyebright *Euphrasia rostkoviana*.

10. The medicated soap in addition to sulphur had verdigris or acetate of copper used as an escharotic to erode the scurf. Oil of tartar was potassium carbonate liquefied by deliquescence.

Huddington Court, Worcestershire, the home of John and Margaret Winter

upon English Bodies. 43

the following Powder : ℞ *Cloves, Galingal. Nutmegs, Cinamon, each* ℥ ſ. *Seeds of Coriander prepared, Roots of Elicampana, each* ℥i. *Seeds of Anis, Fennel, each* ℥ß. *Carraway* ℈i. *Liquoris* ℥ii. *Ginger* ℥i. *Powder them groſly,* and add *Sugar of Roſes* ℥ii. *Mix them.* The Region of the Heart was anointed with this: ℞ *Succ. Cardiacæ, Ol. Nardin.* ā ℥ ſ. *boyl them a little, and add Sugar of Cloves* ℈ſ. *Camph.* ℈i. *Saffron* ℈ß. *Wax a little to make a Liniment.* Being after troubled with the ſwimming of the Head, the reſt of the Symptoms ending by degrees, I counſelled to uſe theſe Tablets : ℞ *Pul. Diacydon. ſine Spec. Nuc. Moſch.* ā ℥i. *Fol. Euphraſ. Majoran. Flor. Lavendulæ,* ā ℈i. *Coral. rub.* ℈ii. *Raſ. Ebor.* ℈i. *Sacch. diſſolut. in Aq. Roſ. f. Tab.* Take them in the Morning, after take ſome Broth wherein is boiled Marjoram and Mace, or in a rear Egg, adding Carraway ſeeds with ſalt. The Leeches were applied to the Hemorrhoid Veins. For the Morpheu, which was very filthy, it was removed by the following: ℞ *White Sope* ℥ii. *Quick Sulphur* ℥i. *Verdigreaſe* ℥i. *Camphire* ℈i. *with Oil of Tartar make a Globe, and moiſten it in a little Vinegar, and anoint the Face with it, and let it dry by it ſelf, the morning after waſh it off with Milk.* With this ſhe was delivered, the which I have experienced an hundred times. For her weeping Eyes was uſed our Opthalmick Water, ſet down Obſerv. 3. to the Temples. For ſtaying the Rheum was applied this : ℞ *Bole Armoniack* ℥ii. *Maſtick* ℥ ſ. *Dragons blood* ℥i. *Powder of Galls* ℥ ſ. *with Whites of Eggs and Vinegar make a Plaſter, which apply to each Temple.* By theſe ſhe was ſpeedily cured.

OBSERV.

Observ. XLVIII.

Mrs. *Symmons* of *Whitelady-Aston*, troubled with a Diſtillation of the right Eye, for a year, without pain and redneſs, by reaſon of which there was diminution of ſight, was cured by me for fifteen years, by the following courſe : For the removing the watering of the Eye, this was uſed : ℞ *Fumatory, Sena,* each ℥iii. They were boiled in Whey for one draught, which was often repeated. After was uſed *Pil. ſine quib. eſſe nolo.* To the Neck was applied *Horſtius's Veſic-catory,* which I have a long time uſed with moſt happy ſucceſs (the preſcript of which you have in the *Marrow of Chirurgery*) above the Eye ef-fected. On the Temples I appointed to be appli-ed *Empl. contra Rupt.* or in place of it, that pre-ſcribed of Bole in the former Obſervation. In the following *Collyrium* were dipt two little Spunges, after wrung out, and applied to the Eye, and there bound till dry ; it is moſt efficacious and ap-proved. ℞ *Pomgranate Pills* ℥i. *boyl them in Wa-ter of Roſes, Plantain, Nightſhade,* each ℥iij. *In the ſtraining diſſolve Bloodſtone* ℥ii. *Stir it till it be red, after caſt away the Fæces, and add Myrrh.* ℥ß. *Sarcocol waſhed in Milk* ℥i. *Ceruſſ. Tutia,* each ℥i. *White Vitriol, Starch,* each ℈i. *Powder them all finely, and mix with the Collyrium.* There may be alſo prepared the Muçilage of the Seeds of Line and Fenugreek, and when you would uſe the

48: ISABEL SIMONDS OF WHITE LADIES ASTON, WORCESTERSHIRE

Hall's patient for fifteen years at White Ladies Aston, a village adjacent to the homes of several of his other cases, was Isabel Simonds. She was the daughter of William Penrice of Crowle, the second marriage to join these old Worcestershire families; only the main road into Worcester separated the two communities.[1]

Isabel was born about 1580–4 and married Thomas Simonds in about 1607; they had four sons and three daughters. Strongly puritan, Thomas Simonds was fined in 1625 for refusing to accept a knighthood and in 1634 disclaimed his right to a coat of arms, stating that both his father and grandfather had been yeomen.[2] In February 1628 their eldest surviving son, George (d. 1664), married an heiress, Jane Russell, whose sister, Mary Hunt, was also a patient (no. 15). George Simonds was a close friend of Cromwell, whom he entertained at White Ladies Aston on the eve of the Battle of Worcester in 1651.[3]

Thomas Simonds died in January 1641 and was buried in St Helen's, Worcester, where he has a monument. Isabel inherited all his goods and possessions (worth £163 14s. 6d.), including card tables and thirty pairs of sheets. In the pattern of local farming, they had equipment at White Ladies Aston for making cheese and perry. Thomas Simonds's will indicates that he feared a family dispute about land between his surviving children, George, Mary and Elizabeth.[4] Isabel Simonds died in 1645 and was buried on 12 August. Their old timbered manor house was pulled down in 1836.

The distillation of the right eye (no. 3) was treated initially with a laxative draught containing senna and fumitory followed by a purgative pill. As a further attempt to draw out the offending humour and relieve the eye, a vesicant or blistering plaster devised by Horstius[5] was applied to the neck. The principal item in the plaster was a substance extracted from the blistering beetle known as cantharides or Spanish fly. Species of beetles crushed and treated to extract a vesicant have been used since antiquity to inflame the skin and raise a blister. In galenic terms they were classified as hot medicines in the fourth degree.

1. *VCH Worcs.*, III, pp. 322–3, 560.
2. *HV Worcs.*, 1634, pp. 92, 79.
3. Ibid., p. 108.
4. (H)WRO, class 008.7 1641/180; Nash, II, p. 438.
5. Horstius was probably Gregor Horst (1578–1639), Professor of Medicine at Wittenberg and Ulm. Another possible candidate is the lesser known Jacob Horst (1537–1600), uncle to Gregor. The formula is given in Hall's manuscript and Cooke included it in his *Mellificium Chirurgiae*, 1648.

the *Collyrium*, mix a little with it, or in want of
thefe, the White of an Egg. And thus fhe was
cured.

O B S E R V. XLIX.

JUlian *Weft*, aged 53, troubled with an immoderate Flux of her Courfes, was cured as followeth : ℞ *Sena* ℥i. *Troches of Agarick* ℨiii. *Sugar* ℨvi. *Ginger* ℥i. *Currants* ℨii. *boyl them on a
gentle Fire in two quarts of Whey till half a pound
be wafted.* Of this Decoction take ℥iſſ. morning and night for three days, which emptied her
Body from ill humors. The fourth day was
given the following : ℞ *Crocus Martis in red Wine*
℥iſſ. After was given the following : ℞ *the Yolk
of an Egg, with a little Sallet-Oil, mix them with
the following Herbs,* viz. *Motherwort,* St. *Johns-
wort, Milfoil, and Celendine, and make a Fritter.*
Take one a day made thus for nine days. To
the Back was applied an Emplafter framed of
Creta and Whites of Eggs, by which fhe was delivered.

Take this from the Tranſlator, which hath
been often experimented by him on feveral Perfons. ℞ *Plantain water* ℥ii. *Rubarb powdered* ℈ii.
Yellow Myrobalans powdered ℈i. *Syrup of dried Rofes* ℥ſſ. *mix them, and give it at feven a clock in the
morning, two hours after, taking fome broth.* The
next day was opened the Liver-vein of the right
Arm,

A plaster was applied to the temple of the patient and a collyrium prescribed containing nightshade,[1] bloodstone, *cerussa* (lead carbonate), *tutia* (zinc oxide) and white vitriol (zinc sulphate).[2]

49: JULIAN WEST OF HONINGTON

Julian was baptised in Honington on 26 November 1574, the daughter of William Hannes and, as Hall recorded her age as fifty-three, he must have treated her in 1627. She was married to a yeoman, John West, whose will of 1633 indicates that they had eight children. When John West died in February 1640 his goods were worth £134 18s. 4d.; he left 3s. 4d. for the poor of Honington.[3] Julian West survived for another quarter of a century and outlived her son, John; she was buried in the parish on 6 April 1652 as a widow.

Julian West was experiencing a menopausal haemorrhage and Hall opened his treatment with a purgative docoction to empty 'her body from ill humors'. To suppress the bleeding *Crocus martis* (iron oxide) was given in red wine, followed by a fritter of herbs fried in oil and egg yolk. The herbs were motherwort *Leonurus cardiaca*, milfoil or yarrow *Achillea millefolium*, both recommended as useful in 'uterine purgations', St John's wort *Hypericum perforatum*, used in uterine disorders, and celandine, *Cheledonium majus*, an aperient. *Creta* or chalk in white of egg was used as a plaster for the back.

Hers was one of the few cases to which James Cooke appended his own treatment for this common condition, including a regime of blood-letting, as Observation 50 in his first edition.

50: JOHN SMITH OF NEWNHAM, ASTON CANTLOW

Not a well-born patient, and with the commonest of all English Christian and surnames, John Smith might well have been untraceable but for Hall's own identification of him. He was noted as 'de Nunã', presumably for future reference and to avoid confusion with others of the same name.

Newnham in fact is just to the east of Aston Cantlow and a hamlet

1. The nightshade, known for its use in ophthalmology, is *Atropa belladonna* or deadly nightshade which contains the alkaloid atropine that dilates the pupil of the eye. This effect was not known in Hall's time and the nightshade in his formula might refer also to woody nightshade or garden nightshade, all three plants being listed under the heading *Solanum* (Lewis, *Experimental History*, pp. 544–6).

2. The term 'faeces' in the prescription for the collyrium refers to the sediment formed after boiling the herbs with the haematite or bloodstone.

3. (H)WRO, class 008.7 1640/230.

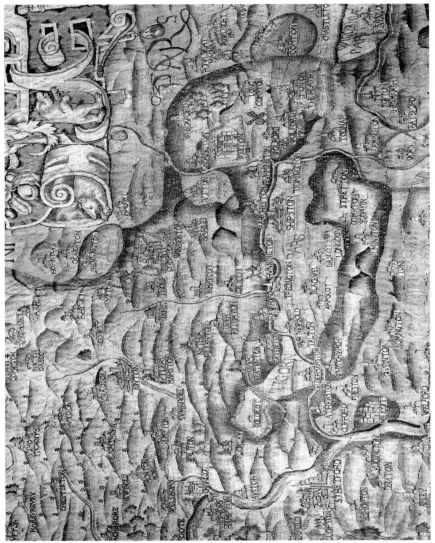

Part of the Sheldon tapestry map of Warwickshire (by kind permission of Warwickshire Museum)

Select Observations

Arm, and there was removed ℥vi of Blood or
more, often ſtopping it. After bleeding was given the following : ℞ *Conſerve of Roſes* ℥iv. *Magiſtral of Coral, and Pearl, of each* ℨi. *Confection of
Jacynts* ℨi. *mix them, and make an Electuary.* The
Doſe was the quantity of a Nutmeg, five or ſix
times a day, taking every morning and evening
an hour after it a ſpoonful of the Tincture or Syrup of Coral, with the Waters of Roſes and Plantain, of each three ſpoonfuls. The following
hath been proved as ſucceſsful : ℞ *the Pulp of Ta-
marinds* ℥ſs. *Mace* ℈i. *Yellow Mirobalans* ℨii. *Rubarb.* ℨi. *Schænanth.* pſs. *boyl them in Plantain water to three ounces ; to the ſtraining add Rubarb torrified powdered* ℈i. *Syrup of dried Roſes* ℥i. *make a
Potion.* Which was given in the morning. The
next, ſix Ounces of Blood were removed, that is,
two ounces at a time, by repetition, ſo much
diſtance of time betwixt, as one might go a
ſtones caſt. After bleeding was taken the following : ℞ *Crocus Martis, Troches de Carab.* each
℈ii. *Conſerve of Roſes, Marmalad of Quinces,* ℥i.
Syrup of Myrtles, ſo much as may make an Electuary.
There was given of it ℨi morning and night ſo
long as was neceſſary, drinking after it of *Plantain water* ℥iij. *Sugar,* and a ſpoonful of the Tincture
of Coral.

Observ. L.

JOhn *Smith* of *Newnam*, aged 60, was miferably tormented with the retention of Urine for three days, caufed by the Stone, in which fell out a total Suppreffion with hazard of Life. For his eafe many things were ufed without any advantage. At laft they fent for me, to whom I fuccefsfully gave the following: ℞ *Winter Cherry-berries* N. vj. *Parfley feed* ℥iij. *boyl them in fufficient quantity of Milk, with which make Poffet-drink, of which he took* ℥vi. *Syrup* of *Marfhmallows* by Fernelius ℥i. *Holland Powder* ℥ii. *mix them.* He drank White-wine, wherein Winter Cherr'es bruifed were infufed. To the Region of the Bladder, and between the Yard and Anus was appl'ed hot the next: *Take a good big Onion, and Head of Garlick, fry them with Butter and Vinegar.* Thefe thus ufed, procured Urine within an hour, with fome ftones and gravel; and fo was he delivered from that long, pernicious and eminent Danger, for which God be praifed.

Observ. LI.

Mrs. *Sheldon* of *Bel-end*, aged 55, was miferably afflicted with an old Cough, and withall, dulnefs of hearing, was cured as followeth: ℞ *Pil. de Succin.* ℥ſ. *Pil. Aurear. fine quib.* ā ℈i.

within the parish. It was an area of extensive lias quarries, whence stone had come to repair Clopton Bridge in Stratford in the 1540s.[1] To be aged sixty, Smith must have been born in the 1550s or '60s, for he was buried at Aston Cantlow on 28 January 1617, when the parish register entered his name as 'John Smythe of Newnham', presumably how he was always known.

John Smith's distressing illness caused by the movement of stones and retention of urine was treated with a prescription involving the fruits of the winter cherry, *Physalis alkekengi*, a plant that grows wild in Europe. The berries of winter cherry were first given in a posset with the diuretic parsley seeds, syrup of marshmallows and the purgative Holland powder, followed by the berries infused in wine. The use of winter cherry for this condition was confirmed by William Lewis a century after Hall. He wrote that winter cherry was a powerful diuretic and used with success 'against suppressions of urine and for promoting the expulsion of gravel'.[2]

A roasted or, as in this case, a fried onion placed between the genitalia and the anus was another remedy for suppression of urine. Garlic applied externally was said to be a stimulant.

51: ELIZABETH SHELDON OF BEOLEY, WORCESTERSHIRE

Few gentlemen can have been reputedly more quarrelsome in Elizabethan England than Thomas Markham (1530–1607) of Ollerton (Notts.), nick-named 'Black Markham' because of his swarthy complexion. About 1586 his daughter, Elizabeth, married Edward Sheldon (1558–1643) of Beoley and, like her daughter-in-law (no. 52), was Hall's patient. Markham was denounced as a papist, chiefly because of his wife, Mary, née Griffin (1540–*c*. 1633), an heiress who was certainly influential in bringing up their eleven children as staunch Catholics.[3] Elizabeth Markham, born in the 1560s, had links with other major recusant families of the Midlands, for her sister, Anne, was married to Sir Francis Smith of Wootton Wawen. The arms of Sheldon impaling Markham were woven into the great Barcheston tapestry map of Warwickshire, dated 1588, which Horace Walpole so admired and bought in 1781 (illustrated, p. 94).[4]

Dugdale noted that the Sheldons had made Beoley their chief seat. It

1. *VCH Warws.*, III, p. 35.

2. Lewis, *An Experimental History*, p. 26.

3. W.J. Tighe, 'A Nottinghamshire Gentleman in Court and Country: the career of Thomas Markham of Ollerton, 1530–1607' (*Thoroton Society Trans*, 90, 1986), pp. 30–45; *HV Worcs.*, 1569, pp. 128–9.

4. Horace Walpole, *Journals of Visits to Country Seats* (Walpole Society, 16, 1927–8), p. 62.

ā Ə̶i. f. *Pil.* 5. She took three at night, and two
in the morning. The day after was exhibited
the following Powder, from Ə̶i to ʒi. for every
day, morning and night, with white Wine, Broth,
or other grateful Liquor. ℞ *Card. Bened. Sinap.*
Sylveſt. ā Ə̶ij. *Piper. long.* Ə̶i. *Sen.* ʒii. *Sem. Aniſ.*
ʒſ. *Diagrid.* Ə̶ſ. *miſc. f. Pul. ſubtiliſ.* It was
taken for three days. The Cough being very
urgent, were given the following Troches, hold-
ing one in the Mouth till it be diſſolved. ℞
Diatragac. frigid. ʒiſ. *Sem. Hyoſc. alb.* Ə̶i. *Sacc.*
penid. ʒi. *Opii diſſol. in Vin. gener.* gr. vi. *cum in-*
fuſ. Gum. Tragac. faɛ̌t. in Aq. Roſ. f. Troch. They
are very profitable between ſleep in the Night. By
theſe ſhe was altogether freed from her Cough.
For her dulneſs of hearing was uſed in the morning a Fume received into the Ear by a Tunnel.
It was framed of the Decoɛ̌tion of *Origanum, Rhue,*
Marjoram, Spica Celtic. Bay berries, Juniper berries,
ſeeds of Fennel, Carraway, Cummin, boiled in Wine.
After which was put in Musk with Wooll in the
night ; but in the day Garlick, being firſt perforated, and after macerated in Honey. In the day
time alſo was drawn into the Noſe the juice of
Pimpernel, Burnet and Beets, which was very profitable, a like quantity of each mixed. By theſe,
with God's bleſſing, ſhe was cured.

was always a place-name with spelling variations (Beley on Speed's map of 1610, Berley in the *Heralds' Visitations*), and 'Bell Ende' must be a mistake made by Hall, for Bell End in Belbroughton (Worcs.) seems to have no links with the family. Edward Sheldon, Elizabeth's husband, was the eldest surviving son of Ralph Sheldon of Weston, who had earlier been imprisoned for recusancy. Having entered the Middle Temple in 1580,[1] Edward succeeded his father in 1613 and inherited considerable estates. Charles I visited the Sheldons at Weston in 1636. The family collection of antiquarian manuscripts was known to both Archer and Dugdale.

Elizabeth Sheldon had six children, the eldest born in 1589, and Hall must have treated her in about 1620. In 1625 a permit was issued for the Sheldons to go to the Low Countries, with a retinue of servants, 'that he might have leisure more freely for God and himself'; they lived at Namur, where she died in 1630.[2] Elizabeth Sheldon was buried at Beoley, outlived by her husband, who survived until October 1643.

To treat Elizabeth Sheldon's cough Hall began by expelling ill humours with a purgative pill and followed this with a *pulvis subtilissimus* or fine powder composed of purgatives mixed with the 'hot' drugs, *sinapi* or mustard and long pepper to temper the phlegm. To ease the urgent cough and procure sleep a *trochiscus* or lozenge was prescribed containing opium, *sem. Hyosc. alb.* the seeds of the white henbane, the soothing *Sacc. penid.* barley sugar and tragacanth gum.

To treat the dullness of hearing Hall prescribed a fume or vapour directed into the ear and formed from a mixture of herbs and seeds, boiled in wine. It must be assumed that it was the vapour from this boiling that was directed into the ear. A mixture of juices was directed to be drawn into the nose. The juices of the roots and leaves of burnet-saxifrage and beets are pungent and when taken into the nose would have acted as a powerful *errhine*, a substance which excites sneezing and increases the secretion of mucous.

52: ELIZABETH SHELDON OF WESTON

William Sheldon's wife, Elizabeth, was the daughter of William Lord Petre of Writtle (Essex), a noted Catholic, who sheltered at least two priests in his family house.[3] She was born on 27 September 1592 and in 1611 married William Sheldon (1589–1659) of Weston, a member of one of the leading Midland recusant gentry families.[4] She was thus the daughter-in-law of another Elizabeth Sheldon (née Markham) of Beoley (no. 51), but she and her husband did not succeed to the estates until Edward Sheldon's death in

---

1. *RAMT*, p. 47.
2. E.A.B. Barnard, *The Sheldons* (Cambridge, 1939) p. 43.
3. Bossy, *The English Catholic Community*, p. 254.
4. Nash, I, opp. p. 64; Dugdale, I, p. 584; Hughes, pp. 47, 63, 135, 268.

OBSERV. LII.

Mrs. *Sheldon, Wife to the Son,* being corpulent,
well coloured, was wont to mifcarry often, the fecond month after conception, yet fuf-
fered no other accident with it, required my
counfel. I advifed her to purge, and ftrengthen the
Womb, for which fhe took *Sage* in her drinks
and meats, alfo a little of the following Powder
in a rare Egge. R̵. *Gran. tinctor. Margarit. Tormentil. ana* ʒ i. *Maftic.* ʒ ſs. *Mif. f. pul.* There was
given as much as would lie on a groat. For the
retaining the Infant, this is the beft Plafter. R̵.
Labd. purif. ʒ i ſs *Gallar. Mof. Quercin. Bol. Arm.
Nuc.Cupref.Ter. Sigil. Mirtil. Rof. rub. Sang.Dracon.
Balauft. ana.* ʒſs. *pic. Naval.* ʒ ii. *Tereb.* ʒ vi. *Malax.
omnia fimul, f. Empl.* Part of which fpred on leather, and applied to the Loins, *Os facrum,* and the
bottom of the Belly. This fhe ufed all her time,
and after brought forth a lufty hearty Son, and after that more.

OBSERV. LIII.

Mr. *Baker* aged 24, greivoufly vexed with a
long cough ; by divine affiftance was cu-
red as followeth. R̵. *Venice Terbintine wafhed in Hyffop water* ʒ i. *diffolve it according to Art with the yolk
of an Egg, to which add* ʒiii *of Hyffop water, as alfo*

E

ʒi *of*

1643, three decades later. Her waiting-woman, Elizabeth Stoker, was also treated by Hall (no. 142).

Hall noted that Elizabeth Sheldon had difficulty in carrying a pregnancy to full term, tending to miscarry in the second month. Her eldest child, Elizabeth, was not born until 1619, after eight years of marriage, confirming Hall's notes, and the heir, Ralph, in August 1623, presumably when Hall attended her. She had three more sons, Edward, who became a Benedictine monk at Douai, George and William, all of whom died without issue, and two other daughters.

The Civil War years were harsh for the Sheldons, fulfilling their motto *optimum pati* (to suffer is best). William Sheldon claimed that they were forced to leave Weston for Worcester and finally took refuge in a farmhouse, their goods and horses seized by Parliamentary soldiers.[1] Elizabeth Sheldon died on 20 July 1656, three years before her husband; they are both buried at Beoley. William's epitaph records that he was 'faithful to an unhappy king . . . deprived of the rich estate on account of his inviolable loyalty to his King, he never mourned for it'.[2]

Hall in this observation described a regime to prevent a miscarriage. He advised her to purge but, as in all pregnancy cases, he refrained from prescribing any of the purgative drugs. To strengthen the womb he advised sage *Salvia officinalis*, a herb, hot in the first degree and dry in the second, which was highly regarded as a remedy in classical and medieval times.[3] The powder prescribed to be taken in an undercooked egg contained garnets, pearl, the corroborant or strengthening resin mastic and tormentil *Potentilla erecta*, an astringent herb believed in the seventeenth century to be an assured remedy against abortion.

A plaster composed of astringent drugs melted with turpentine and pitch[4] was applied over the loins, belly and *Os sacrum*, the bone at the base of the spine. This regime was successfully followed by Elizabeth Sheldon throughout her pregnancy.

53: [HENRY] PARKER OF [TALTON IN TREDINGTON]

Although Hall noted this young gentleman as aged twenty-four and thus born in the period 1587 to 1611, he cannot be positively identified. A possible candidate is Henry Parker (*c.* 1607–70), a wealthy London mercer,

1. M. Warriner, *A Prospect of Weston* (1978), pp. 16–17.

2. Ibid., p. 17.

3. Pliny (AD 23–79) in Book XXII of *Natural History* lists a number of uses for salvia including the treatment of uterine disorders; Loeb Classical Library (1951), VI, p. 399.

4. *Pic. Naval.* in the plaster refers to common pitch prepared by heating wood tar. Among its several names are *Pix arida*, *Pix sicca* and *Pix navalis*.

50   *Select Observations*

℥ i. *of Syrup of Liquoris.* This purged him. After he took every morning the following Mixture :
℞ *Flower of Sulphur* ℥ii. *Roots of Elicampana, Oris,
Liquoris,* each ℥i. *Hony sufficient to make an Electuary, add Oil of Sulphur ten drops, and make a Licking.* When he went to bed, he used this Fume :
℞ *Storax, Mastich, Terbentine, red Arsnick,* each
℈iv. *Incorporate them with the Yolk of an Egg* : After
with it anoint little Bits of Juniper, and dry
them ; the Fume of which is to be received into
the Mouth by a Tunnel.

OBSERV. LIV.

R Eceive two or three brief Observations of
Thonerus, as to the former Disease, which I
could not pass, because much approved ; of which
this is the first :

A Son of a Citizen of *Ulm,* being fourteen
years old, was molested with a long Cough by the
flowing of a thin Catarrhous matter, so that there
was a Consumption feared ; the Counsel of other
Physicians proving fruitless, he was cured as followeth : ℞ *Roots of Elicampana, Polypody of the
Oak, Oris,* each ℥ii. *Hyssop, Betony, Carduus benedictus,* both the Maiden-hairs, each p. i. *Liquoris*
℥ii. *Figs, Jujubes, Sebestens,* each ℥ii. *Sena* ℥vi.
Troches of Agar. Mechoac. ã ℥ii. *Rubarb* ℈iv. *Cinam.*
℥i. *Galang.* ℥ii. *Make a Bag for* ℔ii *of Hydromel.*
Of which take ℥i every day. Being it was a dry
Cough, and conjectured to be produced from a
thin

upon English Bodies. 51

thin ferous matter, there was prescribed this : ℞
Syrup of Jujubes, Corn-Poppies, each ℥iſs. Olibanum
Ɔiiſs. Myrrh Ɔi. Liquoris Ɔii. White Sugar candy,
Penidies, each ʒvi. mix them. Of this was taken
a small spoonful morning and evening, upon a
White-bread Toast moistend in Sack. Thus he
was wholly cured, although there was no small
danger of a Consumption.

Observ. LV.

ANother was of the Noble Lord of *Schellen-*
berg, dwelling in *Kiseleckt*, aged 80, who
was grievously tormented with a Cough, abhor-
ring Medicament ; for whom was prescribed the
following : ℞ Spec. Diair. simp. Diatrag. calid. ā
ʒi. Sacch. in Aq. Salu. diſſol. ℥iv. f. Confeckt. in
Rotul. oblin. Ol. Cinamom. They promoved abundance of Phlegmatick Excretion by Cough. He
commended them for their Affeckts and Pleasant-
nefs.

Observ. LVI.

ACertain Woman of *Uline*, being troubled
with a long Cough from a salt Rheum, was
thus cured : ℞ Coriander seeds prepared ℥ſs. Spec.
Aromat. Rosat. ʒi. Dianth. ʒſs. Spec. Diatrag. frig.
ʒi. Aniseeds Ɔii. the Tablets of Sugar of Roses
℥v. make a Past, and of it Troches, which are to
E 2
be

be taken. Ŗ *Spec. Diair. S. Diatrag. calid.* ℨi.
Extrac. Liquor. ℨſſ. *Sacch. in Aq. Farfar. diſſol.* ℥iv.
Aq. Aſthm. ℨii. *& f. Rot.* By theſe was expecto-
rated abundance of viſcid matter, ſhe was delivered, and praiſed the Medicines.

OBSERV. LVII.

EDward *Rawlins*, aged about two years, had
a hard Tumor of one of his Stones to the big-
neſs of a Hen's Egg, which was cured as followeth: Ŗ *Linſeeds, powder them, and with Linſeed
Oil make a Pulteſs, which was applied hot.* After
there was a little Bag made of Cloth to keep it up
in, with which he was cured.

OBSERV. LVIII.

GOod-wife *Palmer* of *Alceſter*, afflicted grievouſly with Pain of the Head and Heart, from
obſtruction of the Courſes, was delivered by the
following: Ŗ *the Syrup of the five Roots* ℥i. *Rubarb powdered* ℈i. *Diacath.* ℥vi. *Manna* ℥ſſ. *Mugwort water* ℥iv. *mix them.* This gave eight ſtools
after the *Saphœna* was cut. After ſhe took the
following : Ŗ *Troches of Myrrh* ℈ii. *Cinamon, Caſtory, each* ℈i. *Syrup of Mugwort and White-wine,
each* ℥ii. *mix them.* This is moſt excellent for the procuring of the Courſes,
often proved.

OBSERV.

whose eldest son, Sir Henry (1638–1713), purchased Talton manor and mill in 1663,[1] and the Honington estate in 1670.[2] If Henry Parker were Hall's patient, he would have been treated in about 1631.

This observation introduced another variation into Hall's treatment for a cough. He begins as usual with a purge but instead of the normal purgative drugs employed Venice turpentine,[3] which was made into an emulsion 'according to the art' with the yolk of an egg. Turpentine was usually exhibited as a diuretic, but the dose of one fluid ounce prescribed would have been sufficiently irritant to purge. A honey-based electuary involving sulphur and a fume completed the treatment. The fume took the unique form of pieces of juniper dipped into a mixture of gums, turpentine and red arsenic[4] mixed with the yolk of an egg. These were dried and ignited to produce a vapour which was directed into the mouth of the patient.

CASES 54 TO 56

Following Hall's regime of medication for Mr Parker's long-lasting cough, Cooke interpolated three observations on treatments for the same illness, taken from Thonerus, each recording soothing and expectorant medicines for coughs with various symptoms.

Thonerus was the Latin name of Augustus Thoner (1567–1655), who was Director of the College of Medicine at Ulm. He was a great admirer of Galen and galenic therapy. He was, however, opposed to blood-letting.

57: EDWARD RAWLINS

The Rawlins family were important local landowners in both Salford Priors and Long Marston, and by the 1620s they were also becoming prominent in Stratford. Hall's young patient is difficult to identify from the surviving evidence; the case notes give this boy's age as one year not two, and neither place nor status was indicated by Hall. However, he may have been the son of Edward Rawlins, gentleman, of Salford, a child whose baptism was not recorded there but who was buried in the parish on 19 July 1628. Dugdale

1. *VCH Worcs.*, III, pp. 542–5.
2. Sir Richard Hyde Parker has kindly provided invaluable details of his family's history taken from biographical notes made by his great-grandfather.
3. Venice turpentine was a thin pale product from the larch tree. It was not produced in the Venetian territories but imported from parts of Germany.
4. Red arsenic or *Realgar* was the name for a sulphide of arsenic; when burnt, a sulphurous smell was produced.

The tomb of Mary and Richard Murden in Moreton Morrell church
(by kind permission of the Vicar and Churchwardens)

commented on the striking number of seventeenth-century Rawlins memorials to be seen in Salford parish church.[1]

A hot linseed poultice was used to treat the child. Hall described the condition as a swelling of one of the testicles, but it has been suggested that he may have been treating a hernia.[2]

58: JANE PALMER OF ALCESTER

Although it is easy to appreciate how, through social activities and a positive class cohesion, Hall's wealthy patients formed a distinct network of family ties, it is perhaps surprising to find a similar pattern in humble sufferers. It is, of course, far harder to trace such links after three and a half centuries. However, Hall had a small group of patients in the Alcester area, including Jane Palmer, who was the sister-in-law of another patient, Julian West of Honington (no. 49). Hall gave no indication of her status or title in his notes. John West, a yeoman, in his will of 1640 left a bequest of 10s. to his sister, Jane Palmer of Alcester, towards enabling her to apprentice her younger son, John.[3]

Hall's notes unusually recorded how satisfactory the prescription was. Jane West had been baptised in Honington on 26 March 1608 and had married [John] Palmer (b. 1611) of Alcester in about 1630. Details of her son's apprenticeship have not been found. She was buried, a widow, at Alcester on 14 September 1644.

The patient was experiencing amenorrhoea or suppression of menstruation. Hall treated her first with a purgative[4] followed by a mixture containing preparations of myrrh, castor and mugwort *Artemisia vulgaris*, all three recommended as drugs to relieve uterine obstruction and promote the menses.[5]

After purging, the patient was bled. It is apparent that Hall was not consistent in his records with regard to the taking of blood. In Observation 8 he merely said that he let blood and in no. 14 'I caused a vein to be opened'. In nos 23 and 25 he gave the volume of blood taken, but not which vein was opened. In this case he stated that the saphenous vein (in the leg) was opened but failed to record the volume. He was more precise in no. 29, where he noted that on the sixth day eight fluid ounces of blood were taken from the cephalic vein.

1. Dugdale, II, p. 886.

2. Joseph, p. 64.

3. (H)WRO, class 008.7 1640/230.

4. In the purgative mixture, syrup of the five roots *Syrupus de quinque radicibus* was attributed to Mesue. The roots are the aperient or opening roots (no. 47).

5. Lozenges of myrrh *Troschisci e myrrha* were attributed to Rhazes and syrup of mugwort *Syrupus de arthemisia* to Matthaeus de Gradi or Gradibus, a Milanese physician who died about 1480.

Observ. LIX.

Mrs. *Barnes* of *Tolton,* being troubled with the over-flowing of her Courſes a month after Birth, was cured only by the following Remedy: ℞ the *Shavings of Hartshorn* ℥ſſ. *taken in drink, in the morning for four days.* She felt preſent eaſe, and was altogether reſtored and cured.

Observ. XL.

T*Albot,* the Firſt-born of the Counteſs of *Saliſbury,* aged about one year, being miſerably afflicted with a Feaver and Worms, ſo that Death was only expected, was thus cured. There was firſt injected a Clyſter of Milk and Sugar. This gave two ſtools, and brought away four Worms. By the Mouth was given *Hartſhorn burnt,* prepared in the form of a Julep. To the Pulſe was applied *Vng. Populeon* ℥ii. *mix'd with Spiders webs, and a little Powder of Nutſhels.* It was put to one Pulſe of one Wriſt one day, to the other the next. To the Stomach was applied *Mithridate* ; to the Navel, the Emplaſter againſt Worms. And thus he became well in three days, for which the Counteſs returned me many thanks, and gave me a great Reward.

Observ.

59: [MARY] BARNES OF TALTON, IN TREDINGTON

This gentlewoman, the second wife of William Barnes (III), must have been born in about 1589, for Hall noted she was aged twenty-eight in 1617, in the late stage of pregnancy (no. 66). Hall did not date this particular note. William's first wife had died in Stratford following childbirth in March 1615. He must have remarried about 1616 and then presumably moved from Stratford to Talton after he inherited at the death of his uncle (no. 94) in 1621. William Barnes (III) was also Hall's patient (no. 85). Mrs Barnes later had five children born at Talton (1620–7). Harvey Bloom considered that a child, William, baptised at Tanworth-in-Arden on 16 February 1619 as the son of William Barnes, was theirs, although this is not confirmed by any suggestion of gentry status in the register.[1]

Mary Barnes was presented at Quarter Sessions for being a recusant in 1636–7 and 1640.[2] No record of her burial has been found.

It has already been noted that Hall was very careful when prescribing for women who were pregnant or had recently given birth. In the case of Mrs Barnes, troubled with excessive menstruation, he restricted his prescription to shavings of hartshorn, a drug for which he had considerable respect and regularly prescribed (no. 26). The reputation of hartshorn was to continue long after Hall's time, although its use was to change. In the early eighteenth century Pomet referred to it as a cordial, cephalic, sudorific and antispasmodic.[3] In the mid-nineteenth century, when most of the animal drugs were no longer used, Jonathon Pereira described it in his encyclopedic textbook as a nutrient, emollient and demulcent.[4]

60: GEORGE TALBOT OF GRAFTON, WORCESTERSHIRE

When Shakespeare's roll-call of great English aristocratic commanders at Agincourt in *Henry V* (1599) included Talbot, he could not have known that only twenty years later John Hall would be treating the infant George, son and heir to a family that claimed descent from tenth-century Welsh royalty.[5] The child was wrongly described by Hall as the son of the Countess of Salisbury.

George (born about 1618 and attended by Hall about 1619) was the eldest son of John Talbot, tenth Earl of Shrewsbury, who had inherited the title and extensive Worcestershire lands, centred on Grafton, from his unmarried uncle. As his first wife, John Talbot married Mary Fortescue, the

1. SBTRO, DR 41/12.
2. WoQS, pp. 633, 612, 614, 647–8, 687.
3. Pomet, *A Compleat History of Drugs*, p. 257.
4. J. Pereira, *The Elements of Materia Medica and Therapeutics* (3rd edn, 1849–1850), vol. II, p. 2258.
5. Nash, I, opp. p. 158.

Observ. LXI.

Mrs. *Sheldon* of *Grafton*, aged 24, was miserably troubled with vomiting her Meat, and Feaver, fourteen days after Birth ; as also she was afflicted with Fits of the Mother, and cold Sweats, was thus delivered : ℞ *Posset drink of rasped Hartshorn, and Marygold flowers.* For the Mother was given Əii *of the white of Hens dung, Tincture of Coral* Əiiss. *Bugloss water* ʒiv. It was given oft in a day, a spoonful or two. To the Navel was applied an Emplaster of *Caranna,* in the midst of which was put three grains of Musk. To the Stomach was applied this : ℞ *Labdan.* ʒi. *Wax* ʒii. *Cloves, yellow Sanders,* each Əi. *Mastick* ʒi. *Myrrh* ʒss. *with Oil of Wormwood and Mace make a Plaster.* By these she was cured.

Observ. LXII.

Mrs. *Davis* of *Quenton,* aged 63, long tormented with Pain in the Stomach by Wind, helped as followeth : ℞ *Spec. Aromat. Rosat. Gabr.* ʒii. *Rad. Enul. Camp.* ʒiii. *Cal. Aromat.* ʒii. *Liquoris* ʒv. *Turbith. præp.* ʒss. *Sena* ʒii. *Sem. Anis.* ʒss. *Santon* ʒii. *Rad. Gentian.* ʒiss. *Sacch. q. s. f. Pul.* Dose, as much as will lie upon a shilling, given in Wine. With this she was cured.

OBSERV.

daughter of Sir Francis of Salden Hill (Bucks.);[1] she was the Countess who expressed her gratitude to John Hall in words and money. She had two other sons, Francis and Gilbert.

The family home, Grafton Manor, near Bromsgrove (Worcs.), had been extended in 1567 by Sir John Talbot, whose inscription carved on the great parlour window frieze reminds us that 'there is non acorde when everi man woulde be a lorde'; remains of the Tudor terraced gardens and stew-pond can still be seen. The house served as headquarters of the region's Catholic mission for two centuries.[2]

In about 1640 George married Mary, the daughter of the second Baron Powis. Soon after his marriage, George Talbot died childless in March 1642 and on their father's death (in February 1653/4) the title passed to the younger brother, Francis, who became the eleventh Earl.

A mild enema and a preparation of burnt hartshorn for the fever was followed by an application to the child's pulse of *Ung. Populeon*, an opiate ointment (no. 37) mixed with spiders' webs[3] and powdered nutshells. Applications to the wrists occur elsewhere in the observations, for example, the case of the pregnant Mrs Barnes (no. 66). Mithridate externally applied and a plaster against worms completed the treatment, with which Hall claimed to have cured within three days a child for whom 'Death was only expected'.

61: MARGARET SHELDON OF TEMPLE GRAFTON

Margaret Sheldon, noted as *Generosa*, was the daughter of Thomas Kempson of Oversley, the youngest of three brothers who had established themselves across south-west Warwickshire by 1600, with George Kempson at Haselor and Richard at Binton.[4] Hall also treated another branch of this extensive family, Leonard and Margaret Kempson at Stratford (nos 31, 82).

Thomas Kempson married Letitia Collier from Stone (Staffs.) and Margaret was the fourth of their six children. A prosperous man, Thomas Kempson rented Oversley Park and, in 1629, sold various lands for the large sum of £1,265.[5] Margaret must have been born early in the seventeenth century and by about 1630 had married Brace Sheldon of Temple Grafton. Their marriage is shown, as are other details, on a

1. *Burke's Peerage* (1915).

2. *VCH Worcs.*, III, pp. 123–7.

3. Spiders' webs or cobwebs *Aranearum telae* were associated in Dioscorides and elsewhere with the treatment of fevers. In folk medicine cobwebs were applied to small wounds where they helped stop bleeding by encouraging the coagulation of blood ('Master Cobweb, If I cut my finger I shall make bold with you', *A Midsummer Night's Dream*, IV, i, 174).

4. *VCH Warws.*, III, pp. 99, 64.

5. Ibid., p. 30.

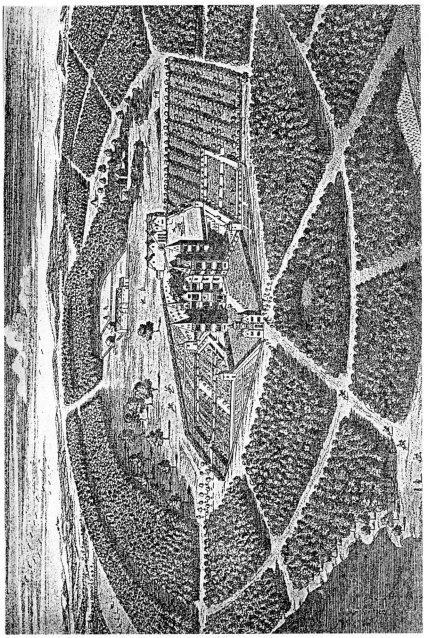

Westwood Park, Worcestershire, the home of Sir John Pakington (from J. Kip, *Nouveau Théâtre de la Grande Bretagne*, 1715)

Sheldon family pedigree prepared early in the nineteenth century, but dates are lacking and neither Brace's nor Margaret's baptism has been found.[1] Their marriage has proved equally elusive.

Brace Sheldon was the second son of William Sheldon of Broadway, who had married Cecily, the daughter of Francis Brace of Doverdale and Droitwich (Worcs.),[2] where their handsome monuments can still be seen. Brace Sheldon had Temple Grafton manor settled on him in 1622 by his uncle, the childless William Draper.[3] He was Treasurer of Barlichway Hundred in 1625.[4]

Margaret Sheldon had four sons (two of whom died young) and four daughters, but their baptisms cannot be verified because unfortunately the bishop's transcripts for Temple Grafton exist for only thirty-four years of the crucial period 1612–69. Margaret Sheldon and her son, also Brace, were accused of recusancy in 1624; he had succeeded to the manor by 1650. Her younger son, Ralph, was born in 1633, for his tombstone recorded his age as ninety-one in 1724. Margaret Sheldon was noted as a widow in the churchwardens' recusancy presentments of 1664; she was buried at Temple Grafton on 16 December 1669. Late into the century the family were paying substantial fines ($£20$ and $£40$) for not attending the parish church.[5]

Margaret Sheldon's was the most serious of the cases listed under the heading *feb. puerpera* in the index to Hall's manuscript. Puerperal or child-bed fever was first described by Hippocrates. It assumed epidemic form in the eighteenth and early nineteenth centuries and was the cause of many deaths in the lying-in wards of hospitals during that period.[6]

Hall prescribed hartshorn for the fever. For the fits of the 'mother' or hysteria he prescribed a mixture composed of hen's dung[7] and the cordials coral and bugloss *Anchusa officinalis*. A plaster formed of drugs with strengthening properties was applied to the stomach.[8] With these preparations Hall claimed to have cured Margaret Sheldon but does not say how long it took for her to recover her health.

1. WCRO, HR 91.
2. *HV Worcs.*, 1634, pp. 91–2.
3. SBTRO, DR 41/23.
4. QSOB, I, p. 20.
5. Ibid., VII, pp. 111, 165.
6. H. Thoms, *Classical Contributions to Obstetrics and Gynaecology* (Springfield, 1935), pp. 161–95; S.A. Seligman, 'The lesser pestilence: non-epidemic puerperal fever', *Med. Hist.* 35 (1991), pp. 89–102.
7. Hen's dung *Stercus gallinaceum* was one of eleven animal dungs in the London *Pharmacopoeia* of 1618, including *Stercus humanum* or human excrement. Dioscorides refers to hen's dung but does not associate it with the symptoms related in this observation. Other sources compare it to pigeon's dung, which was said to be anodyne and to help relieve pain; W.T. Fernie, *Animal Simples* (Bristol, 1899), p. 405.
8. Yellow sanders or saunders wood used in the plaster was an aromatic wood from Timor believed to have strengthening properties.

OBSERV. LXIII.

THE Son of Mr. *Bifhop*, aged 6, being delivered a month before fafely from the Small Pox,
fell into a grievous Cough and Feaver, with
Worms. ℞ *Manna* Əii. *Diacatholicon* Ʒʃs. *Flower
of Caffia* Ʒii. *mix them with Syrup of Liquoris.* This
he licked of often. I gave alfo burnt *Hartfhorn* in
Milk. His Breaft was anointed with the Pectoral
Ointment. There was given him our Julep of
Poppies, and a Clyfter of Milk and Sugar, and fo
he was cured.

OBSERV. LXIV.

Mrs. *Harvy*, now Lady, very religious, five
weeks after Child birth, was vexed with
a great Flux of Whites, as alfo Pain and Weaknefs of the Back, was thus cured: ℞ *Dates as
many as you pleafe, cut them fmall, and with purified
Honey make an Electuary.* This fhe ufed in the
morning. By this only Remedy fhe was cured,
freed from her Pain which came often, ftayed the
Whites, and made her fat.

62: [FRANCES] DAVIES OF QUINTON

A difficult patient to identify, in spite of knowing her status as *Generosa*, her parish and approximate age, because of the commonly-found surname and lack of a Christian name. However, if Hall were treating her in her last illness, she would have been born about 1570 and presumably married some twenty years later.

She was almost certainly Mrs Frances Davies, buried at Quinton on 26 June 1630, the wife of Mr John Davies, both of whom were distinctive by their titles in the register. Her husband was to be buried there on 9 November 1635. Sir Edward Underhill (no. 120) was an executor of John Davies's will (28 February 1632), which contained a 20s. bequest to Edward's niece, one of Davies's eight god-children thus remembered. John Davies made his will eighteen months after his wife's death and there were no children of the marriage mentioned as legatees.[1]

Hall prescribed a carminative powder for Mrs Davies containing cathartic and stomachic drugs including the 'hot and dry' *Radix Enula Campana* or the root of elecampane *Inula helenium* and turbith, the root of turpethum *Convolvulus turpethum*.[2]

The prescription illustrates the fact that Hall did not use the term 'dose' in the modern sense of an accurately measured quantity of a drug. The quantities listed for the preparation represent proportions which can be diluted with sugar *q.ff.Pul* (in sufficient quantity to make a powder). The powdered drugs, diluted to an unspecified quantity, were to be administered 'as much as will lie upon a shilling'.

63: RICHARD/GEORGE BISHOP OF OXHILL or
WILLIAM BISHOP OF BRAILES

There are several possibilities for the identity of this gentry-status child. He could be one of the two sons of Anthony Bishop of Oxhill, where Hall treated other patients. Anthony Bishop (b. 1591) had married a Leicestershire bride, Elinor Farmer, and their four children were baptised at Oxhill in the years 1619 to 1628, Richard on 13 December 1619 and George on 6 January 1623. It is impossible to tell if either boy died young, since the burial register is defective for the years 1617 to 1633. Anthony

---

1. PRO, Prob 11/172.

2. Turbith or Turpethum was the name given by Paracelsus to an emetic yellow mercurial sulphate because it resembled turpethum root in colour. Its greater toxicity would have made it dangerous to dispense turpethum mineral in mistake for turpethum root. See M.P. Crosland, *Historical Studies in the Language of Chemistry* (1962), p. 117.

The tomb of Sir Henry Rainsford and Anne his wife in
Clifford Chambers church

Bishop sold the manor of Oxhill in 1631 and the family appears not to have remained in the parish.[1]

In the same part of south Warwickshire, Hall could have been attending William Bishop, born in 1606, the elder son of John of Brailes (1586–1627) and Dorothy (née Corham). Young William's grandmother was Jane Sheldon of Broadway. William Bishop was buried at Brailes in 1687, having had thirteen offspring by two wives.[2]

Hall must have treated the Oxhill boy in 1625 or 1629, or William Bishop of Brailes in 1612. His note that the child had suffered from smallpox does not clarify the matter, since the disease was endemic at this period.

Hall treated the child with an electuary which had to be licked ensuring that only small amounts of the purgative drugs were ingested. It contained manna, cassia and *Diacatholicon*, a purgative devised to expel all peccant humours, including those from which the worms generated. Hartshorn was prescribed for the fever and an opiate julep was administered.

The formula for pectoral ointment *Unguentum Pectorale*, used here as a remedy for the cough, was given in the London *Pharmacopoeia* of 1618 and attributed to Nicolaus Myrepsus. The ingredients included sweet oil of almonds, duck's grease and hen's grease.[3]

64: MARY, LADY HARVEY OF MORETON MORRELL

Mary Harvey was the daughter of Richard and Mary Murden of Moreton Morrell. Hall had treated her mother in 1626 and Mary herself in 1619 when he noted her age as seventeen (nos 111, 97). On 7 September 1620 she married an attorney, Stephen Harvey (b. 1596) of Milton Malsor (Northants.), only son of Francis (no. 143), also an eminent lawyer. Stephen Harvey had gone to Balliol College, Oxford, entered the Middle Temple and was called to the bar in 1619. He became a Knight of the Bath on 1 February 1625/6.[4] He was MP for Reigate and had acted as steward for John Evelyn's Surrey estates. Sir Stephen served on the Warwickshire bench shortly before his death. He died in 1630 and was buried at Hardingstone (Northants.). From Hall's initial description of her as Mrs Harvey, he must have treated her after the birth of one of her first four children; Stephana was born posthumously.

Mary Harvey had six daughters and two sons in the years 1621 to 1629.

1. *VCH Warws.*, V, p. 126.
2. *HV Warws.*, 1682–3, p. 87.
3. See Observation 83 for information on pharmacopoeial animal fats and greases.
4. *RAMT*, p. 93; Shaw, I, p. 163.

OBSERV. LXV.

Mrs. *Randolph*, aged about 27, troubled with Wind in the Stomach, and too much Flux of her Courses, being discolour'd with torment of her Stomach after Meat, was thus cured: To the Back was applied this Emplaster: ℞ *Bole Armoniac. Creta, with the Whites of Eggs make a Plaster.* For the staying of the Flux of the Courses was given a Penny-weight of *Allum* in red Wine. There was also used the Powder prescribed *Observ.* 46. Thus in the space of four days she was cured.

OBSERV. LXVI.

Mrs. *Barnes,* being great with Child, and near delivery, fell into a Tertian Feaver, which was accompanied with Thirst, Watching, Pain of the Head, a miserable pricking Pain on the left side. She was aged about 28, was cured as followeth: ℞ *the Powder of white Hellebore a sufficient quantity, apply it with slit Figs to the Pulse of each Wrist:* It was removed every four and twenty hours. For ordinary drink, ℞ *Barley* ʒiii. *Succory* M i. *Roots of Succory* ʒiii. *Syrup of Roses and Violets,* each ʃi. *Liquoris sliced* ʒiii. *Figs* iii. *Currants* ʒii. *Sugar-candy* ʒii. *Boyl them all in eight quarts of Water, till a quart be wasted, after strained, it was drank cold.* To the Side was used this Ointment,

Mary, the first child, was baptised on 13 July 1621 but the second, Elizabeth, died in infancy in 1623, possibly in a current fever epidemic, and is commemorated on a tablet alongside her grandparents' tomb in Moreton Morrell church (illustrated, p. 106). Both sons died bachelors, but two daughters married into the Temple and Holbeche families.

In her widowhood, Lady Harvey entertained the puritan minister, Thomas Dugard, who noted visits to her in his diary until December 1639.[1] She was still alive in January 1645, when she loaned money to Parliament.[2] Records of her burial have been difficult to trace, because the Moreton Morrell register was lost in the 1950s and the bishop's transcripts have major gaps.

However, on 30 November 1650 Mary, daughter of Richard Murden, esquire, was buried at Moreton Morrell and it is perhaps possible that this is Lady Harvey.

The treatment in this case was simple in contrast to Hall's regimes for other cases involving the uterine discharge known as whites or leucorrhoea (nos 32, 114, 126, 152). It is probable that the patient's having recently given birth determined the treatment. Dates, which occur in the contemporary *materia medica* under the name *dactylus*, had a reputation for the control of fluxes.[3]

65: ELIZABETH RANDOLPH OF WOOD BEVINGTON, SALFORD PRIORS

Elizabeth was the wife of Ferrers Randolph of Bevington, and their eldest son, Thomas, was baptised at Salford Priors on 27 August 1620. Hall was treating her perhaps after this delivery or the birth of another child, Elizabeth. He also attended her mother-in-law (no. 103) and her husband, Ferrers (no. 25). Elizabeth Randolph must have been born about 1593, but her maiden name and marriage have not been traced. Her husband was dead by 1651 and on 15 September 1657 an entry, 'Elizabeth Randolph of Bevington', appears in the admission register of St Peter's Franciscan Mission, Birmingham.[4] This may, of course, be her daughter, who as late as 1651 was unmarried. Because of her recusancy, Elizabeth Randolph may not have been buried at Salford Priors and, in any case, both parish registers and bishop's transcripts are faulty after 1646.

To cure the flatulence, Hall prescribed for Elizabeth Randolph the carminative powder used for Mary Cooper (no. 46). A plaster was applied

1. BL, Add. MS 23146.
2. Dr Ann Hughes kindly provided this reference.
3. Lewis, *An Experimental History*, p. 427.
4. W.P.W. Phillimore (ed.), *Warwickshire Parish Registers: Baptisms*, II (1904), p. 63.

ment: ℞ *Vng. Dialth.* ℥i. *Ol. Amygd. dulc.* ℥iii. *Miſc.* The Side being anointed with it, there was applied a Linnen Cloth ſpread with Butter, it was applied hot. There being very great pain of the Head, there was uſed the following Ointment: ℞ *Ointment of Alabaſter* ℥ſ. *Opium* gr.vii. *mix them.* With this were the Temples anointed, and to them ſome of it applied. By theſe means ſhe was cured, and delivered from danger of Miſcarriage. She was cured in ſeven days ſpace.

O B S E R V. LXVII.

RObert *Sartor* of *Stratford* upon *Avon*, aged about 34, fell into a violent bleeding at the Noſe, which intermitted for four hours, and returned again, was ſtopt as followeth: I cauſed Tents made of new Cloth, often dipp'd in *Frog-ſpawn* in *March*, and dried, to be put up his Noſtrils, made ſtrong Ligatures below the Shoulders. After the following Plaſter was ſpread upon Linnen, and applied to the Forehead, Temples, and Neck very often, cold: ℞ *burnt Argil, and powdered,* M ii. *Wine vinegar* ℔ſſ. mix them to conſiſtence of an Emplaſter: And thus within half an hour the Flux was ſtayed.

to her back. To check the menstrual bleeding a penny-weight[1] of alum in red wine was prescribed. In the seventeenth century alum, a powerful astringent, was used both internally and externally to stop bleeding (no. 92).

66: [MARY] BARNES OF TALTON, IN TREDINGTON

This appears to be the same [Mary] Barnes, a young gentlewoman, recorded as having recently given birth (no. 59).

Mrs Barnes was suffering from a tertian fever,[2] pains in the head, thirst and watching or wakefulness. She was in an advanced stage of pregnancy and Hall avoided the emetic and purgative regimes prescribed in other cases of tertian fever (nos 22, 28). Except for a cooling drink, all remedies were applied externally.

Powder of white hellebore *Veratrum album* on slit figs was laid over the pulse of each wrist. White hellebore was regarded as a drug hot and dry in the third degree and when taken internally purged 'upwards and downwards'. It was not recommended internally for delicate persons.

The side of the patient was anointed with *Unguentum Dialthaea* or marsh mallow ointment mixed with oil of sweet almonds. To treat the pains in the head Hall prescribed an ointment for the temples composed of opium mixed with ointment of alabaster *Unguentum de Alabastro*, which was composed of powdered alabaster (sulphate of lime) with the juice of rose, betony and other ingredients.

67: THOMAS ROBERTS, TAILOR OF STRATFORD-UPON-AVON

One of the more difficult of the patients to identify, Hall's manuscript appears to read *Roberts Sartor* (or tailor), suggesting he was Thomas Roberts, described by Hall as a townsman, baptised in the town on 2 July 1579 and buried there on 13 January 1617. He had one son, who died in 1613 as an infant, the year in which Hall treated Roberts.

To stop the bleeding from the nose Hall inserted into the nostril a small roll of cloth, called a tent, which had been dipped into frog-spawn and dried. It would appear that the cloth for these tents was prepared in advance each spring when frog-spawn was available. Frog-spawn *Sperma ranarum* was regarded as a cooling, anodyne remedy used for burns, inflammations, fluxes, and some skin diseases.

1. The weight of a silver penny was 22.6 grains, which was $^1/_{240}$ of the Saxon or Tower pound and equivalent to 24 grains in the apothecaries' measure.
2. In the manuscript this case was indexed under *feb. puerpera* or child-bed fever, an inaccurate description for a tertian fever in late pregnancy (no. 61).

Observ. LXVIII.

BAron *Compton*, now Earl of *Northampton*, aged
55, in 1617, was cruelly tormented with
Pain of his Teeth, and very much molested with
swelling of his Gums, which was removed by the
following Remedies : ℞ *Pil. de Succ. Crat.* ℥iii. *f.*
Pil. N° 18. Of these he took three every morning and night for three days, which purged very
well. This *Gargarism* was used : ℞ *the Decoction
of the Bark of Guaiacum, and of Barley, each,* ℥iv.
Syrup of Mulberries, and Honey of Roses, each ℥ii.
*Spirit of Vitriol so many drops as will make it taste
sharpish.* In this also was there often in a day a
piece of Spunge, applied to the pained Gums, and
there it was held the whole day. By these Medicines he was delivered from all his Symptoms;
the second day he could eat meat, and the third
day he was perfectly healed.

   Thonerus hath some short Observations concerning Pain of the Teeth, which receive here :
   I have (saith he) tryed on my self, if the Tooth
be hollow, as also on many others to stop the
Tooth with a little *Camphire* : But if they be not
hollow, then he boiled ℥ß *of Camphire in half a
pint of Vinegar*, which was held hot in the Mouth.
Both which he found successful.
   One who had Pain of the Teeth, and Tumor
of the left Jaw, from a hot defluxion, was thus
cured : ℞ *Mas. Pil. Aurear. Cochear. sine quib.* ā ℈i.
                                Extract.

Ligatures were tied around the upper arms and a 'cold' plaster applied to the forehead, temples and neck. The plaster was made with burnt argil, which may have been *Cimolia alba*, the clay used to make tobacco pipes, or *Cimolia purpurascens*, better known as Fuller's earth. Hall recorded that these measures stayed the bleeding within half an hour.

68: WILLIAM COMPTON, FIRST EARL OF NORTHAMPTON

Hall attended William Compton (1562–1630) in 1617 before he was created Earl of Northampton on 2 August 1618, but obviously wrote up the Casebook later. On two other occasions (nos 83, 87) Hall treated the Earl for similar conditions. Hall also attended him in 1622 (no. 2).

The patient's symptom of swollen gums was attributed to a distillation of phlegm from the head. This required an initial treatment with a purgative pill. A gargle prepared from a decoction of guaiacum bark mixed with soothing preparations was prescribed. When the condition occurred again some years later Hall imposed a more rigorous purgative regime (no. 83).

Cooke added some observations from Thonerus (no. 54) on remedies for a painful hollow tooth and what was probably a dental abscess.

69: THOMAS UNDERHILL OF LOXLEY

Thomas Underhill (b. 1622), treated by Hall in 1634, was the eldest of the four children of Thomas and Elizabeth, née Daston, of Dumbleton (Glos.). This is one of the few cases when John Hall included comments from the patient's family, in this instance the parents' anxiety that their son could be cured; Hall had also attended the boy's father (no. 136). Thomas's father had sold Loxley manor in October 1622, but retained a house in the parish.

Thomas junior later served as one of the King's Life Guards. He lived at St Giles-in-the-Fields, London, with his uncle, Sir John Underhill, who was separated from his wife, Alice, Viscountess St Albans (d. 1650).[1] Dugdale considered Thomas Underhill to be a royalist in 1642;[2] he died unmarried after 1679.

Thomas Underhill had survived malign spotted fever (typhus) and measles within the previous year. The description of his condition clearly indicates that he was left grievously weak and ill. Hall, in discussing the case with the boy's parents, warned of a long and difficult treatment.

Hall interpreted the symptoms as those of scurvy and the treatment that

1. J.H. Morrison, *The Underhills of Warwickshire* (Cambridge, 1932), pp. 130–1.
2. NRO, Finch-Hatton 4284.

upon Englifh Bodies. 59

Extract. Catholic. Theophr. gr. vi. *cum Aq. Betonic. f. Pil.* 27. which was taken. The middle Vein of the left Arm was opened, and the outward Jaw anoint with the following : ℞ *Camphire* ʒi. *diffolved, Oil of fweet Almonds.* By the ufe of thefe was a defired effect.

Observ. LXIX.

THe eldeft Son of Mr. *Underhil* of *Loxley,* aged about 12, having laboured the fummer before of a *malign Spotted-Feaver,* after fell into the *Meafels,* of which he was cured *Jan.* 1. 1634. Being fent for to him, I found him grievoufly afflicted with the Scurvy ; on the right fide he had a Tumor without difcoloration, fo that I judged there was a Tumor of the Liver. He was grown as lean as a Skeleton, was Melancholy, with black and crufty Ulcers appearing in the Legs. He had a loathing of Meat, a difpofition to Vomit, and an Erratic Feaver ; his Urine was red, as in a burning Feaver, yet without thirft or defire to drink. The Pulfe was fmall, weak, and unequal, fcarcely to be perceived with the Finger ; all Signs of a confirmed Scurvy. His Parents were very earneft with me to cure him ; I told them, I would do my utmoft to do it, but it would require fome time, and it would be difficult. I proceeded as follows: ℞ *Cryftal.Vener.* ʒii. *Spec. Diatrion. Santal.* ʒi. *Pul. Holland.* a ʒii. *M. f. Pul.* for four dofes. It gave him every day three or four ftools without any gripings. The affected Part was anointed with
Unguent.

60 *Select Observations*

Unguent. Fido variol. To the Ulcers was ufed *Diapalm.* After for three days was given *Cream of Tartar* ℥i, in the morning; and an hour after was taken the following: *Take of our fteeled Wine* ℥iiij. *the Effence of Fumitory and Germander,* (which you have in *Bald. Ronf.* fol 259. with *Senertus in 8vo*) each ℥ſſ. *Syrup of Brooklime* ℥ii. *of Water-creffes* ℥i. *Juyce of Scurvy-grafs prepared* ℥vi. *mix them.* The Dofe given was four fpoonfuls, after which to ufe exercife: With which he had two ftools, and caft up by vomit the firft day fome Phlegm. The next day in the morning he took *Diacurcum* ℥ſſ. after the fteeled Wine. Every third day he purged with *Diatart. Quereet.* ℈ſſ. in the pap of a roſted Apple. After he ufed our Antifcorbutic Beer. To his Spleen was applied *Empl. de Ammoniac. Foreft.* Sometimes he ufed the next: *Take Juyce of Scurvy-grafs* ℔ſſ. *Syrup of Brook-lime and Water-creffes,* each ℥iſſ for three mornings. The *Chalibiat* Wine was continued for a whole Month, with the Juyce of Scurvy-grafs, &c. as before. He purged with *Pil. Ammoniac. River.* Of ℥ſſ. was made three Pills, one of which he took every third day, which gave him two or three ftools. The Side fwell'd and pained, was anointed with the following: ℞ *Unguent. Splanch. Magiftr. Dialth.* ā ℥i. *M.* morning and night. In the ufe of the Scorbutic Beer all other was forbidden. After the ufe of the former Pills twice, there fell out a painful Tumor of the Foot, which hindred his Sleep by night, and moving by day; with which were joined Faintings. Therefore to corroborate was ufed the following: ℞ *Pul. Pannon. rub.* ℈i. *Magift. Coral.* ℈ſſ. *Lap. Bezoard.* gr. iij. *M.* To
the

the Foot was ufed the next : *Take Brook-lime,*
M iv. *Wormwood, Melilot, Chamomel, Sage,* each
M i. *Boyl them in fufficient quantity of Beer for a
Bath.* Which ufed for three days, he was almoft
altogether freed from the Pain and Tumor. Then
I purged him with the following : R *Pill. Ruffi.
Stomach. Hier. cum Agaric.* ā ℈i. f. *Pil.* 6. He
took one at Bed-time. The Foot being well,
there fell out a miferable Pain in the right Shoul-
der, which he was freed from in twenty four hours,
by the ufe of *Ung. Fido.* He never left off the Steeled Wine, except thofe days he purged. After meals
he took of the next fo much as would lie upon a
fhilling : R *Plerifar.* ℥ß. *Sacch.* ℥ii. *Mifc.* Efpecially
he purged twice with *Pil. River.* And fometimes
he took in a morning two of the following, which
gave three or four ftools : R *Pil. de Ammoniac.* ℈i.
Gum Gamb. pp. gr. ix. *fine quib.* ℈ß. *M. f. Pill.* By
this method he was cured, God be praifed.

Observ. LXX.

ANne Green, the Daughter of Mrs. *Green,* aged
22, was troubled with Pain of the Head,
fometimes a vivid Colour through all the whole
Body, after that white, with an univerfal Itch
over the Body, with painful Puftles, fo that fhe
could not walk without great Pain, was thus
cured : R *Sarfaparilla* ℥ii. *Hermodactiles* ℥iß. *Guaicum, Liquoris,* each ℥i. *Polypody of the Oak, Sena,*
ā ℥ii. *Agaric.* ℈ii. *Roots of Fennel, Parfly,* each ℥i.
Betony, Sage, each Mß. *Rofemary* p. i. *The Seeds of*
Anis,

followed was along the lines he normally adopted to treat that condition. A series of purgative preparations to expel the morbid humours was combined with strengthening preparations such as steeled wine and the use of the three scorbutic drugs, scurvy-grass, brooklime and water-cresses in various forms, including the juices, a syrup and a beer. *Diapalm.* or iron sulphate was applied to ulcers on the patient's legs. To treat the tumours or swellings ammoniacum was prescribed. The gum-resin ammoniacum was imported from the East Indies and was reputed to resolve obstructions when given internally and disperse hard tumours when applied externally. Hall employed it both ways, prescribing a pill and a plaster.

The treatment involved several remedies that appear for the first time in the Observations.[1] Recovery was, as Hall predicted, long and difficult, with additional complications along the way. Eventually Thomas Underhill was declared cured and was to live for many years.

70: ANNE GREENE OF STRATFORD

Hall's notes described this patient as the eldest daughter, aged twelve, of Lawyer Greene, an entry Cooke clearly misread. Hall would have treated her in 1616. There were three surviving children of Thomas and Letitia Greene of Stratford, where Anne was baptised on 18 March 1604.

Her father was the son of a Warwick gentleman and entered the Middle Temple in 1595; he was called to the bar in 1602.[2] By 1603 he had married Letitia Chandler, a Leicester widow, and become town clerk in Stratford, a post he held until 1617.

In 1613 his brother, John, married to Margaret Lane, became deputy town clerk and four years later Greene sold his tithes and his Stratford property to go and live in Bristol. Greene claimed to be 'cosen' to both Shakespeare and Daniel Baker. The attorney, Francis Collins, visited him at home and Greene hunted at Alveston with Sir William Somerville.

Thomas Greene must have known Hall well and in 1613 they acted as joint trustees in a property settlement made by Richard Lane of Alveston. After leaving Stratford, Greene had a successful career in law; in 1621 he became Reader at the Middle Temple, Master of the Bench in 1623 and

---

1. *Crystal veneris* was the name given to copper sulphate; *Species Diatrion Santalon* was a corroborant powder attributed to Nicolaus Myrepsus; *Diatart. Quercet.* was an aperient tartar preparation attributed to Quercetanus (Joseph du Chesne); *Unguentum Splanchnicum Magistrale* was an ointment to treat the spleen; Plerisar was Hall's shorthand for *Pleres Archontichon*, a corroborant or strengthening powder of thirty-one ingredients including pearl, red coral and musk.

2. *RAMT*, p. 69.

Anis, Carraways, and *Coriander,* each ℥ß. *Cinamon*
℥i. *Boyl them in eight pints of Water, till half be
wasted; after strain it, and of the strained Liquor
take* ℥iiß. *Syrup of Roses solutive* ℥i. *Oil of Vitriol
so much as will make it sharpish.* It was given, and
procured five stools. This being continued five
days, the Body was well purged. After was given
this Decoction : *Take of China sliced* ℥iii. *Infuse it
in three pints of Spring water for twenty four hours,
after boil them on a gentle Fire till half be wasted.*
After being strained, there was given a Draught
in a morning five hours before Dinner, and also
three hours before Supper, hot, till all was
drunk. It was given every third day. After the
use of this *Sudorifick Decoction*, the following Bath
was used : ℞ *Oak leaves* M xx. *Fennel* M xv. *Roots
of Briony, Elicampane sliced*, each M iv. *Brimstone,
Allum, Sea salt*, each ℔i. *Boyl them in sufficient Water for a Bath.* From the Bath she went into her
Bed, and sweat. After, her Body was anointed
with the following : ℞ *Roots of Elicampane, Briony*, each *as much as pleased, Alum a little, make an
Ointment with May Butter.* By these means she became fair and smooth.

Observ. LXXI.

JOhn *Nason* of *Stratford* upon *Avon,* Barber, aged
40, always after Meat suffered most bitter
Pains of the Stomach, as also cruel Misery in the
Loins, so that he had seldom any Sleep at nights,
was entring into the Yellow Jaundice; his Urine
was

Treasurer six years later. His son, William (b. 1608), followed his father into the law. Thomas Greene died in 1640.[1]

Anne Greene's cutaneous affliction was treated first with a decoction of purgative and stomachic drugs[2] followed by a sudorific or sweating decoction of China root.[3] The bath was made from astringent oak leaves and alum, together with sulphur and sea salt. Included in both the bath and the ointment were the roots of elecampane and bryony *Bryonia dioica*, both recommended for the treatment of scabs and itch.

71: JOHN NASON OF STRATFORD, BARBER

John Nason appears to have married a Stratford girl, Elizabeth Rogers (b. 1582 or 1583), on 28 October 1600. He was buried at Stratford on 12 November 1624. Two entries in the baptismal register, in 1604 and 1613, describe children born to John Nason, 'tonsor' (or barber) and 'barber'.

Nason was noted by Hall as a townsman of Stratford, a professional but lower status medical competitor. Apprenticed as a barber-surgeon, Nason was licensed in 1622 by the Bishop of Worcester to practise as a surgeon,[4] and thus able to undertake a far wider range of medical procedures than the barber was permitted. Hall treated him in 1624, a year with a high death rate. Elizabeth Nason, widow, was buried at Holy Trinity on 22 May 1653.

Nason's distressing symptoms were treated with an emetic, which made him vomit six times. This was followed by a medicinal wine with aperient properties which contained, among other things, eupatory *Agrimonia eupatoria*, recommended to promote all secretions. The wine was directed to be mixed with half a pint of goose dung. Goose dung occurs in the Saxon leechdoms as a cure for small wounds and canker, but was not listed among the animal excrements of the London *Pharmacopoeia* of 1618. The volume prescribed (and the use of the term 'juice') makes it possible that goose dung was a common name for the juice of goose-grass or aparine used to feed geese. Lewis observed that 'The leaves and stalks of aparine yield upon

1. E.K. Chambers, *William Shakespeare, A Study of Facts and Problems* (Oxford, 1943), pp. 151–2.

2. Hermodactylus root, a species of colchicum, was imported from the Middle East and used as a purgative (no. 89). Polypody *Polypodium vulgare* is a fern that grows in the clefts of walls, rocks and decayed trees. The polypody growing on the oak was highly regarded and used as an aperient and expectorant.

3. China root China *smilax*, related to sarsaparilla, was introduced into Europe in the sixteenth century and recommended as a treatment for venereal disease. In Hall's time it was prescribed to promote sweating in the treatment of a variety of maladies.

4. Brinkworth, p. 148.

was thin, red, the Crown yellow and frothy. ℞ *our Emetick Infusion* ℥i. It gave six Vomits, and four Stools. The following day, ℞ *Horehound* ℥ii. *Hops* ℥i. *Roots of Bugloss, Elicampane, and Eupatory,* each ℥ß. *Rubarb grosly sliced* ℥i. *Wood of Aloes* ℥iß. *Boyl them all in three pints of White-wine, till the third part be wasted; after strain it without expression; to the straining add the Juyce of Goose-dung half a pint.* Of this he took ℥iii with *white Sugar* ℥ii. This quantity he drunk betimes in the morning. And thus in few days space he was cured, and well coloured.

Observ. LXXII.

BAron *Compton,* aged 55, was infested with bitter Pain by the heat of Urine, was cured by the following Water, often proved by me in this Disease : ℞ *the Whites of eight Eggs well beat, Cows milk* ℔i. *Red Rose water* ℔ß. *distill them in a common Still.* Of this *Water* ℞ ℥iv. *Syrup of Alth. Fernel.* ℥i. *mix them.* It is to be given cold, fasting. And so he was perfectly cured, so that he rode with King *James* in his Progress into *Scotland.*

expression a large quantity of turbid green juice. . . . The juice of this herb has been given, in doses of two or three ounces, as an aperient in obstructions of the viscera'.[1]

72: WILLIAM COMPTON,
FIRST EARL OF NORTHAMPTON

Hall was able to record that his successful treatment enabled his illustrious patient to join the king's visit to Scotland in 1617, although the condition was later to return (no. 2) in 1622. In both observations Hall recorded a cure. On this first occasion Hall employed a cooling mixture formed from a liquor distilled from whites of eggs, rose-water and milk, mixed with syrup of Althaea or marsh mallow, attributed to Jean Fernel.

73: ELIZABETH BOUGHTON OF LAWFORD

This patient was not the sister but the mother-in-law of William Combe of Old Stratford. Cooke mistranslated the phrase *socrus Gs Combes de Lawford* and, noting that Hall thought her 'fair', added the adjective to her place of residence, Lawford. She was Elizabeth Catesby of Lapworth Hall, born in 1575, the daughter and heiress of Edward Catesby, the younger son of Sir Richard of Ashby St Ledgers (Northants.), a family heavily implicated in the Gunpowder Plot. She married Edward Boughton (1572–1625) of Lawford near Rugby on 28 October 1593 and they had three children, Katherine (b. 1595), William (1599–1660, knighted in 1641) and Thomas (1602–66).[2] Hall must have treated her in 1611, the earliest case in his notes. A year later her daughter, Katherine, married Combe (no. 134).

When their sons married sisters, who were heiresses, in 1623, Edward Boughton extended Bilton Hall, the family home; the date was recorded on the porch, although now the only internal evidence of seventeenth-century work is timber-framing in the attics.[3] Edward Boughton made his will in September 1620, just after his wife's death. It is an extraordinary document, not merely because he left all his substantial estate to the second son, Thomas, but that the eldest, William, was to receive only £100 a year since he had spent his time in 'riotous and disorderly courses, breaking both the bounds of Lawe and nature'. Katherine Combe, his married daughter, was one of the witnesses.[4] Elizabeth Boughton died at the age of forty-four

1. Lewis, *An Experimental History*, p. 70.

2. *HV Warws.*, 1682–3, pp. 113–14; B.G.F.C. Ward-Boughton-Leigh, *Memorials of a Warwickshire Family* (1906), pp. 51, 56–9.

3. *VCH Warws.*, VI, pp. 30, 32, 265.

4. LJRO, B/C/10/Edward Boughton, 1624

Observ. LXXIII.

Mrs. *Boughton*, Sifter to Mr. *Comb* of *Lauford-fair*, aged about 36, very handfom, was afflicted with a moft grievous Difeafe, and bitter Symptoms, for above two years; and although many expert Phyficians did lend their help, yet there was no Profit, yea rather all was more bitter and grievous. She could fcarce fwallow or breath, fhe felt fomething hard in her Throat to the big-nefs of a Dove's Egg, fo that fhe could fcarce fwallow either Meat or Drink. This was caufed from Wind; for fhe felt it move, and in its mo-tion it was fometimes more and lefs painful. The tumor of the Almonds was not great, from a Rheum which diftilled from the Head, which vexed her moft in the night. Her Illnefs and Pain hindred her Sleep, and fhe feared fhe fhould be choaked; yet her Head was afflicted with a nota-ble numnefs, and an incredible pronenefs to fleep; her Body was fo alfo afflicted, by which fhe could fcarce walk, and natural Action was deprived; hence there were a long time of Symptoms. By in-tervals her Hands would be livid, not without coldnefs; the Thighs tumified, and a *Scorbutick Dropfy* broke forth; all thefe being caufed from the Spleen, Liver, and fuppreffion of the Cour-fes. ℞ *Sena* ʒiiſ. *Cream of Tartar* ʒii. *the beft Turbith, Hermodactils, each* ʒi. *Rubarb, Troches of Agarick, each* ℈ii. *Scamoni* ℔p. ʒſ. *Mace, Cina-mon, Galangal, each* ʒiii. *Sugar of Violets the weight of of all, make a Powder.* Dose from ʒi to ʒii in Broth, wherein was boiled *Peniroyal, Mugwort, Horehound, Sage, Betony.* This ended, the next Decoction was taken: ℞ *China sliced* ʒi. *Sassafras* ʒiii. *Spring water* ℔vi. *Juyce of Limons* ʒii. *Infuse them for twenty four hours, after boil them till a third part be wasted, and then let it pass through an Ippocras bag.* Of which there was drunk ʒv morning and night, with ʒii of the *Juyce of Scurvy-grass prepared.* Every third day, if the Body was not open, was given a Clyster framed of ʒxii *of the former Decoction, red Sugar* ʒii. *and Honey of Rosemary flowers* ʒiii. For her Mouth, ℞ *Spring water* ʒii. *Oil of Vitriol so many drops as made it very sharp, in which Water was dipp'd a Feather, and so conveyed to the swell'd Fauces.* This was done often in each hour, by the use of which there ran out, and was spit forth continually very much Phlegm. After was used a Fume of Amber, which was received by a Tunnel into the Mouth. To the Stomach was applied our Plaster for the Stomach, *Observ.* 19. ℞ *Diamor. simp.* ʒv. *Mel Rosar.* ʒiv. *Succ. Matris sylvæ* ʒviii. *Aq. Hord.* ʒxii. *Ol. Sulph. q. s. ad gratam acidit.* This Gargarism was often used in a day. Thus she was cured, and lived eight years after.

F

Observ. LXXIV.

ESquire *Beaufou*, (whose Name I have always cause to honour) at the end of his Supper eating great quantity of Cream, about the age of 70, after his first sleep he found himself very ill, and so continued. The second day he sent for me, I found his Pulse quick, and his Urine red and little, often pissing, his Stomach full of Phlegm and Choler, as appeared: for falling into a voluntary vomiting, there came up a great quantity of Choler, like the Yolks of Eggs putrified. This considered, I gave him an ℥ of our *Emetick Infusion*, which gave ten Vomits and three Stools, which answered desire. To drink, he had prescribed the Decoction of Hartshorn with Sugar and Limon. And thus he was cured in four days.

Observ. LXXV.

ESquire *Packinton* was troubled with want of Appetite, to whom I prescribed the following Powder, which was taken for many days: ℞ *Sena* ℥iii. *Ginger, Mace, each* ℈i. *Cinamon* ℥ß. *Cream of Tartar* ℥ii. *mix them, and make a Powder.* Dose ℥i in Broth. This restored his Appetite, for which he thanked me, desiring the Receipt. The next year after he also used it with good success.

The

on 12 April 1619, six years before her husband; they are both commemorated by a tomb in St Botolph's church, Newbold-on-Avon.

The fact that Elizabeth Boughton recovered and lived for eight years rules out the possibility that the 'something hard in her throat to the bigness of a dove's egg' was a tumour. Other possibilities to account for her symptoms are some form of hysteria or a remitting neurological disease. Hall accounted for the symptoms by a distillation of rheum from the head which caused her almonds or tonsils to swell, suppression of menses and a disturbance of the liver and spleen.

The treatment followed methods used to deal with a severe disturbance of the humours. First a purgative powder was to be taken with a herbal broth, followed by a diaphoretic decoction to make her sweat, with the juice of scurvy-grass to treat the patient's 'scorbutic dropsy'. The decoction was also used as an enema. A plaster was applied to the stomach, and for local treatment of the throat there was an acidified water to be applied with a feather to the fauces or throat, a vapour of burning amber to the mouth and a gargle. The ingredients of the gargle, which was slightly acidified with sulphuric acid, were *Diamoron*, a preparation of mulberries, *Melita rosarum* or honey of roses, the juice of *Matris sylvae* or meadowsweet, *Filipendula ulmaria* and *Aqua hordeata*, a water made from pearl-barley.

74: SIR THOMAS BEAUFOU OF EMSCOTE

The Beaufous had acquired the manor of Emscote, near Warwick, by marriage in the mid-fifteenth century. Sir Thomas Beaufou, Hall's patient, lived to be eighty-six and therefore must have been treated about 1614. He married an heiress, Ursula, the daughter of William Hudson of Guy's Cliffe, in 1563. Their family conformed to the regular Beaufou pattern of three sons and four daughters. Thomas, knighted in 1603, was Sheriff in 1607.[1]

However, during Ursula's last years, he lived 'overfamiliary acquainted' with her sister, Dorothy Aldersey (widowed by 1580), who ruled Thomas's household and estate. When a widower, Thomas clandestinely married his niece, Dorothy's daughter, Ann, with whom he 'lyved cohabited and conversed together at bed and bord as if . . . lawfull man and wief', having 'Carnall knowledge of each others bodies'. Dorothy continued to live with them as a 'p[ro]curer and abettor'. The case reached the Worcester consistory court in 1617 and Sir Thomas sold land (some to Sidrak Davenport, also a patient) to pay his fines. In 1626, after Ann's death, he received a general pardon by Letters Patent.[2]

The court heard that the Beaufou affair was common gossip in the area,

---

1. BL, Add. MS 29264; *HV Warws.*, 1619, pp. 203–4.
2. Gwendolyn Beaufoy, *Leaves from a Beech Tree* (Oxford, 1930), pp. 51–4.

The following hath cured many of the like Affect : First purge with a Potion framed of the Decoction of *Wormwood* and *Agrimony*, and ℥ſs of *Diaphæni-con*. After was drunk the following : ℞ Leaves of *Agrimony*, *Wormwood*, and *Centaury*, each Mi. Boil them in water to ℔ſs of the ſtraining ; add a little Sugar, drink it every morning for three or four mornings.

Observ. LXXVI.

MR. *Rogers*, Clerk, aged about 40, was troubled with Pain in the Throat, Tumor of the Tonſils and Palat ; he could hardly either ſwallow or breath, and was almoſt ſtrangled, to whom I coming preſcribed the following : ℞ Figs, *Liquoris*, *Raiſins*, *Aniſe ſeeds*, each ℥j. *Spring water* ℔iv. *Boyl them till half be waſted, and uſe it for ordinary drink.* Take the Fume of Amber oft in a day. To the Neck and Tumor appearing, I commanded this Cataplaſm : ℞ *Green Wormwood* M ii. *Hogs greaſe as much as will make a Pultis, being well beat together.* In one nights ſpace he was cured, and had his ſwallowing again. This was proved an hundred times.

which makes Hall's loyal comment about always having honoured Sir Thomas puzzling. The 1694 fire at St Mary's, Warwick, destroyed important Beaufou monuments and both registers and transcripts are defective. Sir Thomas died in 1630 and was succeeded by his eldest son, also Thomas (b. 1579), who died only five years after his father. From evidence in the imperfect register transcripts, the possibility that there were offspring of this second marriage cannot be discounted.[1]

The elderly self-indulgent Sir Thomas, having made himself ill by eating too much cream, was dosed with Hall's emetic infusion which made him vomit ten times. A less vigorous medicine was the decoction of hartshorn, which he drank during the four days it took him to recover from the cream (and the emetic). Hartshorn was among the medicines recommended to soothe irritated states of the intestine.

75: SIR JOHN PAKINGTON OF WESTWOOD PARK, WORCESTERSHIRE

Sir John Pakington was treated twice by Hall, on this occasion for inappetance and later for gout (no. 89). The family were originally from Buckinghamshire. Sir John was born in 1548 and had been a favourite of Queen Elizabeth I, at whose court he enjoyed the nickname of 'Lusty Pakington'.[2] The Queen had met him on her progress to Worcester in 1575; she created him a Knight of the Bath and granted him the monopoly on starch. A very wealthy man, he served as Lord Lieutenant of Worcestershire and married Dorothy (née Smith), daughter of the Queen's silkman. They had four children, a son (d. 1624) and three daughters.[3] Westwood Park, site of a former Benedictine priory near Droitwich, was acquired soon after their wedding in 1598 and considerable building work was carried out there from about 1600.[4] Hampton Lovett nearby had formerly been the family home; by 1603 Pakington was second among Worcestershire gentry only to John Talbot of Grafton in taxes paid.[5] In 1618 Sir John acquired a licence to impark 1,000 acres; he created two parks at Westwood, one of red and the other of fallow deer. The burgesses of Droitwich objected, as they had formerly had a right of way there.[6] Originally a hunting lodge, Westwood was the only Worcestershire house depicted by Kip in his *Nouveau Théâtre de la Grande Bretagne* (see p. 112). In the 1650s it sheltered several eminent divines.

Hall treated Pakington with senna mixed with ginger, mace, cinnamon

1. WCRO, DR 447/34.

2. Grazebrook, II, p. 420.

3. *HV Worcs.*, 1569, p. 103; *Complete Baronetage*, I, p. 148.

4. Pevsner, *Worcs.*, p. 286.

5. John Amphlett (ed.), *The Worcestershire Lay Subsidy Roll of 1603* Worcs. Hist. Soc. (1901), pp. 10–11.

6. *VCH Worcs.*, III, p. 237.

Observ. LXXVII.

THe Lady *Beaufou*, godly, honeſt, being of a noble Extract, continuing healthful till the age of 28, which was 1617, *July* 1. fell into a burning malign continual Feaver, with great Pain of the Head, moſt vehement Heat, Pain in the Stomach ; the Body all over, eſpecially the Arms, was full of ſpots ; the Urine was red and little. It was then called the *New Feaver*, it invaded many, I was called the third day of its Invaſion. The Stomach being ſtuffed and burdened with ill humors, as I perceived, I adviſed the following Vomit : ℞ *Emetick Infuſion* ℥ix. This gave twelve Vomits without any great trouble. The day before ſhe had (unknown to me) drunk much Milk to quench her thirſt, by reaſon whereof the Vomit at firſt drew forth a wonderful quantity of curdled Milk, ſo that ſhe was almoſt choaked, after came Choler mixed with Phlegm, afterward burnt Melancholy. She had alſo ſix Stools Phlegmy, mixed with green Choler and much Seroſities. Her vomiting ending in three hours, I gave a Pill of *Laudan. Paracelſi* gr. vii. (ſure he miſtook her, for four is a good Doſe) after which ſhe ſlept four hours, the Pain of her Head ceaſing. Then to me unknown her Servant gave her a draught of Whey, which being drunk, ſhe preſently had three Vomits of black Stuff without any trouble, and two ſuch like Stools, and was cruelly afflicted with the Hiccough, to allay which

I

and cream of tartar. The spices would have masked the unpleasant taste of the senna and also tended to reduce its griping effects. The treatments noted at the end of the observation involve the very bitter wormwood, since bitters were traditional to stimulate appetite. These remedies were inserted by Cooke and did not occur in Hall's manuscript.

76: JOHN ROGERS, VICAR OF STRATFORD-UPON-AVON

John Rogers served as vicar of St Nicholas, Warwick, for seven years (1599–1606) and he was also a visiting preacher at Tysoe three times a year during this period.[1] Rogers was appointed to Stratford in 1606 and seems to have been disliked by the townspeople. He made powerful enemies there, including Daniel Baker, whom he fined in a bastardy case in the Peculiar Court in 1606. He lived in the Old Priest's House in Chapel Quad and was thus a near neighbour of Shakespeare, at whose funeral he would have officiated in 1616. In the same year he sentenced Thomas Quiney on a bastardy charge.[2]

Rogers was not always on bad terms with the borough authorities, for the Corporation sent him wine in 1616 when his brother preached in Stratford and two years later gave him a new gown. However, in 1618 he was presented to a second benefice and, until he was paid £5, he refused to leave. He was dismissed from his living in 1619 by eighteen votes to seven and replaced by Thomas Wilson (no. 4) of Evesham, for which the permission of the Lord Chancellor, Sir Francis Bacon, was required. Scurrilous verses against Wilson and a mob demonstration (with shouts of 'Hang him!') were recorded in Stratford.[3] John Rogers had a family of six, four daughters and two sons born in Stratford between 1606 and 1615, one of whom died as an infant. He was attended by Hall in the period 1617 to 1619.

Hall treated Rogers's inflamed and swollen tonsils with an emollient drink, a vapour of burnt amber and a wormwood cataplasm (poultice) to his swollen glands. Hall ended by commenting 'in one nights space he was cured', but this referred only to the fact that his condition was sufficiently relieved to enable him to swallow.

77: ANN, LADY BEAUFOU OF EMSCOTE

This patient was Ann, née Aldersey, daughter of the first Lady Beaufou's sister, and thus Sir Thomas's niece.[4] When Hall first attended her in July 1617, she was suffering from what he described as the new fever (typhus or spotted fever).

1. WCRO, DR 288/1.
2. Brinkworth, pp. 137, 143.
3. Fogg, p. 49; Hughes, *MH*, pp. 62–3.
4. *HV Warws.*, 1619, pp. 203–4; BL, Add. MSS 29264. See also no. 74.

I gave Claret wine burnt with Aromatick, which ſucceeded ; ſhe was quieter the reſt of the Night, but did not ſleep well. In the morning I gave Chicken-broth, made with appropriate Herbs, and ſo for four hours ſhe reſted. At the end of that time I gave a draught of the Decoction of Hartshorn hot. On Munday morning having ſome evacuation, I appointed the ſame Decoct. ſhould be given cold. She was miſerably afflicted with *Puſtles*, with great heat of the Tongue and Throat, that ſhe could not drink without great difficulty, for which ſhe uſed the following Gargariſm : ℞ *Diamoron. ſimp.* ʒiv. *Honey of Roſes* ʒii. *Roſewater* ℔j. *Oil of Sulphur, ſo much as made it ſharpiſh.* After the uſe of the *Hartshorn Decoction*, the ſeventh day, the Pox appeared, yet the foreſaid Gargariſm was uſed for the Throat, and ſhe drunk of the Decoction of Hartſhorn cold four times a day, and ſo ſhe was cured. I ordered that the Pox after the eighth day ſhould be anointed with this : ℞ *common Oil, and Carduus water,* well ſhaked together, and ſo there were left no Scars.

Observ. LXXVIII.

MR. *Farman*, afflicted with the Small Pox, whilſt being at my Lady *Beaufou's*, ſo that he could not go to his Father's at *Leiceſter*. To expel them, I gave him this : ℞ *Diaſcordium* ʒi. *Mithrid.* ʒſſ. *Croc.* Ɔſſ. *Aq. Dracuncul.* ʒiii. *Corn. Cervi* Ɔi. *f. Hauſtus.* This cauſed him to ſweat, and the ſame day began to appear his Pox. This

F 3　　　　 cauſed

Hall noted curing Mr Farman's smallpox while he was visiting Lady Beaufou (no. 78), but it has not been possible to prove a family link between these two patients. The fragmentary nature of the parish registers for St Mary's, Warwick, in the early seventeenth century makes it uncertain if there were children of this second prohibited marriage. However, two baptisms in the bishop's transcripts suggest that two sons were theirs, George (b. 1615) and Thomas (b. and d. 1622), each noted as a son of 'Milesii [Knight] Beaufou'. Lady Beaufou died aged thirty-seven in 1626, making possible Sir Thomas's pardon in that year (no. 74).[1]

Lady Beaufou's continual fever, severe pain in the head, vomiting bile and rash of spots were symptoms of typhus fever, also called new fever, camp fever, gaol fever, putrid or malign spotted fever. An eruption of pox or pustules was regarded as a favourable sign.[2] In this case Hall recorded explicit details of the morbid humours expelled by the emetic infusion. He identified choler or yellow bile, phlegm and burnt melancholy, which was believed to be an unnatural form of black bile converted by the fever from a cold dry to a hot dry humour.

Hall's treatment after the stomach had been unburdened of its 'ill humours' consisted of an opiate pill *Laudanum Paracelsi*,[3] hartshorn, his favoured remedy for fevers, a gargle and carduus benedictus water shaken with oil and applied to the pustules, which he said healed without scarring. An attack of hiccup was treated with claret wine burnt (heated or perhaps distilled) with aromatic. Aromatic was the collective name for drugs having a grateful spicy scent and pungent taste. They included spices, gums and resins such as myrrh.

78: [THOMAS] FARNHAM OF LEICESTER

As early as the thirteenth century there were members of the Farnham family living in various parts of Leicestershire and by the sixteenth century they were well established at Quorndon, about 7 miles from the county town, where some fine tombs reflect their wealth and importance.[4]

1. Beaufoy, *Leaves*, pp. 47–58; WCRO, DR 447/34.
2. Buchan, *Domestic Medicine*, 2nd edn. (London, 1772), pp. 245–9.
3. In recent times laudanum is the name given to a tincture of opium. The original formula is attributed to Paracelsus. J.R. Partington in *A History of Chemistry* (1961), Vol. II, p. 150, observes that there was more than one recipe, not all of them containing opium. Hall prescribed the solid form obtained by extracting opium with spirits of wine, mixing it with saffron, castor, ambergris and other drugs, then evaporating to a soft mass. Cooke noted that the dose of seven grains was excessive and quoted a dose of four grains. Sir Walter Ralegh, in a collection of medical recipes roughly contemporary with Hall's, quotes a dose of three grains (MS 13, fol. 12, item 749 in S.A. Moorat, *Catalogue of Manuscripts in the Wellcome Historical Medical Library* (1962).
4. Pevsner, *Leics.*, p. 355.

caufed no fmall joy to his Sifter, and thankfulnefs
to God, that he was delivered from the Jaws of
Death.   For his thirft, he drank at his pleafure
the Decoction of Hartshorn, and ufed the fame
Gargarifm prefcribed for the Lady *Beaufou*; as alfo
anointed his face often in a day, when it began
to dry, with this: ℞ *Carduus water* ℥ii. *Sallet Oil*
℥iſs. *Stir them much together.* This removed the
Pits.

Observ. LXXIX.

THE Lady *Rouſe* of *Rouſelench*, aged 27, fell
into a Quotidian Feaver two days after
Child-birth; in the very Fit fhe was moft vio-
lently afflicted with the Head-ach, as alfo cruel
Pain in the Neck, was thus cured: ℞ *Diaſcord.*
℥i. *Magiſt. Perlar. Tinctur. Coral.* ā gr. xii. *Aq.*
Card. benedict. ℥ii. It was given two hours before
the Fit, it was reiterated before the next Fit, and
fo for two days.   She was delivered from the
Pain of her Neck with this Plafter: ℞ *Caran.* ℥i.
diſſol. in Vino Hiſpan. Pic. alb. ℥i. *f. Empl.* Spread
it upon Leather, and apply it to the Neck.   And
thus fhe was delivered from her Pain and Feaver.

Hall specifically noted that Mr Farnham was prevented from returning to his father in Leicester by smallpox at Emscote. Although this patient has not been positively identified, he seems to be the son of Thomas (b. 1563), the fourth generation of this surname in Leicester. Described by Hall as *Generosus*, he could reasonably be Thomas (b. 1593), who married in 1622. His sister cannot be identified.

The patient was a victim of smallpox. Hall's treatment has features in common with his treatment of Lady Beaufou's fever. A *haustus* or draught included opium (in the *Diascordium*) and hartshorn. These were mixed with other drugs including *Aqua Dracunculus*, a water made from tarragon *Artemisia dracunculus*. Carduus mixed with sallet oil (olive oil) was used to anoint the 'pits' (pustules) on the face, which apparently healed without scarring.

79: ESTHER, LADY ROUS OF ROUS LENCH, WORCESTERSHIRE

Hall recorded attending Esther, Lady Rous on three occasions. She was the sixth of the thirteen children of Sir Thomas Temple of Stowe (Bucks.) and named after her mother, Hester Sandys of Latimers (Bucks.).[1] Lady Rous was connected to several patients in Hall's network, so that, for example, her brother's son, Peter, married into the Tyrrell family, whose letters survive about Hall's success at growing vines in his Stratford garden.[2] Her daughter-in-law was the widowed Mary Wagstaffe (no. 144) and her husband's aunt, Isabel Woodward, was Mary Murden's mother (no. 111).

John Rous inherited in 1611, at his father's death, a substantial Worcestershire manor that the family had held since the late fourteenth century. The timbered house Esther occupied was large, its two quadrangles linked by a great hall; a moat remains in the park.[3] Sir John Rous was Sheriff of the county in 1610 and 1636. Baptised on 23 November 1589 and married when she was only sixteen on 21 November 1605, Esther had seven children in fourteen years.[4] On this occasion Hall attended Lady Rous when she suffered from fever (1616) and in her last pregnancies in 1617 and 1620 (nos 93, 96). She died, aged only thirty, in 1620. Her fifth child, Mary, may well be the Mrs Savage for whom Hall later prescribed (no. 151), for Mary Rous in 1633 married a local gentleman, John Savage of Cookhill.

The Rous family were consistently wealthy, with a landed income of at

1. *HV Bucks.*, 1634, pp. 115–16; *VCH Bucks.*, IV, pp. 232–3, 237.

2. Joseph, p. xi.

3. *VCH Worcs.*, III, pp. 497–500; E.A.B. Barnard, 'The Rouses of Rous Lench', *Trans Worcs. Arch. Soc.* N.S.9 (1932), pp. 31–74.

4. *HV Worcs.*, 1569, pp. 114–15; *HV Worcs.*, 1634, p. 82; I am most grateful to Mr Hugh A. Hanley of Bucks. CRO for his help.

OBSERV. LXXX.

WIlliam *Clavel*, troubled with a virulent *Go-norrhea*, and extream heat of Urine, ha-ving been under anothers hands for a month with-out Profit, was cured with the following Reme-dies in fifteen days ſpace, being in the Month of *November* : R *Gum. Guaiac. pul. ℥i. It was given in Beer.* It gave five ſtools. Afterwards he took a pint of the following Decoction, morning and night : R *Sarſaparilla ℥ii. Hermodactiils ℥iſs. Guai-acum, Liquoris, each ℥i. Sena ℥ii. Seeds of Anis, Carraway, and Coriander, each ℥ſs. Boyl them in eight pints of Water, till half be waſted.* After the ſtrained Liquor was taken, Doſe ℥iv. there was given the following Electuary : R *Gum. Tragacant. ℥ſs. diſſolve it in ſufficient quantity of Plantain water, ſtrain it, add Gum. Guaiacum powdered ℈ii. Ter-bentine burnt ℈i. mix them. Doſe ℈iſs.* By the uſe of the Decoction of *Sarſaparilla* he was very well purged, and delivered altogether from the pains of the Loins, and the heat of Urine in four days, and by the uſe of the Electuary he was altogether cured of his *Gonorrhea.*

least £1,000 a year in the period 1603 to 1642.[1] Hall noted Lady Rous as 'religious' while her eldest son, Thomas (1608–76), strongly anti-royalist, was patron of John Trapp and of Richard Baxter, who both dedicated works to him.[2] Sir John Rous died aged seventy-two on 10 April 1645 at Warwick; his body was removed to Rous Lench on 23 February 1653. Their monument with a 'crude Doric entablature' survives among the family tombs in St Peter's, Rous Lench.[3]

In the index to Hall's manuscript this case was listed under puerperal fever but Lady Rous was reported to be suffering from an intermittent malarial type quotidian fever, where the fever fits recurred daily, and not from the serious infection now called puerperal or child-bed fever. A quotidian fever was attributed to morbid phlegmatic humours. As in all cases involving pregnancy and childbirth Hall refrained from prescribing purgative or emetic medicines.

Two hours before the fit of fever was due he arranged for a draught to be given composed of the opiate *Diascordium*, the cordial strengthening medicines pearl[4] and coral, mixed with a water prepared from carduus benedictus, which was a hot and dry drug used here to counter the cold wet phlegm.

The painful neck was treated with a plaster using caranna, a resin from New Spain dissolved in Spanish wine with white pitch, which was prepared from turpentine or some other form of resin.

80: WILLIAM CLAVELL OF FECKENHAM, WORCESTERSHIRE

In the Latin text this patient is called William Clavell *de Fecknã*, with neither status nor age recorded. Unlike Francis Harvey (no. 143), Clavell was not a gentleman and not of sufficient status that his identity had to be protected. The Latin version also seems to give October as the month when Clavell was treated, rather than November.

Searches in Feckenham registers and in Worcestershire generally have failed to find any records of this patient; he may have been a traveller. There could, of course, have been an initial misunderstanding of his place of origin.

William Clavell was suffering from a venereal infection, gonorrhoea, an inflammatory urethral discharge. Hall's treatment involved guaiacum and sarsaparilla, drugs imported from the West Indies in the sixteenth century as specifics for the treatment of syphilis (no. 7).

1. J.T. Cliffe, *The Puritan Gentry* (1984), p. 194.
2. Ibid., pp. 10, 194.
3. Pevsner, *Worcs.*, p. 255; Barnard, 'The Rouses', pp. 33–7.
4. *Magisterium Perlarum* or magistery of pearl. Magistery comes from the language of alchemy and means the work of the master. It was applied to preparations requiring special skills and knowledge.

Observ. LXXXI.

RIchard *Wilmore* of *Norton*, aged 14, vomited black Worms, about an inch and half long, with six feet, and little red heads ; when he was to vomit, he was almoſt dead, but in a little time after he revived, I gave him *Merc. Vitæ.* The next day after his Father brought ſome wrapped up in Paper, they crept like Earwigs, and were very like, ſave in colour, he earneſtly deſired my beſt advice. I conſidering the ſtate of the Diſeaſe, the ſtrength of the Party, and that for moſt part he was thus cruelly afflicted every New Moon, unleſs he devoured abundance of Meat, inſomuch that he was ready to tear himſelf in pieces, I gave the following Remedies : ℞ *Merc. Vitæ* gr. iii. *Conſerv. Roſ. parum.* This gave ſeven Vomits, and brought away ſix Worms, ſuch as I never beheld or read of. The following day I gave this : ℞ the *Emetick Infuſion* ʒv. It gave five Vomits, and brought up three Worms. The third day I gave the following : ℞ *Spec. Diaturb. cum Rhab.* ʒi. *Pul. Sen. lax.* ʒſ. *Aq. Portulac.* ʒ iii. *Syr. Roſ. ſol.* ʒii. *Ol. Vitriol. gut.* 8. *Miſc.* This purged well, but brought away no Worms. Thus he was delivered, and gave me many thanks. I met him two years after, and asked him whether he had any Eroſion of the Stomach, or an Ejection of Worms, and he told me he had never been troubled with it ſince.

Guaiacum or *Lignum vitae*, used in this case in the form of the resin extracted from the wood, enjoyed a considerable reputation in Hall's time for the treatment of syphilis and other venereal conditions. In time its value was questioned and by the eighteenth century it was used only as an adjunct to the more efficient mercurial remedies. Various reasons were put forward to account for the failure of the drug to live up to its reputation. It was argued that a drug of proven value in the warm West Indies would be of less use in the European climate. It was also said that the drug, when used to treat syphilis, was given in the early stages of the disease and the passing of the primary phase was falsely interpreted as a complete cure.[1]

Clavell was treated one month after the onset of the disease. The urethral discharge cleared up in fifteen days under the prescribed purging and sweating regime and the patient was said to be 'altogether cured of his Gonorrhoea'. Not all urethral discharges are due to the gonococcus organism and this would explain the complete cure that Hall claimed. If, however, this were a true gonorrhoea then complications might set in and cause considerable distress, as in the case of Francis Harvey, another of Hall's patients who suffered from gonorrhoea (no. 143).

81: RICHARD WILMORE OF NORTON CURLIEU, BUDBROOKE

Richard Wilmore's home was in Norton Curlieu, a hamlet in Budbrooke parish, just outside Warwick. In 1588 Edward, second Lord Dudley, had granted the manor of Budbrooke to, among others, Thomas Wilmer. However, this grant was declared fraudulent and the estate was then given to the Dormers, well-known recusants who lived at Grove Park.[2] Wilmers were living at Budbrooke as early as 1570.

On 24 June 1603 Hall's patient, Richard Wilmore, son and heir of Richard the younger (d. 1626),[3] was baptised and therefore must have been attended by Hall in 1617; Hall noted that they met again in 1619. A year after his father's death Richard Wilmore married Joan Awry and their two children were baptised in the parish, Mary in 1630 and Richard two years later. Richard Wilmore was buried at Budbrooke on 14 February 1649/50.

This is an intriguing case-history with the reference to the new moon adding a bizarre touch to the account. The creatures vomited were probably some type of insect larvae. It was not unusual to describe larvae as worms. The buccaneer explorer William Dampier (1651–1715), when in the West Indies, recorded that he extracted two white worms from a boil in

---

1. Lewis, *An Experimental History*, p. 301; J.S. Forsyth, *The New London Medical and Surgical Dictionary* (1826), p. 328.

2. *VCH Warws.*, III, p. 66.

3. (H)WRO, class 008.7 1626/211.

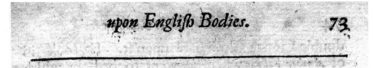

Observ. LXXXII.

Mrs. *Kempſon*, being for many days and nights cruelly tormented with a hollow Tooth, and had uſed many Medicines, as alſo Charms, and yet not profited, came running to me, to whom I preſcribed the following Water, which being uſed, removed the Pain, provoking a great deal of ſpitting, which was very thin : ℞ *Water of Corn Poppy* ℥ii. *Oil of Vitriol ſo much as made it ſharp, being well mixed.* There was dipp'd in it Lint, and applied to the hollow Tooth, it was reiterated often. This ſpeedily removed the Tooth-ach, yet Pain in the Head continued, for which was preſcribed the following Pills : ℞ *Pil. Coch.* ℥ſ. *Aurear.* ℥i. *Troch. Agaric.* ℈ſ. *cum Aq. Betonic.* f. *Pil.* 7. Theſe gave ten Stools, and three Vomits, and brought away four great long Worms by ſtool. And thus was ſhe delivered from her foreſaid Symptoms.

Observ. LXXXIII.

Baron *Compton*, Preſident of *Wales*, being much afflicted with ſwelling of the Face ariſing from Rheum, which made his Face very ill-favoured, was thus cured : ℞ *Vnguent. Dialth.* ℥ſ. *Ol. Chamomel. Viol. Amygd. d.* ā ℥ii. *Axung. Gallin.* ℥i. f. *Vnguent.* With this his Face was anointed, and a
double

his leg, about three quarters of an inch long, invested with three rows of black, short, stiff hair, running clear round them.[1] In more recent times worms in the diapers of young children, reported by mothers from immigrant populations living in New York, were shown to be insect larvae. In one case they proved to be maggots, in another the slender brown 'worms' were the first stage larvae of a moth.[2] In the latter case it was easier to identify the larvae than to explain their presence.

For treatment Hall used strongly emetic and purgative medicines to expel the putrescent matter from which the 'worms' were generated. He used the chemical remedy *Mercurius vitae* (no. 39), emetic infusion and another purgative containing *Species Diaturbith cum Rhabarbo*, which was a powder containing terpethum and rhubarb together with *Aqua Portulaca* or water of purslane *Portulaca oleracea*.

82: MARGARET KEMPSON OF STRATFORD-UPON-AVON

Margaret Kempson had been baptised in Stratford on 24 November 1589, the third of five children born to John and Isabel Sadler in the years 1587 to 1594. Her mother, also a patient of Hall, was the daughter of Peter Smart (no. 105). Hall noted that she was a gentlewoman.

John Sadler was a prosperous miller, aspiring to gentle status, and marriage for his daughter, Margaret, to such a long-established landowning family as the Kempsons must have been regarded as advancement, although she was some twenty years younger than her husband, Leonard Kempson of Stratford (no. 31). The date of their marriage has not been found.

The Kempsons lived with the Sadlers at their Church Street house, very near New Place. Eight months after Leonard Kempson's death, on 20 April 1626, at the age of thirty-seven, Margaret Kempson remarried. Her second husband was John Norbury of Alcester (baptised 21 April 1599), ten years her junior, and it may be presumed that her mother approved of the arrangement, for a year later Isabel Sadler bequeathed a 'best grosgrain gown' and 20s. each to buy rings to the newly married John and Margaret Norbury.[3]

They left Stratford for Alcester after their marriage. Margaret was buried there on 11 October 1643 and John Norbury on 23 June 1651.

Hall's remark 'came running to me' suggests a possible frosty reception for a patient who had tried self-medication and charms before seeking the advice of a physician! He treated Margaret Kempson with an anodyne

1. G. Norris, *William Dampier* (1994), p. 13.
2. *Pediatrics*, 71 (1983), p. 466.
3. (H)WRO, class 008.7 1627/138.

double Linnen Cloth laid upon it. He took ʒiß
of *Amber Pills*, when he went to bed, by which
the Tumor of the Face was removed. There
was uſed as a Gargariſm, the following : ℞ *Syrup
of red Poppies* ʒß. *Water of the ſame* ℈iii. *Oil of
Vitriol ſo much as made it ſharp.* And thus he was
wholly cured in two days.

OBSERV. LXXXIV.

ESquire *Rainsford*, aged 35, being miſerably
afflicted with a malign Feaver, Thirſt, Wind,
Pain of the Spleen, Tumor of the Stones, and
Hypochondriac Melancholy, was cured as followeth : ℞ *Manna* ʒß. *Rubarb* ʒi. *This he took in
Poſſet-drink.* It gave five Stools without any eaſe,
with this he purged himſelf. I being called, applied the following Plaſter to the Region of the
Spleen : ℞ *Labdan.* ʒii. *Ceræ flav.* ʒi. *Empl. Melilot.* ʒii. *Emplaſt. ex Saturn. rub.* ʒß. Being well
freed from the Wind, for the flatuous Tumor in
the Scrotum was *firſt* applied a Pultis made of *Rue,
Chamomel, Parſly,* boiled in Claret-Wine. This
removed, was applied a Plaſter framed *ex Empl.
Noſtr. Saturnali, & Melilot.* ā part. *æqual.* By theſe
that Tumor was removed. To mollify the Belly
was uſed the following Clyſter : ℞ *Ol. Sem. Lin.*
ʒviii. *Ol. Rutæ, & Cham.* ā ʒi. *Diaphœn. & Diacath.* ā ʒß. *in Vin. Hiſpan. diſſol. f. Clyſt.* It gave
two Stools with Wind. He after complained of
his Stomach, for which the third day I gave him
this : ℞ *Emetick Infuſion* ʒi. *Aqua Cæleſtis three
drops.*

water involving the corn poppy *Papaver rhoeas*, which was applied on lint to the hollow tooth. A strong purgative and emetic pill was prescribed for the head pains which, when it worked, revealed a worm infestation.

83: WILLIAM COMPTON, FIRST EARL OF NORTHAMPTON

Hall was treating William Compton before he was created Earl of Northampton at Salisbury on 2 August 1618 and he was attended twice more (nos 68, 87) for this condition. Hall attributed his patient's swollen gums (no. 87) to a distillation of rheum from the head. There is no precise indication of the chronological order of the consultations except for the patient's changes of title.

On this occasion Hall treated the swelling of the face locally with a marsh mallow ointment mixed with the oils of chamomile, violets and sweet almonds. *Axungia gallinae* or hen's fat[1] was mixed in and the ointment applied to the side of the face. Amber pills containing the purgative aloes were administered and an opiate gargle prescribed.

In Observation 87 Hall treated the swollen gums by prescribing a rigorous purgative regime beginning with an infusion using senna, rhubarb and agaric followed by the strongly purgative *Pilula Aureae*, containing aloes, scammony and colocynth. This treatment, intended to expel the morbid humours, was supplemented by the administration of a sweating decoction involving China root and sassafras.

84: SIR HENRY RAINSFORD OF CLIFFORD CHAMBERS

Sir Henry, the eldest surviving son of the twelve children of Hercules Rainsford of Clifford Chambers, inherited the manor on the death of his father in August 1583; he became the ward of his mother and step-father, William Barnes of Talton, whom Hall also attended (no. 94). Henry entered the Middle Temple in 1594.[2] In about 1595 he married Anne Goodere (no. 168); their two surviving sons were the heir, Henry (born in 1599), and Francis (1601). Henry Rainsford was knighted at the coronation of James I in 1603. He was remembered in the will of John Combe of Stratford in

---

1. Animal fat (*Axungia*) and grease (*Adeps*) featured prominently in the *materia medica* of the seventeenth century. The London *Pharmacopoeia* of 1618 listed twenty-six such items including the fat or grease of the camel, dog, hen, lion, serpent and bear. *Adeps hominis* or human grease was also listed.

2. *RAMT*, p. 67.

drops. It gave fix Vomits. This removed his Illnefs, and want of Appetite. The fame day he
took the Vomit, at the hour of Sleep was given
the following: R *Diafcordium* ʒi. *Syrup of Limons* ʒi. It was given in Poffet-drink. The next
day after the Vomit, he received a Clyfter framed
of *Diacatholicon,* red Sugar, and Milk, which gave
two Stools, and thus was cured.

Observ. LXXXV.

MR. *Barns,* aged 36, being long lame of a
Canker in the Leg, was thus cured: Firft,
I purged his Body with Pills, after I ufed a Decoction of *Guaiacum.* After I applied the following: R *White Copperas* ʒii. *Bole Armoniack* ʒi, ʒii.
Camphire ʒiii. *Make a Powder, of which take* ʒi.
*which was caft in hot Smiths Forge-water; after
a while it was taken from the Fire, and taken from
the fetling.* With this Water (I may fay) the
fame Ulcer was wafhed, and a Cloth laid upon it
wet in the faid Water; with which being almoft
cured, to cicatrize it I ufed the following Plafter:
R *White Lead* ℔ſſ. *Cretæ* ʒiv. *Powder them, and
with Hogs greafe make a Plafter.* It was applied
the thicknefs of ones Finger, and lay on nine
days. Before it was applied, the Canker was
wafhed with the following: Take *white Copperas,
and boil it in water.* After the Plafter was removed, another was applied for fix days, a third was
applied three days, and always it was wafhed before. By thefe he was cured.

OBSERV.

1614 with a bequest of a silver salt or £5. In 1616 he was granted a licence to impark at Clifford Chambers.[1]

The question of when Sir Henry was born has been confused by the citing of erroneous information from his monument in Clifford Chambers church (illustrated, p. 116).[2] However, as Hercules Rainsford died intestate in 1583, an inquisition *post mortem* was taken on 11 December stating that Henry, the heir, would be aged eight on 18 December 1583.[3] Hall noted his patient's details correctly in the manuscript as aged thirty-five in 1618. Sir Henry died on 27 January 1621/2 and his burial was recorded in the parish register three days later, when he was thirty-nine, the age at which his father had died.

Rainsford was suffering from a virulent fever, pains in the region of the spleen, swollen testicles and hypochondriac melancholy. Before calling Hall to attend him he purged himself with a posset drink of manna and rhubarb. Hall's treatment was directed to each of the symptoms. A plaster[4] was applied to the spleen and a poultice, followed by a plaster, to the swollen testicles. The stomach illness was treated first with an enema, then with an emetic composed of Hall's emetic infusion mixed with three drops of *Aqua Coelestis*,[5] which caused the patient to vomit six times, thus removing his 'illness and want of appetite'. An opiate of *Diascordium* and an enema containing *Diacatholicon*, a preparation to purge all humours, completed the treatment. The manuscript ends with the comment 'he praised God that he was restored to his former health'.

85: WILLIAM BARNES (III) OF TREDINGTON

The Barnes family were well established on the Warwickshire–Worcestershire border by the mid-sixteenth century. Their arms were approved at the 1634 *Heralds' Visitation*.[6] William Barnes (I),

1. John MacLean, 'The Manor and Advowson of Clifford Chambers', *Trans Bristol and Glos. Arch. Soc.*, XIV, part 1 (1890), p. 19.

2. Ibid., p. 44; Emily A. Buckland, *The Rainsford Family* (Worcester, 1932), p. 322.

3. MacLean, 'Clifford Chambers', pp. 16–17.

4. The plaster was composed of *Emplastrum de Meliloto* named after the herb melilot *Trifolium melilotus officinalis* and composed of this herb, together with twenty-one other ingredients made up of herbs and resins. *Emplastrum ex Saturn rub.* and *Empl. Nostr.Saturnali* refer to a plaster made with salts of lead. In the alchemical nomenclature lead was associated with the planet Saturn.

5. *Aqua Coelestis* was a compound water composed of over forty ingredients, mostly herbs and spices, but also musk and ambergris. It was attributed to Pietro Mathioli (1501–77), who was also the author of the electuary *Antidotus magna Mathioli adversus venena & pestem*, an antidote against poisons and pestilence composed of 120 crude drugs and nine preparations, each preparation having from 20 to 50 ingredients.

6. *HV Warws.*, 1634, p. 8.

OBSERV. LXXXVI.

GOod-wife *Sheffeild*, a Husbandman's Wife of *Old Stratford*, aged 48, was cruelly afflicted with a Dysentery, and much weakned with the Flux of her Courses ; having been retained for five years before, was cured as followeth: ℞ *Laud. Parac.* gr. vi. *Mithrid.* Эß. Conserve of *Roses* ʒiß. *Crocus Martis* Эi. *mix them.* By this she was freed from her Dysentery, and Flux of Courses; yet being vexed with thirst, this was given: ℞ red *Poppy Water* ʒiv. *Syrup of Violets* ʒß. *mix them.* And thus she was freed from all.

OBSERV. LXXXVII.

THe most Illustrious Lord, Lord *William Compton*, President of *Wales*, being troubled with a Distillation from the Head to the Gums ; he had also want of Appetite, which I cured as followeth: ℞ *Sena well picked from the stalks* ʒß. *Rubarb* ʒii. *Agarick* ʒi. *Cinamon* ʒvi. *Infuse them all for twelve hours in Borage and Succory Water warm, of each* ʒx. *In the morning they were boiled to the wasting of four ounces, after being strained six or seven times, and sweetned with four ounces of Sugar :* He took of this ʒii when he went to bed, with which in the morning he had a great stinking Stool, that being
the

grandfather of Hall's patient, acquired Tysoe manor in 1555 and at his death in May 1561 he was said to be of Talton, which was the residence noted by Hall (no. 59). His son, William (II), was aged fifteen at his father's death when he inherited Tysoe, only to dispose of it in 1603. Hall's patient, William (III), held Tredington manor after Francis Sheldon (*fl.*1612).[1]

William, son of Richard Barnes (d. 1632), the younger brother of William (II), was baptised in Stratford on 8 November 1587. Although no record of his first marriage has been found, his daughter, Elizabeth, was christened there on 15 March 1615, and her mother, Mary, was buried at Holy Trinity only nine days later. His servant, Philip Cook, had died two months before at a time of rising mortality in the town. William Barnes must have remarried in about 1616, for a year later Hall was attending his wife in a difficult pregnancy (nos 59, 66). He inherited a considerable estate at the death of his uncle, William of Clifford (no. 94), in 1621. Hall was treating William Barnes in 1623; the date of his death has not been found, although he was still alive in 1647.

The manor of Talton passed, by purchase, in 1663 to Henry Parker (d. 1670), whose family also acquired Honington Hall.

Barnes had canker or an eroding ulcer on his leg.[2] Hall expelled the morbid humours with a purging pill (not specified) and the sweating decoction of guaiacum. A lotion was prescribed using white copperas, Armenian bole and camphor. White copperas was one of the names given to zinc sulphate, an astringent salt. The three ingredients were heated in water in which a blacksmith had cooled his iron, one of the forms of steeled water (no. 9). The water separated from the undissolved residues was used to cleanse the ulcer.

To cicatrise or heal the ulcer, Hall directed that it should be washed with a solution of white copperas and then a plaster applied composed of white lead (lead carbonate), creta (chalk) and hog's grease. After nine days the plaster was removed, the ulcer cleansed with the white copperas solution, and another plaster applied for six days, then a third plaster applied for three days. In this treatment Hall was careful to remove the plaster at prescribed intervals and cleanse the ulcer. He would have known that if the plaster were not removed from time to time and the ulcer cleansed it would, like Shakespeare's 'flattering unction' in *Hamlet* be apt to 'skin and film the ulcerous place/Whilst rank corruption, mining all within/Infects unseen', III, iv, 138.

1. *VCH Worcs.*, III, pp. 543–4; *VCH Warws.*, V, pp. 18–19, 176.

2. The heading to this observation in Hall's manuscript was *Cancri tibia curi*. In the selective index at the end of the manuscript the case of William Barnes was listed under Cancer.

the 21th of *April.* The 22th in the morning he took ℥v of the faid Decoction, by which he had eight Stools. The 23th, ℞ *Pil. Aurear. de Ru-barb.* ā ℥i. By which he had thirteen Stools. After the third Stool he began to be better, there being taken Broth. The Body well purged, the following Decoction was adminiftred : ℞ *China fli-ced* ℥ii. *Saffafras cut into thin round pieces* ℥ſſ. *Boyl them in eight pound of Water till half be wafted.* Of this he took ℥iv at the leaft for eight days, every fourth day taking Episilon ii of *Pil. Ruffi.* And thus he was cured.

Observ. LXXXVIII.

MY Lady *Beaufou*, troubled with Indigeftion of Meat, and Wind after eating, with Obftructions of the Liver, was cured with the following Prefcriptions; ℞ *the Roots of Docks pithed* ℥iv. *Leaves of Agrimony* M v. *The Leaves of Succory with the whole* M ii. *Boil them in three gal-lons of new Beer, till half a gallon be wafted, ftrain it, and put Barm to it; after put it in a Veffel, and into it the following Bag :* ℞ *Sarfaparilla, Saffafras, Shavings of Ivory, each* ℥i. *Sena, Polypody, each* ℥v. *Hermodactils* ℥ii. *Liquoris* ℥ſſ. *Galangal, Rubarb, each* ℥ſſ. *Mecoachan* ℥i. *Cinamon, Cloves, each* ℥i. *Cut them all grofly, and mix them, and put them into a Canvas bag, with a ftone in the bottom, being put in-to the Beer, tye it at the top of the Barrel.* After ten or twelve days fhe took a draught morning, and at four in the afternoon. By this fhe was well purged,

86: ELINOR SHEFFIELD OF OLD STRATFORD

Elinor, wife of John Sheffield, a local farmer, had married in about 1594 and had ten children in sixteen years (1595–1611), three of whom died young. She must have been born in about 1574. John Sheffield was baptised in Stratford on 26 November 1568, the second son of Thomas; his mother died when he was aged fifteen. Thomas Sheffield of Old Stratford was described as a husbandman in 1601 in his inventory, with goods worth £10 10s., of which corn and hay were the most valuable.[1].

Elinor's husband, John, frequently served as a churchwarden at Holy Trinity and in 1596 the Sheffields had a household of six.[2] Hall must have attended her about 1622; she died some two years later and was buried on 24 September 1624. Her husband survived her by five years. Her son, Thomas, later married Ann Austin, also a patient (no. 43).

The patient was suffering from a uterine haemorrhage and 'a dysentery', which Hall defined (no. 116) as a condition resulting from food being digested but not separated from unwholesome matter. He treated Elinor Sheffield with six grains of laudanum (no. 77), Mithridate which also contained opium[3] and *Crocus martis* or iron oxide.

87: WILLIAM COMPTON, FIRST EARL OF NORTHAMPTON

Although Hall noted that he attended the Earl in April, no year was recorded, but it must have been after November 1617, when Compton became President of the Council of Wales. Lord Northampton was treated for dental problems on two other occasions (nos 68, 83).

88: ANN, LADY BEAUFOU OF EMSCOTE

Hall did not record a date for treating Lady Beaufou's indigestion, nor her age, although he did so on another occasion (no. 77). There is no indication which was the earlier consultation.

Lady Beaufou's indigestion and flatulence were treated with a medicated beer composed of purgative and stomachic drugs, among them leaves of succory or chicory *Cichorium intybus*, roots of dock or lapathum *Rumex acutus*,

---

1. (H)WRO, class 008.7 1601/118g.
2. *Mins & Accts*, V, p. 68.
3. The narcotic effects of opium are due to its morphine content. Other alkaloids present have a relaxing action on the intestinal muscle, which causes constipation, an effect which may have been instrumental in freeing the patient from her 'dysentery'.

purged, and digefted her Meat very well.

Obferv. LXXXIX.

ESq; *Packinton*, as he was riding to *London*, in his Inne was fuddenly and miferably afflicted with the Gout in hands and feet, fo that he could neither ftand nor handle any thing. Being called to him, I thus cured him : ℞ *Mallowes with the roots cut fmall, they were boyled in equal parts of Wine and Vinegar, to the wafting of the third part, to which was added Rye bran after a light boyling.* They were laid to the pained Joints, with which he was well eafed in one day, and delivered from the Inflammation by fomenting the parts with *Water of the fpawn of Frogs.* After was applied *Emplaſt. Diachalcit.* The fame day I gave ʒii *Pul. Sen. Montag. cum Hermodact.* gr. xv. He was reftored the third day, and rid towards *London*.

Obferv. XC.

WIlfon of *Stratford*, aged about 48, was miferably afflicted (for a long time) with Pain of the Stomach, and Indigeftion, fo that he durft fcarce eat ; to whom being called, I cured with only the following Powder : ℞ *Sena* ʒvi. *Ginger, Fennel feed, Zedoary, Cummin feed, each* ʒii. *Cloves, Galangal, Nutmegs, each* ʒi. *Rubarb* ʒii. *Sugar Candy* ʒvi. *make a Powder.* Dofe, the quantity of

both said to open obstructions of the viscera, and agrimony *Agrimonia eupatoria* recommended to amend an infirm liver.

Given that the preparation of the medicinal beer took between ten and twelve days, we may assume that the patient's illness was not particularly distressing.

89: SIR JOHN PAKINGTON OF WESTWOOD PARK, WORCESTERSHIRE

Hall had already treated the elderly Sir John for inappetence (no. 75). There is no direct evidence to indicate when Hall was attending Sir John for gout, but he was reputed to have died of it on 18 January 1625, aged seventy-seven. He was buried at Aylesbury (Bucks.).[1]

In Hall's manuscript this case was headed *chiriga et podagra* meaning gout of the hands (*chiragra*) and feet (*podagra*). The term gout was derived through the French *goutte* from *gutta*, Latin for 'drop' in allusion to the dropping or defluxion of humours into the joints. Wirsung defined gout as 'the passion or payn of the joynts which falleth into them, and the sinews of mans bodie by some humor or wind from above.'[2] In the seventeenth century any painful swelling of the joints would be called gout and would have included what we would now define as synovitis, arthritis, rheumatism and the painful disease (now specifically called gout) resulting from an excess of uric acid (nos 120, 165, 169).

Hall treated his patient with a poultice of mallows, a fomentation of frog spawn and a plaster.[3] He was purged with *Pulvis senae*, which contained senna, attributed to the Paduan physician Bartolomeo Montagnana (d. 1460). To this powder Hall added the purgative hermodactylus, a species of colchicum, recommended by Paul of Aegina (AD 625–90) for the treatment of pain in the joints.[4]

90: [ROBERT] WILSON OF STRATFORD-UPON-AVON

If this patient were born in Stratford between the years 1563 and 1587, of the two surviving males from this period Robert Wilson seems to be the man Hall treated. Hall noted him as a townsman. He was baptised, the son

1. Nash, opp. p. 352.

2. Wirsung, *Praxis Medicinae Universalis*, p. 529.

3. *Emplastrum Diachalcitis* was a plaster made from chalcitis loosely defined as a kind of mineral vitriol. It may have been copper sulphate but was more likely to have been green vitriol or ferrous sulphate. See John Quincy, *Lexicon Physico-Medicum or, a New Medical Dictionary* (10th edn, 1787), p. 187.

4. Pereira, *Elements*, vol. I, p. 1,059.

of a Bean spread on a Toast, first moistned in Wine, morning; and at night when he went to bed, the quantity of a Filbert with a little Wine, by which he was cured.   Thus the Author.

I remember that both *Riverius* and *Thonerus* cured each one, cruelly tormented with Pain in the Stomach, with letting blood: the latter cured several others, two with *distilled Oil of Carraway feed, five drops in two spoonfuls of hot Broth*; two other with the like quantity of *Oil of Amber*, given in like manner for some days.

O B S E R V. XCI.

Mrs. *Hanberry* of *Worcester*, aged 30, cruelly tormented with the Cholick, and Pain of the Back, that she could not stand upright, was thus cured: ℞ *Emplast. Nost. Caran.* which was applied to the Loins.   To the Belly was applied the following: ℞ *Featherfue, Rhue, Chamomel, each* M i. *Seeds of Carraway, Cummin, Lovage, Anis, Carrots, each* M ß. *Boil them all in sufficient quantity of Claret Wine, after strain them, but not too hard:* Which apply to the Belly till they be cold; after they are cold, heat them again in the same Wine, and so do twice or thrice, or as need is.   There was given inwardly *Seeds and Tops of red Nettles boyled in White-wine*, I mean the Decoction, it was given in a morning hot.   And thus she was delivered from all her Symptoms.

O B S E R V.

of William, on 19 September 1570 and married Frances Smith on 23 June 1590. They had eight children born in the years 1591 to 1609 and Frances died in 1614. Hall attended Wilson in 1616, who lived on for many years; he was buried on 3 April 1635.

Wilson was another of Hall's patients who was diagnosed as suffering from indigestion. The prescription was for a powder composed of the purgative senna mixed with carminative drugs designed to break wind. The formula included powdered zedoary root,[1] a bitter aromatic Indian drug used as a warm stomachic for strengthening and stimulating the stomach.

The powder was taken on toast. The patient had to measure it himself and Hall devised a simple domestic measure. The powder was moistened with wine and shaped into the size of a bean for taking in the morning and into the size of a filbert (hazelnut) at bedtime.

The observation ends with a note by Cooke on treatments by Lazare Riviere and Augustus Thoner.

91: ANNE HANBURY OF WORCESTER

On another occasion when Hall treated this young gentlewoman (no. 11) he had not recorded her age or other details. In this note, he entered her age as thirty. However, this is impossible as she was born in 1614. He was attending her on this occasion for colic and back pains.

Hall used local applications to the loins and belly and a decoction of nettles in white wine.[2] The plaster applied to the loins was probably the same as that Hall prescribed for his own wife when she was suffering from colic (no. 19). The poultice of herbs included featherfue or fever-few *Matricaria parthenium* and lovage *Levisticum officinale*, both carminative, aromatic and believed serviceable in female disorders.

92: SISTER OF NEIGHBOUR SHEFFIELD

The positive identification of this patient is impossible, since, although Cooke suggested that she was Hall's neighbour, the manuscript described her only as *soror vicini Sheffeld's*, omitting 'my' entirely. It seems likely that she was a sister or sister-in-law of another patient, Elinor Sheffield of Old Stratford (no. 86).

Hall treated this case of uterine haemorrhage with alum, as in the case

1. A member of the genus *Zedoaria*, generally identified as *Koempferia rotunda*.
2. Hall was prescribing a nettle which may have been one of the three nettles used in medicine: Common nettle *Urtica dioica*, Roman nettle *Urtica pilulifera* or small stinging nettle *Urtica urens*.

Observ. XCII.

THe Sister of my Neighbour *Sheffeild*, much debilitated with too great a Flux of her Courses, to whom I gave of *Alum the weight of two
pence in Rose water, for three days, fasting.* Two
hours after she took Broth made of Mutton, altered with *Milfoil, and the inner Bark of an Oak.*
She drunk her Drink steeled. With which she
was cured safely and quickly.

Observ. XCIII.

MY Lady *Rouse*, being in the eight Month of
Child-bearing, was infested with Convulsion of the Mouth, very ill-favoured; she was aged
28. ℞ *Rosemary ashes what quantity pleased, with
which was made a Lye with Whitewine, with which
the affected part was fomented with four double Linnen.*
After to anoint was used the Unguent, with the
Oils in the beginning of *Observ. 36.* There was
held in her Mouth *Rose water sharpned with Oil of
Vitriol.* And so she was cured, as in the foresaid
Observation.

OBSERV.

of Elizabeth Randolph (no. 65). In addition he prescribed the astringent oak bark with milfoil, which was recommended for treating excessive uterine flux (no. 49). Drink containing iron in an unspecified form was also prescribed.

93: ESTHER, LADY ROUS OF ROUS LENCH, WORCESTERSHIRE

In Hall's manuscript, Lady Rous's age was noted as twenty-nine, not twenty-eight, as given by Cooke, and the date 29 September was added to the first line of his notes. He must have been treating her in 1618. Hall also attended Lady Rous in two other pregnancies (nos 79, 96).

In the eighth month of pregnancy Lady Rous suffered from convulsions of the mouth. The evidence suggests that she had a history of a nervous complaint affecting her neck and face. When Hall was attending her for a quotidian fever shortly after childbirth, he prescribed a plaster to relieve a pain in her neck (no. 79).

In 1619, a year after she had been treated for convulsions of the mouth, she was reported to have been troubled with a Tortura-Oris, the same nervous complaint that afflicted Hall's own daughter, Elizabeth (no. 36). In 1620 Hall attended her in her last pregnancy (no. 96).

Except for rose-water sharpened with acid to be held in the mouth, no medicines to be taken internally were prescribed because of the patient's advanced state of pregnancy. The ointment with oils used in the case of Elizabeth Hall was prescribed and a fomentation applied to the face.

The fomentation was in the form of a lye, the name given to a liquid impregnated with a salt, in this case ashes of rosemary. Rosemary *Rosmarinus officinalis* was recommended for the treatment of nervous complaints. It was usually prescribed in the form of the whole herb, the oil or a distillate. Gerard wrote that it 'comforteth the brain and inward senses' and that it 'restoreth speech unto them that are possessed with the dumb palsie'.[1]

94: WILLIAM BARNES OF CLIFFORD CHAMBERS

William Barnes was born in 1547, the eldest son of William Barnes (d. 1561) of Barcheston and Talton; he entered the Middle Temple in 1566.[2] Hall noted him as of gentleman status. His mother was Alice Middlemore of Edgbaston and both his parents were buried at Tredington. As his first

1. Gerard, *The Herball* (1633), Lib. 3, Chap. 185. Rosemary was still being recommended as a stimulant for the nervous system in the early nineteenth century. See Forsyth, *Medical and Surgical Dictionary*, p. 742.
2. *RAMT*, p. 30.

Observ. XCIV.

MR. *Barns* of *Clifford*, after the pulling out of a rotten Tooth, was troubled with a Flux of Blood from the fame place, two days after, which I cured in a fhort fpace: he having bled twenty four hours, having no Remedy for prefent at hand; I bid him to hold cold water in his Mouth, and often caft it out, and fo he continued till other Medicines were provided: After I ufed this: R *White Vitriol,* part ii. *Bole Armoniack,* pa.i. *Camphire* pa.ſs. *Rofe water hot, fufficient to make a Lotion;* In which dip a Linnen Cloth often, and apply cold to the place. This was ufed five hours, and then it ceafed. But after a time it bled again, which I ftayed with a Spunge dipped in the aforefaid Lotion, and *Crocus Martis* put upon it: And fo he was altogether cured.

This Obfervation of the Author's calls to mind a like Accident, which befell to a Maid in *Cornhil,* near *Popes-head Ally, London,* which when other means proved fuccefslefs, I ftayed, by keeping my Fingers only upon the Mouth of the Artery, removing them feveral times.

G   Observ.

wife, William Barnes had married Jane Smith at Charlecote on 10 October 1567; the marriage was childless.

After Jane's death, William married a far more distinguished lady, the widowed Elizabeth Rainsford of Clifford Chambers. She was the daughter of Robert Parry of Denbigh, related to Tudor Trevor, Lord of Hereford, and she had married Hercules Rainsford of Clifford, second son but heir to a substantial estate. Hercules Rainsford had served as Governor of the castles of both Limerick and, in 1579, of Dublin. At his death, aged thirty-nine, on 2 August 1583, his heir, Henry, was only eight. Elizabeth Rainsford married William Barnes, who became Henry's guardian, early in 1584 and, though formal, the affectionate phrases of William's will (22 August 1621) suggest that the relationship was a satisfactory one.[1] The notebook of Thomas Greene, town clerk of Stratford-upon-Avon from 1603 until 1616, confirms other evidence that William Barnes was, with the Rainsfords, involved in the town's affairs.[2]

Hall's manuscript gave the date that he was treating William Barnes as 1 January 1619; he was buried at Clifford on 26 September 1621. Childless, his lands passed to his nephew, also William Barnes.

Hall stemmed the bleeding from the tooth cavity by applying a styptic lotion made from white vitriol (zinc sulphate),[3] Armenian bole and camphor in rose water. When the bleeding started up again the treatment was repeated adding *Crocus martis* (iron oxide) to the sponge which had been dipped in the lotion. The astringent lotion was the same as that used some years later for the patient's nephew (no. 85), but with rose-water replacing steeled water.

The observation ends with a note by Cooke indicating how he had stayed a similar haemorrhage.

95: HUDSON, A PAUPER

Although Hall did not state that the pauper Hudson was from Stratford, it seems very unlikely that he would have attended a poor man anywhere other than in the town itself. However, without his age or Christian name, it is impossible to identify this man, although his gender is clear. Accounts of the Stratford Overseers of the Poor for this early period do not survive.

Hall treated this patient's vertigo first with bleeding to relieve the head, taking ten fluid ounces (half a pint) of blood from the anterior vein of the right arm, then called the cephalic vein. This was followed by a strong purgative pill.

1. Buckland, *Rainsford*, p. 221.
2. *Mins & Accts*, V, p. 139.
3. Hall used two names for zinc sulphate. In Observation 85 he referred to it as white copperas and in this observation as white vitriol.

OBSERV. XCV.

ONe *Hudson*, a poor Man, labouring of a ſwimming in his Head, called *Vertigo.* I cauſed ℥x of Blood to be taken from the *Cephalica,* purged him with *Pil. Aurear. & Cochear:* ā Ɔii. *Troch. Alhand.* gr. viij. f. *Pil.* 7. They gave nine ſtools. Laſtly he took *Peacock dung dried* ℨi. infuſed in White-wine for a night, and after ſtrained. And this he continued from New Moon to Full Moon, and was cured.

OBSERV. XCVI.

THE Lady *Rouſe*, being with Child, was miſerably troubled with the Mother, and Faintings, and extreme Pain in the Head: Firſt, ſhe had a Fume of *Horſe hoofs burnt*, which reſtored her as ſoon as it was drawn into her Noſtrils. Then ſhe had a Suppoſitory put up, framed of Honey, and *Pul. Sanctus*, which gave two ſtools, and brought away much Wind. She had a Fume of Odorificks below, and ſmelt to ſtinking things. Her Neck was anointed with *Oil of Spike*, after with *Unguent. Martiatum*. She having the year before been troubled with *Tortura Oris*, and now much fearing it, in a morning faſting ſhe took the quantity of a Nutmeg of the following Electuary: ℞ *Species Dianthoſ. Conſerve of Borage, each* ℥i.
Mithridate,

Peacock's dung dried and infused in white wine was prescribed and directed to be taken over two weeks as measured by the phases of the moon. The peacock featured in the medieval *materia medica* but was not included in the list of animals or animal parts in the London *Pharmacopoeia* of 1618. The meat in a broth was given for pulmonary complaints, the powdered bones were used to cure morpheu and the feathers when burnt were used as a fume against hysteria. The dried dung was among the medicaments recommended for the treatment of epilepsy and presumably related conditions such as vertigo.

96: ESTHER, LADY ROUS OF ROUS LENCH, WORCESTERSHIRE

Hall had already recorded attending Lady Rous twice (nos 79, 93) in connection with her pregnancies. When Hall visited her on 20 March 1620, she was, aged thirty, in her seventh pregnancy in fourteen years. This last child, William, and his mother were both buried at Rous Lench on the same day, 12 August 1620.

Lady Rous was troubled with the 'Mother' (hysteria), faintness and pains in the head. Part of the treatment was to prevent the neck and facial problems she had experienced over several years (nos 79, 93). Her neck was anointed with oil of spike (lavender) and Soldier's ointment. An electuary was prescribed containing among other things *Species Dianthos*, a powder with rosemary recommended for nervous complaints (no. 93), and *Diacymini*, a powder with cumin.[1]

To treat the faintness and hysteria Hall prescribed a suppository containing *Pulvis Sanctus*, which contained, among other things, senna and tartar. The patient was also required to smell a fume of burnt horse's hoof[2] and other 'stinking things'. Treatment with strongly smelling vapours was comparable to the use of a burning feather wafted under the nose, or the more recent phial of smelling salts to act as stimulants and restoratives in cases of fainting. Hall also directed a vapour from 'odorificks' to be directed to the genitals.

97: MARY MURDEN OF MORETON MORRELL

Hall was later to treat this young gentlewoman after her marriage to Stephen Harvey (no. 64) and also her mother (no. 111), Mary, wife of Richard Murden in 1626.

1. The formulae for *Species Dianthos* and *Species Diacyminum* were included in the London *Pharmacopoeia* of 1618.
2. The London *Pharmacopoeia* listed *Ungula alces, asini, caprae* and *porci* (hoofs of elk, ass, goat and hog). It is unlikely that the compilers of the formulary would have regarded the hoof of *equus* as an unreasonable substitute for the hoof of *asinus*!

Warwick Priory, the home of Sir Thomas and Lady Puckering (from W. Niven, *Mansions of England in the Olden Time*, 1839)

upon Englifh Bodies. 83

Mithridate, Diacymini, each ʒii. *Harts-horn prepa-*
red ʒiii. In Broths fhe took Hartshorn prepared.
To her Navil was applied a Plafter of *Caranna,*
in the middeft of which was put *Musk* gr. iii.
Thus fhe was cured, and at due time was brought
to bed, *March* 16. 1620.

OBSERV. XCVII.

Mrs. *Mary Murden,* aged 17, labouring of a
few and ill coloured Courfes, Pain of the
Head, and Rednefs of the Face after Meat, was
cured as followeth : ℞ *the Roots of Fennel and*
Parfly, each ʒii. *of Sparagus, and Butchers broom,*
each ʒiii. *Calamus Aromaticus* ʒ ſs. *Betony, Mugwort,*
Avens, Water-creffes, Hyffop, Rofemary, Penyroyal,
Nettles, each M ſs. *Elicampana roots* ʒſs. *Liquoris*
ʒii. *Seeds of Anis, Fennel,* each ʒiii. *Raifins fto-*
ned, M i. *Sena, Polipody,* each ʒiv. *Hermodactils*
ʒii. *Rubarb, Agarick,* each ʒii. *Boyl them all in a*
gallon of Water till half be wafted; in the ftrained
Liquor was diffolved Syrup of Mugwort, Au-
guftanus, Succory with Rubarb, each ʒii. Dofe ʒiii
to v. By the ufe of which fhe was prefently
cured.

OBSERV. XCVIII.

D*ixwel Brunt* of *Pillerton*, aged 3 years, had a Tumor of the Navil, out of which broke five long Worms out of a little hole like a Fiftula ; the Nurfe pulled out four dead, but the fifth was fomewhat alive, the fore-part not moving, the hinder part ftirred, as witneffed the Nurfe, Father, Mother, and Maid. The Tumor being hard, I appointed a Platter of Hony to be applied. The fame day was given a Suppofitory of Honey, but no Worms appeared. The next day was applied a *Cataplafm framed of green Wormwood, beat with the Gall of an Ox, and boyled.* There was given a Suppofitory. After thefe the Navil was cured, and he lived.

OBSERV. XCIX.

THe Countefs of *Northampton, March* 6. 1620. fell into that Dropfey called *Anafarca,* with fwelling of the Face and Feet, and was cured as followeth : ℞ *the Decoction prefcribed for Mrs.* Murden, *Obferv. 97. adding of Rubarb* ʒii, *Sena* ʒ*ſſ.* The Dofe given was ʒiv for three days. The firft day it gave eight Stools, the fecond day eighteen, and the third fifteen, without any lofs of ftrength. After fhe took for five mornings the quantity of a Nut of *Electuar. Diacubeb.* After
                                                        fh e

Hall treated Mary Murden's symptoms, on this occasion (1617), with a complex mixture corresponding to the galenic principle of administering large numbers of drugs and allowing the body to choose those needed to temper the morbid humours and restore the patient's normal constitution. Twenty-three drugs were used to make a decoction, to which were added three syrups: syrup of chicory with rhubarb, *Syrupus Augustanus*, which also contained rhubarb, and syrup of mugwort, for which formula in the London *Pharmacopoeia* of 1618 there were forty-three ingredients.

98: DIXWELL BRENT OF PILLERTON PRIORS

Dixwell Brent was the youngest of the ten children born to John Brent of Pillerton Priors and Barbara Dixwell of Coton, the daughter of Charles Dixwell and Abigail (née Herdson), in the parish of Churchover. Dixwell was baptised on 9 December 1617. His mother was the eldest of five children in this armigerous north Warwickshire family.[1] This was one of the cases for which Hall, in his manuscript, noted a precise date of treatment, 27 April 1620.

The Brent family, some of whom were papists, were widely scattered across the Felden area of south Warwickshire, and their monuments survive in Barcheston and Ilmington churches.[2] No evidence of Dixwell Brent's later life has been found.

Hall's use of the suppository in this case suggests that he was of the opinion that these were intestinal worms which had emerged via a fistula (a tube-like passage) in the swelling of the navel. There is no indication in the report that he saw the worms for himself. It is possible that these were larvae or maggots from eggs laid in a lesion in the vicinity of the navel. Hall would have considered them as being spontaneously generated. Later in the century Francesco Redi (1626–97) was to demonstrate in a brilliant, controlled experiment that maggots in flesh were not spontaneously generated but developed from eggs laid by flies.[3]

99: ELIZABETH, COUNTESS OF NORTHAMPTON

This consultation took place two years earlier than Hall's other treatment of Lady Northampton in 1622 (no. 1) when she suffered from cacochymia and scorbutic symptoms. On this occasion he was attending her for *anasarca* or edema, where the patient's face and feet were particularly affected. Edema

1. *HV Warws.*, 1619, p. 297.
2. Dugdale, I, p. 630; *VCH Warws.*, V, p. 10.
3. F. Redi, *Esperienze intorno alla generazione degl' insetti* (Florence, 1688).

ſhe uſed the following Decoction : ℞ *Guaiacum* ℔i.
Soldanellæ ſiccæ M i. *Cinamon* ℥ii. *Currans* ℥ii. *Boyl*
them in ℔ix *of Water till half be waſted ; being kept*
in a hot place, there were poured in three pints of White-
wine. Of this was taken ℥vi in the morning hot,
and ℥iv in the evening, covering her well to ſweat.
Every morning after ſhe had ſweat, an hour after
ſhe took of the foreſaid Electuary, and every third
day ſhe was purged with the following : ℞ *Mecoa-*
chin ℥iſſ. *Syrup of Roſes ſolutive* ℥i. *Wormwood wa-*
ter ſimple, and Sack, each ℥ii. It gave firſt two
Stools, after that two Vomits, after that three
Stools, after that one Vomit, at laſt twelve Stools,
after which the Tumor was altogether removed.
After which ſhe took *Elect. Chalyb. Crat.* By which
ſhe was perfectly cured, and brought to a good colour in twenty days ſpace.

Observ. C.

M rs. *Goodman,* aged about 54, was troubled
with a Pain of her Head and Stomach, and
was cured as followeth : ℞ *Maſſ. Pil. Maſtic.* Əii.
Aloes roſ. Əi. *cum Syr. Roſ. ſol. f. Pill.* They
were taken before ſupper, and ſo continued for
three days. After upon a faſting Stomach take of
the following Electuary the quantity of a Filbert :
℞ *Conſerve of red Roſes* ℥iv. *Spec. Aromat. Gabr.*
℥iſſ. *Cloves ſliced* ℥i. *Amber-greaſe* gr. vi. *Mix them*
with the Syrup of Citron Pills. By theſe ſhe was
perfectly cured.

The

is the accumulation of serum in cellular tissue. The treatment was a vigorous regime over twenty days involving purging, sweating and vomiting. It began with the poly-pharmaceutical decoction prescribed for Mary Murden, fortified with the purgatives senna and rhubarb (no. 97). Hall recorded the drastic effects of this remedy over three days and observed that there was no loss of strength. A respite of five days followed during which the patient took an electuary containing cubebs, a pungent, warming, aromatic spice.

Treatment to expel the morbid humour resumed with a decoction of guaiacum taken hot to cause sweating. This was combined with a mixture containing mechoacan (no. 27) every three days which brought about further purging and vomiting. When the swelling had subsided Hall completed his treatment with a restorative electuary containing iron salts devised by Crato von Krafftheim.

100: [SARA] GOODMAN

The sparse details noted by Hall make this patient difficult to identify positively; he recorded that her status was *Generosa* and she must have been born sometime in the years 1563 to 1581. Her surname, not particularly common in Warwickshire, is frequently found in Northamptonshire and she could have been connected to the Compton family, whose steward, William Goodman, was a gentleman member of the Castle Ashby household in 1616 and was prominent in the estate accounts for the period 1629 to 1636. He may indeed be the William Goodman baptised at Yardley Hastings (Northants.), adjacent to Castle Ashby, on 22 November 1582.

However, another possibility is that the patient was Sara, the wife of Thomas Goodman, to whom Lady Hunks left £20 in her second will of 1641; the sum was substantial compared with the bequests to her family (only a few pounds each) and in the light of Lady Hunks's comments about her own lack of wealth (see no. 138). The will mentioned Sara Goodman's 'love and good service to me' and she may have attended Lady Hunks only after the move to Ireland,[1] for she was not a legatee in the first will. She would presumably have had her medical expenses included with Hall's account for her mistress.

Hall treated this patient with pills similar in composition to *Pilulae Stomachicae* (no. 15) and an electuary of a carminative and cordial nature. These remedies suggest that he regarded the head pains as being 'by consent' from the stomach (no. 29).

1. PRO, Prob 11/197.

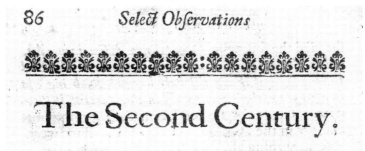

The Second Century.

OBSERV. I.

MAfter *Penil*, Gentleman to Esq; *Grevil* of *Milcot*, was troubled with Spots and Pustles, that broke forth in his Hands, which being broke, there dropp'd forth a clear venemous Water, which inflamed and excoriated the Hands greatly. Many Remedies being used in vain, the Head also was enflamed and burned, and full of scales; being aged about 38, was thus freed: ℞ *Agrimony, Scurvygrass, Water-cresses,* each M i. *Sage, Cichory, Fumitory,* each Mß. *Elicampana* root ℥ß. *Polipody of the Oak* ℥iii. *Roots of Sassafras* ℥ß. *Boyl them all in* ℔xii *of Water till half be wasted. In the straining add Rubarb, Agarick,* each ℥ß. *Sena,* and *Liquoris,* each ℥i. *Seeds of Anis, Carraway, Coriander,* each ℥ii. *Cinamon* ℥i. *Boyl them again till* ℔ii *be wasted: to the straining, add Syrup of Roses solutive* ℥ii. *Oil of Vitriol* 12 *drops.* The Dose was ℥iv, continuing it for four days. Every day he had six or seven stools. To anoint, he used this: ℞ *White Ointment camphorated, mixed with the Juyce of Housleek, as much as you please,* with which the Hands were anointed.

101: EDWARD PENNELL OF LINDRIDGE, WORCESTERSHIRE

Milcote House at Weston-on-Avon was owned by Sir Edward Greville (d. 1634), cousin to the Warwick Castle family, a man whose finances could not support his grand lifestyle; even as early as 1610 he had lost £1,000 in a company formed to exploit salt mining.[1]

One of the large Greville household was Edward Pennell, whose armigerous family held land in Lindridge, Mathon and Woodson (Worcs.).[2] Edward Pennell married Margaret Greville, his master's coheiress, and niece to Sir Charles Greville, a Worcestershire recusant, who had bought part of the manor of Leigh from Pennell.[3] Edward and Margaret Pennell had three daughters and two sons; she died in 1625. The royalist Edward was at the surrender of Worcester in 1646 and paid £60 to compound for his Lindridge estate.[4] Edward Pennell was buried on 5 August 1657; his and Margaret's brass monuments are in St Lawrence's church, Lindridge.

The cutaneous affliction affecting the patient's hands and face was treated first with a decoction containing scorbutic drugs, purgatives, spices and drugs used for the treatment of skin conditions, for example, fumitory. Seven fluid ounces of blood were taken from the liver vein, now called the basilic vein of the right arm. (The corresponding vein of the left arm was known as the splenetic vein.) Wirsung wrote that to open the liver vein 'unburdeneth all parts below the neck . . . of their superfluous blood'.[5]

For local treatment to the hands Hall prescribed camphorated white ointment *Unguentum album*, its formula attributed to the Arabian physician, Rhazes, and composed of oil of roses and lead carbonate in a base of white beeswax.[6] It could be prescribed with or without camphor. Hall added the cooling juice of houseleek.

102: FRANCES ROGERS OF STRATFORD-UPON-AVON

On 4 April 1621 Hall treated the young Frances Rogers, daughter of Philip and Eleanor (d. 1613). Rogers was a town apothecary, dealing in medicines,

1. Menna Prestwich, *Cranfield: Politics and Profits under the Early Stuart*, (Oxford, 1966).

2. *VCH Worcs.*, III, p. 446.

3. Nash, II, p. 94; *HV Worcs.*, 1634, p. 78.

4. Grazebrook, II, p. 193.

5. Wirsung, *Praxis Medicinae Universalis*, p. 24.

6. The compilers of the revised London *Pharmacopoeia*, published in 1746, omitted the lead salt from this ointment because of the danger the 'corroded' lead posed when used on the skin of children. *The Dispensatory of the College of Physicians, London*, trans. by H. Pemberton (1746), p. 363.

upon Engliſh Bodies. 87

anointed. The Liver Vein was opened to ℥vii. Thus he was quickly cured, and delivered from his Scabs.

OBSERV. II.

ROgers of *Stratford*, aged 17, did labour of Vomiting, Jaundice, ſtopping of the Cour-ſes, and bleeding at the Noſe, on *April* 4. 1621, was cured as followeth : ℞ *Emetick Infuſion* ℥vii. *Syrup of Violets, half a ſpoonful.* This given, gave ſeven Vomits, and five Stools. After this, ℞ *the Decoction of Sarſaparilla* ℥iii. *the laxative Pouder of Sena* ℥iſs. This purged very well. The third day there was given ℥iſs of the *white of Hens dung in White-wine, with Sugar.* And ſo ſhe was cured.

OBSERV. III.

MIſ. *Randolph,* aged 55, being vexed with a burning Feaver, in which ſhe fell into the yellow Jaundice ; her Urine was red, and Saffron-like, having Pain of her Stomach, with Tumor and hardneſs, Pain of the Loins, Tumor of the Spleen, and the Dropſy, deſired my advice, which was given as fol'oweth : ℞ *Emetick Infu-ſion* ℥vi. *Oxymel of Squils* ℥ii. *Syrup of Violets, half a ſpoonful: mix them.* It gave three Vomits, and four Stools the next day. ℞ *Elect. è Succ. Roſ.*
G 4   ℥ii.

tobacco and ale, with premises in Chapel Street and High Street. John Hall probably knew the girl. In the spring of 1604 William Shakespeare had sold Rogers twenty bushels of malt, perhaps for his pharmaceutical activities, and in June lent the apothecary 2s. Rogers paid 6s. of the debt but Shakespeare sued him for the remaining £1 15s. 10d. and also for 10s. damages.[1]

Frances was baptised on 6 January 1605. Her social status is marked by lack of a title, but is noted as *oppidana* or townswoman by Hall. Her sister, Margaret, died as a child in 1609 but her brother went to Oxford and obtained a licence to practise surgery.[2] She does not appear to have married in the town.

Hall's prescriptions for emetics and purgatives were his treatment for cacochymia or a depraved state of the body humours. This is the second case in which he recommended hen's dung. In Observation 61 he prescribed it for the 'Mother' and it is probable that he detected hysterical symptoms in this illness of Frances Rogers.

103: ELIZABETH RANDOLPH OF WOOD BEVINGTON, SALFORD PRIORS

Edward Ferrers of Rowington died in 1578, leaving no sons but five daughters to inherit his substantial estate. His sister, Ursula, was the wife of John Beaufou of Emscote, whose eldest son, Sir Thomas, was also Hall's patient (no. 74). The inheritance included Bevington, in Salford Priors, which Ferrers had gained by marriage to Elizabeth Grey (d. 1602). Hall's patient, the eldest Ferrers daughter, Elizabeth, in about 1580 married Thomas Randolph of Bevington, and the widowed Elizabeth Ferrers settled this estate on her daughter and son-in-law in 1585. Thomas Randolph's father was a gentleman from Cuddington (Bucks.).[3]

Their Bevington manor house was demolished in 1821, but evidence existed of a chapel there (used by fugitive priests) that was later turned into a little parlour, its chancel becoming a study.[4]

Elizabeth Randolph bore four sons and three daughters. Hall also treated her son, Ferrers Randolph, in 1619 (no. 25), and her daughter-in-law, another Elizabeth (no. 65). Her husband, Thomas, was buried at Salford Priors on 6 April 1628. Records of her death have not been traced, but there is a gap in the Salford burial register from 1646 to 1655; there are no Randolph memorials in the church.

1. SBTRO, ER 27/5.
2. E.I. Fripp, *Shakespeare's Stratford* (Oxford, 1928), p. 37.
3. *HV Warws.*, 1619, p. 303; *VCH Warws.*, III, p. 160; Henry Morris, *Baddesley Clinton, its Manor, Church and Hall* (1897), p. 119.
4. Gunn, *Wood Bevington*, p. 12.

℥ii. *Diacath.* ℥iſſ. *Diaphænic.* ℥iiſſ. *Rub. elect.* ℈ſſ. *Spic.* gr. v. *Syr. Cichor. cum Rhab.* ℥ſſ. *Aq. Cichor.* ℥iii. *f. Hauſt.* It gave eighteen ſtools. For ordinary Drink, the quiet days ſhe drunk the Decoction of *Harts-horn.* And thus her Feaver left her, the Jaundice yet remaining: for the removing of which was uſed the following, ℞ *White-wine* ℔i. *Celendine water* ℥vi. *Saffron* ℥i. *Theriac. Androm.* ℥iii. *Bezoar.* ℈i. the *Juyce of Goose dung, six spoonfuls* : *make a sweating Drink.* She took it four days, Doſe ℥iv faſting. At night ſhe took the following Electuary : ℞ *red and white Sanders, each* ℥iii. *Currans infuſed in White wine, and after pulped,* ℥iv. *Rubarb* ℥i. *Saffron* ℈i. *make an Electuary.* The Doſe was the quantity of a Nutmeg. For the Tumor of the Belly, ℞ *Unguent. Agrip.* ℥i. *Arthanitæ* ℥ſſ. *Martiat.* ℥iii. *Ol. Nard. Rut. Scorp.* ā ℥ij. *Aq. Vitæ parum, Aceti. gut. aliquot. f. Ungu. Ar. Sect.* Thus ſhe was cured beyond the expectation of her Friends.

Observ. IV.

MR. *Broad* of the *Grange,* vexed with a deſperate Squincy, with a burning Feaver, heat and excoriation of the Tongue, aged 42, left of all, was thus cured : ℞ *the common Decoction for a Clyſter* ℔i. *Diacath. & Diaphæn.* ā ℥i. *make a Clyſter,* which injected gave four Stools. He was let blood under the Tongue, uſed the following Gargariſm, ℞ *Honey of Roſes, Plantain and Roſe water, each alike; to which was added a little Oil of Vitriol.* For a
licking

The emetic infusion Hall employed in this case was one of his standard methods for the treatment of fever with dropsy and jaundice. He also employed a *haustus* or draught composed of *Diacatholicon* and *Diaphoenicum* with *spica* or lavender and preparations of chicory to expel humours by severe purging. The decoction of hartshorn was frequently prescribed by Hall in cases involving fever. There was also a sweating drink containing saffron, which was used to treat yellow jaundice (no. 6), and juice of goose dung, which was employed in the case of John Nason (no. 71), where the symptoms and appearance of the urine were similar to Elizabeth Randolph's.

The ointment applied was made from a mixture of Soldier's ointment, the root of cyclamen *Cyclamen Europaeum* and *Unguentum Agrippae*, which contained the root of bryony which, externally applied, was believed to reduce swellings. There were three oils added to these ingredients: oil of nard, oil of rue and oil of scorpions.[1] The apothecary was instructed to make the ointment adding a small but sufficient volume of *Aquae Vitae* and *Acetum* or vinegar.

104: WILLIAM BROAD OF BIDFORD-ON-AVON

William Broad of Bidford (1583–1653) had married a local heiress, Frances (baptised 2 January 1594), the daughter of George Badger, and through her in 1616 had acquired a substantial estate, Bidford Grange, originally a corn-growing farm belonging to the Abbots of Bordesley (Worcs.). Broad had three children, Elizabeth, George and Frances. Dugdale noted Broad's connection with two Stratford families,[2] for Frances Badger was the grand-daughter of Thomas Nash and the niece of John Lane, both men of standing in the town.

In 1625, the year when Hall treated him, William Broad served as Treasurer of Barlichway Hundred.[3] His name does not appear in Quarter Sessions again and he may have declined further office because of his health. Broad lived on for nearly another three decades; his death is recorded on a monumental slab in St Laurence's church, Bidford. Although a gentleman, he rejected the opportunity of becoming a knight in 1625. His young daughter, Elizabeth (1620–4), has a brass plaque to her memory in

---

1. Oil of nard could have been either Celtic nard *Valeriana Celtica* or Indian nard, also known as spikenard *Andropogon nardus*. The medicinal virtues were the same for both. *Oleum Scorpionum* was included in the London *Pharmacopoeia* of 1618 and prepared by infusing scorpions in oil of bitter almonds for forty days. Culpeper referred to scorpions as provoking urine and breaking the stone (*A Physicall Directory*, p. 62).

2. *VCH Warws.*, III, p. 53; Dugdale, II, p. 725.

3. QSOB, I, p. 2.

licking this : ℞ *Syrup of Liquoris and Hyssop, each* ℥ii. *Oxymel of Squils* ℥ß. *best Honey* ℥i. *mix them.* It was used after the Gargarism. To the **Throat** was applied the following : ℞ *Green Wormwood, with Hogs grease, make a Cataplasm.* I commanded he should be let blood, but he would not, although I told him the danger, which fell out, for he fell into continual burning. For ordinary drink he had the following : ℞ *Liquoris, Anis seeds, Figs, Raisins of the Sun, each* ℥i. *Boyl them in two quarts of Water till a pint be wasted.* And so I left him. The next day his Feaver increased, and his Strength abated, and he said he could not possibly live, and I was sent for speedily. When I came, I found his Life in danger, he could scarce speak, I presently had a Vein cut, and took away ℥x, with which his speech returned, and he said he found great ease. The same day at the hour of Sleep, I gave him our Julep against the Feaver, and he rested pretty well ; for his ordinary drink, the *Decoction of Harts-horn.* And thus he was delivered from his Feaver, and danger of Suffocation, and became very well ; for which God be praised, that can only work wonderfully.

OBSERV. V.

Mrs. *Sadler* laboured of a grievous Cough, with difficulty of breathing, and loathing of Meat, she was aged 60. ℞ *Oxymel of Squils* ℥ii. *Syrup of Violets* ℥ß. *Emetick Infusion* ℥ii. *mix them.* This gave seven Vomits, and twelve Stools,

by

the church porch and there is a slab commemorating his only son, George, who died at the age of seventeen.[1] After Broad's death the estate went out of the family.

Although no other details were given, Hall noted in Observation 10 that he had also treated Broad's family tutor (*paedagogus*), not, as in Cooke's translation, a servant, but a man who presumably taught the three young children.

A quinsy is an attack of tonsillitis where an abscess forms near the tonsil. Hall recommended bleeding, an enema containing purgative drugs, emollient gargles and a poultice applied to the throat.

The evidence from the cases that make up the *Select Observations* indicates that Hall was a moderate in the use of bleeding as a therapy. In this case he employed it twice. First he had blood taken from the vein under the tongue, in the vicinity of the quinsy. He later ordered the patient to be bled to relieve the fever. Broad initially refused to undergo this second bleeding but a sharp deterioration in his condition brought Hall once again to his bedside and he was able without opposition to remove ten fluid ounces (half a pint) of blood presumably from a vein in the arm.

Hall noted 'I commanded that he should be let blood' and 'I presently had a vein cut', indicating that he did not carry out the bleeding himself but left it to an assistant, a barber-surgeon or apothecary.

105: ISABEL SADLER OF
STRATFORD-UPON-AVON

John Hall treated Isabel Sadler, *Generosa*, in 1621, as he noted in his manuscript. She was the daughter of Peter Smart (d. 1588) and on 27 August 1584 she married John Sadler (1561–1625), a Stratford miller. He was later wealthy, accorded the status of gentleman and served as both Bailiff (twice) and as alderman. He was landlord of the Bear in Bridge Street.[2]

They had five children, one of whom who died in infancy, born during the years 1587 to 1594; John Hall later attended members of their families. In 1606 John Sadler was accused in the church court of fathering a bastard;[3] he was buried on 1 July 1625. Isabel Sadler made her will in 1627, although she did not die until February 1636. Apart from the usual household goods and bequests of small jewellery items, Isabel Sadler left cash to all her grandchildren on marriage, a silver bowl to her eldest son and the best items of clothing to her daughters, including Margaret

1. Dugdale, II, p. 727.
2. *VCH Warws.*, III, p. 269.
3. Brinkworth, p. 131.

by which she found her self much eased : ℞ *Pil. de
Succin. Cochear.* ā ℈i. *Rhab. Pul.* ℈ß. *f. Pil. cum
f. q. Oxymel Scill.* These gave seventeen Stools.
The Lincture was this : ℞ *Lohoch. San. & expert.
de Pulm. Vulp. Syrup. Liquorit. Tussilag,* ā ʒi. *Oxymel. Scill.* ʒii. *f. Linct.* It was taken with a Liquoris stick. She also held in her Mouth one of
the following: ℞ *Succ. Liquor.* ʒiiß. *Farin. Amyli,* ʒiß. *Croci, Myrrh.* ā ℈iß. *Opii* gr. iii. *Styrac.
Calam.* ʒiii. *Syr. Viol. q. f. f. Pil.* 24. One of them
was taken when she went to bed. And thus in
one week she became well.

Observ. VI.

Mrs. *Brown,* young, of a very good habit of
Body, was for three years troubled with a
watery Flux of the Belly, especially in the night,
having every night no less than six or seven stools.
It brought her to extream danger, with great dejection of strength ; she was also much griped,
and was sleepless ; who desiring my advice, I prescribed as followeth : ℞ *Pil. de Succin.* ʒß. *Rhab.
opt. Pul.* ʒi. *cum Syr. de Stœchad. f. Pil.* 7. By
which she had eight stools. ℞ *Sarsaparilla, the
Bark of Guaiacum,* each ʒii. *Saffafras* ʒi. *Guaiacum* ℔ß. *Coriander feeds prepared* ʒiii. *Cut and bruise
them, after infuse them in Spring water* ℔xiv. *for
twenty four hours, after boyl them till half be wasted.
At the end of boyling, add Cinamon bruised* ʒiv. Of
this Decoction strained she took three draughts
every day, one in the morning hot, at four a clock
in

Norbury, formerly Kempson (no. 82). Eleanor Quiney was a particularly favoured grandchild, for she also inherited pewter and embroidered table-linen.[1]

Isabel Sadler, sixty years of age, was suffering from a cough, breathing difficulties and loss of appetite. Hall prescribed a strong emetic and purgative medicine, which was severe in its effects but resulted in the patient's announcing that she was 'much eased'. To relieve her further Hall prescribed a purgative pill that gave seventeen bowel evacuations.

The cough was treated with a linctus, which included in its composition two lohochs. Lohoch was another name for a linctus and the two preparations prescribed were *Lohoch Sanum et Expertum* and *Lohoch e Pulmone Vulpis*. The former was made from soothing mucilaginous substances and pectoral drugs such as liquorice and hyssop. The principal ingredient in *Lohoch e Pulmone Vulpis* was dried fox lung *Pulmo vulpis*. Fox lung was recommended to cure breathing difficulties and to strengthen and preserve the lungs.[2] There is a discernible sympathetic association here between the drug and the condition it was said to cure.

A pill containing liquorice, *Farin[a] amyli* or wheat starch, one eighth of a grain of opium and other drugs, was prescribed to be sucked at bedtime.

106: BRIDGET BROWNE OF RADFORD SEMELE

This patient, noted simply as 'young' and of gentry status in Hall's case notes, appears to be Bridget, the daughter of Lady Browne of Radford (nos 110, 167), whose melancholy he had recorded when attending her soon after the young woman's death in childbirth.

Bridget Browne was born in about 1602 and on 6 November 1623 she married Clement Throckmorton of Haseley (1604–71), his first wife. The Haseley branch of the family was descended from Sir George Throckmorton (d. 1553), whose eldest son, Robert, lived at Coughton and whose third son, Clement, bought the manor of Haseley in 1554.[3] His grand black-lettered tomb-chest, with brasses, can still be seen in the parish church.[4] Job Throckmorton (d. 1601), a notorious Puritan, added an elaborate porch to Haseley Old Manor (demolished in about 1966); the estate descended to his grandson, Clement, whom Bridget Browne was to marry.

Hall must have treated her in about 1620, before her marriage. She had three sons, Clement (d. 1664), Francis (died childless) and Robert, who

1. (H)WRO, class 008.7 1627/138.

2. Culpeper, *A Physicall Directory* p. 70; W.T. Fernie, *Animal Simples* (Bristol, 1899), p. 186.

3. *VCH Warws.*, III, p. 106.

4. Pevsner, *Warws.*, p. 308.

the afternoon, and at going to Bed, both cold. Of the *Fæces* was made a second Decoction. Her Head being covered, the following Fume was received: ℞ *Roman Nigella, Storax, Calamus, Benjamin,* each ℥iii. *Mace, Cloves,* each ℥i. *Make a gross Powder for a Fume.* ℞ *Leaves of Sage, Marjoram, Stæchados,* each M ß. *Seeds of Anis, Fennel, Cummin,* each ℥ii. *Bayberries bruised* ℥ß. *Milij.* ℔i. *Common Salt* ℔ß. *torrefy them all in a Frying-pan, and put them into Bags,* which apply very hot to the Head and Neck: when they are cold, after use the Fume. With these she was cured.

Observ. VII.

Mrs. *Mary Talbot,* Sister to the Countess, a Catholick, fair, was troubled with the Scurvy, with swelling of the Spleen, erosion of the Gums, livid Spots of the Thighs, Pain of the Loins and Head, with Convulsion and Palsy of the Tongue; her Pulse was small and unequal, her Urine was troubled and thick. The Countess asked me whether there were any hopes of Life? I answered, Yes, if she would be patient and obedient, although her Scurvy was confirmed. I first purged her Body with *Pil. Ruffi,* and *Tart. Vitriol.* She used with her Meat Salt of Scurvy-grass, and in her Broths Salt of Wormwood. All other Drinks being forbid, she drunk the following: ℞ *Garden Scurvy-grass* M iv. *Water-cresses, Brooklime,* each M ii. *Juniper-berries bruised* M i. *Wormwood* M ß. *Boyl them in sufficient quantity of new*

Beer

married Elizabeth Mordaunt of Walton. Bridget had died by 1633. In her will, Lady Browne bequeathed £10 to Bridget's son, her grandson, the young Clement.[1] Clement Throckmorton, Bridget's husband, had a close political relationship with his brother-in-law, George Browne, both firm parliamentarians, and he did not become a magistrate until the Restoration.[2] The Coughton–Haseley links were not severed until 1830, when the family portraits at Haseley were finally removed in a cart to Coughton Court.[3]

Bridget Browne appears to have been suffering from a chronic catarrhal diarrhoea. Treatment began with a purgative pill made from amber, rhubarb and *Syrupus de Stoechade*, a compound syrup attributed to Mesue and containing the flowers of *Lavendula stoechas* or French lavender. This was followed by a sweating decoction containing guaiacum, sarsaparilla and sassafras.

Hall regarded the condition as being due to phlegm descending from the head and to counteract this he prescribed an unusual preparation that doubled up as a poultice and a fume. A mixture of aromatic resins, dried herbs and seeds was roasted with common salt and applied hot in bags to the head. When cool the mixture was ignited and the patient required to inhale the vapour.

107: MARY TALBOT OF GRAFTON, WORCESTERSHIRE

One of Hall's grandest patients was, in fact, sister to the Earl of Shrewsbury (*soror comitis*) and not to his wife, as Cooke mistranslated. She was Mary, third and youngest daughter of Sir John Talbot of Grafton and his first wife, Catherine Petre. Her elder brother, George (1567–1630), had been ordained as a priest before he became the ninth earl in 1618.[4] Worcestershire's wealthiest Catholics, the Talbots were linked by marriage to virtually all the other contemporary Midland recusant families, such as the Giffards, Fortescues and Winters, their local standing enhanced by their earlier sufferings.

Mary Talbot's eldest sister was Gertrude, who had married Robert Winter of Huddington, executed in 1606 for his part in the Gunpowder Plot. By the time Mary's father died in 1611 he had spent long periods in prison for recusancy. In 1587 he was in the custody of Henry Whitney at Mitcham (Surrey), whose daughter, Joan, also a recusant and a patient (no. 18), was later to marry Richard Lane of Alveston.[5] Mary Talbot's great-nephew was the infant George, whom Hall treated (no. 60).

1. PRO, Prob 11/213.
2. Hughes, p. 53.
3. WCRO, CR 1998/Drawer 8 [8]
4. *Complete Peerage*, XI, p. 717.
5. Humphreys, *Studies*, pp. 174–84; *VCH Worcs.*, III, p. 126.

Beer to four gallons, of which make Beer. After fourteen
days she begun to drink it in the morning, exercising
an hour after. After she swallowed for the space of
six days the quantity of a Nutmeg of an Electuary,
made of the Flowers of Scurvy-grass; afterward
she began to walk, and at last was very well.

OBSER. VIII.

MR. *Handslop*, aged about 61, afflicted with
the Scurvy, with which there was straitness
of the Breast, difficulty of breathing, Thirst, yellow Jaundice, hard Tumors of the Thighs, being
livid and black, Retraction of the Sinews of the
Ham, so that he could not go without a staff, the
Appetite lost, and troubled with vomiting, his
Pulse was little, scarce perceived to move; the
Urine was various, sometimes thin, the next day
yellow without sediment, the Belly was loose; was
thus cured : ℞ *Elect. Diacath. & Venterflu. Solenand.*
à ʒii. *Confect.Hamech.* ʒß. *Pul. Senæ, cremor. Tart.* à
Əß. *cum Sacch. f. Bol.* This gave six stools, but
being weak, he was ready to faint. The next
day, ℞ *prepared Harts-horn, Shavings of Harts-
horn, each* ʒi. *Powder of Earth-worms* ʒiii. *Conserve of Barberries, a sufficient quantity to make an E-
lectuary.* Dose the quantity of a Filbert. After
take six spoonfuls of the following Wine : ℞
Wormwood Wine ʒiv. *the Syrup against the Scurvy by*
Forest. ʒii. *mix them.* The livid Tumors of the Thigh
I bid to foment twice a day with a Decoction of
Brook-lime made in Beer, it is to be with doubled
Clothes

Mary Talbot must have been born in the 1570s; there is a marginal date, 1628, in the Latin case notes establishing that this was when Hall saw her. It seems that she did not marry but lived at the family home, Grafton Manor. The Grafton parish registers do not exist before 1676 and the bishop's transcripts are defective for the years 1642 to 1662. The date of Mary Talbot's death has not been traced.

The livid spots on the thighs, erosion of gums and other symptoms indicate that Mary Talbot was suffering from acute scurvy. Hall's regime of treatment was similar to that used for the Countess of Northampton (no. 1), first purging with *Pilula Ruffi* and *Tartarus vitriolatus*.[1] She was required to drink only medicated beer containing scorbutic drugs and salt of scurvy-grass was to be added to her food. This salt was obtained by evaporating the juice of scurvy grass to a thick consistency and then allowing it to cool.[2] An electuary made from flowers of scurvy grass was also prescribed.

108: ROBERT HANSLAP OF SOUTHAM

Originally from Northamptonshire, the Hanslaps were a substantial family in Southam by the mid-sixteenth century and figured prominently in the town's activities.[3]

Hall's patient was Robert Hanslap, the third of the eight children of Nicholas and Dorothy; his elder brother, Thomas, inherited an estate at Aynho (Northants.).[4] Robert Hanslap was baptised at Southam on 11 July 1568 and, aged thirty-five, married a local girl, Margaret, the sixteen-year-old eldest child of Ralph and Elizabeth Hill. Robert and Margaret Hanslap had a son and two daughters, of whom only one, Elizabeth, survived, and who inherited a marriage portion of £300.[5]

The family took a leading part in church affairs at Southam and held various parish offices; they gave a silver chalice and paten to St James's church in 1633.[6] Hall must have attended Robert Hanslap, clearly very ill, early in 1629; Hanslap was buried in Southam on 1 March 1629. Hall also treated Christian Basse, Joan Judkin and Thomas Holyoak as patients in the town (nos 9, 39, 164).

---

1. *Tartarus vitriolatus* was a name for potassium sulphate, a mild laxative. It was one of the chemical remedies supported by the teaching of Paracelsus. One of its many names was *specificum purgans paracelsi*.

2. The method for preparing salt of scurvy-grass was later described by A.V. Molimbrochius, *Cochlearia curiosa*, trans. Tho. Sherley (1676). The Vitamin C content would have been destroyed in the process.

3. *VCH Warws.*, VI, p. 222.

4. *HV Warws.*, 1619, p. 257.

5. PRO, Prob 11/155.

6. *VCH Warws.*, VI, p. 224.

upon Engliſh Bodies. 93

Cloaths hot, ℞ *New Worms prepared, bruiſe them in a Mortar with two ſpoonfuls of Wine, after ſtrain them through a Cloth, to which add a quart of White-wine.* Of this was given three ſpoonfuls morning, four in the afternoon, and night, and an hour after it ℥ii of the following: ℞ *Syrup. Sceletyrſ. For.* ℥vi. *Vin. Abſynth.* ℔ſſ. For the tumor of the Thighs was uſed this: ℞ *the Powder of the Flowers of Chamomel, the tops of Wormwood, each* ℥iii. *Briony root and Dazies, each* ℥ſſ. *Meal of Wheat, Orobus, and Beans, each* ℥iii. *Crums of white Bread* ℔ii. *mix them altogether with Cows milk, or rather Goats milk, and by gentle boyling make a Pulteſſ.* For ordinary drink he took the following: ℞ *Scurvy-graſſ* Miv. *Brook-lime, Water-creſſes, each* Mii. *Wormwood* Mſſ. *Juniper berries* ℔ſſ. *Calamus Aromaticus* ℥iii. *Roots of Saſſafras* ℥ii. *Boyl them in five gallons of Beer till a gallon be waſted, after tun them up:* he began to drink of it fourteen days after. For the contraction of the Hams, ℞ *Juyce of Scurvy-graſſ* ℥i. *Oil of St. Johns-wort, Mullen, Elder, each* ℥ſſ. *Boyl them to the waſting of the Juyces: being ſtrained, there was added Tacamahacca* ℥iſſ. *Balſam of Peru* ∋iv. *Melt them at a gentle Fire, ſtirring them; at the end add a little Wax.* He had this Cordial Electuary: ℞ *Conſerv. Cochlear.* ℥ii. *de Abſynth. Diaſorios Horſtii, Bugloſs, Caryoph. hortenſ. Roſ. Damaſ. Rad. Helen. condit.* ā ℥ſſ. *Lign. Rhod. Calam. Aromat. Rad. Aroniſ. præp. Spec. Diarrhod. Abbat. Diapler. Confect. Alker.* ā ℥ſſ. *cum Syr. Sceliturb. Foreſt. f. Elect.* Doſe, the quantity of a Filbert. To the hard Tumors was applied this Pulteſs: ℞ *Wormwood poudered, a ſufficient quantity, beat it with new Eggs, ſhells and all, to the form of a*

Cata-

This is another case of scurvy and from the number of prescriptions employed we may assume that the treatment was over a long period of time. Thirteen preparations were prescribed for Hanslap: a bole, two electuaries, two syrups, a wine, a medicated beer, three poultices, a plaster and two ointments. The first treatment was the purgative bole, which appears to have distressed the patient, who was very weak. Other treatments involved the use of the scorbutic herbs as in other cases of scurvy. ν

A large part of the regime was directed to the symptoms which had crippled the patient, swollen thighs and contracted sinews at the back of the leg. *Syrupus sceletyrs*, according to the formula of Pieter Foreest, was prescribed. *Sceletyrbe* was the name given to the wandering pain in the legs proceeding from scurvy. Also prescribed were earthworms, in a wine, in an electuary and as an oil in one of the ointments. Earthworms were listed in the London *Pharmacopoeia* of 1618 under *Lumbrici, seu vermes terrestres.*[1] They had a wide application in seventeenth-century medicine and the number of conditions to be treated by earthworms had increased steadily since classical times. They were recommended as antispasmodics to treat convulsions in children, for diseases of the ear, of the lungs, of the urinary passages, to cool inflammations and to heal cut sinews.

There are three other drugs of interest among the very large number employed in this observation. Balsam of Peru and Tacamahacca in the plaster to correct the 'contraction of the Hams' were both American tree resins or balsams. The balsams or balms from America were well received in Europe and represented a considerable advance in the treatment of wounds.[2] *Medulla Cruruis [et] Vituli* in the ointment, also for the contraction of the ham, were the bone marrow from the cow and the calf. Both were included in the marrows recommended by Dioscorides. The London *Pharmacopoeia* specified marrow taken from the shinbone.

109: ELIZABETH, LADY PUCKERING OF WARWICK PRIORY

Elizabeth Puckering was born in 1598, the youngest daughter of Sir John Morley of Halnaker (Sussex); she was married to Sir Thomas Puckering (nos 139, 161) of Warwick Priory on 2 July 1616 and contemporary gossip cited her dowry as £5,000.[3] Her mother was Cecily (née Caryll) of Ladyholt, near Harting (Sussex), related by marriage to the Smiths of

1. In addition to the whole animal the London *Pharmacopoeia* employed earthworms in three plasters and two oils.
2. F. Guerra, 'Drugs from the Indies and the political economy of the sixteenth century', *Analecta Medico-Historia, I. Materia Medica in the XVIth Century*, ed. M. Florkin (Oxford, 1966), p. 38.
3. Chamberlain, II, p. 15.

94.   *Select Observations*

Cataplasm, and apply it cold to the *Tumors*. This was admirable, and highly praised, it removed the Tumor. For the Contraction of the Ham was used the following : ℞ *Unguent. Dialthæ, Ol. Chamom. de Castor. & Lumbric.* ā ℥ß. *Medul. Crur. Vitul. Ol. Lini*, ā ℥iii. *Succ. Raphan. Cochlear. Nasturt. Aquatic.* ā ℥ß. *cum s.q. Ceræ & Ammoniac. sol. f. Lin.* He found much ease by this. ℞ *Uuguent. Dialth.* ℥ß. *Lilior. albor. Cham. Aneth.* ā ℥ii. *Granor. Juniper. contus.* Əi. *f. Unguent.* ℞ *Elect. Chalyb.* ℥vii. *Conserv. Absynth. Cochlear.* ā ℥i. *Misc.* There was given ℥iii fasting, after the use of which he was cured, so that he was both able to ride and walk; and he said himself he was perfectly cured.

Observ. IX.

THe Lady *Puckering*, being often vexed with the beating of the Heart, was thus cured : ℞ *Diambr. Diamosch. dulc. Aromat. Ros.* ā ℥ii. *Confect. Alker.* ℥i. *Diacoralli* ℥i. *Theriac. mag. Mithrid. opt.* ā Əii. *Conserv. Bugloß Cochlear.* (because she had the Scurvy) ā ℥i. *Misc. f. Elect.* Dose the quantity of a Filbert, by which she was eased.

Mrs. *Iremonger's* waiting Maid was cured as followeth, both of the beating and trembling of the Heart : ℞ *Castor.* ℥i. *Rad. Diptam.* ℥ß. (because her Courses did not flow rightly) *Diambræ, & Diamosch. dulc. Spec. Aromat. Ros.* ā ℥ii. *Theriac. mag. Mithrid. opt.* ā Əii. *Conserv. Bugloß* ℥i. *cum Syr. Artem. q.s.f. Opiat.* By that time she had taken half of this she was freed, although she had
been

Wootton Wawen. The Puckerings had two daughters, Cecily and Jane. Cecily was born in 1623 but died, aged only thirteen, in 1636, shortly before her father; her monument in St Mary's, Warwick, notes her religious nature and fortitude. No date is recorded when Hall treated Lady Puckering.

Lady Puckering's other daughter in 1649 went to London to stay with her uncle, Sir Adam Newton, only to be kidnapped at Greenwich, and carried off to a forced marriage at Erith by one James Welsh, protesting his love for her.[1] Finally restored to her family, the marriage was declared null and Jane later married Sir John Bale (1617–*c.* 1653) of Carlton (Leics.). She died in childbirth in 1652.[2] The Warwick Priory estate passed to Sir Henry Newton, who took the name of Puckering, but at his death in 1701 the line became extinct.[3] When she was widowed, Lady Puckering settled at Ladyholt. At her death in 1652 she founded a charity in Sussex to support five poor widows and four fatherless boys, for which funds came from her family inheritance.[4]

The Iremongers were a distinguished legal family throughout the seventeenth century, with Throckmorton and Bedfordshire connections. Hall described this patient as *Generosa Iremonger pedisequa*, a gentlewoman who acted as a companion. No actual identification has been possible.

This observation reported on the use of an opiate electuary for two patients, Lady Puckering and Mrs Iremonger's companion, both experiencing 'beating and trembling of the heart'. The principal ingredients of the electuary were theriac, mithridate (no. 9), *Diamoschum* and *Diambra*.[5] *Diamoschum* was a mixture of nineteen drugs including pearl, amber, coral and the antispasmodic cordial musk. *Diambra* was a mixture of mostly spices with *ambrae griseae* or ambergris, the waxy substance secreted by the sperm whale. This was a rare and very expensive drug and was recommended as a cordial and antispasmodic.[6] Hall recorded patient satisfaction for this electuary.

In each case he added supplementary items to the formula. In the case of Lady Puckering he included scurvy-grass (*Cochlearia*) because she had scurvy, for the companion castor and the root of *Dictamus albus* or fraxinella to resolve a menstrual problem.

1. *Worthies*, p. 591.

2. Hamper, p. 98.

3. John Nichols, *The History and Antiquities of the County of Leicester* (1804), II, pt II, p. 546.

4. *VCH Sussex*, IV, p. 215; J. Shirt, 'Dame Elizabeth Puckering's Charity', *West Sussex History*, no. 20 (1981), pp. 13–15.

5. Both of these preparations were included in the London *Pharmacopoeia* of 1618 under 'Species'.

6. In 1604 ambergris was listed as twice the price of musk per ounce (no. 38).

been afflicted for a long time, and said the Electuary was worth Gold. This hath cured many, for
which I have had many hearty thanks.

Observ. X.

THE Lady *Brown* of *Radford*, was oppreffed
with thefe Scorbutic Symptoms, as with
binding of the Belly, Melancholy, Watchfulnefs,
troublefom fleep, Obftruction of the Courfes, continuing for a year, and by thofe Obftructions was
miferably tormented with Wind, and fwelling of
the Belly, efpecially about the Spleen, when fhe
broke wind, fhe was eafed ; fhe felt a continual
beating at the mouth of her Stomach, fo that it
might be felt with the hand, as if there had been
fome live thing leaping in her Belly. All thefe
happened from the death of her Daughter, dying
in Child-bed. By the following Prefcriptions fhe
was cured : ℞ *Scurvy-grafs*, *Water-creffes*, *Brook-
lime*, *Maiden-hair*, *Ceterach*, ã M ii. *Scabious*, *Harts-
tongue*, ã M ß. *Cordial Flowers*, each p. i. *Liquoris*
fhaved ʒvi. *Sena* ʒi. *Polypod.* ʒvi. *Rubarb, the Bark*
of Cappar roots, *Bark of Myrobalane Ind. prepared*,
ã ℈iv. *Cream of Tartar* ʒii. *Raifins ftoned* ʒx. *Barly*
p. i. *Squinanth.* ℈i. *Boyl them in fufficient quantity*
of the Waters of Wormwood, *Agrimony*, *Fumatory*,
to ℔i ʒiv. *After they are boyled*, *let them ftand*, *in-
fufing for all night* : *to the ftraining add* *Syr. Sceletyrs*
Foreft. ʒii. *Diafireos*, *Syr.Cichor. cum Rhab.* ã ʒi. *mix*
them with ʒii *of Cinnamon water.* *Dofe feven fpoonfuls*, which gave fix ftools. After to the Region
of

110: ELIZABETH, LADY BROWNE OF RADFORD SEMELE

Elizabeth Browne was the widow of Sir William, whose father, John, of Barnham Manor (Sussex) had bought the Radford Semele estate in 1589.[1] Sir William, who died on 11 March 1637, had been a magistrate and Treasurer of Knightlow Hundred.[2] Hall attended Lady Browne twice and on 1 January 1633 he noted her aged forty-nine (no. 167). She was therefore born in about 1584 and must have married after 1600.

She had at least three children. George, the heir, in 1636 had married Margaret Littleton, daughter of Sir Edward of Pillaton (Staffs.) and to her, as the only close female relative, Lady Browne bequeathed plate and linen. Thomas, her second son, was left £100. Hall recorded that Lady Browne's daughter had recently died in childbirth. This was Bridget, also his patient (no. 106), who had married Clement Throckmorton of Haseley on 6 November 1623; they had three sons, Clement (to whom Lady Browne left £10), Francis and Robert.[3]

As a widow, Lady Browne regularly entertained the puritan Thomas Dugard (1608–83) of Barford, in the years 1637 to 1641.[4] She continued to live at Radford, and in 1640 was in dispute with parishioners about local levies.[5] Sir George succeeded to the estate and, with his brother-in-law, Clement Throckmorton, was to be a leading supporter of Parliament in 1642.[6] In her will, proved on 10 August 1650, Lady Browne noted £300 was owed her by Sir Richard Tichborne and the same sum was on loan to Sir Kenelm Digby (1603–65), both known recusants; John Aubrey had recorded that Digby had 'great debts'. After Sir George Browne's death in January 1660, with no direct heirs, the estate passed to the Throckmortons of Haseley.[7]

This is the first of two observations devoted to Lady Browne. Here Hall described a clutch of 'scorbutic symptoms' which he said began after the death of her daughter in childbirth. He treated her with scorbutic drugs including preparations used for Robert Hanslap, who was suffering from scurvy (no. 108). In 1633 Hall referred to 'scurvy long confirmed' and treated her for a scorbutic fever with hartshorn and the scorbutic drugs

1. *VCH Warws.*, VI, p. 201; I am grateful to Dr T.P. Hudson, editor *VCH Sussex*, for his help.

2. WCRO, DR 295/1; the date has been changed in the burial register from 1632 to 1636 in a different ink; PRO, Prob 11/174.

3. Ibid., Prob 11/213.

4. BL, Add. MS 23146.

5. *QSOB*, II, p. 70.

6. Hughes, pp. 58, 124, 295, 302.

7. BL, Add. MS 29264.

of the Spleen was applied *Cera de Ammoniac. Foreft.* This difcuffed the Tumor, and eafed the Pain. Yet although well purged, there remained the Scorbutic Pain of the Belly. After purging, the Urine was troubled, and the fediment was various. To the Beer ufed for Mr. *Handflop,* was added M ii of *Fumatory.* The Leeches were applied to the Hemorrhoids. After was ufed the Electuary for Mr. *Handflop, Obferv.* 8. *Cent.* 2. framed of *Harts-horn, Ivory, Worms,* &c. By the ufe of thefe fhe was freed from the Scurvy, and came to enjoy perfect health.

OBSERV. XI.

Mrs. *Murden,* aged about 53, troubled with *Vertigo,* Pain in the Head and deafnefs, was by me cured prefently : ℞ *Aloes Rof.* ʒi. *Rhab. Pul. & Aq. Cinam. afperf.* ℈ii. *Agarick, Recent. tro.* ℈i. *Maftic. Myrrh.* ā ℈ß. *cum Syr. Betonic. f. Pil.* N°. 25. *Dofe Pil.* 5. *hor. ante cœnam.* Thefe were adminiftred *April* 17. 1626. by the ufe of which there was the defired effect, and they were much praifed ; they were after given for prevention.

(no. 167). In both cases the critical symptoms of scurvy are absent and this throws some doubt both on the nature of Lady Browne's illnesses and Hall's use of the term 'scorbutic' (no. 1).

111: MARY MURDEN OF MORETON MORRELL

Mary Woodward married Richard Murden (1573–1635) of Moreton Morrell on 4 May 1591. She was the fourth child of Thomas Woodward of Butlers Marston, who in 1567 had married Isabel, daughter of Sir John Rous of Rous Lench. Richard and Mary Murden had only one child, Mary, born in 1602,[1] a considerable heiress, who later married Sir Stephen Harvey and was also attended by Hall (nos 97, 64). Unusually, Hall noted the actual date of treatment.

There is a splendid monument to Mary Murden and her husband in Moreton Morrell church. Richard Murden served as Sheriff of Warwickshire in 1634 and is appropriately shown in full armour; Mary Murden wears a mantle, gown and deep ruff. They kneel on cushions, facing each other on either side of a *prie dieu*. Traces of colour can still be seen on their near-lifesize figures (illustrated, p. 106). Richard Murden had levied Ship Money for the first time for Charles I. Warwickshire, completely land-locked, not surprisingly had the worst county record for collecting the tax, which was finally reduced following Murden's bitter dispute with Coventry. Contemporary rumours suggested that in October 1635, aged sixty-two, he had died following a robbery at his house.[2] The puritan Dugard visited his widow on 12 August 1637.[3]

Mary Murden's symptoms were treated with a formula for twenty-five purgative pills, five to be taken *hor.ante coenum*, an hour before supper. Another case of vertigo (no. 95) was treated by bleeding from the cephalic vein. In this case for some reason Hall confined his therapy to purgatives.

112: GEORGE UNDERHILL OF OXHILL

Hall treated George Underhill (1567/8–1650) in 1630–1, already an elderly member of this widespread gentry family. By then he had moved to Oxhill, which he inherited from his brother, Francis, in 1613. George was the youngest son of Thomas Underhill of Ettington in this branch of the family.[4] He went to Oxford and matriculated at Gloucester Hall in 1583. He lived at Alderminster until acquiring the Oxhill property. He never married and bequeathed Oxhill to his nephew, Thomas Underhill of

1. *HV Warws.*, 1619, p. 319.
2. Hughes, pp. 15, 105–7.
3. BL, Add. MS 23146.
4. *HV Warws.*, 1619, p. 31.

Observ. XII.

MR. *George Underhil*, aged about 64, was much weakned with an immoderate loofnefs of the Belly, and cruelly tortured with the Cholick, by eating Herrings, was thus cured : R *Elect. Ventriflu.* ʒvi. *Cremor. Tart.* Ɔi. *Rhab. pul.* Ɔii. *cum Sacch. f. Bol.* It gave nine ftools. At the hour of Sleep he took this : R *Diafcord.* ʒi. *Aq. Scabiof.* ʒiij. *Syr. Lim.* ʒi. *Syr. Papav.* ʒſs. *Mifc.* He took the Shavings of *Harts-horn* twice a day. For the Stomach, R *Conferv. Rof. rub.* ʒii. *Spec. Aromat. Rof. Gab.* ʒi. *Caryophil. incif.* ʒſs. *Amber-greafe* gr. iii. *Mifc. cum Syr. Cortic. Citr. q. f. f. Elect.* Dofe, the quantity of a Filbert. After Meat he took the following Pouder : R *Sem. Coriand. præp. Sem. Fœnic. Anifi. Carvi,* ā Ɔii. *Cor. Cer. præpar. Coral. rub. præp. Cinam. Nuc. Mofch.* ā Ɔi. *Spec. Aromat. Rof. lætific. Gal.* ā Ɔſs. *Sacch. Rof. tab. ad pond. omnium, f. Pul. grof.* He alfo had applied *Scutum noft. Stomach.* and fo he was cured.

Observ. XIII.

MR. P. afflicted with a Flux of Semen, and Night-pollutions, by which he was much weakned, was cured as followeth : R *Pulp. of Caffia* ʒvi. *Pulp of Tamarinds* ʒii. Red *Coral,*

H   *Maftich,*

Loxley,[1] also a patient (no. 136). In 1642 Dugdale noted his political persuasion as neutral.[2]

Underhill's illness resulted from eating too many herrings, and was treated first with a good purge. Hall also recommended hartshorn, which he had prescribed for Sir Thomas Beaufou, another elderly patient, who had had a surfeit of cream (no. 74).

After the purge Hall prescribed an opiate mixture of *Diascordium* and syrup of poppies to be taken at bedtime, with a stomachic electuary and a carminative powder to be taken after meals. *Scutum nost. Stomach* refers to a shield-shaped plaster devised by Hall and applied to the stomach.

113: 'MR PSAMIRE'

Although Cooke referred to this patient only as Mr P., in Hall's notes his status was recorded as *Generosus*, presumably the reason for the tactful entry. His pseudonym, 'Psamire', was both a contemptuous term and a colloquial word for an ant. No other clue to the identity or place of residence was given.

Hall initially treated this man's sexual problem (as almost every other problem) with a purgative, this time using the pulp of the fruits of cassia (no. 13) and tamarind *Tamarindus indica*.

A pill was prescribed with gum arabic, tragacanth gum, Armenian bole, carabe (another name for amber), mummy powder[3] and *Mandibule Lucii piscis* or jaw of pike,[4] all items believed to hinder or stop fluxes. The instructions directed three pills to be taken at first, then one each morning. Chalybiated or steeled milk was prescribed, presumably to treat the weakness exhibited by the patient, and lead plates were applied to the 'Reins', the region of the kidneys and loins.

1. Morrison, *The Underhills*, p. 126.

2. NRO, Finch-Hatton, 4284.

3. Mummy *Mumia* was included in the London *Pharmacopoeia* of 1618. It was said to pierce all parts, restore wasted limbs, cure consumptions and ulcers, hinder blood coagulation and stop fluxes and rheums. A shortage of the genuine article resulted in recipes for making artificial mummy from the newly dead. Webster in *The White Devil* expressed what many might have thought when he described mummy as an unnatural and horrid physic (I, i, 17–20). See Pomet, *A Compleat History*, p. 229; Fernie, *Animal Simples*, p. 297.

4. Jaw of the pike in addition to stopping a flux was also recommended to abate fever, cure agues and expel plague (Fernie, *Animal Simples*, p. 163). This was one of the animal drugs included in the London *Pharmacopoeia* of 1618.

Maftich, each ℈iß. *make a Bole with Sugar.* This
purged well. After ℞ *Gum. Arabic. Tragacanth.*
Carab. Mum. Bol. Arm. Mandibulæ Lucii, ā ℈ii. *f.*
Pil. & cum Syrup. de Rof. ficc. vel Myrtin. f. Pill.
pondere ℈i. *Cap. prima vice Pil.* iii. afterward one
Pill for many days in a morning. He ufed alfo
chalybiated Milk. To the Back were applied Plates
of Lead, on the region of the Reins. And thus
he was cured.

Observ. XIV.

Mrs. *Kenton* of *Northampton,* aged 48. weakned and difcoloured with the Whites, was
cured as followeth : ℞ *Venice Terbentine* ʒß. *diffolve*
it with the Yolk of an Egg, adding of the pureft Ho-
ney. ʒi. *Sugar of Rofes* ʒii. *White-wine* ʒvi. *mix*
them: of which take every day ʒi. She drank her
ordinary Drink warm, which was a Decoction of
Barly, with Liquoris and Mallows. After
the former Potion, fhe ufed this Bole : ℞ *Oliba-*
num, Bole Armoniack, and fealed Earth, of each
ʒß. *make them into a very fine Pouder, and with two*
Whites of new-laid Eggs make a Bole. This is an
admirable Secret, it is to be ufed for divers days,
fix hours before Meat. She alfo had this Drink :
℞ *Guaiacum chips* ℔i. *of its Bark bruifed* ʒiv. *infufe*
them eight days in Spring water ℔viii. *with a drachm*
of Oil of Sulphur, in Horfe dung, being in a Glaß
Veffel well ftopt with Wax and Brimftone; after ftrain
it : in the ftrained Liquor put a frefh quantity of the
Guaiacum, &c. and infufe it as before; after three
                                                  days

114: [MRS] KENTON OF NORTHAMPTONSHIRE

A patient of genteel status, born in the period 1565 to 1587, suffering from 'Gonorrha', she has been impossible to identify. Kentons do not seem to be recorded for Northamptonshire and her name may in fact be Kington.

Hall's treatment of Mrs Kenton in its use of a turpentine preparation and a plaster for the back resembles the regime prescribed for Mrs Garner, who was also suffering from leucorrhoea (no. 32).

In this observation Hall reported on the use of two medicines which may have been numbered among those he would not have wished to be made public during his lifetime.[1] One he described as an 'admirable secret' and the other he regarded as of great value in a number of serious diseases.

The first was a bole composed of olibanum or frankincense, a gum-resin from Turkey and the East Indies recommended for uterine flux, Armenian bole and sealed earth, the latter also used for Mrs Garner. The second preparation was made from guaiacum wood infused with acidulated spring water and horse dung in a stoppered vessel. The product was to be sweetened and 'aromatized' to the patient's palate. Horse dung, *Stercus Equinum* in the London *Pharmacopoeia*, was quoted as being of value in floodings of the womb.[2] The principal ingredient, guaiacum, was first introduced into Europe for the treatment of syphilis or French pox. Hall claimed that this preparation of guaiacum cured dropsy, apoplexy and other grievous diseases of the head. It is an illustration of how a foreign drug, introduced as a specific for one disease, quickly became a remedy for a variety of illnesses. Sassafras was treated likewise by Hall's contemporaries.

115: MARGARET DELABERE OF SOUTHAM, GLOUCESTERSHIRE

Margaret Newman, a gentlewoman, was married at Badsey (Worcs.) on 12 May 1608 to Richard Delabere (d. 1636) of Southam (illustrated, p. 206).[3] He paid a composition of £25 rather than take a knighthood at the coronation of Charles I in 1625. Margaret Delabere was one of Hall's few patients to undertake hydrotherapy, for which she travelled to Bath, some 20 miles from her home. It seems unlikely that Hall attended her so far from Stratford, although he treated other patients from nearby parts of Gloucestershire, such as Henry Izod (no. 121). However, in Worcestershire

1. Dr John Bird in his introduction to the first edition of Cooke's *Select Observations* wrote that the manuscript 'was intended by the Author [Hall] not to be published til his decease, when men more willingly part with what they have'.
2. Fernie, *Animal Simples*, p. 249.
3. *HV Glos.*, 1623, p. 49.

days strain it, and after sweeten and aromatize it to the *Patients* palat. The Dose is two, three, or four ounces, according to the strength and nature of the sick. Two ounces of this doth more than ℥ß of the ordinary Decoction. It is safe in the *Spleen, Picrocholis,* and *Jaundice* confirmed; cures the *Dropsy, Apoplexy, French Pox,* and other grievous Diseases of the Head. Of the *Fæces* may be made a second Decoction, which may be used with Meat, instead of Drink. To the Back was applied, ℞ *Empl. contra Rupt. & pro Matrice,* ā ℥i. *Ungu. Comit.* ℥ii. *Mastich. Sang. Drac. & Coral. alb.* ā ℥ii. *Ros. rub.* p. i. *Rad. Bistort. Musc. Querc.* ā ℥ii. *Ter. sigill.* ℥iß. *Malax. omnia simul cum Ol. Myrtil. f. Emplast.* Of this spread so much upon Leather as may be for a Plaster for the Back, and *Os sacrum,* and another to the lower Belly, which are to be continued on betwixt the time of the Courses, and then removed. By these she was cured.

OBSERV. XV.

Mrs. *Delaberr,* of *Southam* near *Glocester,* having been long sick with loathing of her Meat, insomuch that no sooner she had eaten, but it came up, her Urine often changing; and although she was pretty well whilst in Bed, yet when she rose she was troubled with swooning: having also the Scurvy, was cured as followeth: ℞ *Pil. Hier. cum Agarick, Ruffi,* ā ℈ii. *de Succin. aggregat. Crem. Tart.* ā ℈iß. *Oxymel scil. q. s. f. Pil.* 15. *deaurent.* She took two at a night, and three

100 *Select Observations*

in the morning, every third day, she being well purged. To the Spleen was applied this Plaster, ℞ *Cerat. de Ammoniac. Forest.* ℥i. *Emplast. de Me-lilot.* ℥ß. *Misc.* Spread it upon Leather, and a red Sarcenet upon it. Those days she purged not, she took of this Electuary : ℞ *Conserve of Damask Roses* ℥i. *Conserve of Scurvy-grass* ℥iii. *Conserve of Bugloss,* ℥ii. *Spec. pleresarch.* ℥ß. *Cream of Tartar, prepared Steel, each* Əii. *Wake-robbin roots prepared* Əi. *Confect. Alkerm.* ℥i. *with sufficient quantity of Sugar make a soft Electuary.* Dose, in the evening the quantity of a Bean, and in the morning before she rose, the quantity of a Nutmeg, and so for two days, the third she purged, by which she came to be so much better, as that to walk and ride, and then would to the *Bath*, where she used the following Decoction, when she came out of the Bath, and went to bed and swet : ℞ *Chips of Guaiacum* ℥iii. *Bark of the same* ℥ii. *Sassafras* ℥i. *China cut thin* ℥ß. *Shavings of Ivory* ℥iii. *Liquoris* ℥i. *Agrimony, Carduus benedictus, Scurvy grass, Water-cresses, Brook-lime, each* M ß. *the tops of Fumitory, Flowers of Bugloss, Stæchados, Rosemary flowers, each* p.i. *Nutmegs, Cinamon, each* ℥ii. *Infuse them upon the Fire for twelve hours in six quarts of Water, after boyl them to the half, and then strain it, and being sweetned with Sugar, Dose was* ℥iv. It was used in the morning every fourth day, purging with these Pills: ℞ *Pil. Hier. cum Agar. Russi.* ā Əii. with which being well purged, she used no other Physick, but went home very well.

Observ.

Observ. XVI.

*J*Acob *Ballard,* aged 60, being cruelly vexed with
a bloody Flux, and ſpumous, and ſometimes
chylous, with a *Teneſmus* for three months, was
cured as followeth ℞ *Ordinary Barly* p. i. *the
Seeds of Line and Fenugreek beaten, each* ℥i. *Flowers
of Chamomel, Melilot, each* p. i. *Rie bran* p. ii.
*make a Deco*ꜩ*ion of all in Water to* ℔ß. *In the ſtraining diſſolve the Yolks of two Eggs, Hony of Roſes* ℥iii.
and red Sugar ℥ii. *mix them, and make a Clyſter,*
which was injected. After which he took this
Potion at night : ℞ *Philon Perſ.* ℈ii. *Aq. Plantag.*
℥iii. *Syr. Cydonior.* ℥i. *f. Pot.* This profited ad-
mirably, for he ſlept well, his Pain was eaſed,
and his Flux was ſtayed. After was uſed an Aſtrin-
gent Clyſter to ſtay the Flux, and heal the Ulcer :
℞ *the tops of Briars, Plantain, Purſlain, Coriander
ſeeds prepared, Cummin a little torrefied and beaten,
each* ℥i. *Starch torreſied* ℥ß. *Galls, Cypreſſe-Nuts
beaten groſly, each* iv. *Bran* p. ii. *Boyl them in ſteeled
Water to* ℔i. *To the Straining add Goats Sewet* ℥i.
prepared Bole Armoniack ℨii. *Juyce of Plantain* ℥iv.
Mucilage of Tragacanth ℥i. *Honey of Roſes* ℥ii. *mix
them for a Clyſter.* To the Belly was applied the
following Plaſter : ℞ *Maſſ. Empl. contra Ruptur.*
℥iii. *Empl. Diaphœnic.* ℥ii. *Maſtich, Olibanum, Coriand. præp. Bol. Arm. præp. Sang. Drac.* ã ℈iv.
Lap. Hæmatit. ℨii. *Succ. Plantag.* ℥iv. *Vin. rub.
craſſ.* ℥iii. *Ol. Myrtil. & Cydonior.* ã ℥ii. *Miſc. cum
Cer. & Terebin.* with your hands moiſtned with red

Wine,

she could have been visiting a wide kin network that included the Hobys and Hackets, her mother's family.[1]

Margaret Delabere's loss of appetite, vomiting and scorbutic symptoms were treated by Hall's usual methods for expelling ill humours. He prescribed a sweating decoction containing guaiacum and sassafras to be taken when she emerged from the hot springs.[2]

The instructions for the plaster to be applied to the area of the spleen was that it was to be 'spread upon Leather and red Sarcenet upon it'. Sarsenet is a fine soft silk material and used in this case to lie between the plaster and the skin.

116: [JAMES] BALLARD

This patient cannot be positively identified, since no place of residence was noted and families named Ballard were widely scattered across Worcestershire and south Warwickshire; yeomen named Ballard, for example, lived in Inkberrow and Ilmington. His status was not given as *Generosus*.

Although the Cooke edition listed him as Jacob, in Hall's Latin notes his name was written as 'Jacob⁵', and he might therefore have been baptised James. No other Hall patient has this particular first name for comparison. However, in the Ombersley (Worcs.) register for 1576, a James Ballard married Margaret Hadley on 26 May and, if he is this man, he must have been born in the early 1550s and have been treated by Hall in about 1616.

The condition described is one where there was blood in the faeces, which were spumous or frothy and sometimes chylous (white and milky). There was tenesmus or rectal pain. Hall attributed the patient's symptoms to an ulcer.

Treatment began with an emollient enema followed by an opiate potion containing *Philonium Persicum* (no. 45) and *Syrupus Cydoniorum* or syrup of quince, which was described as a binding and stomachic medicine of service in cases of alvine flux or diarrhoea. Astringent enemas to stop the flux and heal the ulcer were supported by a plaster to the stomach and an opiate suppository to ease the pain. Towards the end of the treatment Hall controlled the patient's diet and prescribed olibanum (no. 114).

The observation ends with medical dicta relating to the process of concoction. This may be defined as the process of digestion and the subsequent separation of healthy fluids from unwholesome matter, which

1. Nash, I, p. 53; Pevsner, *Worcs.*, p. 74.

2. Margaret Delabere was at Bath about the time it was becoming known to the higher ranks of society. The visit of the Queen, Anne of Denmark, in 1616 is said to have been the significant event that was to lead to the popularity of the spa and its golden age in the eighteenth century.

Wine, and make Rolls, and spread Plasters upon
Leather, which apply to the Belly. For *Tenesmus*,
℞ *best Myrrh, Saffron, Storax, Calamint*, each ℨß.
Opium ℈i. *Bdellium, Aloes*, each gr. xviii. *Wax
liquified, sufficient to make a Suppository* ; one of
which put into the Fundament. That night the
former Potion of *Philon Perf.* was reiterated, and
after that he took the following astringent Electuary : ℞ *Bole Armoniack præp.* ℈iv. *Pearls, red Coral,
each* ℈ii *Pouder of Rose seeds, Spec. Diarrhod. Abbat.* ā ℨß. *Conserve of Cumfrey, Citron Pills candied,
each* ℨi. *with Sugar dissolved in Rosewater make an
Electuary.* Dose ℨii in the morning, and so much
before supper. He also before meals took some
grains of the best *Olibanum*, his Diet was spare and
drying. And thus he was cured.

Observe well, 1. *If there be a good Digestion,
and not the like separation, then there is a Dysentery.*
2. *If there be Separation and not Digestion, then it is
Lientery.* 3. *If neither Separation, nor Digestion,
there is present a Diarrhea. If the matter in the Stomach be putrified, then there is a Flux of the Belly, with
various colour.*

Observ. XVII.

Mrs. *Layton*, born of a noble Stock, long laboured of a Scorbutic Epilepsy, always at
her first falling into it, it was with a Feaver, and
convulsive motions, the rest of the Signs in *Eu-
gal, fol.* 86. and *Senertus, fol.* 60. In the Fit she
was most miserably vexed with cold horror, and
concussi-

would be excreted. Hall shows how variations in digestion and separation lead to dysentery, diarrhoea and lientery or *lienterica*, when food passed through the alimentary system and was excreted with little or no alteration.

117: MARGARET LAYTON OF SLEDWICH, COUNTY DURHAM

The second child of John Clopton of Sledwich (Durham) and Elizabeth (née Ashton), Margaret Layton's connection with Warwickshire was through her elder brother, William, who married his Stratford kinswoman, Anne Clopton (b. 1577).[1] Hall not only recorded her status as *Generosa* but also the fact that she came of noble stock (*ex nobile stirpe nata*).

Margaret Layton had been in Stratford in early January 1594, when she received two quarts of white wine from the Corporation,[2] while visiting Clopton House, the family home. Linked to the local recusant network, her father had leased a house in Old Town in 1589 from Ralph Sheldon of Beoley;[3] there is no evidence, however, that she ever lived in Stratford.

Margaret was born in about 1575 and lived at Sledwich from 1582 when her father inherited it from her maternal grandfather, Ralph Ashton of Great Lever (Lancs.). The manor house is in the parish of Whorlton in a 'lonely and sequestered' position, originally with fine interior plasterwork of 1584.[4] John Clopton, her father, was Queen Elizabeth's Receiver for several of the northern counties; some of his correspondence survives for 1587.[5] In 1589 he negotiated a settlement of £700 when his son married the substantial heiress, Anne Clopton.[6] Their son, Thomas (d. 1643), eventually inherited the Stratford estate. Margaret's family had sold Sledwich by about 1622.[7]

The identity of Margaret Layton's husband, the date of their marriage, if there were children and their deaths have not been found; the Whorlton parish registers begin only in 1626 and the bishop's transcripts not until 1765. Her father was still alive at the Heralds' Visit in 1615.[8] As Hall noted that Margaret Layton lived on for many years, he must have been treating her in the earlier part of the period 1611 to 1635, when she was visiting Stratford.

1. Robert Surtees, *The History and Antiquities of the County Palatine of Durham*, 1840, IV, p. 48; Sydney E. Harrison, *Sledwich, Co. Durham* (1944).

2. *Mins & Accts*, V, p. 20.

3. SBTRO, ER3/285.

4. Surtees, *The County Palatine of Durham*, p. 48.

5. *CSPD, Add.*, pp. 218–20, 222.

6. SBTRO, ER3/10.

7. Surtees, *The County Palatine of Durham*, p. 47.

8. *HV Durham*, 1615, p. 77.

Southam, Gloucestershire, the home of Margaret Delabere (from Joseph Nash, *Mansions of England in the Olden Time*, 1839)

concuſſion of the Members, for half an hour, ſo
that the whole Bed ſhook ; the Fit laſted ten hours,
ſhe not knowing nor feeling any pain. After in the
ſame day ſhe laboured of another Fit for ſix hours,
and yet was delivered from it beyond the expectation of the By-ſtanders. After ſhe fell aſleep, a-
nother Fit ſhe had, wherein ſhe ſaid ſhe had cutting pain. She was alſo afflicted with a Jaundice,
with diminution of the Courſes. I cured her
with the Preſcriptions following : ℞ *Elect. Ventri-*
flu. ℥vi. *Crem. Tart.* ℈i. *Rhab. pul.* ℈ii. *f. Bol.* It
gave ſix ſtools. For the Jaundice, which was
filthy, ſhe took this: ℞ *Mithridate* ℥i. *prepared*
Harts-horn ℈ii. *Pouder of Worms* ℥ii. *Conſerve of*
Barberries ℥i. *mix them,* for two mornings ; by
which ſhe was pretty well delivered from the Jaundice. Afterward I thus purged her : ℞ *Pil. fætid.*
Alephang. Coch. ā ℈i. *Agar. Troch.* ℈ſſ. *Caſtor.*
gr. vi. *cum Syr. de Stœchad. q. ſ. f. Pil.* 7. She took
three of them at night, going to bed, and four
in the morning. After I uſed the following neezing Pouder : ℞ *Nuc. Moſch. Rad. Pæon.* ā ℥ſſ. *El-*
leb. Nig. ℈i. *Pyrethr. Piper. alb.* ā ℈ſſ. *Miſc. f. Pul.*
a Portion of which was blown into the Noſtrils.
Whilſt the time of the Fits was expected, there
was given every morning ℥ii of this Opiat : ℞
Conſerve of Scurvy-graſs ℥ii. (which I always uſed
to mix with other Medicines in Scorbutic Affects
to infringe the Ill of the Diſeaſe) *Dianthos, Con-*
ſerve of Betony, each ℥ i. *Old Mithridate, Venice*
Treacle, each ℥i. *Miſſeltoe of the Oak,, Shavings of*
Harts-horn, Piony ſeeds, Man's ſcull pulverized, each
℈iv. *mix them.* It is to be taken of it ſelf, or with
Betony water, to which is added Oil of Vitriol.

By thefe fhe was fully delivered from her Fits for many years.

Observ. XVIII.

LYdia *Trap*, the Daughter of Mr. *Trap*, aged about two years, labouring of a burning Feaver, want of fenfe and motion in fome parts, and the Worms, infomuch that Death was daily expected, by me through God's blefling was thus reftored : R *prepared Harts-horn ʒiii. Spring water* ℔i. *Boyl them to the half; after was added a little Rofe water, an ounce of Syrup of Limons, a fpoonful of Sugar, and fo much Oil of Vitriol as made it fharpifh.* She took this for her drink, forbearing all other. To the region of the Heart was applied this : R *Old Treacle ʒi. Pouder of Piony root ʒſ. make a Plafter.* About her Neck fhe wore round flices of the fame Root ; and the Pouder of the fame Root was ftrewed upon her Head ; her Neck was anointed with the Oil of *Amber and Saffafras,* each ʒſ. *Spirit of Rofemary* vi *drops.* To her Navil was applied this Plafter : R *Aloes ʒſ. Pil. fine quib. Ɔi. Worms Ɔi. Myrrh. Ɔi. with Ox-gall make a Plafter.* To extinguifh thirft, and provoke ftools, was given the following : R *Syrup of Rofes folutive ʒi. boyled Water ʒii. Oil of Vitriol, fufficient to make it fharpifh.* For the Stomach was ufed *Ung. pectorale.* By thefe in a few days fhe became well.

Margaret Layton fell into fits lasting several hours when there was a fever, 'cold horror' or shivering and convulsions of the limbs. She was jaundiced and had menstrual problems. Hall, referring to the works of Eugalenus and Senertus (no. 1), diagnosed scorbutic epilepsy.

Treatment began with a purgative followed by an electuary for the jaundice, which included conserve of barberry *Berberis vulgaris* used to treat putrid dispositions of the humours. A sneezing powder was prescribed similar to that used by William Fortescue, also suffering from an epileptiform disorder (no. 29). An opiate was added including conserve of scurvy grass, which Hall stated he always used with other medicines in scorbutic cases 'to infringe the Ill of the Disease'. The opiate contained three drugs recommended·for the treatment of convulsions: clove gillyflower *Dianthus caryophyllus*, mistletoe *Viscum album* and betony *Stachys officinalis*. There were also two drugs used to treat epilepsy, paeony root (no. 35) and 'Man's scull pulverized'. Human skull was one of the items recommended by Galen for epilepsy. Nicholas Culpeper stated that powdered skull given with betony 'helps palsyes and falling sickness'.[1]

118: LYDIA TRAPP OF STRATFORD-UPON-AVON

Lydia, baptised on 2 September 1629 at Stratford, was the third child in John and Mary Trapp's family of ten, born in the town during the years 1625 to 1643. Four of the children died young. Hall also attended Lydia's father (no. 181) and noted him in the manuscript of the present case as a schoolmaster. He treated Lydia in 1631. In 1646 she married, at St Nicholas, Warwick, a local minister, William Potter. No record of her later life has been found.

Lydia Trapp was suffering from a fever, partial paralysis and worms. In the manuscript Hall described this case as a *Hemiplagia*. The term 'hemiplegia' as used today means a paralysis limited to one side of the body. Cooke translated Hall's term as 'want of sense or motion in some parts'.

The principal medicaments prescribed were hartshorn for the fever and paeony root, as used for baby John Walker (no. 35). Hall avoided purgatives taken internally to treat worms in so young a patient. He used instead a plaster applied to the navel which contained the purgative aloes, the ingredients of *Pilula Sine Quibus* (no. 29) and worms made into a plaster with ox bile. Fernie quotes medieval sources that prescribe earthworms for the treatment of convulsions in children and the expulsion of worms.[2]

1. Culpeper, *A Physicall Directory*, p. 71. Human skull appears in the London *Pharmacopoeia* under the title *Cranium Humanum, In Eo Os Triquemtum* (human skull containing the triangular bone).

2. Fernie, *Animal Simples*, p. 533.

OBSERV. XIX.

THe Lady *Underhil*, aged 53, was troubled
with Pain of the Joynts in the hands, and
when fhe rubbed one with another, there arofe
a flatuous Tumor; fhe had alfo on a fudden a
red Face, her Voice was alfo much loft, fo that
when fhe fpake, the By-ftanders could not un-
derftand her; fhe felt as it were the fenfe of
biting of Ants in many parts of the Body, and
thefe from the Scurvy. ℞ *Sarfaparilla* ℥ iv.
Saffafras ℥i. *Agrimony, Scurvy grafs, Water-creffes,
Brook-lime, each* M i. *Bark of Capar root, Myrobalans of India, each* ℈iv. *Polypody of the Oak, and
Liquoris, each* ℥ſs. *Raifins ftoned* ℥x. *Infufe them in
fix pints of Water for a night, after boil them to the
half: to the ftraining, add Sena* ℥i. *Rubarb* ℥i.
*give them two or three walms, adding Syrup againft
the Scurvy by* Foreſius ℥iv. *mix them.* The Dofe
was fix or eight fpoonfuls, which purged her
well, and fhe became very well, and fo highly
praifed the Apozeme, as if it wrought by inchantment.

119: CATHERINE, LADY UNDERHILL OF ETTINGTON

Catherine Uvedale was born in about 1580 and married Sir Edward Underhill of Ettington on 17 May 1613. The Uvedales' family home was at Wickham (Hants.), where remains of a sixteenth-century family monument survive.[1]

Lady Underhill must have been treated by Hall in 1633; her husband was also a patient (no. 120). She had had two daughters, Jane, who was buried at Ettington in 1623, and Anne, baptised in 1622 but who died young. After her husband's death in 1641, Lady Underhill continued to manage the estate, and in that year a case was brought to Warwickshire Quarter Sessions when four men were accused of entering her close in Over Ettington.[2] Lady Underhill made her will in June 1658 and died four years later.

Lady Underhill's symptoms, attributed to scurvy, were pain and swelling in the hands, loss of her voice and some form of irritation of the nerve-endings which was compared to the biting of ants.

Hall prescribed only one medicament, an *apozeme*, the name given to a preparation made by infusion and decoction. In this case the drugs were the scorbutic herbs, purgatives, the bark of the root of capar *Capparis spinosa* and myrobalans, a dried plum-like fruit brought from the East Indies. These fruits, of which there were several species, had a bitter taste and a gentle purgative action. The comment that the *apozeme* was highly praised 'as if it wrought by inchantment' suggests that the patient's recovery was swift.

120: SIR EDWARD UNDERHILL OF ETTINGTON

Sir Edward Underhill (1573–1641) was the eldest son of Edward Underhill of Pillerton Priors. He matriculated at Magdalen College, Oxford, aged fourteen in 1587, receiving his BA in 1595 and an MA four years later; he remained in Oxford until his father's death.[3] He was knighted in January 1612/3 and at Wickham (Hants.) on 17 May 1613 he married Catherine (no. 119), daughter of Sir William Uvedale, who became Treasurer of the King's Household.[4]

Sir Edward was a magistrate and served as High Sheriff of Warwickshire in 1638; he was attended by Hall in 1623, the year in which his daughter, Jane, was buried at Ettington in a period of the widespread and fatal spotted fever epidemic. Dugdale noted that he too was buried at Ettington, on 13 November 1641, intestate at his death.[5]

1. Pevsner, *Hants.*, pp. 652–3.
2. QSOB, VI, p. 71.
3. Morrison, *The Underhills*, pp. 130–1.
4. Chamberlain, I, p. 606.
5. Dugdale, II, p. 626.

Observ. XX.

ESquire *Underhil*, aged 50, was miserably tormented with the running Gout, which pained all the Joynts of his Body, as Ancles, Knees, Arms, Neck, &c. Which was by the ensuing Medicines cured in a few days. ℞ *the Pouder of the Root Sarsaparilla, Sena, each* ℨvi. *Cream of Tartar* ℨiii. *mix them.* The Dose was from ℈ii to iv. which gave him three or four stools a day. The Body being well purged, the following Bath was used : ℞ *Salt* ℔i. *Quick Brimstone* ℥iß. *Alum* ℔ß. *Bay berries* ℥iv. *Boyl them in sufficient quantity of Water : he sat in it daily up to the knees morning and evening.* This delivered him not only from the Pain in his Feet, but from that callous hardness under his Toes. For preservation in the month of *October* was used the following : ℞ *Caryocost.* ℨiiß. *Elect. de Tamarind.* ℥ß. *Cryst. Tart.* ℈i. *f. Bol. cum Sacch.* After was used *Pil. Podagr. Plater.* As ℞ *Hermoductils skinned* ℥ß. *Aloes, Turbith, Mecoachan, Rubarb, yellow Mirobalans, also Chebuls, Mastich, each* ℨi. *Roots of round Birthwort* ℈i. *St. Johns-wort, Seed also of Cummin and Ginger, each* ℨß. *Salt gem.* ℈ß. *with the Juyce of Ground-pine make Pills, adding Diagrid.* ℨß. Dose, sometimes every month was taken ℨi. and so he was delivered from that Pain begun, but yet wholly it was removed by the former Pouder : to which was added *Betony* ℥ß. *Sugar of Roses* ℥i. And thus for
many

Hall described the patient's pains in the joints as running gout (see no. 89 for a discussion of the term 'gout' as used by Hall). The initial treatment was a purge and a medicated bath. After this two preparations were prescribed for 'preservation in the month of October' and afterwards taken monthly. The first was a bole composed of tartar, an electuary of tamarind and *Electuarium Caryocostinum* which contained scammony. This was followed by *Pilula Podagra*, which Hall attributed to Felix Platter (1553–1617). Podagra means gout of the feet. The formula contained purgatives, spices, hermodactils (no. 89) and two species of myrobalans, yellow myrobalan and the chebule myrobalan (no. 119). Hall supplemented Platter's formula with *Diagrydium* or scammony.

121: HENRY IZOD OF TODDINGTON, GLOUCESTERSHIRE

The Izod family had built Stanton Court, Gloucestershire, in the reign of James I.[1] Henry Izod of Toddington, who Hall in his manuscript tells us was a gentleman, was born in about 1568, the son of Henry senior, of Toddington (Glos.) and, as his first wife, had married Ann Gunn of nearby Saintbury. They had four children, Francis (b. *c.* 1593), Henry (*c.* 1595–1650), later Rector of Stanton, Dorothy (b. *c.* 1597) and Mary. Dorothy became the wife of Edward Randolph of Bevington. This family was also attended by Hall (nos 25, 65, 103), who may have treated Izod when he was visiting Warwickshire, but he also had another patient in the area, Margaret Delabere (no. 115). Henry Izod remarried in 1626; his second bride was Bridget Penny of Sedgeberrow (Worcs.), who outlived him.[2]

Henry Izod died at Toddington on 1 April 1632. He had made his will on 20 May 1629, leaving bequests to the church and the poor of Toddington, as well as to his four servants.[3] His heir, Francis, entered the Middle Temple in 1614[4] and later succeeded to the estate; Henry, junior, was left plate and livestock, while Mary, then married, had £10 in cash. Dorothy Randolph was not mentioned, nor were her children; she may not have been remembered in her father's will because of the Randolphs' known recusant status. In Stanton church there is a painted stone tablet, with a coat of arms and inscription, as a monument to the Reverend Henry Izod (d. 1650).

Henry Izod was passing blood in his urine and this was brought on by the slightest exercise. Hall treated two other similar cases, Robert Butler (no. 125) and Thomas Underhill (no. 136). Blood in the urine has several

1. Pevsner, *Glos (Cotswolds)*, p. 43.
2. *HV Worcs.*, 1682–3, p. 96; *HV Glos.*, 1623, p. 95.
3. Gloucestershire Record Office, Wills 1632/42.
4. *RAMT*, p. 102.

many years he was cured, and it never returned again.

Observ. XXI.

MR. *Izod*, being upon light motion troubled with pissing blood, was thus cured : ℞ *a Mass of Terbentine Pills with Rubarb ʒii. clear Terbentine ʒi. with Liquoris pouder make fifteen Pills, which was given in a spoon with Syrup of French-Mallowes.* He used the following Tablets : ℞ *Troches of Winter-cherries with Opium ʒſſ. Roots of Comfrey, Terbentine hard boiled, each ʒi. Sugar ʒiiſſ. with the infusion of Gum Tragacanth, make Tablets weighing Əii.* He often drank *Cream of Barly,* as also Milk boiled with Eggs, and so became well.

Observ. XXII.

THe Lady *Smith* (a Roman Catholick) being greatly afflicted with Wind of the Stomach, after it much more tormented her by taking a strong Infusion of *Stibium* from an Emperick, so that for a month together she was forced to take 3 or 4 draughts of Broth in a night, for expelling the Wind, otherwise she could not sleep, nor rest in Bed for Pain. She was about the age of 27. ℞ *Pil. Hier. cum Agaric. de Succin. Ruffi.* ã Əi. *f. Pil. sex, deaur.* She took three of them
when

causes including stone in the kidney, stone in the bladder and inflammation of the urethra. Butler and Underhill were both said to have 'heat of the urine', an indication of an inflammation.

In modern medicine identification of the site of the haemorrhage would indicate the measures to be taken for treatment. If Hall came to any decision concerning the cause of the symptoms it is not readily discernible in the treatments he applied. Winter cherry, which was used for the treatment of stone (no. 50), was prescribed for Izod and Underhill. Turpentine (no. 2), used for symptoms indicating an inflammation of the urethra, was also prescribed, although these symptoms were not recorded in the case of Izod. Butler, whose symptoms differed only in intensity from those of Underhill, was prescribed a decoction of sarsaparilla and a wine containing the astringent herb tormentil.

Underhill and Butler had only one treatment in common, the application to the back of perforated plates of lead moistened with vinegar. In addition to acting as a form of lead plaster these plates, when in place night and day, as directed for Underhill, prevented the patient from lying on his back, a posture believed to be a contributory cause of kidney disease.

122: ELIZABETH, LADY SMITH OF WOOTTON WAWEN

Elizabeth was one of six patients Hall recorded as recusants. She was born in about 1600, the daughter of Sir John Carryl of South Harting (Sussex),[1] where a family chapel was built in 1610.[2] Her mother was Mary, the daughter of Robert, later first Lord Dormer of Grove Park, Warwick, a noted Catholic. In 1620 Elizabeth Carryl married Charles Smith of Wootton Wawen; born in 1598, he too was connected with leading papist families. Charles Smith was the eldest of four sons of Sir Francis (1570–1629) and Anne Markham of Ollerton (Notts.).[3]

Charles Smith was knighted in 1619. When Elizabeth's father-in-law died he left her £10 to buy a jewel in his memory and £10 to each of her sons. Sir Charles inherited the Harewells' old family house at Wootton in 1629, on the site of the present mansion, which his eldest son built in 1687.[4] Charles sought to improve the estate by enclosing the commons and creating a new watercourse there.[5]

Lady Smith gave birth to four sons and five daughters. Hall noted that she requested more of the powder he had prescribed to be sent to the

1. *HV Sussex*, 1633–4, p. 161.
2. Pevsner, *Sussex*, p. 237.
3. Tighe, 'A Nottinghamshire Gentleman', pp. 30–45.
4. William Cooper, *Wootton Wawen, Its History and Records* (Leeds, 1936), pp. 28–9.
5. Ibid., p. 33.

when she went to bed. In the morning she took
the quantity of a Nutmeg of the following Electuary : ℞ *Elect. Chalyb. Craton.* ℥iſſ. *Elect. Ventriflu.* ℥ſſ. *Miſc.* After she took it she used exercise : ℞ *Sem. Coriand. præp. Fœnicul. de Aniſi. Carvi.* ā ℥iſſ. *C. C. præp. Coral. Rub. præp. Cinamom.
Nuc. Moſch.* ā ℈iſſ. *Spec. Aromat. Roſ. Lætific. Gal.
Diamoſch. dulc.* ā ℈ſſ. *Sacch. ad pond. omnium f.
Tragea.* This she took after Meals. The 24th
of *October* she sent to me for the same Pouder,
which was for the Countess of *Leiceſter*, who took
it, and for it returned me many thanks. And by
these was she delivered from those bitter Tor-
ments, and they did not return.

Observ. XXIII.

Mrs. *Winter*, Widow, (Roman Catholick) aged
28, was troubled with the Flux of the
Belly, Inflammation of the Reins, with great
abundance of Urine, even almost to fainting ; she
was also troubled with the Stone and Scurvy
confirmed, and was much weakned, was thus
cured : ℞ *the beſt Mithridate* ℈ii. *Diaſcordium* ℥ſſ.
Confectio Alkerm. ℈i. *Harts-horn prepared* ℈ſſ. *Bezoar ſtone* gr. vi. *Manus Chriſti perlat.* ℥i. *Magiſtral
of Pearl* gr. iv. *Coral prepared* ℈ſſ. *El. Lætific.
Gal.* ℥i. *Mix them with Syrup of Corn-Poppy, to
make an Electuary.* She took half of it upon a
knifes point, with which the Flux was bridled,
with great ease and chearfulneſs of mind : at bed-
time she took the other half, and reſted that
night.

Countess of Leicester, presumably Lettice, who died on 25 December 1634 and is buried at St Mary's, Warwick.

In 1642, although formerly indicted for recusancy, Sir Charles's conformity was certified and a year later he was created Viscount Carrington. During much of the Protectorate he lived abroad, although in 1648 he was accused at Warwickshire Quarter Sessions of not paying his share of constables' levies for the parish.[1]

In 1645 Lady Carrington was presented as a recusant at Warwickshire Quarter Sessions[2] and in her husband's absence she moved to Ledwell Park in Oxfordshire with her children. Lord Carrington had fled abroad, but was murdered at Pontoise by his valet in 1665.[3] Elizabeth Carrington's Midland recusant connections were wide; for example, her sister-in-law was Mary, the second wife of Sir Robert Throckmorton, and her eldest daughter the second wife of Sir George Winter of Huddington. Both families were also Hall's patients (nos 42, 123). Lady Carrington died at Wootton and was buried there on 21 March 1658.

Before calling in Hall, Lady Smith's flatulence had been treated by an 'Empirick', a man who practised medicine according to experience, while ignorant of its principles. The use of stibium or antimony suggests she had consulted either a physician who followed the doctrines of Paracelsus, or a quack doctor exploiting the new chemical remedies.

Hall treated the patient with a purgative pill, a 'steeled' electuary and a carminative in the form of a *Tragea* or coarse powder.

123: MARGARET WINTER OF HUDDINGTON, WORCESTERSHIRE

Prominent among Worcestershire's Catholic families, the Winters were further distinguished by their part in the Gunpowder Plot and the severity of their later treatment as recusants. Three Winters were executed in 1606, Robert, Thomas and John, the sons of George Winter of Huddington. Their Catholic connections were impeccable, for their grandmother was Catherine Throckmorton of Coughton and George's first wife had been Jane Ingilby of Ripley, whose brother was the Yorkshire martyr, Francis (d. 1586).[4]

Robert Winter (1567–1606) inherited the Huddington estate at his father's death in 1594 and married Gertrude Talbot, whose family home at Grafton was also a Catholic centre. As a widow, Gertrude Winter had to

1. Ibid., p. 30
2. QSOB, VI, p. 71.
3. Cooper, *Wootton Wawen*, p. 30.
4. Henry H. Spink, *The Gunpowder Plot and Lord Mounteagle's Letter* (1902), p. 26.

night. For drink she had the Decoction of *Harts-horn*. To the mouth of the Stomach was applied this : ℞ *Spec. Aromat. Rof. Cab.* ℨſſ. *Labdan.* ℨſſ. *Mithridat. opt. Theriac. Andromac.* ā ℨi. *Cer. flav.* ℨii. *diſſol. Ol. Stomach. Craton.* *f. L. A. Empl.* By thefe the Belly being bound, she took the following Pills : ℞ *Pil. Ruffi. de Succin.* ā ℨi. *f. Pil.* N°.10. She took three at bed-time. After the former Cordial was repeated. After I gave the following Potion : ℞ *Aq. Antiscorbut. Doncrel.* ℥iv. *Spleneticæ ejuſ* *dem* ℥ii. *Syr. Sceletyrb. Foreſt.* ℥iii. *Miſc.* She took eight fpoonfuls of it in mornings. Afterward she ufed the following Electuary : ℞ *Conſerve of Bugloſs, of Clove Gilly flowers, Dianthos,* each ℥i. *Conſerve of Scurvy-graſs* ℥ii. *Elicampana root candied* ℨiii. *Spec. Diarrhod. Abbat.* ℨi. *Diapleresarchont* ℥ſſ. *Confectio Alkermes* ℈ii. *with the Syrup againſt the Scurvy by* Foreſt. *make an Electuary.* The Dofe was the quantity of a Filbert, fafting. The *Decoction of Harts-horn* was repeated. And fo she was cured, and freed from all her Symptoms.

OBSERV. XXIV.

THe Lady *Jenkinſon* (fair, pious, chaft,) was vexed with Pain of the Head, and a light Vertigo, Pain of the Mouth, of the Stomach and Sides, fainting, watching, heats in hands and feet, languishing without caufe, the Flefh of the Gums loofe, and often bleeding, all being a difco-

forfeit the manor for her recusancy.[1] In about 1617 her eldest son, John, married Margaret Russell, the eldest of the three daughters of Sir Thomas Russell (d. 1632) of Strensham (Worcs.).[2] Hall noted her age as twenty-nine in his manuscript.

Margaret Russell seems to have been baptised on 27 March 1595; she had three sons, John (d. 1628), Robert (d. 1630) and George, who was born in October 1621. Hall must have attended her in 1623/4. Her husband (no. 40) had died in 1622. George succeeded and became a baronet in 1642. Although he married three times (his second wife was Mary Smith of Wootton Wawen), his children all died as infants and the title became extinct at his death in June 1658. There is a family monument in the parish church.[3] Margaret Winter died in 1629 and was buried at Huddington. The inventory of her personal possessions, made on 29 July, includes clothes valued at £30, a watch and a small striking time-piece, worth £7.[4]

Margaret Winter was treated for flux of the belly (diarrhoea), inflammation of the reins (kidneys) and scurvy. A cordial electuary and a plaster to be applied to the upper part of the stomach were prescribed. Other preparations included the scorbutic drugs and hartshorn. When the diarrhoea had abated *Pilula Ruffi* and *Pilula de Succino* (no. 1) were prescribed to counter the depraved condition of the body humours.

Hall ended by observing that the patient was cured and freed from all her symptoms. No further reference was made to the stone said to be troubling her.

124: ANNE, LADY JENKINSON OF WALCOT, NEAR CHARLBURY, OXFORDSHIRE

There is no indication whether Lady Jenkinson was treated by Hall, who clearly admired her, at her home in Walcot, some 25 miles from Stratford. Her husband, Sir Robert, was descended from Anthony Jenkinson, a distinguished diplomat, who had twice been Elizabeth I's ambassador to Russia.

Lady Jenkinson's connection with Warwickshire was as the daughter of Sir Robert Lee (*c.* 1572–1637) of Billesley, near Alcester,[5] and she may have been visiting her father when attended by Hall. Sir Robert's father was also Robert Lee (d. 1605), knighted in 1603 after a year as Lord Mayor of London; he had bought Billesley manor in 1599 for £5,000 from the

1. *VCH Worcs.*, III, p. 410.
2. *HV Worcs.*, 1634, p. 84.
3. (H)WRO, BA 4610(v).
4. HMC, *Var. Coll.*, ii, p. 299.
5. *HV Oxon.*, 1634, p. 270; *HV Warws.*, 1682–3, pp. 70–1.

diſcovery of the Scurvy. ℞ *Pil. Hier. cum Aga-ric. Ruffi.* ā ʒi. *Alephang.* ♋ii. *cum Aq. Betonie.* ſ. *Pil.* There was added *Diatartari.* ♋ii. and it made fifteen Pills. She took three of them when ſhe went to bed. In the morning ſhe took a ſmall draught of the following: ℞ *Roots of Oris, Elder bark, of Danewort, and of Capers, Ta-maris, Succory, Squich graſs, Fennel, Sparagus, Madder,* each ʒſſ. *Gentian.* ʒii. *Wormwood* M i. *Soldanella, Mugwort, Agrimony, white Horehound,* each M ſſ. *Tops of Centaury* ʒiiſſ. *the Cordial Flow-ers,* each ʒiſſ. *Calamus Aromaticus* ʒ ii. *Liquoris* ʒi. *Sena* ʒii. *Agaric.* ʒſſ. *Mechoac.* ʒiii. prepared *Steel* ʒſſ. *Cream of Tartar* ʒi. *Rubarb* ʒiii. *Ginger* ʒi. *Cinamon* ʒſſ. *Anis ſeeds* ʒii. *Infuſe them for three days in four pints of White-wine in* Bal. Mar. *well ſtopped up in a double Veſſel, after boyl them at a gentle* Fire *for an hour, the Veſſel being ſtill ſhut.* Of this when cold take ʒiv. *Syrup againſt the Scurvy by* Foreſtus ʒi. For three mornings after ſhe took the Beer againſt the Scurvy, preſcribed *Obſerv.* 7. of this Century; adding to the Ingre-dients, of *Saſſafras* ʒſſ. *Sarſaparilla* ʒii. *Betony, Agrimony, Fumatory,* each M i. Whilſt it was rea-dy, ſhe took the following: ℞ *Conſerve of Scurvy-graſs* ʒii. of *Wormwood, Diaſerios,* of *Buglosſ, Clove Gilly flowers, Damask Roſes, Elicampana root* candied, each ʒſſ. *Wood of Rhodium, Calamus Aro-maticus, Wake robbin root prepared, Spec. Diarrhod. Abbat. Diaplereſar. Confectio Alkermes,* each ʒ ſſ. with Foreſtus's *Syrup againſt the Scurvy, ſo much as will make an Electuary, cover it with a leaf of Gold.* After the taking of the quantity of a Nutmeg of this, ſhe drank of the following; ℞ *the Water*

againſt

Crown.[1] Sir Robert (II) had loaned money to Edward Conway and was one of the local gentlemen to escort his corpse from Honeybourne (Glos.), en route to Ragley in 1631.[2]

Anne Mary Lee was born in about 1600 and married Robert Jenkinson in about 1620; she had two brothers and three sisters. Their manor house at Billesley, Dugdale noted admiringly, was built as Lee's chief seat during the years of Anne Mary's childhood; her father was Sheriff in 1620. In spite of a fire at the house in 1986, the hall survives; there is also a dovecote and the remains of a village, although the old church fell into disuse and was rebuilt in 1692.[3]

Lady Jenkinson had six sons and four daughters born at Charlbury in the years 1621 to 1640. She herself had political connections of some importance, for her father's sister, Joan, was married to Sir John Coke of Melbourne, Principal Secretary for some eleven years before the Civil War. Hall may have had links with Billesley, for it was there that his daughter, the widowed Elizabeth Nash, was to marry John Barnard in 1649. Lady Jenkinson was buried at Charlbury on 9 November 1686 and her husband on 10 April 1677.

Hall treated Lady Jenkinson, suffering from scurvy, as in similar cases, with a regime of purgatives and scorbutic drugs, including a beer against scurvy and, during the time the patient was waiting for this to be prepared, she was prescribed an electuary containing scurvy grass and other drugs[4] covered 'with a leaf of gold'. This is the only example of an electuary covered with gold leaf, but Hall on more than one occasion instructed the apothecary *fiat Pil. deauro* (make gilded pills). Gold and silver were both employed as cordials, having qualities to strengthen the heart and vital spirits (no. 126).[5]

Other prescriptions were a purgative pill,[6] a mixture to be held in the mouth to relieve tooth-ache and a powder for catarrh. Hall attributed the head pains to the catarrh and wrote 'For her Catarrh there was used the following powder for the Coronal Suture'. The coronal suture extends from one temple across to the other uniting the frontal bone to the two parietal bones.

1. Dugdale, II, p. 718; *VCH Warws.*, III, p. 60.

2. *CSPD, 1631*, p. 498.

3. *VCH Warws.*, III, p. 61.

4. Other drugs in the electuary were: Rhodium wood or rosewood believed to have cordial properties, *Species Diarhodon* which contained red and white saunders wood and wake robin root, the acrid root of *Arum maculatum* also known as cuckoo pint.

5. Gold and silver leaf were used to coat pills long after these metals had been abandoned as cordials. Coatings were used to improve the appearance of the pills and mask a bitter taste.

6. *Pil. Alephang.* refers to the pills listed as *Pilulae Alephanginae sive Aromatice* in the London *Pharmacopoeia* of 1618. The formula was attributed to Mesue. Aloes was one of the many ingredients.

againft the *Scurvy* ℥iii. that *againft the Spleen* ℥ii. the *forefaid Syrup of* Foreſtus ℥iii. Doſe eight ſpoonfuls. For her Catarrh there was uſed the following Pouder for the Coronal Suture: ℞ *Maſtich, Myrrh, Amber, Cloves, Sandarac, Wood of Aloes,* red *Rofes,* each ℥i. mix them, and make a *Pouder.* As there was need ſhe was thus purged, ℞ *Pil. Ruffi. Alephang. Diatartari* ā ℈i. *Pil. Hier. cum Agaric.* ℈ii. *Aq. Antiſcorb. q. ſ. f. Pil.* N. 6. There was three given at Bed time. The fifth of *December* ſhe was cruelly tormented with the Tooth-ach, ℞ *Scurvy grafs water* ℥vi. *Red Rofe water, and of Plantain,* each ℥iii. *Honey of Rofes, Honey of Mulberry ſimple,* each ℥i. *Spirit of Vitriol fufficient to make all tart.* Of this ſhe took in her Mouth, which delivered her from the Tooth-ach, and other Symptoms. And by theſe ſhe was cured.

Observ. XXV.

BUtler of *Stratford,* from gentle motion of his Body, was much troubled with piſſing blood, which came in abundance, with Pain in the Kidneys; his Urine was ſo hot, that it very much tormented him, eſpecially about the Prepuce, which I thus cured: Firſt he drank of the Decoction of *Sarfaparilla* for eight days. After he drunk *Tormentil in Wine.* To his Back were applied Plates of Lead, full of holes, moiſtned with Vinegar; it was often changed, and ſo in
                                                                the

125: [ROBERT] BUTLER OF
STRATFORD-UPON-AVON

In John Hall's notes, the date he attended this man, 1629, was added in the margin. Fripp considered that the patient was Robert Butler, the son of an important town figure, also Robert (d. 1637), who had served as a Bailiff, churchwarden and alderman. Both father and son were glovers by trade.

However, it seems unlikely that Hall would refer to such a man only as 'Butler, op^s', as he did for other humble inhabitants. Aldermen were regarded with considerable respect in the town, and Hall noted one, who was his patient, as 'Alderman^s Tyler' (no. 162) and an alderman's daughter, Margaret Smith (no. 163), was described as such. Social distinctions were also recorded in the parish registers, with the titles 'Mr', 'Alderman' and 'gent.' regularly added to such men's names.

It seems possible that this patient was Robert Butler, described as *chir* (surgeon) in the parish register for 1606, when his son, William, was baptised on 17 November. The infant William was buried two days later. Record of the burial of Hall's patient has not been found.

The symptoms and treatments used in this case are discussed in the notes for Henry Izod (no. 121).

126: [ELIZABETH] RICHARDSON [OF SHOTTERY]

Hall noted this Catholic patient was *Generosa*, a social status that suggests she was Elizabeth, née Burman, who had married William Richardson, a yeoman of Shottery, on 8 August 1607. She was the daughter of Thomas Burman of Shottery and she had been baptised in Stratford on 5 October 1569. Her husband's father, John Richardson, had been a surety for Shakepeare's marriage-bond.[1] Neither her age nor her place of residence was given.

Her children, two sons and a daughter, were baptised in Stratford in the period 1607 to 1611. William Richardson was buried on 18 November 1624, when a serious epidemic with some seventeen deaths raged in Shottery. His widow was required to prove his will to the diocesan authorites. Including livestock, his goods were worth £153 5s. 8d.[2] However, Elizabeth did not die until twenty years later and was buried on 6 March 1646 at the age of seventy-six. She was one of only six patients that Hall noted as a Roman Catholic.

Hall gave an explicit account of Mrs Richardson's symptoms, which he treated initially with a dietary restorative including China root and

1. (H)WRO, BA 2648, B 716.093.
2. Brinkworth, p. 170; SBTRO, BRU 15/1/58.

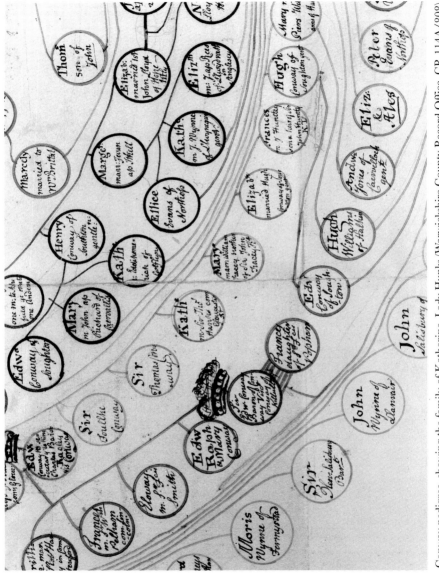

Conway pedigree, showing the family of Katherine, Lady Hunks (Warwickshire County Record Office, CR 114A/808)

the ſpace of eight days he was much amended, and after cured.

Observ. XXVI.

Mrs. *Richardſon* (a Roman Catholick) was troubled with Wind in the Womb, ſo that when ſhe went to make water, the Womb ſent forth the Wind, as if one had broke wind backward ; ſhe alſo had the Scurvy, ſwooning, Pain of the Head, over-flowing of her Courſes, alſo abundance of Whites. She was alſo troubled with much heat in her Loins, weakneſs of her whole Body, ſhe could eat well, but could not endure Phyſick or the Light. She was thus cured, Firſt ſhe had a Reſtorative made of a Leg of Veal, a Cock, Harts horn ſhaved, and *China*, ſhe took of it every morning, firſt drinking our Milk water with *Manus Chriſti perlatæ*. To ſtay the Flux was uſed the following, ℞ *Water of Milk* ℥iii. *Spawn-Frog water two ſpoonfuls*, *Manus Chriſti perlat. Confect. Alkerm.* each Ɖij. To her Back were applied Plates of Lead perforated and moiſtned in Vinegar. To the region of the Womb was applied *Emplaſt. pro Matrice*. ℞ *Harts horn burnt* Ɖi. *Confectio Alkermes* Ɖſſ. *Bezoar ſtone* gr. iii. *Scabious water* ℥ii. *Syrup of Limons* ℥ſſ. *mix them*. It was given whilſt ſhe was cold, for ſhe had an Erratic Feaver. ℞ *Snail water of my preparation, of Spawn Frog water, each* ℥iv. *Confectio Alkermes* Ɖii. *Manus Chriſti perlatæ* ℥ſſ.

℥ß. *Water againft the Scurvy* ℥vi. *againft the Spleen* ℥ii. *mix them.* This was reiterated, and to it added ℥iß of *Syrup. Lætific. Rod. à Fohfe.* By the ufe of this fhe gained ftrength very much, and faid it was as good as *Aurum potabile*, and would never be without it. And thus fhe was cured wholly.

Obser. XXVII.

Mrs. *Peerfe* of *Aufon*, (Roman Catholick) aged about 28, was vexed with a fruitlefs endeavour to vomit, Melancholy, Tumor of the Feet at night, Weaknefs of the whole Body, a Scorbutic daily Feaver, with light horror, Pain of the Spleen and of various Joints of the Body, her Urine was like clear Water. She was cured as followeth : ℞ *Elect. de Tamarind.* ℥ß. *Syr. Dyaferios* ℥i. *Oxymel. Noft.* ℥ß. *Aq. Buglofs* ℥ii. *Ol. Vitriol.* gut. vi. *Mifc.* This gave fix ftools. The following day the Urine was filthy, and fhe took the faid Potion, only there was added *Spec. Arom. Rof.* ℈i. and ℥ii taken off from the Electuary. At the hour of fleep was exhibited the follow.ng : ℞ *Bezoar.* gr. iii. *Laudanum Paracelfi* gr. ii. *Confectio Alkermes* ℈ß. She refted quietly. The next day there was given this : ℞ *Syrup of Poppies* ℥ i. *Scabious water* ℥ iß. *Bezoar.* gr. iv. *Rofewater a little, and Spirit of Vitriol fufficient.* After fhe ufed the Chalybiated Wine, prefcribed *Obferv.* 24 of this Century. To which was added, *Syrup. Schelet. Foreft.* ℞ of the *Wine* ℥vi. of the

I

Syrup

hartshorn. To stop the flux he prescribed a water containing frog spawn, the many uses of which included the treatment of whites or leucorrhoea (no. 67). External treatments involved the application of perforated plates of lead moistened in vinegar (no. 121) and *Emplastrum pro Matrice* or plaster for the womb.

Hartshorn was used to treat the fever and this was followed by a cooling, antiscorbutic restorative containing among other things the water of snails and frog-spawn. When this was repeated *Syrupus Laetificans* was added, prepared from an exotic mixture of spices, *os cordis cervi* (heart bone of a stag), pearl, musk, gold and silver leaf. Hall reported that the patient compared this remedy to *Aurum potabile*, a well-known cordial consisting of gold in a fine state of subdivision suspended in a volatile oil.

> Therefore thou [the crown] best of gold art worse than gold.
> Other, less fine in carat, is more precious,
> Preserving life in medicine potable;
>
> (2 Henry IV, IV. v. 161)

127: CLARE PEERS OF ALVESTON

Clare Peers was one of Hall's acknowledged recusant patients. Her husband, Thomas (1587–1646), was the great-grandson of Robert Peers, a Bristol merchant (d. 1550), who acquired the Alveston estate through the good offices of his brother, William, the sub-prior of Worcester. In 1576 Edmund Peers, having inherited, established himself in the county by marrying Margaret Underhill of Ettington, a family Hall was later to attend.[1]

Clare Peers was the daughter of a gentleman, Andrew Benlow. She married on 10 June 1612 and had three sons and three daughters, two of whom died as infants. Her youngest boy, Philip, became a physician and died in Maryland. In the mid-1630s both Clare and her husband were to suffer for their Catholic faith; in 1633 Thomas was fined for not attending church for over a month and two years later they were both summoned for being absent on forty Sundays.[2] Dugdale noted Thomas Peers as a royalist in 1642.[3] Clare Peers was buried at Alveston on 8 April 1636 and her husband a decade later, on 26 August 1646.

Their daughter, also Clare (baptised on 29 May 1626), was indicted for recusancy in 1647, a year after her father's death.[4] She and her sister later married into a prominent Worcestershire Catholic family, the Attwoods.

1. Dugdale, II, p. 675; *HV Warws.*, 1619, p. 233.
2. QSOB, I, p. 225; VI, pp. 15, 22, 24.
3. NRO, Finch-Hatton 4284.
4. QSOB, I, p. 78.

114　　　　*Select Observations*

Syrup ℥iv. *Water againſt the Scurvy* ℥ii. *againſt the Spleen* ℥ii. *Syr. Lætif.* ℥iii. *mix them.* ℞ *burnt Hartsborn* ℈i. *Confect. Alker.* ℈ii. *Magiſt. of Pearl, Tinct. of Coral, each* gr. vi. *Man. Chriſti perlat.* ℨſſ. *Bezoar.* gr. vi. *Conſerve of Scurvy-graſs, ſufficient. Make a ſoft Electuary, adding Spec. Plereſarchon.* By theſe ſhe was freed from her Symptoms. From her Melancholy ſhe fell into the Mother : ℞ *Caſtor* ℨi. *Fæcul. Brion.* ℈ſſ. *cum Aq. Hiſtoric. f. Pil.* Nº 5. They were given at night. To the Navil was applied *Emplaſt. è Caranna, cum Moſc.* She drew into her Noſe the Fume of *Aſſa fœtida.* By theſe ſhe was well eaſed. After ſhe was purged thus : ℞ *Pil. Ruffi. Spec. Hier. ſimpl.* ā ℈iſſ. *Caſtor* ℈i. *Fæcul. Brion.* ℈ſſ. *cum Aq. Hiſt. q. ſ. f. Pil.* 5. She took them at night. And thus ſhe was recovered.

OBSERV. XXVIII.

ALice *Collins*, Servant to my Lady *Puckering*, aged about 24, was tormented with the Mother, Obſtruction of her Courſes, and at the end of her Fit ſhe ſhed tears. Her Urine was like Spring water. For the removing of the Diſeaſe and Symptoms, I preſcribed the following : ℞ *Briony roots* ℥ſſ. *Sena* ℨſſ. *Ginger* ℨſſ. *Cinamon* ℨi. *Sugar* ℨvi. *They were infuſed for a night, in a pint and half of Whey, and in the morning boyled a little, and then ſtrained* ; *to which was added the compound Syrup of Mugwort* ℥ii. Of this ſhe drank for ſome days in a morning ℨv. hot ; by which ſhe was well purged and cured.

　　　　　　　　　　　　　　　　OBSERV.

The patient's symptoms were treated with a regime of purgatives, opiates, restoratives and scorbutics using drugs noted in earlier observations.

Hall commented that as a result of this treatment Clare Peers was freed from her symptoms but her melancholy fell into the 'Mother'. He treated the hysteria with a pill composed of castor, *Faecul. Brion.* with *Aq. Historic* [*sic*]. The *faecul.* was the deposit obtained when root of bryony was bruised in water. This was mixed with the castor and made into a pill using *Aqua Hysterica* (no. 159). The fume of asafoetida was prescribed. Asafoetida, a gum resin with an unpleasant odour, would have been included in Hall's list of 'stinking things' (no. 96).

128: ALICE COLLINS, COMPANION TO LADY PUCKERING OF WARWICK PRIORY

Although described in translation as a servant, in his Latin notes Hall recorded her as *pedisequa* or waiting-woman, clearly a higher social category. Alice was the fourth of the six children of Francis Collins; she was baptised in Stratford on 11 July 1602 and would thus have been attended by Hall in 1626.

Her father, a Warwick attorney, was William Shakespeare's legal advisor and acted for the poet when he bought land and tithes in 1605. Collins prepared Shakespeare's will in 1616 and, as its overseer, he was bequeathed £13 6s. 8d. by his client. He had also drawn up the wills of Thomas Combe in 1609 and in 1613 of William Combe, who left him £10.[1] In 1612–13 Collins was deputy Clerk of the Peace for Warwickshire.[2] He served as deputy Town Clerk of Stratford in the years 1602–8 and in April 1617 was elected as Steward to succeed Thomas Greene. However, he was buried on 27 September 1617, having made his own will only the day before.[3]

Alice Collins is not recorded in Sir Thomas Puckering's account books (1613–32), but her younger sister, Mary (b. 1607), may be the Marie Collins named as part of the Warwick Priory household.[4] On 25 May 1633 Alice Collins married Thomas Greene, junior, at St Mary's, Warwick; their son, William, was baptised there in June, 1634. The registers are faulty for the next decades, but she was buried, a widow, at St Mary's on 10 October 1656.

This was a case of a suppression of menstruation (amenorrhoea) and fits of hysteria. Hall prescribed a hot drink, which included the purgative

1. *Life*, pp. 191, 242.
2. QSOB, VI, p. xxxiv.
3. Fogg, p. 49.
4. SBTRO, DR 37/vol. 17: I am grateful to Dr Levi Fox for access to his transcription before publication.

Observ. XXIX.

HEster Sylvester, Daughter to Mrs. *Smith* (now *Marit*) of *Burford*, being grievously troubled with the Worms, was cured twice with the following Pouder : ℞ *Coraline, Worm seed, each ℨi. white Dictamny, Bistort, Tormentil, each ℥ß. make them all into a fine Pouder, which besprinkle with the sharpest Wine Vinegar, and after dry it in the shade.* Dose from ℨß to ℨiii. (but she took a drachm) according to the age of the Patient, and strength of the Disease. It is to be given either in Wine, Purslain water, or the Pulp of a rosted Apple.

Observ. XXX.

LYnes of *Stratford*, aged 53, in 1630, was troubled with a Timpany, her Belly being much swelled, so that she could scarce go, with hoarsness of her Voice, and loathing of Meat, insomuch that she was left by her Friends as hopeless, yet by God's blessing she was cured as followeth: ℞ *Roots of Oris, and Assarabacca, each ℨii. Pellitory of Spain, Elicampana, and of Brier, also the Bark of the Roots of Spurge, each ℨiii. Origanum, Calamints, each p. i. Soldanella ℥ß. Mecoachan ℨiii. Anis seeds, Bay berries, each ℥ß. boyl them altogether in B. M. in a quart of White-wine (the Vessel being well stopp'd) for four hours ; after*

being

senna, the root of bryony *Bryonia dioica*, one of the principal drugs used to treat hysteria, and mugwort *Artemesia vulgaris*, which was used for uterine obstructions and to calm hysterical spasms.

129: HESTER SYLVESTER OF BURFORD, OXFORDSHIRE

This patient was the grand-daughter of Alderman Francis Smith (died 1625), a haberdasher of Stratford, and his wife, Ursula. Their daughter, Margaret (born in 1599), whom Hall had noted as *Generosa* (no. 163), married Paul Sylvester at Stratford on 3 February 1623. Hester was their daughter, aged ten or younger when Hall attended her, possibly when she was visiting Stratford.

The Sylvester family were prominent merchants in Burford, having become wealthy from textiles;[1] they held public office in the town and five of their great tomb chests (1568–1654) can still be seen in the parish church there.[2]

Hester Sylvester, Hall's patient, married Richard Cox in Burford in 1649. No children of the marriage have been traced nor has any record of her death.

This case of worms Hall treated with a powder composed of wormseed, corallina, white dittany *Dictamus albus*, bistort or snake weed *Polygonum bistorta* and tormentil *Potentilla erecta*. Wormseed *Semen santonicum* is specific against roundworm (no. 166). Corallina was known as white wormseed. It was a white coral, the best samples being brought from the Mediterranean.

130: JOAN LYNES OF STRATFORD-UPON-AVON

This townswoman, for whom Hall noted a specific date when she was cured, 4 January 1630, can be identified as Joan, née Richardson, the wife of Humphrey Lynes, whom she married at Stratford on 16 May 1598. She therefore seems to have been the daughter of John Richardson, baptised in the town on 30 November 1575, and the mother of a son, also Humphrey.

Joan Lynes had a tympany or tympanites, a distension of the abdomen due to the presence of gas in the intestine or peritoneal cavity. The name is derived from *tympanum* (drum), as the belly of the patient sounds like a drum when struck.

Hall treated the condition with a potion, a pill and an electuary in which soldanella featured prominently. Soldanella occurs in the literature under the following names: Sea cole-wort, Scotch scurvy-grass, *Brassica marina* and

---

1. *HV Oxon.*, 1634 p. 126; W.H. Hutton, *Burford Papers* (1905), p. 20.
2. Pevsner, *Oxon.*, p. 506.

being ſtrained, it was ſweetned with Sugar. Of this was drunk ℥vi morning and evening. After eva-cuation was made with *Pil. Soldanellæ,* thus made : ℞ *the tops of Soldanella* Ɔii. *Cinamon* Ɔi. *Pil. ag-gregativa* ℨi. *Troch. Alhand.* Ɔſs. *Elaterii* gr. iv. *with the Juyce of Oris roots make Pills,* 5 *of* ℨi. There were three taken about midnight ; as there was need they were reiterated. To ſtrengthen the Stomach, and the reſt of the Bowels, was uſed the following Electuary : ℞ *the Juyce of Oris roots* ℨiij. *Galangal, Cinamon, each* ℨii. *Cloves, Mace, each* ℨi. *Zedoary* Ɔii. *Soldanella* ℨſs. *Pouder them to be poudered, and with Honey purified make an Electuary.* Doſe, the quantity of a Nutmeg. After meals I appointed the following Pouder, to free the Stomach from crudities, to gently heat it, to help Concoction, and diſcuſs Wind : ℞ *Coriander ſeeds prepared* ℨſs. *of Fennel and Anis, each* ℨii. *Carawaies* ℨi. *Cinamon* ℨii. *Roots of true Acorus, Galangal, Citron Pills dried, each* ℨi. *red Roſes* ℨſs. *Sugar, the weight of all* ; *make a Pouder.* Doſe, half a ſpoonful. Thus ſhe was cured, *Jan.* 4. 1630.

Observ. XXXI.

Mrs. *Baker* of *Stratford,* aged 38, had much pain in her Loins, and was cruelly torment-ed with a deſire to piſs, yet little Urine came, and that while ſhe was troubled with the Mother, Me-lancholy, and the Scurvy was feared. To whom the following was uſed with deſired ſucceſs : ℞

Convolvulus soldanella. It is a purgative and its root was used in the nineteenth century as a hydragogue, a drug that promoted the removal of water from the body.[1]

A carminative powder was prescribed to be taken after meals to free the stomach from 'crudities', help concoction (no. 116) and discuss or disperse wind.

131: KATHERINE BAKER OF
STRATFORD-UPON-AVON

Katherine Baker was the third wife of Alderman Daniel Baker, a woollen draper. Henley-in-Arden is often noted as his birthplace, but his name does not appear in the parish registers, although he was presumably the son of Daniel (d. 1601) and Philippa Baker and born in about 1565. He bequeathed money for a clothing charity at Henley in his will.[2] In 1586 in Stratford he married his first wife, Joan (née Taylor); she died aged thirty-four in 1600, leaving him three sons whom he outlived. His second wife, Eleanor, died with her second infant in 1605. A year later, although a leading Puritan, responsibility for a bastard was laid against him in the church court.[3] Daniel Baker moved in the community's circles of power; Thomas Greene referred to him as 'my cosen' and he figured prominently in the opposition to enclosing the common land of Welcombe, declaring himself to be one of the 'sworne men for the good of the Boroughe'.[4]

In about 1619 he married Katherine, although no record of their marriage has been found; they appear to have had no children. Not a local bride, she was, however, a gentlewoman from a prosperous family and included in her dowry were six silver spoons and a great chest. Daniel Baker made his will on 10 March 1637, four years before his death in June 1641. All Baker's land went to his grandson, but he bequeathed to Katherine, his 'well-beloved wife', furniture, household linen, utensils and twenty nobles a year, forfeit if she remarried. She also received £400 and was allowed to live in his new house for a year as a widow.[5] The date of her death has not been found.

Hall treated this urinary disorder with a purgative regime followed by a restorative electuary, which was taken for thirty days, after which she became well.[6] Among the symptoms were the 'Mother' and melancholy.

1. S.F. Gray, *A Treatise on Pharmacology* (3rd edn, 1824), p. 63.
2. PRO, Prob 11/186.
3. Brinkworth, p. 135.
4. Cooper, *Wootton Wawen*, p. 76.
5. SBTRO, BRU 15/13/26a–29.
6. In the electuary the apothecary sign to indicate the weight of *Sacch. alb.* (white sugar) to be used is missing. In the manuscript Hall made an amendment after *Sacch.alb.* and put the ounce apothecary sign in the margin. Cooke appears to have missed it.

℞ *Syr. Lætific. Rodor. à Fonſeca* ℥ii. *Diata⸱tar. ejuſdem* ℨi. *Aq. Bugloſ.* ℥ iii. *Miſc.* It gave ſix ſtools. After ℞ *Pil. Ruffi.* ℈i. *Hier. cum Agaric.* ℈i. *Pil. fætid.* ℈i. *Caſter* ℈ſ. *cum Aq. Artemiſ. f. Pil.* N° 7. *deaurent.* Theſe gave ſeven ſtools. ℞ *Lign. Saſſafr. inciſ.* ℥iſ. *Cinam. opt.* ℥i. *infund. in Aq. fontan.* ℥xiv. *per hor.* xij. *deinde bull. ad dimid. adde Sacch. alb.* ℥xii. *bul. ad conſiſt. Syr. cui adde Dianth. Conſer. Bugloſs,* ā ℥vi. *Flor. Caryoph.* ℥ſ. *Rad. Enul. Cam. condit. Zinzib. condit.* ā ℨii. *Spec. Aromat. Roſ.* gr. vii. *Confect. Alkerm.* ℥ſ. *Ambræ griſ. Moſc.* ā gr. vi. *Miſc. f. Elect.* After ſhe had taken of it fourteen days, ſhe was much better; and continuing it thirty days, ſhe became well.

Observ. XXXII.

S*Mith* of *Stratford*, aged 38, being long troubled with an immoderate Cough, and Pain of the Head, was thus cured: ℞ *Flower of Brim-ſtone* ℨii. *Roots of Elicampana, Oris,* and *Liquoris, all poudered, each* ℨi. *Honey ſufficient to make an Electuary*; *to which was added twelve drops of Oil of Sulphur, and ſo licked.* After ℞ *Orpiment* ℨi. *Yolk of an Egg, as much made a Maſs, which after it was dried, it was poudered*; *to which was added of To-bacco* ℨſ. *Coltsfoot* ℨi. *Anis ſeeds* ℈iiii. *Oil of Anis ſeed three drops.* Of this he took in a Pipe, and ſo was cured.

I 3

Hall added that scurvy was feared. A noticeable difference between this treatment and those of patients with similar symptoms is that for Katherine Baker there were none of the preparations or drugs Hall used to treat hysteria and melancholy, while the scorbutic drugs regularly prescribed to deal with scurvy are absent.

132: [MRS] SMITH OF STRATFORD-UPON-AVON

Although this Stratford patient cannot be identified, Hall's original Latin notes indicate that Smith is female, not male, as given by Cooke, as the words *curata* (cured) and *op*ᵃ (townswoman) make clear. However, she was of only modest status and nearly twenty girls named Smith were baptised at Stratford in the years 1573 to 1597. She could also, of course, be a married woman or widow, making her even more difficult to trace from the brief information in Hall's notes.

For the patient's immoderate cough Hall prescribed the electuary to be licked that he used for Henry Parker (no. 53). A fume was prescribed using orpiment or yellow arsenic sulphide (instead of the red arsenic used for Parker) mixed with egg yolk, which was then dried and powdered. Aniseed, coltsfoot and tobacco were added to the mixture, which was smoked in a pipe.

Gerard's herbal gives a long list of the medicinal virtues of tobacco and its uses. The list includes the relief of head pain.[1]

133: SUSANNA HALL OF STRATFORD-UPON-AVON

Cooke's suggestion that this patient could be the wife of the preceding case (no. 132) cannot be sustained, as he has mistranslated Smith's gender as male, when a female patient is clearly described. Hall gave a precise date for attending Susanna in 1630, when she would have been aged nearly forty-five.

This is another case of scurvy treated with a purgative bole (relatively mild on this occasion), an electuary devised by Sennert containing scorbutic herbs and ending with a restorative steeled wine, also including the scorbutic herbs.

The pain in the back and joints was treated with an ointment made with capon's grease, oil of sweet almonds and other items. A plaster *Emplastrum Oxycroceum* was applied to the back.[2]

1. Gerard, *The Herball*, Lib. 2, Chap. 90. Gerard states that tobacco was also known as Henbane of Peru.

2. The formula for *Emplastrum Oxycroceum* in the London *Pharmacopoeia* of 1618 contained saffron, pitch, turpentine, colophony, myrrh and other resinous items. It was attributed to Nicolaus Myrepsus.

Observ. XXXIII.

Wife (whether of the Author, which is most probable, or of the Man that went before, or of some other, I know not, because not mentioned) was troubled with the Scurvy, accompanied with Pain of the Loins, Corruption of the Gums, stinking Breath, Melancholy, Wind, Cardiac Passion, Laziness, difficulty of breathing, fear of the Mother, binding of the Belly, and torment there, and all of a long continuance, with restlesness and weakness. There was given this Bole : ℞ *Electuary of Tamarinds* ℥ß. *Cream of Tartar* ℥i. *mix them.* To the Back was applied *Emplast. Oxycroceum*, which freed her from pain of the Loins and Belly, *Febr. 9. 1630.* The tenth day taking cold, she had again miserable pain in her Joints, so that she could not lye in her Bed, insomuch as when any helped her, she cried out miserably ; for which I used this Ointment : ℞ *Capons greafe, Oil of sweet Almonds, of Dil. and Roses, Mucilage of the Roots of Althæa, drawn with Mallow water*, each ℥i. *mix them.* After anointing, the foresaid Plaster was applied with good success, for she was quieter all night ; but yet in the morning she was troubled with Wind. Then I gave of *Sennertus's* Electuary, which is thus framed : ℞ *the Conserve of the tops and leaves of Scurvy-grass* ℥iii. *the Flowers of Buglofs, Clove Gilly-flowers, and Damask-Roses*, each ℥ß. *the flesh of Candied Nutmegs, Citron Pills candied and cut*, each ℥i. *Honey*

of

upon English Bodies.   119

Juniper-berries Ʒiii. *Confectio Alkermes* Ʒß. *Syrup of Cinamon* Ʒvi. *Syrup of Scurvy-grass*, or that of Foreſtus, *ſufficient to make an Electuary, to which was added Oil of Sulphur, ſufficient to ſharpen it.* For the conſtipation of the Belly, was uſed this Suppoſitory, ℞ *Honey* Ʒi. *Spec. Hier. Pic.* Ɔii. *Troch. Alband.* Ɔß. *Cummin ſeed* Ʒß. *make a long Suppoſitory.* For the Cardiac Paſſion was uſed *Elect. Pleriſarchon.* Doſe Ʒ ß. faſting; yea, at any hour it was uſed, drinking the following ſteeled Wine after it: ℞ *Fumatory, Brook-lime, Water-creſſes, Scurvy-graſs, Betony, Agrimony, Harts-tongue,* each Mß. *Bark of Capparis, Aſh, Tamaris,* each Ʒß. *Roots of Elicampana, Polipody,* each Ʒiii. *Madder, Liquoris, Calamus Aromaticus, Eringoes,* each Ʒß. *yellow Sanders, red Coral, ſhavings of Ivory,* each Ʒvi. *Cloves, Mace, Cinamon, Ginger,* each Ʒiii. *Ceterach, Flowers of Broom, Roſemary, Marygolds, Epithymum,* each p.i. *Juniper berries* Ʒi. *Steel prepared according to* Crato Ʒiv. *White-wine* ℔viij. *infuſe them together at the Fire in* Bal. Mar. *for eight days at leaſt, ſtirring them twice a day; after ſtrain it three or four times, and to the ſtraining add Saffron* Ʒß. *firſt drawn out of Scurvy-graſs water, Confect. Alkermes* Ɔii. *Sugar ſufficient to ſweeten it.* Doſe is two or three ſpoonfuls in the beginning, which may be increaſed, if there be need. And by theſe ſhe was cured.

I 4   OBSERV.

Observ. XXXIV.

Mrs. *Combs*, aged about 36, being troubled
with a long confirmed Scurvy, accompanied with the like and more dreadful Symptoms,
than are in the former Observation described, was
cured as followeth: To prepare the humors, ℞ *our*
Oxymel ℥iii. *Syr. Diaserios* ℥ii. *Syr. Schelet. Forest.* ℥ii.
Water of Water-cresses ℥iii. *Dose* ℥iiij, with White-
wine for three mornings together, which gave two
or three stools a day. After I purged her thus: ℞
Pil. Hier. cum Agarick, *Alephang. Ruffi.* ā ℈ii.
Ol. Salv. Chym. gut. vii. *cum Aq. Bet. f. Pill.*
7. *Deaurat.* She took three at the hour of sleep.
Being well purged, she used that *Chalybiated Wine*,
prescribed in the former *Observation*, as also the
Electuary in the same. After was taken the *Anti-*
scorbutic Water, prescribed *Observ.* 26 of this Cen-
tury. For the Loins was used the Ointment in
Observ. 33. After which was applied *Emplast. de*
Ammoniac, Forest. For the corruption of the Gums
we used this: ℞ *Scurvy-grass water*, *Water wherein*
Iron was quenched, ā ℥vi. *Honey of Roses and Mulber-*
ries simp. ā ℥ii. *Oil of Vitriol, sufficient to make it sharp.*
With this she washed her Mouth. She drunk the
Antiscorbutic Beer, prescribed, *Observ.* 7. and 24. of
this Cent. For the Stomach was prescribed this: ℞
Spec. Diamb. Aromat. Ros. ā ℈iß. *Ol. Mastic.* ℥i. *Cer.*
fluv. ℥v. *Labdan.* ℥iii. *f. Emplast.* To the Back was
applied *Oxycroceum.* There were often used at
the hour of sleep five Pills framed of *Cyprus Tur-*
pentine,

Hall referred to his treatment of the Cardiac Passion, an ancient term for a fainting fit, where the patient became pale and cold with diminished respiration and pulse. Treatment was the administration of an electuary made from *Species Pleres Archontichon*, a strengthening preparation containing the cordials pearl, red coral and musk.

134: KATHERINE COMBE OF OLD STRATFORD

Katherine, baptised on 3 December 1595, was the only daughter and eldest child of Edward and Elizabeth Boughton of Little Lawford in north Warwickshire. A gentlewoman, she was married in June 1612 to William Combe of Old Stratford (1586–1666), a leading magistrate, parliamentary supporter and twice Sheriff of the county. Her brother, William (b. 1599), recalled that so many disputes had arisen as a result of the marriage that their father had been led to wish that Katherine had 'been buried when she went to be married',[1] for the Boughtons were firm royalists. However, divided political loyalties must have troubled other contemporary families.

She was the mother of one son and nine daughters, of whom the eldest child, Mary, was also later treated by John Hall (no. 144). Katherine was buried in Stratford on 21 June 1652 aged fifty-seven, four years before her husband, not in 1662 as noted by Dugdale in his description of Holy Trinity Church.[2] Hall was presumably attending her following the birth of Constance, who was baptised on 4 October 1632 and buried eight days later.

Katherine Combe was suffering from a 'long confirmed scurvy' exhibiting the symptoms described in observation 132. A number of the treatments prescribed in that observation were also used in this. Hall finally noted that she was 'freed [of her symptoms], and brought forth a goodly Daughter, beyond all expectation'. Elsewhere in the *Select Observations*, whenever Hall had to treat a pregnant woman or one who had recently given birth, he avoided giving purges and emetics. Early in his treatment of Katherine Combe, however, he prescribed a purgative pill and reported that she was 'well purged'.

135: DOROTHY, LADY CLARK OF BROOM COURT

Dorothy Clark was the daughter of Thomas Hobson (1544–1630) of Cambridge. A wealthy carrier and local philanthropist, he is generally credited with the origin of the phrase 'Hobson's choice'. In his will Thomas

1. Hughes, p. 39.
2. Dugdale, II, p. 686.

pentine, and *Cream* of *Tartar.* By thefe fhe was
freed, and brought forth a goodly Daughter, beyond all expectation.

Observ. XXXV.

THe Lady *Clark*, aged about 44, afflicted with
a Baftard Tertian, was cured as followeth :
I gave the following Vomit upon the coming of
the third Fit ; ℞ *Emetick Infufion* ʒ vi. It gave
eight Vomits and one Stool, and fhe had a gentle
Fit. After the heat coming on, fhe drank of the
Decoction of Harts-horn. The intermitting day
fhe had the following Clyfter : ℞ *Mallowes, Beets,
Mercury, Origanum, Calamints,* each M ß. *Seeds of
Anis and Fennel,* each ʒii. *Whole Barly* p. i. *Flowers of Chamomel and Melilot,* each p. i. *make a Decoction in water to* ʒx. *in the ftraining diffolve Diacatholicon and Diaphænicon,* each ʒi. *Spec. Hier. Picr.
Holland Pouder,* each ʒi. *make a Clyfter.* Which
purged well. Before the fit fhe took the following : ℞ *Confect. Alkermes* Ɔß. *Laudanum Paracelfi* gr. ii. *Magiftery of Pearl* gr. iii. *mix it.* After
which fhe became well.

Observ. XXXVI.

MR. *Thomas Underhil* of *Lamcot,* aged about
39, was exceedingly weakned with piffing
blood, with pain from very light motion of the
Body,

Hobson noted that he had already given Dorothy (b. 1585) and her sister, Elizabeth Parker, 'large portions whereby my estate is much less than heretofore it was' and so left her only £6 13s. 4d. as a 'Fatherly remembrance and token of my love'.[1] Dorothy's first husband had been William Hay, who bought the manor of Guilden Morden (Cambs.) and who died in February 1617.[2]

Dorothy married as her second husband the widower, Sir Simon Clark (no. 140), within the year. Both her marriages were childless. However, in Warwickshire she had five step-children to care for and Broom Court, a large family home, to administer, sometimes in straitened circumstances. Hall must have attended her in about 1629.

At his death in 1652 Sir Simon bequeathed the manor of Newbold Revel to her.[3] Dorothy Clark continued to live at Broom and four years later was accused at Warwickshire Quarter Sessions of locking a gate and preventing access to the Evesham–Stratford road.[4] She died on 8 November 1669 at the great age of eighty-four; a monument in Salford Priors church commemorates both her and the first Lady Clark.[5]

In the case of Lady Clark, Hall diagnosed a bastard tertian fever also known as a 'counterfeit tertian' and a 'false third day ague'. Wirsung believed this fever to involve phlegm as well as the choler that characterised a true tertian. In this fever the fits were sometimes longer than in the true tertian but the paroxysms not so vehement and it 'heateth not the body so greatly'.[6]

Hall prescribed the emetic infusion he favoured in other cases of tertian fever. On the intermitting day, when the patient was free from a fever fit, a purgative clyster or enema was prescribed. An opiate preparation was to be given just before the onset of a fit. This was composed of laudanum, pearl and *Confectio Alkermes*, made from the juice of kermes grains[7] mixed with sugar and rose water and including a number of the more exotic remedies, such as lapis lazuli, gold leaf, pearl, musk and ambergris.[8]

1. Downing College, Cambridge; I am grateful to the Master and Fellows of Downing College for access and to Mrs O.J. Miller for her help with Hobson material.

2. *VCH Cambs.*, VIII, p. 99.

3. *VCH Warws.*, VI, p. 175.

4. QSOB, II, p. 120.

5. Dugdale, II, p. 865.

6. Wirsung, *Praxis Medicinae Universalis*, p. 637.

7. The kermes grain is the nidus of an insect found adhering to the branches of the scarlet oak in Spain, Italy and the southern parts of France. The grains are reddish-brown in colour and about the size of a pea. The juice has a pleasant smell and pungent taste. It was employed as a corroborant and a cordial.

8. The formula in the London *Pharmacopoeia* of 1618 was attributed to Mesue.

Body, as alſo heat of the Urine, who was cured as
followeth : Ҥ *Maſſ. Pil. de Tereb. cum Rhab. Craton.*
ʒii. *form. Pil.* vi. *of a drachm.* Three were given
in the morning rolled in the Pouder of Liquoris,
in a ſpoonful of ſome Syrup of *Althæa.* Theſe taken, Ҥ *Troch. Alkekengi cum Opio* ʒſs. *Rad. conſolid.*
Terebint. coction. indurat. ā ʒi. *Sacch.* ʒiſs. *cum infuſ.*
Gum. Tragac. Aq. Malv. f. Tab. pond. Ɉii. Take one
morning and night. Ҥ *Tereb. Limpid.* ʒſs. *diſſol.*
cum Vitel. Ovi, ut artis eſt ; adde Mel. ʒi. *Sacch.*
Roſ. ʒii. *Vin. generoſ.* ʒvi. *Miſc.* Of this was
drank ʒi every morning, which gave three or four
ſtools, at night he took the *Troches.* He wore at
his back a Plate of Lead perforated, and moiſtned
in Vinegar, both night and day, and by theſe he
was cured.

OBSERV. XXXVII.

KAtherine *Sturley* of *Stratford*, aged 44, being
fat and corpulent, caſt out altogether bloody
Urine without any pain of the Loins, or Neck of
the Bladder, yea, there was little ſenſe in its
coming away, was thus cured : Ҥ *Liquoris ſhaved*
ʒvi. *French Barley* p. i. *Jujubes, five leaves of Wa-*
ter-Lillies, Violets, Roſes, each p. i. *Seeds of Pur-*
ſlain, and Sorrel, alſo four greater cold Seeds, each
ʒi. *Roots of Succory* ʒi. *Endive, Sorrel, Plantain,*
Fumitory, each Mi. *Boyl them in Cicer-broth, with*
water to ℔i. *after ſtrain them ; to which add Sugar-*
candy ʒii. *and make an Apozeme.* Of which give
the third part at a time faſting, it was taken for
eight

136: THOMAS UNDERHILL (II) OF LAMBCOTE IN ETTINGTON

Thomas Underhill (II) must have been attended by Hall in 1629. He inherited on the death of his father, Thomas (I), in 1622 as the second son, for his elder brother, Richard, had died in 1608 at the age of twenty-two. His son, Thomas (III), was also treated by Hall (no. 69). On 9 October 1616 Thomas Underhill had married a twenty-year-old Gloucestershire woman, Elizabeth, the daughter of Richard Daston of Dumbleton; they had two sons and two daughters, of whom Anne died young in 1649.[1]

As lord of the manor of Loxley in 1632 Thomas Underhill agreed to bear the cost of providing a house in the village for a poor man, Robert Slater, his wife and two children.[2] Underhill sold the manor of Pillerton Hersey in 1637 and later disposed of Loxley to Sir Simon Clark (no. 140) of Broom Court.[3]

In 1650 he inherited a house in Oxhill from his uncle, George Underhill (no. 112), and moved there, where he died in 1669 at the age of seventy-nine. He and his wife, who died in August 1667, were both buried in St Laurence's Church, Oxhill.[4] The symptoms and treatments used in this case are discussed in the notes for Henry Izod (no. 121).

137: KATHERINE STURLEY OF STRATFORD-UPON-AVON

Katherine Sturley was the eldest daughter of a prominent Stratford citizen. Abraham Sturley came from Worcester and attended Queens' College, Cambridge, until 1569. Before settling in Stratford he served Sir Thomas Lucy of Charlecote on his Bedfordshire estate at Pavenham and may thus have known John Hall's family.[5] John Hall bought a close near Evesham from Abraham Sturley in 1612. Sturley was a churchwarden at Holy Trinity in 1589 and a bailiff six years later.[6] Hall noted her as *opidana*, or townswoman.

In 1575 Sturley had married Anne, the daughter of Alderman Richard Hill, and Katherine was baptised at Stratford on 19 September 1585. The Sturley family connections included Richard Quiney, who was Abraham's brother-in-law. Katherine presumably grew up in the fine house in Wood

1. Morrison, *The Underhills*, pp. 140–1.
2. QSOB, I, p. 143.
3. *VCH Warws.*, V, p. 134.
4. Morrison, *The Underhills*, p. 141.
5. Fripp, *Quiney*, p. 37.
6. Brinkworth, pp. 26, 123.

eight days. To ftrengthen the Kidneys I appointed this Electuary, ℞ *Harts-born prepared,*
red Coral prepared, each ʒi. *Old Sugar of Rofes,*
Marmalad of Quinces, each ℥ iß. *Syrup of dried*
Rofes, *fufficient to make an Electuary.* Of which
was taken ℥ß two hours before meat daily, twice
a day. By thefe fhe was cured. Firft I applied
the following: ℞ *Sanicle, Ladies mantle, Golden*
rod, Sen-green, Betony, Agrimony, each M i. *Althæa,*
M ii. *Fearn, Flowers of Chamomel, St. Johns-wort,*
Mugwort, Bryers, Origanum, Tormentil leaves and
roots, each M i. *They are all to be in three Bags of*
half a yard long a-piece, being equally laid and bafted,
after they are to be boiled in the Fæces of red Wine,
and applied to the Loins, the Patient lying upon her
Belly. Thefe were ufed one after another, till
the Flux of blood was ftayed.

Observ. XXXVIII.

THe Lady *Hunks,* aged *69,* cruelly vexed with
a continual burning Feaver, with torment of
the Side, and pain of the Stomach, as alfo with
binding of the Belly for eight days; the Urine was
confufed, and there was great danger of death,
yet fhe was recovered as followeth : ℞ *Mallowes,*
Althæa, Mercury, each M i. *make a Decoction in*
Water, of which ℞ ℥ xii. *Diaphænic. Diacathol.*
ā ℥i. *Pul. Sanct.* ʒi. *make a Clyfter.* This gave
her two ftools. After we gave our Antifcorbutic
Julep. To the pained Side, the following: ℞
Unguent. Dialth. ℥ii. *Ol. Amygd. dulc.* ā ℥ß. *diffol.*
&

Street that her father built after the 1594 town fire.[1] Abraham Sturley was buried on 25 August 1614.

Hall treated the obese and unmarried Katherine Sturley in 1629. Records of neither her marriage nor her death have been found in the Stratford register.

Katherine Sturley was passing blood in her urine. There was no pain in the loins or in the region of the bladder and Hall was unable to assign a cause for the bleeding.

Treatment began with a poultice to the loins made from herbs packed in a bag and heated in the faeces (lees or dregs) of red wine. Included in the drugs used for the poultice were sanicle *Sanicula Europea*, a herb believed to stay a flux of blood in the urine, and goldenrod *Solidago virgaurea* used to treat nephritic disorders.

An *apozeme* or decoction was prescribed. It included sorrel *Rumex acetosa* recommended to stay a flux of blood. Also included were the four greater cold seeds *Quatuor semina frigida maiora*, which were the seeds of cucumber, gourd, melon and pumpkin.[2] An electuary with hartshorn and coral was prescribed to strengthen the kidneys.

138: KATHERINE, LADY HUNKS OF ARROW

Lady Hunks was Katherine, wife of Sir Thomas Hunks and eldest of the four daughters of Sir John Conway of Ragley (d. 1603) and Eleanor (d. 1588), the daughter of Sir Fulke Greville. Although long-established in north Wales, the Conways became Warwickshire landowners when Sir Edward (d. 1546) gained a large estate at Arrow by marriage.[3] Katherine Conway was born in about 1565, and around 1587 married Thomas Hunks, a professional soldier whose family came from Preston-on-Stour and Radbrook on the Gloucestershire border.[4] Hunks had served in Ireland with his brother-in-law, Fulke Conway, from 1599 and he was knighted there in 1605.[5]

As Secretary of State to James I, Sir Edward Conway (1573–1631), Lady Hunks's younger brother, was an important political figure and she was often mentioned in his substantial correspondence. When Conway died, in February 1631, his corpse lay in a lower room set aside for the purpose in her house at Arrow, adjacent to the church.[6]

Katherine Hunks had ten children. Of these, Conway was buried as an

1. *VCH Warws.*, III, pp. 230, 249.
2. The four lesser cold seeds *Quatuor semina frigida minora* were the seeds of endive, lettuce, purslane and succory.
3. *VCH Warws.*, III, pp. 28, 9.
4. WCRO, CR 114A/808.
5. Shaw, II, p. 139.
6. *CSPD, 1629–31*, p. 498.

& misc. ad ignem. With this was the pained Side anointed; after which was applied a double Linnen Cloth, anointed with Butter, by which the Pain remitted. The next day was taken of the former Decoction ℔ß. the *Emetick Infusion* ʒii. *make a Clyster.* Which injected, gave three stools. For expectoration, ℞ *the Magistral Syrup of Scabious* ʒi. *Loboch of Currants by* Quercetan ʒii. *f. Linct.* Which was taken with a Liquoris stick. The Diet was moistning. The Drink was this: ℞ *French Barly* ʒiii. *Roses, Violets,* each p. i. *shaved Liquoris* ʒiii. *Raisins* ʒii. *Figs three,* 'Sugarcandy ʒii. *boyl them in two gallons of Water to the consumption of a third part*; and drink the strained Liquor. Thus the Fever ended, Thirst remitted, Appetite was restored, she was freed from difficulty of breathing, and she slept well, and all this beyond all expectation within fourteen days: praise to God alone.

Observ. XXXIX.

BAronet *Puckering*, aged about 38, very learned, much given to study, of a rare and lean Constitution, yet withal phlegmatick, was troubled with a *Vertigo*, and after Meat with sudden dejection of strength; sometimes there was present pain of the Head, and darkness of Sight; his Appetite was mean, his Urine well-coloured, but spumous. There were other Accidents from consent, by reason of the fault of Concoction, therefore first Concoction was helped; secondly the Head
and

infant in 1597 at Arrow and in 1601 Hercules was baptised at Stratford; he still owned a house there in Church Street in 1634.[1] In about 1608 her daughter, Eleanor, married Dr John Archbold (1579–1623), a Worcester cleric who had been chaplain to James I and whose younger brother, Thomas, served Lord Conway.[2] When Eleanor was left an impoverished widow with ten children to support, Lady Hunks actively pressed Bishop Thornborough and Secretary Conway to dispose of two Worcestershire livings in Eleanor's favour.[3] Lady Hunks had her grand-daughter, Catherine Archbold, at Arrow as a companion until Catherine's death in 1635.[4] Lady Hunks had five surviving adult sons, all soldiers, Fulke, Henry, Francis, Hercules and Thomas, and two other daughters, Elizabeth and Mary, alive in 1654 when there was an acrimonious dispute over her will.[5] As early as 1634 Viscount Conway had written that he would continue to support his aunt, Lady Hunks, but have nothing to do with her son.[6] This must have been Hercules, later quartered in Stratford as a colonel in the parliamentary army and who, associated with the regicides, received Monkstown Castle, County Cork, as a reward.[7]

Lady Hunks, widowed by early 1631, received a £50 annuity from her brother and later from her nephew, even though he was 'in great want of money'.[8] However, she had been unwell, and on 10 May 1630 Foulke Reed, the agent, wrote from Ragley that she had 'been ill of a fever' but was recovering.[9] This could have been the eight-day 'continual burning fever' of which Hall cured her. On 13 June 1634 she made her first will. In this she left £500 and her papers to her son, Henry, her executor, although six years later she made a second will, not altering the bequest but with Viscount Conway as executor. She referred in this second will to her 'smale and meane estate' and moveable goods 'nothing worth the naming'.[10] As well as the one large bequest and the discharge of family debts, other legacies included her 'Turkois ring' (worth £6), but most were below £5, except £20 to her servant, Sara Goodman. She left 40s. to her grand-daughter, Elizabeth Archbold, if still serving Lady Brooke; in the years 1654 to 1657 Elizabeth Archbold was still receiving an annuity of £1 5s. in the Warwick Castle accounts.[11]

1. SBTRO, BRU 8/5/23.
2. *VCH Worcs.*, II, pp. 58–9.
3. *CSPD, 1623–25*, pp. 130–2, 214, 233, 240, 362.
4. (H)WRO, class 008.7 1634/3.
5. *CSPD, 1654*, p. 37.
6. Ibid., *1634*, p. 148.
7. Brian de Breffny and Rosemary ffolliott, *The Houses of Ireland* (1984), pp. 47–8.
8. WCRO, CR 114A/769.
9. *CSPD, 1629–31*, p. 254.
10. PRO, Prob 11/197.
11. WCRO, CR 1886/4771–4777.

and Nerves were ftrengthned, and their offending caufe removed. But firft of all, the firft ways were gently emptied with ℥ i ß of *Manna diffolved in Broth, altered with Agrimony and Succory, roots and all.* After he was purged thus : ℞ *Pil. de Pæoni.* ℥i. *de Succin. Ruffi.* ã ℈i. *Cephalic. Fern.* ℈ii. *cum Aq. Betonic. f. Pil.* 15. He took three at the hour of fleep, and had three ftools in the morning. Thefe ended, he took the Carminative Pouder prefcribed *Obferv.* 12. of this Century. After meals, adding to it *Diamofch. dulc.* ℈i. I appointed the following Capital Roll : *Spec. Diamofc. dulc.* ℥i. *Ol. Nuc. Mofch. per expr.* ℈i. *Ol. Succin. alb. gut.* iii. *Ambr. grif.* gr. iv. *Sacch. in Aq. Lavend. diffol.* ℥iv. *f. Confect. in Rotul.* Of which he took two or three fafting, by which he fcund much eafe. After he had the Leeches, and fo became well. For prefervation, in the Fall, he ufed the following : ℞ *Roots of Fennel and Parfly, each* ℥i. *of Butcher-broom and Sparagus, each* ℥iß. *Calamus Aromaticus* ℥ii. *Agrimony, Betony, Maidenhair, each* M ß. *Roots of Elicampana* ℥ii. *Raifins of the Sun ftoned, each* M i. *Liquoris* ℥i. *Flowers of Broom and Rofemary, each* p. i. *Seeds of Anis and fweet Fennel, each* ℥ii: *make a Decoction, in which was infufed Sena* ℥iß. *Rubarb* ℥ii. *Cinamon* ℈ii. *in Embers for a night ; in the morning being ftrained, there was added Syrup of Succory, with Rubarb* ℥iiß. *Syrup Auguft.* ℥i. *Oil of Vitriol fufficient to make it fharp.* It was divided into two equal parts ; the firft Dofe gave four Stools, the other feven. The Humor thus prepared, he took the forefaid prefcribed Pills, three at night, and two in the morning, which gave five Stools. When thefe were
ended

In 1632 Lady Hunks was about to sail for Ireland to join Viscount Conway. Her house at Arrow, inherited from her brother, was let, although she retained an orchard there. She was reported as being well at Lisburn, near Belfast, in September 1634. Letters of 11 March 1636 and 14 April 1637 appear to be written by her.[1] Her son, Henry, secured probate of her will on 7 July 1646, when she was said to be of Lisnagarvey, Antrim, but to have died in Worcestershire.[2] She must then have been aged about eighty-five. It seems feasible that she was visiting her Archbold relations in the county, but burial registers and transcripts have gaps for the relevant parishes for the crucial period, Harvington (gap for 1633–60), St Michael, Bedwardine and St John, Worcester (both 1642–65).

For her fever, stomach pains and constipation Hall prescribed a regime of treatment that relieved her 'beyond all expectation' within fourteen days. The elderly patient was greatly weakened by the fever and it was presumably for this reason that the purgative medicines were all administered by enema.

139: SIR THOMAS PUCKERING OF WARWICK PRIORY

Hall attended Sir Thomas twice, in 1629 and in 1635 (no. 161). Puckering lived at the Priory in Warwick, an estate acquired by his father, Sir John, in 1582. Thomas had inherited land in six counties at the death of his father, an eminent lawyer who had been Queen Elizabeth I's Lord Keeper. Puckering entered the Middle Temple in August 1605.[3] Thomas, the youngest son, was aged only four when his father died in 1596. He spent two years as a young man travelling in Europe, and for four years was a companion of Henry, Prince of Wales. Returning to England in 1611, he was made a baronet that year and was knighted in 1612. After an unseemly dispute with Warwick Corporation because of his 'natural malignancy' and lack of 'noble hospitality', he became MP for Tamworth. He served as High Sheriff for Warwickshire in 1625.[4]

Puckering added a new range to the Priory in 1620 and in 1630 established a charity to provide for the poor of Warwick.[5] His household accounts for the years 1613 to 1632 show that he had also received quite extensive medical attention when he was in London, where he was treated by the distinguished physician, Sir Theodore Mayerne, and attended by

1. *CSPD, 1635–6*, p. 289; *1625–49 Add.*, p. 555.
2. PRO, Prob 11/222.
3. *RAMT*, p. 84.
4. Hughes, pp. 33, 36.
5. *Worthies*, pp. 589–92.

ended, he took the Carminative Pouder, adding *Pul. Diamosc. dulc.* ℈i. *Confect. Alkerm.* ℈ii. In the morning he used the aforesaid *Rotula's*, to which was added *Confectio Alkerm.* By which means he was perfectly cured.

OBSERV. XL.

BAronet *Clark* of *Broom-court*, aged about 57, being troubled with a burning Tertian, with pain of the Stomach and Head, his Urine was red. Being called, I cured him in three days, as followeth: ℞ *Emetick Infusion* ℥ ß. *Oxymel nostr.* ℥ iv. This gave five Vomits and eight Stools, by which all was well remitted, and he enclined to health. The following day I gave the Decoction of Harts-horn, which he took often in a day, which he much extolled. This administred for three days, with a convenient Diet, he became very well.

OBSERV. XLI.

THe Lord of *Northampton*, aged about 29, was vexed with a desperate Squinsy, insomuch that he could scarce draw his breath, could not swallow, from his Mouth flowed abundance of viscid humidities. He would not admit of bleeding, although pressed unto it. Therefore I thus purged him: ℞ *Sena* ℥i. *Rubarb* ℥iii. *Agarick*

his apothecary, Mr Depleurs. At one point there were daily visits from Sir Theodore and Mr Pridgeon, a young physician, stayed with Sir Thomas for three nights.[1] Puckering's local friends included Anthony Stoughton of St John's, Warwick, whom he supported politically, and the puritan Thomas Dugard of Barford.[2] Sir Simon Archer, his executor and brother-in-law, noted in his diary that Puckering died on 20 March 1637 at the house of his brother-in-law, Sir William Morley, in Halnaker, near Chichester.[3]

In this observation Hall recorded the constitution and humoral temperament of the patient, something that he must have observed in all his cases. Puckering was described as a learned man 'of a rare and lean constitution, yet withal phlegmatick'. A lean constitution was an attribute more of a melancholic than a phlegmatic person.

The patient was troubled with vertigo and lassitude after meals, accompanied by pains in the head. 'There were other Accidents from consent,[4] by reason of the fault of concoction [digestion]'. This fault in the digestion was the cause of the other symptoms and Hall's therapeutic objective was to help the 'first concoction' and then strengthen the head and nerves. Hall was referring to the first concoction which takes place in the stomach.[5] A gentle purge to empty the 'first ways' was followed by a pill containing cephalic drugs (no. 23). A carminative powder was prescribed and a capital roll, composed of drugs for the treatment of the head, made into a confection and shaped into a rotula, which resembled a pastille in shape. These medicines were followed by the application of leeches.

An additional regime was prescribed for the preservation of health. A purgative decoction was administered to prepare the humour after which he took the cephalic pills, the carminative powder and the rotulae.

140: SIR SIMON CLARK OF BROOM COURT

Sir Simon Clark's fame rests on his antiquarian interests and scholarly correspondence with other like-minded contemporaries, including Sir Simon Archer and Sir William Dugdale.[6] He was born in 1579 and must have been younger than Hall's estimate because Hall died in 1635. His

1. SBTRO, DR 37/Box 105.
2. Hughes, p. 36.
3. SBTRO, DR 37/vol. 28.
4. The meaning of 'consent' is given in Observation 29.
5. 'Alterations are made in the blood vessels which may be called the second concoction, and in the nerves, fibres and minutest vessels, not improperly called the third, and last concoction' (Quincy, *Lexicon Physico-Medicum*, p. 223).
6. Philip Styles, 'Sir Simon Archer', in *Studies in Seventeenth Century West Midlands History* (Kineton, 1978), pp. 1–41.

Spencer Compton, second Earl of Northampton, by Cornelius Johnson
(by kind permission of the Marquess of Northampton)

family originated in Kent, where his maternal grandfather had created a house from the deserted buildings of St Radegund's Abbey. In 1604 Simon Clark was fortunate enough to marry a Warwickshire heiress, Margaret Alderford, whose father, John, had built new ranges to extend Salford Priors Hall in 1602. Margaret Clark died in 1617, having borne a daughter and six sons, of whom Thomas was buried on the same day as his mother.[1]

Simon Clark was created a baronet in 1617, when he bought the manors of Bidford and Broom. A year later he built Broom Court, a mile north-west of Bidford-on-Avon, on a moated site. A large house, with fourteen hearths in 1663, it was demolished in the eighteenth century and only a porch survives; there is now a farmhouse on the site.[2] Sir Simon also owned two manors, Loxley and Newbold Revel.[3] He enlarged the parish church at Salford Priors in 1633 and, during his lifetime, had his own stone coffin carved in readiness for his death. In 1633 he served as Sheriff, a less prestigious appointment than that of a magistrate, but avoided a second term five years later. He had considerable antiquarian interests and among his collection of manuscripts was the great cartulary of Kenilworth Priory.[4]

A firm royalist, by 1646 Sir Simon was ready to submit to Parliament, but was nevertheless still fined £800; the Civil War left him with debts of £1,500, three times his annual income. The Clarks were so impoverished that by 1682, at the Heralds' Visitation, Sir Simon's grandson asked to be excused paying fees, as 'our family have been great sufferers in His Majesty's father's service'; in fact, much of their estate was mortgaged before war broke out.[5]

A widower at thirty-eight, with a family of young children all under fourteen, Sir Simon had remarried by 1618 (no. 135). He obtained a pass to travel abroad in 1620. He died at Broom Court on 15 January 1652, his death noted in Dugdale's diary;[6] James Cooke was one of the witnesses to his will. Sir Simon was buried at Salford Priors, his best epitaph Dugdale's opinion, that he had 'found none more knowing in, and forward to encourage' the history of Warwickshire.[7]

Hall's emetic infusion with oxymel was one of his standard treatments for a tertian fever and he regularly prescribed decoction of hartshorn in cases of fever.

1. *HV Warws.*, 1619, p. 200.
2. Geoffrey Tyack, *Warwickshire Country Houses* (1994), p. 232.
3. *VCH Warws.*, III, pp. 50–1, 56, 99, 132, 155–6, 159, 161, 164.
4. Styles, 'Archer', p. 31.
5. Hughes, pp. 31, 268.
6. Hamper, p. 98.
7. Ibid., p. 9.

rick ℥ii. *Cinamon* ℥ß. *Seeds of Anis and Fennel,*
each ℥i. *Calamus Aromaticus* ℥ ß. *Liquoris* ℥iii
they were infused for twelve hours in ℔iij of *Water,*
after boiled at a gentle Fire, till a third part was wasted ; to the straining was added *Syrup of Succory, Ru-*
barb, Diaferios, each ℥i. Of this, being at hand,
I took ℥iv. *Syr. Diaferios,* and *Succory* with *Rubarb,*
each ℨvi. *mix them.* Much ado he had to swallow
it, it gave him six stinking stools. This being
reiterated, gave eight stools. For the first day I
prescribed this Gargarism : ℞ *Honey of Mul-*
berries simple, *Honey of Roses,* each ℥ii. *Waters of*
Plantain, Barly, and *Honey-suckles,* each ℥iv. *Spi-*
rit *of Vitriol* and *Sulphur,* sufficient to make it sharp.
Some of this was kept hot in the Mouth as long
as he could, wasting all the parts by moving of
it gently in the Mouth. Outwardly was applied
a Cataplasm of green *Wormwood* and *Hogs grease,*
morning and night, with happy success. That
night being restless, he sent for Dr. *Clayton* from
Oxford, yet would not be let blood, who prescribed the following Cataplasm , which delivered
him from pain and danger ; ℞ *Swallows nests,*
straw, dirt, dung and all, N. ii. they were boiled
in *Oil of Chamomel* and *Lillies,* afterward they were
beaten, and passed through a *Sive* ; to which was added
white *Dogs turd* ℥i. the Meal of *Linseed* and *Fenu-*
greek, each ℥i. *Unguent. Dialthæa,* and *Hens grease,*
each ℥ß. and so make a *Pultess.* It was applied hot.
There was used a Fume of *Amber,* and at bed-
time was held in his Mouth one of the following
Troches : ℞ the *Juyce of Liquoris,* white *Sugar,*
each ℥i. seeds of *Purslain, Cucumbers, Melons, Gourds*
cleansed, ā ℈i. *Starch, Trag.* ā ℨß. *Penid.* ℈iv. *f. Troch.*

For

141: SPENCER COMPTON,
SECOND EARL OF NORTHAMPTON

The eldest son of William Compton, who had been created an earl in 1618, Spencer was born on 5 May 1601 and inherited when he was twenty-nine. However, family finances obliged Spencer to mortgage his Middlesex and Somerset estates in 1633 and by the outbreak of war his debts approached £50,000. He was acknowledged as heading the county's court interests. Queen Elizabeth I was his god-mother, and as a young man he was a great favourite of Prince Charles, who later, when crowned, made Spencer his Master of the Robes. Spencer followed the king to York in 1642 and was impeached by Parliament for refusing to return. He was appointed Commissioner of Array for Warwickshire, but lacked the support of the trained bands or their captains.[1]

King James was a guest when Spencer married Mary Beaumont (no. 149) in October 1621.[2] They had six sons and two daughters. Spencer and three of his sons fought at Edgehill. He was killed on 19 March 1643 at the battle of Hopton Heath (Derbys.) and interred in All Saints, Derby, 'in the vault with the old Countess of Shrewsbury', as Dugdale recorded.[3] He was described in his own time as a 'perfect cavalier, brave, generous, faithful to death to his King, and of remarkable talents' (illustrated, p. 252). Hall must have treated Spencer in 1630 and again in 1633 (no. 182).

Lord Northampton had quinsy. In a similar case Hall had bled the patient from veins under the tongue (no. 104) but Northampton refused to be bled 'although pressed unto it'. Hall responded with a vigorous purgative medicine repeated. A gargle and a poultice were applied 'with happy success'.

The success was short-lived and the patient sent for Dr Clayton, whose recommendation to bleed was again refused. Clayton applied a poultice, arranged for the vapour of burning amber to be inhaled and prescribed lozenges. Dr Thomas Clayton (1575–1647) was a distinguished Oxford physician, prominent in the new philosophical approach to medicine.[4] Clayton was paid a fee of 10s. in 1634.[5]

There is some contrast between the poultice prescribed by Hall, which consisted simply of green wormwood in hog's grease, and that prescribed by Clayton, which illustrates some of the excesses of seventeenth-century *materia medica*. Included in the formula for this poultice were two swallows' nests 'straw, dirt, dung and all' and white dog's turd. One cannot be certain

1. Hughes, p. 60.
2. Chamberlain, II, p. 402.
3. Dugdale, I, p. 549.
4. Harold J. Cook, *The Decline of the Old Medical Regime in Stuart London* (Ithaca, New York, 1986), p. 10.
5. WCRO, DR 556/274.

128 *Select Observations*

For his Wife and others troubled with the Squin-fy, I prepared thefe following : ℞ *Seeds of white Poppies* ℈ii. *Gum Tragacanth and Arabick,, each* ʒß. *Seeds of Purflain, Melons, Cucumbers and Gourds, each* ʒß, *Juyce of Liquoris* ʒi. *Sugar of Rofes and Penidies, each* ʒii. *with Syrup of Poppies make Troches.* But he contented himfelf with the for-mer. After the application of the Cataplafm he had this Gargarifm ; ℞ *Plantain water* ℔iß. *Scabious water* ʒiv. *red Rofes* ʒi. *Pomegranate Pills* ʒß. *after they were gently boiled and ftrained there was added Syrup of Mulberries, and Honey of Rofes each* ʒii. This he wafhed his Mouth withal of-ten in a day, and taking after half a fpoontul of the following ; ℞ *Syrups of Liquoris and Maiden-hair, each* ʒß. *Diatrag.frig.* ʒiß. *Syrup of Mulberries and Poppies* ā ʒß. *mix them, and make a Licking.* For ordinary drink he took this ; ℞ *Seeds of Anis, Figs, Raifins of the Sun, and Liquoris boyled in* ℔iv *of water, till a pint be wafted.* By thefe all the Tumors were removed, and he cured.

Observ. XLII.

Mrs. *Stockpn,* Servant to Mrs. *Sheldon* of *Wefton,* aged about 44, was grievoufly afflict-ed with the Jaundice, accompanied with Pain and Torment on the right Side, being in danger of Death, was thus cured : ℞ *Electuary of the Juyce of Rofes* ʒii. *Diacatholicon* ʒiß. *Diaphænicon* ʒiiß. *Rubarb* ℈i. *Spike* gr. v. *Syrup of Succory with Rubarb* ʒß. *Succory water* ʒiii. *make a Potion.* This gave

if the reference to swallows' nest with 'straw, dirt and dung' was the form of Clayton's prescription or Hall's critical comment. Swallows' nests *Nidus Hirundinum*, which were listed in the London *Pharmacopoeia* of 1618, were used for the mucous humour secreted by the birds when building the nest. After treatment they were applied externally for quinsy. Dried excrement of the dog, known under the name of *Album Graecum*, was one of the disgusting excremental items of the contemporary *Pharmacopoeia*. It had its origin in Greek medicine and Dioscorides recommended it to be taken in wine to bind the belly and, when tempered with honey, applied to the throat to treat quinsy.[1]

The observation ends with a prescription by Hall for lozenges for Lady Northampton, who was also troubled with quinsy, with a gargle, a lick and a drink for Lord Northampton.

142: ELIZABETH STOKER, COMPANION TO ELIZABETH SHELDON OF WESTON

The true status of this patient, noted by Hall as *Generosa*, and *pedisequa* (companion), was certainly far above that of 'servant'. She lived at Weston Hall, near Cherington, a magnificent house set in 300 acres of parkland, newly built by Ralph Sheldon of Beoley (Worcs.) in 1588–9. The Sheldons' wealth had been founded on a fortunate marriage and enhanced by tapestry manufacture. The house, one of the largest in Warwickshire, was demolished in 1934 (illustrated, p. 258).[2]

Elizabeth Stoker acted as companion to William Sheldon's wife, Elizabeth (1592–1656), after their marriage in 1611. She must have been a woman of means, because in 1680 Ralph, 'the Great Sheldon', recorded that he held £100 remaining in his hands as executor of Mrs Elizabeth Stoker. This was to be paid to the convent of English Benedictines at Douai after the death of his brother, Edward, a priest there, who received the interest during his lifetime.[3]

Hall directed that this patient should be bled and purged in order to restore and adjust the humours. After this he prescribed a jelly made from worms and containing hartshorn and saffron, one of the drugs used for the treatment of jaundice. Another was celandine *Chelidonium majus*, which was given in broth and in the sudorific or sweating potion. Celandine was recommended in cases of jaundice when not attended by inflammatory symptoms.

Two electuaries were prescribed, the first taken during the course of the treatment and the second on completion. Both contained the corroborant

1. Gunter, *Greek Herbal*, p. 123.
2. M. Warriner, *A Prospect of Weston* (1978), pp. 9–23.
3. Barnard, *The Sheldons*, p. 65.

The South-east Prospect of WESTON in Warwickshire, The Seat of Edward Sheldon.

Weston House, the Sheldon family home, by Henry Beighton, 1716
(from William Dugdale, *Antiquities of Warwickshire*, 1730)

upon English Bodies. 129

gave two ftools. She was (all the time of her Jaundice) miferably afflicted with binding of the Belly. I caufed a Vein to be opened, and there were removed ℥iv of Blood. By this fhe was freed from the pain of her Side. After fhe was purged thus : ℞ *Ammoniacum* ℨi. *Oxymel* ℥ii *Agrimony water* ℥i. *mix them ; and fo for four days.* Being well purged, I prefcribed a Gelly framed of *fhaved Harts-horn* ℥i. *with ten Worms wafhed in White-wine, after boiled all in* ℔ifs *of Water, till half were wafted ; at the end of the boyling I added Saffron finely poudered* ℈i. Of this was given two fpoonfuls in Broth, altered with *Celendine, Barberry bark,* and *Mary-gold flowers.* Her Drink was a Decoction of Harts-horn. She alfo took the following : ℞ *White-wine* ℥iv. *Celendine water* ℥iii. *Saffron* ℨfs. *Venice Treacle* ℨifs. *Bezoar* ℈fs. *the Juyce of Goofe-dung three fpoonfuls ; make a Sudorifick Potion.* Dofe ℥iv, at four a clock in the morning. At night fhe took the following Electuary : ℞ *yellow and white Sanders* ℨiii. *Currants infufed in White-wine, and after paffed through a Sive,* ℥iv. *Rubarb* ℨi. *Saffron* ℈i. *f. Elect.* Dofe, the quantity of a Filbert. By thefe fhe was cured. After I advifed to ufe the following : ℞ *Elect. Chalyb.* ℥ii. *Rhab. Pul.* ℨi. *Ammoniac. Pul.* ℈iv. *Elect. de Tamarind.* ℨ fs. *Diatrionfant.* ℨiii. *Mifc. f. Elect.* Dofe ℨfs. ufing exercife. And thus in twenty days fhe was delivered from Death.

K OBSERV

Observ. XLIII.

ONe of *Northampton*, aged about 65, was much troubled with the heat of Urine, and Strangury, with an Ulcer in the neck of the Bladder, was cured as followeth : First I gave him the Terbentine Potion, prescribed *Observ.* 14. of this Century. For eight days for ordinary Drink, he took the same appointed there. All this while he wore Plates of Lead much perforated, and often changed, to his Back. I appointed the following Injection : ℞ *Troch. alb. Rha. sine Opio* ʒiß. *Lap. Calamin. & Tutiæ præp.* ā ʒi. *Plumb. ust. lot. in Aq. Plantag. Bol. Arm. purif.* ā ʒii. *f. Pul. subtilif. cujus* ʒi *Misc. cum Decoct. seq.* and inject it, adding ʒi of the *Mucilage of Gum Tragacanth, made in Plantain water.* ℞ *Horse-tail, Plantain, each* M i. *Comfrey roots* ʒii. *red Roses* p. i. *Pomegranate Pills* ʒii. *first beat them, and after boyl them in steeled Water.* At the end of these was used the following Tablets : ℞ *Troch. Alkekeng. cum Opio* ʒ ß. *Rad. consolid. Terbent. coct. indurat.* ā ʒ i. *Sacch.* ʒiiß. *cum infuf. Gum Tragac. f. Troch.* Ɔii *pond.* One was taken with Milk, or the Water distilled off Whites of Eggs, *&c.* For many days a Leaden Pipe was put into the Yard, and there kept (which was anointed with *Ung. Rubrum*) as long as he could. His Cods being tumified, were anointed with *Unguent. de Minio,* for which also he drank the Decoction of *Sarfaparilla.* Thus was he freed from the heat of his Urine.

But

or strengthening saunders woods. The second electuary included *Diatrionsantalum*, which was formed of yellow, white and red saunders woods.[1]

When Hall attended Elizabeth Stoker she was very ill. He claimed to have delivered her from death in twenty days although it may have taken longer for her to be restored to full health.

143: SIR FRANCIS HARVEY OF HARDINGSTONE, NORTHAMPTONSHIRE

The most cryptically edited by Cooke of all Hall's cases, in the Latin manuscript this patient is named as '*Generosus* Harvey' of Northamptonshire, his well-recorded venereal symptoms the reason for editorial discretion.

Francis Harvey was the father of Stephen, who in 1620 had married Mary Murden of Moreton Morrell, another patient (nos 64, 97). Francis Harvey was the third son of Stephen senior, whose monument of 1606 can be seen in St Edmund's church, Hardingstone, where the family were lords of the manor.[2] Francis Harvey was born in about 1567 and educated at Cambridge (admitted 1583, BA in 1586, MA in 1589); he entered the law in 1624 and became a Justice of Common Pleas.[3] He was knighted on 2 July 1626. He bought the manor of Milton Malsor (Northants.) and settled it on his son, Stephen, on the occasion of the young man's marriage to Mary Murden. Francis Harvey also had Hertfordshire connections, having inherited family land at Braughing through his mother, Anne Greene,[4] and he married Elizabeth Hemming, apparently of Bengeo. Stephen predeceased his father in March 1630 and the estate passed to the seven-year-old Francis (1623–43).[5]

Francis Harvey's treatment is one of the most detailed of the cases, noted as *ulceris gonorrhae virulentae*. Hall presumably attended Harvey when he was visiting the Murdens at Moreton Morrell, not long before his death, although Hall recorded the patient's recovery. Sir Francis died in 1632 and was buried at Hardingstone on 2 August.

Harvey's gonorrhoea had resulted in a stricture, a narrowing of the urethra, caused by inflammation and resulting in a strangury, the name given to a condition where urine can only be voided drop by drop. Other symptoms were swollen cods or testicles, and a 'virulent gonorrhoea', meaning a purulent discharge from the urethra. To relieve the strangury

---

1. *Diatrium* was a medicine composed of three simple ingredients.
2. *VCH Northants.*, V, p. 272.
3. Chamberlain, II, p. 585; Venn, II, p. 322.
4. *HV Herts.*, 1564, p. 27; *VCH Herts.*, III, pp. 314–15.
5. *VCH Northants.*, V, p. 272.

But now being vexed with a virulent Gonorrhea, he took the following Pouder for ten
days: ℞ *Sarsaparilla* ℥ i ß. *Bark of Guaiacum*
℥ ß. *Cinamon* ℈ii, gr. v. *Sena* ℥ii. *Dodder, Hel-*
lebore root, each ℥i. *fine Sugar* ℥ii. *mix them, and*
make a Pouder. Dose ℥iß. Sometimes the *Dod-*
der and *Hellebore* was omitted. And by this he
became well. But after riding to *London*, (by
what occasion I know not) it broke forth again,
where he had the advice of Doctor *Harvy*, who
prescribed what follows: ℞ *Troch. Rhasis alb.*
℥ß. *Troch. Gord.* ℈i. *Aloes opt.* ℥iiß. *Penidior.*
℥iß. *Aq. Plantag.* ℔ß. f. *Inject.* The following
Electuary he used at night, the quantity of a
Bean, when he went to bed: ℞ *Troch. Alkekeng.*
cum Opio ℥ß. *Syr. Limon.* q. s. *Gum Tragacanth,*
Mastich, Crystal. præp. Coral præp. ā ℈i. f. *Elect.*
By these he was again restored. After he went
to St. *Vincent's* Well, and was much better by
their use. After this, being hurt with the for-
cing in a Pipe rto remove a Caruncle by a
Chirurgeon, he again relapsed, and never was
cured.

OBSERV. XLIV.

Mrs. *Mary Comb* of *Stratford*, aged about 13,
Febr. 15. 1631. Two years before this
she had her Lunar Evacuations sufficient, they
beginning to flow abundantly in the eleventh
year of her Age ; but now they being stopped,
upon which she felt a light Convulsion in the

right

Hall inserted a leaden pipe into the yard (penis) which was kept there 'as long as he could'.

Hall's treatment began with a turpentine potion and lead plates applied to the region of the kidneys, as in other cases involving urinary problems. Salts of lead featured prominently in the regime. The urethral injection, in addition to herbs, had some minerals including *Plumbum ustum*, burnt lead.[1] *Trochisci Albi* in the injection contained lead carbonate. The lead pipe was anointed with *Unguentum Rubrum*, which contained lead salts, and *Unguentum de Minio*, used to treat the swollen testicles, included tutia, camphor and litharge or lead oxide. Other medicines were a lozenge made from *Trochisci Alkakengi cum opio* lozenge of winter cherry with opium, and a powder composed of sarsaparilla, guaiacum bark, senna, dodder[2] and hellebore root.

Hall recorded William Harvey's treatment and so preserved two prescriptions composed by one of the foremost physicians in the history of medicine.[3] Finally Hall added that a surgeon, unskilfully attempting to removed a caruncle (a painful fleshy growth) in the urethra, brought about a permanent relapse.

144: MARY COMBE OF STRATFORD-UPON-AVON

Mary was noted by the Heralds at their 1619 Visitation as aged ten months, the eldest daughter of William Combe and Katherine, née Boughton (no. 134).[4] She was to marry into two leading local families, whom Hall also attended; he treated her in 1631.

At Stratford on 26 November 1636 she married Thomas Wagstaffe of Bishops Tachbrook, the son of Timothy of Warwick. Elizabeth Wagstaffe, Timothy's widow, was also a Hall patient (nos 44, 177). Elizabeth's son, Thomas, born in 1614/5, became a royal ward at his father's death. Sir Thomas died in 1639, but Mary continued to live at Tachbrook. There was one son of the marriage, Sir Combe Wagstaffe, born on 5 November 1637, who died unmarried in January 1668,[5] and a posthumous daughter, Mary, baptised on 23 August 1639.

1. *Plumbum ustum* or burnt lead occurs in Dioscorides. It was prepared by heating lead and raking off the scum until it was reduced to a dross, or alternatively by placing thin plates of lead in sulphur setting it on fire and stirring until reduced to ashes.

2. Dodder *Cuscuta Epithymum* is a parasitic plant growing on thyme and other plants. It has a strong smell and a lingering pungent taste. It was used for its cathartic properties.

3. Geoffrey Keynes, *The Life of William Harvey* (Oxford, 1966) included these with other surviving prescriptions in Appendix II, pp. 437–45.

4. *HV Warws.*, 1619, p. 291.

5. *VCH Warws.*, V, pp. 161, 164.

right eye (to use her owm word, a twitching)
as though her Eye was pulled inward, and presently it would be gone : after both eyes did suffer
with great pain of the Head, for which I administred at bed-time, *Pil. Cephal. Fern.* ʒ ß. by
which she had three stools, the next day they
were repeated.   Then she became cruelly vexed
with the Mother, continuing in the Fit for nine
hours, with some light intervals of ease, from
which she was delivered by the following Medicines: She had a Fume of *Horse-hoofs.*   There was
also given *Aq. Hysteric.* now called *Aq. Brioniæ
campos.* Dose three spoonfuls, by intervals as she
could take it. I applied *Emplast. Hyster.* below
the Navil. Lastly, I appointed the following
Ointment to anoint the inner part of the Matrix :
℞ *Musk* gr. iv. *Nutmeg* Ɔi. *Oil of Lillies* ʒß. *mix
them.* By this it returned to its place. For a
Fume she had the following, used to the Nose : ℞
Castory, Galbanum dissolved in Vinegar, each ʒß.
Sulphur ʒi. *Assa fætida* ʒi. *make* Troches *with Oil
of Castory.* ℞ *Pil. de Pæon. de Chamæp.* ā Ɔii. *Ol.
Salu. Chy.* gut. v. *f. Pil.* N° 10. Three of these
were given at bed time, to which was added *Extract. Hyst.* Ɔi. By these she had five or six stools.
The following day she had another Fit, but less ;
but by the foresaid Fume and Ointment she was
well amended. Inwardly were given two spoonfuls of *Aq. Brion. comp.* At night she took two
of the foresaid Pills ; coming to her in the morning, I found her eased of her pain of Head and
Stomach. The 11*th* of *Febr.* she was gently afflicted with the Mother, and a light Fever ; to
prevent which I gave *Extract. Hysteric.* ʒii. *cum
Aq.*

Mary remarried in the 1640s, but there is a gap in the Bishops Tachbrook parish register for the period 1635 to 1650. Her second husband was John Rous, the third son of Sir John Rous of Rous Lench (Worcs.), a family Hall also treated. Through his marriage Rous acquired Jury Street House in Warwick. He lived, however, in a fourteen-hearth house at Tachbrook Mallory[1] and died there on 6 November 1680. Mary's death took place six years later on 4 March 1686 at Utkinton (Ches.), where her daughter, Mary, lived, the wife of Sir John Crew.[2] Mary Combe's memorial is in St Chad's Church, Bishops Tachbrook.

Mary Combe, aged thirteen, had menstruated at the age of eleven. When Hall was called to her she was suffering from amenorrhoea and experiencing convulsions about the eyes with pain in the head. Cephalic pills were prescribed (no. 23). During the course of this treatment the girl was afflicted with hysterical seizures lasting several hours. Treatments included the patient being made to inhale vapours formed by burning 'stinking things' (no. 96). In this case shavings of horse's hoof were used and later a mixture made into a troche or lozenge containing asafoetida. *Aqua Hysterica*, a compound water containing bryony root, was prescribed.[3] A plaster used for the treatment of hysteria and known as *Emplastrum Hystericum*[4] was applied to the lower abdomen. An ointment containing musk was used to anoint the inner part of the matrix or uterus. The comment 'By this [the ointment] it returned to its place', indicated some form of displacement of the womb had occurred. These prescriptions were followed by another for a pill containing paeony, used in epileptic states, chamaepitys or ground pine *Teucrium chamaepitys*, recommended as serviceable in female obstructions, and *Olea Salviae Chymica* or oil of sage, also used for uterine disorders.

This is one of the few observations where Hall indicated the timing of his treatments. He saw the patient first on 15 February 1631 when he began the treatment described above. The next date was 11 February which must be an error for 11 March. Then he recorded a slight relapse. A further relapse occurred on 28 March when another pill 'covered with Gold [leaf]' was prescribed. Hall claimed that by these pills she was delivered, presumably from her menstrual problems as well as her hysterical symptoms.

1. WCRO, QS 11/5.

2. Thomas Pennant, *The Journey from Chester to London* (1811), p. 11.

3. *Aqua Hysterica* was a compound water containing bryony root. It was attributed to the court physician Sir Theodore Turquet de Mayerne (1573–1665) who was closely associated with the publication of the first London *Pharmacopoeia* in 1618. As Hall indicated the name of this water was changed to *Aqua Bryoniae Composita*.

4. The formula for Emplastrum Hystericum was published in the London *Pharmacopoeia* of 1618 and attributed to Nicolaus Myrepsus.

Aq. Hist. q. s. f. Pil. 10. She took one of them in the morning fasting, and so she became well. *March* 28. she fell again into the Mother, with Convulsion of the Eyes, the said Convulsion having grieved her two days before she was afflicted with the Mother : ℞ *Pil. de Pæon. Chamæpit. Hier. cum Agarick.*, ā ℈ii. *Pil. de Succin. Ruffi.* ā ʒi. *Extract. Hyster.* ʒii. *cum Aq. Hyster. f. Mas.* Of this there were made five of a drachm covered with Gold ; of these she took three at bed-time. By these she was delivered,

---

OBSERV. XLV.

THe First-born Son of my Lady *Harrington*, after the Pox, laboured of a Tumor of the Nose and Lips, and sometimes the Cheeks, with a Rheum distilling from the Head ; he was about the age of 10, which I cured as followeth : ℞ *Scurvy-grass, Water-cresses, Brook lime*, each M iv. *Juniper berries* ℔ß. *Agrimony* M i. *Wormwood, Carduus benedictus,* each M ß. boyled them in five gallons of Beer, *till a fourth part were wasted.* Of the strained Liquor was taken ℔ii. *Sena* ʒii. *Agarick* ʒß. *Rubarb* ʒii. *Sarsaparilla* ʒ ii. *Sassaphras* ʒ i. *Hermodactils* ʒiß. *Liquoris* ʒi. *Polypody* ʒii. *Seeds of Anis, Carraway, Coriander,* each ʒß. *Cinamon* ʒii. To the straining, add Sugar sufficient to make a Syrup. Of this was taken ʒx. *Syrup of Succory with Rubarb* ʒii. Dose was three or four spoonfuls. For the Lips was used *Aq. Mercur. Ruland.* and at night a Plate of Lead. He drank of the foresaid

K 3   Beer.

145: SARAH, DAUGHTER OF SIR JOHN HARINGTON OF ELMESTHORPE, LEICESTERSHIRE

This ten-year-old child is Sarah, the second surviving daughter of Sir John Harington; as she was born in 1607, Hall must have treated her in 1617 when she was presumably visiting the area. The confusion about the child's sex arose from Cooke's translation rather than Hall's Latin notes, where the feminine gender is consistently used about this young patient. She was not, as Hall noted, the first-born, but had become the heiress on the death of her sister.

Her mother was born Mary Offley, a city merchant's daughter, who married Sir John Harington of Bagworth (Leics.) on 4 January 1604. Sir John died in 1615, aged forty-seven, and Lady Harington in 1623 when Sarah was only sixteen.[1] Sarah served as Maid of Honour to Queen Henrietta Maria and in April 1630 married Sir John Freschville, whose eighteen-year-old first wife had died a year earlier. Freschville was MP for Derbyshire and was raised to the peerage for his loyal support of the king in the Civil War, when he commanded eight troops of horse.

Sarah Harington later had three daughters born in the years 1633 to 1638. She died in 1665 and was buried on 24 June at St Lawrence Pountney, London. A year later, aged sixty, Freschville remarried but, with no male heirs, the title became extinct at his death. His third wife, Anna Charlotte de Vic, did not die until 1717, at a great age. Lord Freschville died at Westminster on 31 March and was buried at Staveley (Derbys.) on 9 April 1682; his monument survives in the family chapel there.[2] Their house, Staveley Hall, had been built by his father in 1604 and was captured by parliamentary forces in 1644. It is now used as local authority offices.[3]

Hall's young patient had recovered from smallpox but was suffering from a swelling of the face mostly affecting the lips. Treatment was with a medicated beer containing scorbutic and aperient drugs. *Aqua Mercurialis Ruland*, a water made with the herb mercury, was used to wash the lips.[4] A plate of lead was applied at night.

This was Observation 141 in Hall's original manuscript to which was added the identical case of Margaret Baker, aged nine, who was treated with an amber pill in place of the medicated beer. Cooke made a separate case out of it (no. 146).

1. Leicestershire Record Office, Exton MSS, DE 321f.

2. Pevsner, *Derbyshire*, p. 327.

3. Maxwell Craven and Michael Stanley, *The Derbyshire Country House* (Nottingham, 1982), p. 64.

4. See Observation 11 for a note on mercury. Ruland probably refers to Martin Ruland (1532–1602) known as 'the Elder' to distinguish him from Martin Ruland (1569–1611).

Beer. Which Courfe having been continued for few days, he was cured of his Lip.

Observ. XLVI.

MArgaret *Baker*, aged *9*, having after the Pox a grievous ugly Tumor upon her Nofe and Lip, was perfectly cured as followeth : ℞ *Pil. de Succin.* ℥ß. *f. Pil.* iij. They were given her at a night when fhe went to bed, and fo for four days. Being well purged, the Lip was wafhed *cum Aq. Merc. Ruland.*

Observ. XLVII.

MY Lady *Rainsford*, (beautiful, and of a gallant ftructure of Body,) near 27, was three days after her being laid of a Child miferably tormented with pain in her Belly, from which I delivered her with the following : ℞ *the white of Hens-dung* ℥i. being put in Beer and Sugar, fhe took it. To the Belly the following was applied hot : ℞ *new Milk and Honey, each* ℔i. *Horehound* M i. *Wheat flower* ℥iii. *Saffron* ℥i. *boyl them to a Pulteß.* By thefe fhe was delivered. The Tranflator hath freed feveral from this Diftemper with Chamomel Poffet-drink.

146: MARGARET BAKER
[OF STRATFORD-UPON-AVON]

This nine-year-old patient may be the eldest and only daughter of the three children of Peter and Frances Baker of Stratford-upon-Avon, baptised there on 6 May 1621.

147: ELINOR, LADY RAINSFORD OF
CLIFFORD CHAMBERS

It is clear that Hall greatly admired Elinor, the young Lady Rainsford. She came from Combe (Hants.), where both parish registers and transcripts are unfortunately incomplete. Her parents married in 1580 and Elinor Boswell must have been born in the period 1595 to 1602. Although from Hampshire, she may have had local connections, at Lenchwick (Worcs.) and at Milcote. Before the marriage, Sir Henry Rainsford leased land to William Barnes in January 1620, presumably to raise cash.[1]

Elinor bore Henry Rainsford of Clifford Chambers four sons and a daughter in seven years: Henry (baptised 12 May 1622), Francis (24 June 1623), Hercules (12 December 1625), Katherine (28 October 1628) and a son (7 December 1629). Hall noted attending her three days after childbirth but he did not indicate which delivery. William Barnes left her £10 in his will to buy a jewel.[2] Elinor Rainsford was buried on 14 October 1640, six months before her husband, and a Hampshire gentleman, Francis Reed, wrote to his cousin that he had just attended 'the funeral of my dear neighbour, Lady Rainsford'. Recent election to the House of Commons, Reed thought, would help the widower recover from grief at Elinor Rainsford's death.[3] Their son, Henry, succeeded to the estate, later in 1649 to be heavily fined for his royalist sympathies.[4]

In the index at the end of his manuscript Hall listed this as a case of puerperal fever, although no reference to a fever occurs in the report. White of hen's dung prescribed for this patient was used in the case of puerperal fever recorded in Observation 61.

148: GRACE COURT, APOTHECARY'S WIFE

The original Latin text identified this patient as *Gratia Court uxor pharmacopei*, but the insertion of 'my' in the printed edition suggests that Court may have

1. SBTRO, DR 33/8.
2. MacLean, 'Clifford Chambers', p. 18.
3. Buckland, *Rainsford*, p. 110.
4. *VCH Glos.*, VI, p. 210.

Observ. XLVIII.

Mrs. *Grace Court,* Wife to my Apothecary, aged
27, being grievously afflicted with a burning Fever, and that continual, Pain in the Loins,
small bleeding at the Nose, Pain of the Head,
with small Delirium, was cured as followeth:
First, I appointed her to bleed four or five ounces,
although she had passed fourteen weeks of her
time, being with Child. The same day I gave
the following Cordial: ℞ *burnt Harts-horn, Spec.*
liberant. pul. Pannon. rub. Confect. Alkerm. ā ℈ii.
Conserve of Barberries ℥i. Of this she took the quantity of a Bean every three hours. She drank no
drink but the following: ℞ *Spring water boyled*
℔iii. *Syrup of Pomegranats* ℥iß. *Julep of Roses* ℥ii.
Spirit of Vitriol, as much as made it sharp. To the
Soals of her Feet were applied Radishes beaten with
Salt, and besprinkled with Rose-vinegar, which
was renewed every fourth hour. For the inflammation of the Tongue, was used the following
Gargarism: ℞ *Spring water* ℔ii. *Julep of Roses*
℥iß. *Honey of Mulberries* ℥vi. *Rose vinegar* ʒi. *Spi-*
rit of Vitriol sufficient to sharpen it. With this she
washed her Mouth, which brought away much
Phlegm. Now and then the dry places were an-
ointed with *Honey of Roses,* and sometimes But-
ter. To the Wrists I caused to be applied *Ung.*
Antifebri. ℞ *Ung. Popul.* ℥i. *Tel. Aranear. multas,*
Nuc. Arbor. parum, Misc. For the Back, ℞ *Ung.*
Popul. Ros. ā ℥ß. *Alabast.* ℥ii. *Ol. Nymph.* ʒvi.
Camphor.

K 4

been Cooke's own apothecary after Hall's death. Grace was married to John Court, the third child and eldest son of William (d. 1634) and Frances (d. 1631). John Court was baptised in Stratford on 21 December 1586; he and Grace had five children born during the years 1623 to 1636. Their third child and the eldest son, John, baptised on 27 November 1631, was the chief beneficiary of his father's will (14 January 1639).[1] In the will, made a week before he died, John Court, senior, left his son the family house after Grace's death or remarriage, £40 when he reached the age of twenty-one, and a half share, with his mother, in the patent for selling tobacco in Stratford. As well as items of silver, all the other children received cash – Susanna £120, Elizabeth £60, Grace £50, and Richard £40; he appears to have been the apothecary who assisted Cooke in preparing Hall's notes for publication.

Two years after Court's death, Grace remarried. Her second husband, Christopher Pargetter, was not approved by all the family, because when John junior made his will in 1655 (aged only twenty-four) he wished his step-father omitted from the arrangements.[2] Like his father, John Court the younger was also an apothecary, although his son, Joseph, attended Merton College and later became vicar of Bretforton (Worcs.).[3] Hall noted Grace Court was fourteen weeks pregnant and a birth would therefore take place in November. Two of her children in Hall's lifetime were baptised in November, Susanna (1629) and John (1631). Grace appears to have moved from Stratford after remarrying and no record of her death has been found.

Hall directed that Grace Court should be bled and four or five ounces of blood removed. After this the treatment, involving ten prescriptions, took into account the fact that she was fourteen weeks into her pregnancy. The preparations to be taken internally were generally of a cooling and cordial nature. Radishes beaten in salt were applied to the soles of the feet to hinder the rising of the vapours (no. 31) and an ointment against fever mixed with spiders' webs *Aranearum Telae* was applied to the wrists (no. 60).

At one point in the treatment Hall prescribed a decoction containing hartshorn and *Species Confectionis Liberantis*[4] to prevent the patient falling into a *carus*, which is a state of deep sleep.[5] Before taking this decoction she was given medicines to strengthen the heart and repel 'malign vapours'. At the end of this long regime Grace Court 'came to a composed mind' and was well. In the manuscript Hall gave 'honor to the omnipotent Lord' for her recovery.

1. SBTRO, DR 133/14.
2. PRO, Prob 11/263, quire 140.
3. Foster, p. 335.
4. The formula for *Species Confectionis Liberantis* contained ambergris, musk, pearl, coral, ivory, sapphire, emerald, garnet and twenty-eight other ingredients mostly roots, seeds and spices.
5. *Carus* is the fourth degree of insensibility. The other three are *sopor*, *coma* and *lethargy* (OED).

Camphor. ℈ß. *Misc.* But becauſe there was no
Oil at hand, the following was uſed: ℞ *Ol.
Scorp.* ℥ii. *Amygd. dulc.* ℥ß. *Ung. Roſ.* ℥i. *Misc.*
For the pain of the Head was uſed the following:
℞ *Aq. Roſ. Plantag. Flor. Sambuc.* ā ℥iii. *Ol. Roſ.
Aq. Lactuc. ablut. aliquot.* ℥iß. *Pul. Santal. rub.*
℥iß. *Misc.* In this were dipped Linnen Clothes,
and applied to the Head. And leſt ſhe ſhould fall
into *Carus*, we uſed the following Decoction:
℞ *pure Spring water* ℔ii. *Seeds and Pills of Citrons,*
each ℥i. *burnt Harts-horn* ℥ß. *Spec. Liberan.* ℥ii.
*boyl them till a quart be waſted ; to the ſtraining was
added the Juyce of Citrons, and Sugar, and after
boyled, being not only ſcummed, but purified with
Whites of Eggs.* Of this ſhe took three draughts
in a day, one in the morning, the other an hour
before dinner-time, and the third at four a clock
in the afternoon. For the ſtrengthning of the
Heart, and repelling malign Vapours, ſhe took
twice a day (before ſhe drank the foreſaid Decoction) the quantity of a Nutmeg of the following Cordial: ℞ *Rob of Barberries, Conſerve of the
Pulp of Citrons,* each ℥i. *Spec. Liberant.* prepared
Pearls and Smaragdines, each ℈i. *with the Syrup of
Citrons make an Electuary.* Of this ſhe alſo took at
night. After her third draught the next day ſhe
took of the Electuary, wherein was *Pul. Pan. rub.*
And afterwards a Clyſter: ℞ *Althea roots* ℥i. *the
four emollient Herbs,* each M i. *Barly* p.i ß. *Gourd
ſeeds* ℥ß. *make a Decoction to* ℥xii. *in which diſſolve
Caſſia* ℥i. *Honey of Violets* ℥i. *Oil of Violets* ℥iii.
with Salt make a Clyſter. The 20th day of *June*
ſhe vomited a Worm with Melancholy matter.
Then I gave of the following Electuary the quantity

tity of a Bean every fourth hour: ℞ *Conserv. Ros.
vitriolat.* ℥i. *Spec. Diarrhod. Abbat.* ℥i. *Pul. Pan.
rub.* ℈i. *Confer. Barb. q. s. f. Elect.* These remitted her Fits, and she came to a composed mind,
and in a short time became well.

Observ. XLIX.

THe Countess of *Northampion*, (born of a noble
Off-spring, notably educated, and of a very
good disposition, very fair and beautiful,) in the
seventh month of her Child-bearing, fell into a
Bastard Tertian, as also a filthy yellow Jaundice,
Torment of the Belly and Head, and Pain of the
Back, being aged about 26, desiring my advice,
being not willing to purge, I prescribed as followeth : ℞ *the Flowers of Marygolds and Rosemary,
each* p. i. *Carduus benedictus* p. ß. *Flowers and leaves
of Melilot* p. ii. *boyl them in sufficient Posset drink to*
℔ß. *with a little Sugar.* She took half of it an
hour before her Fit, hot, by which the Fit was
retarded two hours; it beginning, she took the
other half, which freed her from her shaking,
then her Jaundice appeared in her Water manifest-
ly, after sweat broke forth, the next Fit was less.
In the heat of the Fever and sweat, she took the
Decoction of *Harts-horn*, with Juyce of Limons,
of which she drank liberally, in which Decoction
she would not admit Rose-water. On her quiet
day she took every third hour the quantity of a
Bean of the following : ℞ *Conserve of Barberries*
℥ß. *Pul. Pan. rub.* ℈ii. but after she had taken

of

138 *Select Observations*

of it once, she abhorred it. She had a Gelly of
Harts-horn with *Marygold flowers*, and *Saffron*.
The 22*th* of *July*, before her Fit, she had five
grains of *Bezoar*; and an hour before her Fit the
foresaid Posset-drink. This Fit she was troubled
with shaking, but the hot Fit and sweating was
less by six hours. The 23*th* day, by five in the
morning it left her. She took this: ℞ *Tincture of
Coral, Magistral of Pearl*, each gr. iv. *Pul. Pannon.
rub.* gr. xii. *mix them*. She took it an hour before
dinner, and an hour before supper. The 24*th*
day by three a clock in the morning she took as
before, and the Posset-drink, which mitigated the
Fit; the 25*th*, as the 23*th*. The 26*th* there was
applied hot to the Feet the following : ℞ *Wormwood, Rue, Fetherfew, Nettles*, each *equal parts*.
She also had the Posset-drink, as before. The
foresaid being hot, was anointed with *Ung. Popul.
with Opium*. To the Back was applied *Emplastrum
Oxycroceum*, which removed the Pain of her Back
wholly; that day her Fever was very little. The
28*th* she took the following: ℞ *prepared Hartshorn, Pul. Pann. rub.* each ʒß. *Carduus water* ʒii.
Syrup of red Poppies ʒß. *Bezoar* gr. iv. *mix them*.
It was given five hours before the Fit, and the
Herbs were applied to the Feet. The heat com-
ing, ℞ *Syr. Papav.* ʒi. *Lim.* ʒß. *Aq. Scab.* ʒii.
Ol. Vitriol. gut. v. *Aq. Cælest.* gut. vii. *Misc.* With
these Remedies in twelve days she was wholly
cured. *August* the 5*th* taking cold, she relapsed.
Then before the Fit two hours, were applied the
Herbs to her Feet; to her Pulses this : ℞ *Ung.
Popul.* ʒß. *Tel. aran. multas, Nuc. arbor. parum*.
Her Temples were anointed with *Populeon*. For
her

149: MARY, COUNTESS OF NORTHAMPTON

In 1621 Spencer, later the second Earl of Northampton, married Mary Beaumont, the daughter of Sir Francis of Coleorton (Leics.).[1] Hall noted that she was of noble family (she was related to the royal favourite, the Duke of Buckingham), as well as being 'very fair and beautiful'. She was born in about 1600 and treated by Hall in about 1626. She had six sons born in the years 1622 to 1632 and two daughters. Sir Edward Conway had attended the christening of James, the eldest child, in 1622;[2] by 1634 James and his brothers were at Eton.[3]

Hall recorded her case in considerable detail. She was a patient with decided views about her own treatment, and refused two of Hall's suggestions. James succeeded to the estate and titles at his father's death in 1643. As Dowager Countess in 1645 she was fined £990, although claiming she had not 'contributed to this unhappy War'.[4] She moved to live near Oxford in 1646 with her youngest children and then to Grendon manor, close to the family seat of Castle Ashby (Northants.). She owned a new house in Queen Street, London, where she died on 18 March 1654;[5] she was buried at Compton Wynyates.

The Countess was diagnosed as having a bastard tertian fever (no. 135) and jaundice. Hall's standard treatments for these conditions involved the use of emetics and purgatives, but the patient's advanced pregnancy prevented their use in this case.

The treatment was carefully recorded giving the dates on which various medicines were given or applied and appears to have continued almost to the time the Countess was brought to bed. Some medicines were given just before the fit of fever and others on the intermittent day when the fit did not occur.

150: THOMAS FAWCET, RECTOR OF ASTON-SUB-EDGE, GLOUCESTERSHIRE

Hall treated Thomas Fawcet in about 1619 when he was Rector of Aston-sub-Edge. Born in Yorkshire in about 1564 and a Cambridge graduate (BA, St Catherine's in 1588–9),[6] he became vicar of another Gloucestershire

---

1. Nichols, *Leicester*, III, pt II, p. 744; *HV Leics.*, 1619, pp. 170–1.
2. Chamberlain, II, p. 458.
3. WCRO, CR 556/274.
4. Compton, *Comptons*, p. 103.
5. D.J.H. Clifford (ed.), *The Diaries of Lady Anne Clifford* (Stroud, 1994), p. 103.
6. Venn, p. 126.

her Coldnefs, ℞ *Aq. Bezoar. Coch. f. Lap. Bezoar.*
gr. v. *Succ. Lim. Coch.* ii. It was given two hours
before the Fit. When her heat came, her Temples were anointed with *Unguent. Popul.* ℥ ß.
Opii in Aq. Rof. diffol. ℈ ß. By thefe fhe was
again cured, and after fhe was brought to bed
with a Daughter, which I faw in her Arms.

Observ. L.

MR. *Foffet,* (a Minifter) aged about 55,
was cruelly tormented with the Hemorrhoids, for which many Medicines had been
ufed, yet fruitlefs. After he came to me, to
whom I ufed the following : Firft, I caufed
them to be fomented with warm Milk, after
applied this : ℞ *Oil of Linfeed, and Elder, of
the firft* ℥ii. *the other* ℥i. They were applied with
double Linnen Clothes night and day. After
was ufed *Tapfi valentia.* And after this, ℞ *Ung.
Popul.* ℥i. *Opii torrefact. & pul.* ℈i. *Mifc.* It was
applied to the part. By thefe he was cured.

Observ. LI.

ANne *Ward* of *Stratford,* had black evacuations
both from Mouth and Belly, after fell into
the rifing of the Lungs, fo that all looked on her
as dead ; fhe could not fpeak, her Breath was
fent out with a noife ; for an hour fhe lay thus.
Being

parish, Awre, in 1604, a living he continued to hold jointly with Aston. Fawcet married a local girl, Margaret Sellers, in 1607, the year he was appointed to Aston, where the patron was Christopher Cage, a member of a long-established county family.[1] The church at Aston formerly contained a substantial monument to Fawcet, depicting him in old age. Fawcet died on 27 April 1636. By then a widower, his will recorded only a son-in-law, John Sellers, and a grandchild, Katherine Sellers, as family beneficiaries. John Sellers was left all Fawcet's books at Awre and a third of those at Aston. Apart from £10 each to two male servants and 6s. 8d. to the poor, Fawcet left 10s. for a new communion-table cloth at Aston church. The substantial residue of his goods was divided between Sir Endymion Porter (1585–1649) of Aston and a local gentleman, Edward Ballard of Weston.[2] Thomas Sellers, presumably a relative, succeeded him as the incumbent of Aston.[3]

Hall treated this case of haemorrhoids in a manner similar to that of Lady Sandys (no. 37), using fomentations, application of oils and *Unguentum Populeon*. The haemorrhoids were obviously painful and to the ointment which contained mandragora, Hall directed to be added one scruple (twenty grains) of *Opii torrefact. & Pul.*, Opium dried (by heating) and powdered.

151: ANNE WARD OF STRATFORD-UPON-AVON

Anne Ward was one of Hall's non-gentry Stratford patients. Although he noted her as 'honest, beautiful, good and religious', unusually he did not record either her status or her age. There were two females called Anne Ward in the town at the time of his casebook, a mother and daughter. There is no indication which Anne Ward was Hall's patient; if it were the daughter, she would have been under twenty-five at the time of the treatment.

On 6 August 1608 Edward Ward married Anne Cap in the town; they had three children baptised there, Frances in 1609 (died an infant), Anne in 1610 and Edward (died an infant) three years later. Neither Edward Ward nor his wife appears to have been born in Stratford, but he was buried there on 4 June 1639, having served as a churchwarden four years before. No records of Mrs Anne Ward's burial or the daughter's marriage have been found in Stratford.

Both Mrs Goodyear and Mrs Savage in Hall's original notes were described as *Generosa* and this suggests that Mrs Goodyear may have been connected with Anne (née Goodere), Lady Rainsford at Clifford Chambers

1. Robert Atkyns, *The Ancient and Present State of Gloucestershire* (1768), p. 120.
2. Gloucestershire Record Office, 1636/110.
3. Atkyns, *Gloucestershire*, p. 120.

Being called, I prefently caufed a great Cupping-
glafs to be fet to the Mouth of the Stomach, and
prefently fhe fpake.   And fo twice before I delivered Mrs. *Goodyear*, and Mrs. *Savage*, from danger of Death.   All the night after fhe held in her
Mouth of our pectoral Rolls, and after had this
Clyfter : ℞ *Ol. Carmin. Quer. Diacathol.* ā ℥ ii.
Decoct.Carmin. pro Clyft. ℔ß. It gave two ftools the
following day.   ℞ *Elect. de Tamarind.* ℥ß. *de Succ.*
Rof. ℥iii. *Crem.Tart.* ℈i. *cum Sacch.f. Bol.* It gave
eight ftools, and fo fhe was cured.

Observ. LII.

Mrs. *Fines*, aged 22, 1632. (Wife to the Lord
Say's eldeft Son, a very religious excellent
Woman,) was miferably afflicted with the following Symptoms, *viz.* Obftruction of the Courfes
for the fpace of two months; and when fhe had
them at a fit time in a laudable quantity, they
were of an ill watery colour, with great pain in
the Womb; there was alfo difficulty of breathing,
with trembling and beating of the Heart, as if it
would have burft through; after fleep fhe was
fick, with torment of the Belly, and gnawing
about the Navil, but thefe Pains were moft miferable about the time of her Courfes; upon breaking wind fhe was fomewhat eafed; her Belly was
alfo very hard,and moved,as if with child; but hot
Clothes being applied removed the Pain and
Wind.   She was alfo vexed with pain of the
Spleen, Whites, Leannefs, Pain of the Loins,

a

(no. 168), where Hall certainly visited patients. There are at least three possibilities for the identity of a well-born Mrs Savage, with whose families Hall had links: Simon Underhill of Oxhill married the widow Elizabeth Savage before 1624; Lady Rous's daughter, Mary, in 1633 married John Savage of Cookhill; Anne, sister of Ralph Sheldon of Weston (d. 1613), married Ralph Savage.

Anne Ward was in great distress resulting from a 'rising of the lungs', a term referring to a sense of fullness in the throat with oppressed breathing which led, in extreme cases, to suffocation.

Hall's emergency treatment was to place a large cupping glass over the site of the mouth of the stomach. This involved heating a dome-shaped glass and placing it over the skin. As the glass cooled a vacuum was created raising the flesh. Cupping was an ancient form of therapy and there were two kinds, dry cupping, as used for Anne Ward, and wet cupping, where the glass was positioned over scarified flesh. Wet cupping was a form of bleeding and was used for Anne Jackson (no. 154).[1] Hall referred to two other cases where the application of a cup had been successful. Prescriptions for pectoral rolls,[2] an enema containing carminative and purgative drugs and a purgative medicine completed the treatment.

152: FRANCES FIENNES OF BROUGHTON CASTLE, OXFORDSHIRE

In 1632 Hall attended Frances Fiennes, daughter-in-law to the second Viscount Saye and Sele; she was the fourth and youngest daughter of Edward Cecil, Viscount Wimbledon (d. 1638). Frances was born in 1610 and by 1631 had married James, the young heir to William, created first Viscount Saye and Sele in 1624. The family home at Broughton Castle, near Banbury was a crucial Civil War site, for the Fiennes family were devoted to the parliamentary cause.

Frances and James had three sons, James and William, who both died in infancy, and a second William drowned in the Seine as a young man in about 1658 (no. 172). Hall was treating Frances in 1632 for some form of uterine infection, presumably after James's birth. Her husband succeeded in 1662 and after his death in 1674 the title passed to his nephew, William, the third Viscount.[3]

1. A cupping glass was known as a *cucurbita*, a name derived from the gourd once used for the purpose. For a history of cupping see W. Brockbank, *Ancient Therapeutic Arts* (1954), pp. 67–85.

2. A pectoral roll was a mixture of pectoral drugs (medicines appropriated to disorders of the lungs) mixed with sugar and made *secundum artem* into a form resembling barley sugar.

3. Lord Saye and Sele has kindly provided many details of his family.

a light *Vertigo,* as alfo of the Scurvy, and truly
I judged all thefe Symptoms to arife from it.
Which I cured as followeth: ℞ *Pil. de Succin.* ℥ii.
Ruffi. ℥i. *f. Pil.* N. 15. She took three at bed-
time, and two in the morning, which wrought
excellently. For the Wind, ℞ *Spec. Plerefarc.*
℥ß. *Sacch. Rof.* ℥iv. *Mifc.* Dofe, half a fpoonful
after meat. By the ufe of thefe her Courfes flowed well, with many lumps like Flefh, not diffolu-
ble in water, they were expelled with torment,
as in Child-birth. To cleanfe the Womb, ℞ *Hier.*
cum Agaric. de Succin. ā ℥iß. *Terb. Cypr. Pil. Ruffi.*
ā ℥ß. *f. Pil.* N. 20. She took thefe as the former,
cum cuftodia. Thefe ended, fhe took *Spec. Plere-*
farc. ℥ii. and ufed exercife. The fifth of *March,*
at four a clock in the morning, fhe took *Crem.*
Tart in Broth. An hour after that, of our *Chaly-*
biat Water, thus framed: ℞ *Oil of Sulphur* pint i.
Spirit of Wine pint ii. *boyl them in a great new made*
Iron Spoon at a gentle Fire, till half be evacuated ;
the Pouder remaining, keep very clofe, left it diffolve.
Of this ℞ ℥ii. *to which put Agrimony water* ℥iv.
and infufe them upon hot afhes. Of this fhe took
℥ß in Broth, and ufed exercife ; the firft day fhe
vomited, and the fecond and third days fhe did
not ; fhe ufed it for fifteen days. It is excellent
in all Difeafes arifing from the Liver, as *Dropfy,*
Cachexia, Green-ficknefs. To her Spleen was applied *Empl. ex Ammoniac. Fer. & Oxycroc.* She
ufed every day *Plerifar. and Sugar.* Scorbutic
Beer was not omitted, as *Cent.* 1. *Obferv.* 1. By
thefe fhe was cured, taking in the morning *Dia-*
cubeb ℥ii.

OBSERV.

Hall obviously admired Frances, describing her approvingly as 'very religious' and 'excellent'. Presumably, he was not aware of contemporary rumours that the Banbury puritan writer, Joshua Sprigge, had 'had great familiarity, to the jealousy of her husband [with Frances] during the time James was alive'.[1] It seems they lived together at Highgate and, a year after James's death, Frances, aged sixty-four, married Sprigge, a widower twelve years her junior. Sprigge, a famous parliamentary chaplain, was the author of *Anglia Rediviva* (1647), allegedly written with the help of Colonel John Fiennes.[2] Joshua Sprigge died in June 1684 and Frances two weeks later; they were buried at Crayford, Kent.

The formidable list of symptoms recorded by Hall indicates that Frances Fiennes was anaemic and had a serious uterine infection. Hall attributed the symptoms to scurvy and his treatment resembles that prescribed for the Countess of Northampton (no. 1). Aloes, agaric and amber, all regarded as purgatives to be used to amend depraved humours in a woman's body, were prescribed in pills to be taken *cum custodia*, with care. Scorbutic beer (no. 1) was also recommended.

Hall frequently prescribed iron in the form of chalybiate or steeled water. In this observation he described the preparation of his own form of steeled water which he claimed was excellent in all diseases arising from the liver, such as dropsy, cachexia (a depraved state of the body) and green sickness (chlorosis, a form of anaemia most common in young women). To prepare the steeled water one pint of sulphuric acid was mixed with two pints of alcohol and the mixture heated in an iron vessel. The iron sulphate formed when such a mixture is heated with iron is insoluble in the alcohol that remains after the heating process and comes out of solution. Hall directed that two drachms (120 grains) of the sediment be added to four fluid ounces of agrimony water and half a fluid ounce of this solution (equivalent to fifteen grains of the iron salt) taken by the patient in broth. This was to be repeated for fifteen days.[3]

153: FRANCES FINCH OF STRATFORD-UPON-AVON

Frances Finch was baptised in Stratford on 11 May 1586, the daughter of Robert Jones, who was later in 1590 to be charged with fornication. On 17 October 1612 she married Thomas Finch; the first of their two sons was baptised on 24 March 1613. Hall noted her status as townswoman.

The parish register shows that she was buried on Christmas Day 1632

---

1. Anthony à Wood, *Athenae Oxoniensis* (1813–20), IV, p. 137.
2. *DNB*.
3. The therapeutic dose of ferrous sulphate is 600–900 mg (4.6–13.8 grains) daily in divided doses. Therapeutic doses of the salt have been known to cause vomiting.

Observ. LIII.

FRances Finch of *Stratford*, aged 47, being troubled with the Worms, Pain of the Back and Sides, was thus cured: ℞ *Pul. Dudlian. Scamon. præp.* ā gr. xiv. *Crem. Tartar.* gr. x. *Aq. Boragin.* ℥iſs. *Syr. Roſ. Coch. half.* This being exhibited, gave four ſtools, with abundance of little Worms. The next day being given again, ſhe was cured. It is obſervable, that *Riverius* hath ſeveral Obſervations about Worms, and his ſpecial Remedy is *Mercur. dul. cum Scam. aut Reſin. Jalap.* the which the Tranſlator hath proved very often, given in a due Doſe.

Observ. LIV.

Mrs. *Jackson*, (Wife to Mr. *Jackſon* Jun.) aged about 24, being not well purged after birth, fell ſuddenly into a grievous Delirium, no other Diſeaſe preceding; ſhe was moſt angry with thoſe that formerly ſhe moſt loved, yet her talk was very religious. By intervals there was a Fever acute, which made me fear a Frenzy. By reaſon of much buſineſs I could not have time to viſit her, yet there was a happy ſucceſs by the following Preſcriptions: ℞ *Syr. Artem.* ℥i. *El. Lenit. Diacath.* ā ℥iii. *Rhab. Caſtor.* ā Ə ſs. *Aq. Betonic.* ℥iii. *Miſc.* Her Stomach being full of wind, ſhe vomited
after

and Hall must have been consulted in her final illness. Thomas Finch was buried on Christmas Day 1655.

Hall prescribed for Frances Finch a preparation containing the purgative resin scammony to expel worms. Cooke added a note that Lazarus Riviere used as a special remedy for worms a mixture of jalap, scammony and *Mercurius dulcis* (mercurous chloride, also known as calomel). It was one of the new chemical remedies and became widely used, its low solubility making it a relatively safe mercurial for use in medicine.

154: ANNE JACKSON OF BINTON

Although Anne Jackson was the only one of Hall's patients that he actually noted he was too busy to visit, his description of her as *Generosa . . . religiosa uxor Thelogi junioris* identifies her as Anne, the wife of the Rector of Binton, which was less than 5 miles from Stratford. John Jackson cannot be positively identified from either Oxford or Cambridge *alumni* lists, but he is the only living incumbent of this surname in the diocese in the years covered by Hall's notes.

Hall had already treated other patients, such as the Kempsons, in the area. Dugdale noted that John Jackson was appointed to replace Anthony Gulson from 29 August 1626[1] and Jackson signed the register from 1628 onwards. The register for St Peter's, Binton, recorded the burial of Anne, wife of the rector, on 14 December 1634, and John Jackson's interment nine months later on 14 September 1635. When the church's land was listed on 26 June 1635 Jackson's name did not appear;[2] his successor, James Sheppard, was appointed on 20 October 1635, a month after Jackson's death.

The exact date on which Anne Jackson required medical attention, after her pregnancy, cannot be determined. She must have been born early in the seventeenth century, but curiously no baptisms are recorded in the Binton register for the period 1614 to 1638. Although the bishop's transcripts are complete for these decades, they are extremely damaged and it has not been possible to trace any Jackson baptisms there either.

Hall was unable to visit Anne Jackson and treated her on the basis of reports he had received of her condition. It was not unusual for a physician to prescribe treatment without actually seeing the patient. In 1615 Dr Samuel Taylor wrote to the mathematician Thomas Harriot, who was suffering from an ulcer on the face, and informed him that he had discussed his case with Dr Theodore Turquet de Mayerne. Mayerne was unable to see Harriot at once but promised to send 'the methods that he would advise

1. Dugdale, II, p. 713.
2. WCRO, DR 72/28.

after without Pain, she had five stools. She took
it again.   The 22*th* of *May* there were taken a-
way ʒvi of blood, very black and aqueous ; yet
the Delirium was not wholly removed.   The 23
day,   ℞ *Leaves of Mallows, Violets, Beets, Lettice,
Borage, each* M ii. *Barly* ʒi. *Seeds of Gourds and
Cucumbers, each* ʒß. *make a Decoction with a sufficient quantity of Water, to* ʒxii. *To the strained Liquor
add Oil of Violets* ʒiii. *Caffia new drawn, Diacath.
each* ʒi. *Salt* ʒi. *make a Clyster.*   After for watching and restlesness I gave the following Syrup :
℞ *Syrup of red Poppies* ʒiß. *Syrup of Violets* ʒß.
Scabious water ʒiii. *Rose-water a little, Oil of Vitriol
to sharpen it.*   To the Forehead was applied this :
Oil of Roses omphac. ʒiii. *Vinegar of Roses* ʒi. *Pouder of red Sanders* ʒiß. *Waters of Lettice, Plantain,
and Roses, each* ʒi. *mix them.*   To the Head was
applied a Hen new cut thorow.   To the soals of
the Feet, Radishes bruised with Salt and Vinegar,
every third hour, for revulsion.   The 25*th*, ℞
Caffia newly drawn with Betony water ʒi. *Syrup
of Roses solutive* ʒß. *Waters of Buglofs, Borage,
Violets, each* ʒij. *make a Potion.*   It was given
in the morning.   There were also Scarifica-
tions, with Cups to the Scapula's and Shoulders.   And thus in seven days she was happily
cured.

OBSERV.

you in the cure'.[1] Hall's observation does not exclude the possibility that he found time within the seven days to see the patient and prescribe according to her progress.

The delirium and acute fever was said to be caused by Anne Jackson's not having been well purged after childbirth. A purgative mixture was prescribed and a little later six fluid ounces of blood were taken from a vein. The delirium persisted and a day after the bleeding Hall ordered an enema containing cooling and purgative drugs. He also prescribed an opiate syrup for the watching (insomnia) and restlessness.

Two methods were used to combat the poisonous vapours. Radishes bruised in salt and vinegar were applied to the soles of the feet; a hen cut through was applied to the head. This remedy was an ancient one, for Dioscorides refers to a hen cut through and applied whilst still warm as being a remedy for the bitings of serpents.[2] Later it appears to have been used to draw out other poisons, particularly in the case of delirium. A live pigeon cut open was used to treat Hall's own feverish delirium (no. 160).

Anne Jackson was also ordered to undergo wet cupping, in which small cuts were made on the shoulders and shoulder-blades and heated cups placed over them (no. 151).

155: ISABEL WOODWARD OF AVON DASSETT

Isabel Woodward was the youngest child of John Woodward (d. 1625), who had married Isabella Blencowe of Marston St Lawrence (Northants.), where imposing tombs indicate the family's status.[3] Isabel was born at Avon Dassett and had two older brothers, Richard (1604–84) and John (d. 1665).[4]

Unusually Hall noted that Isabel, a virgin, was *bene morata et optime dotata* (well-mannered and richly endowed), but nevertheless was *gibbous* or hunch-backed. Marriage would have been unlikely for such a gentlewoman at twenty-eight, but in 1641 her distant cousin, Isabel Fetherston, died and two years later she married the widowed John Fetherston to become mistress of Packwood Hall, 11 miles south-east of Birmingham.

John Fetherston (1593–1670) had practised law in London before inheriting at his father's death in 1634. In 1624 he had married his first wife, Isabel, the eldest daughter of John Woodward of Butlers Marston (1570–1623). The Woodwards were of similar status to the Fetherstons and

1. BL, Add. MS 6789.
2. Gunter, *Greek Herbal*, p. 103.
3. Pevsner, *Northants.*, p. 302.
4. *HV Warws.*, 1619, p. 227.

Observ. LV.

MAy the 2d, Mrs. *Woodward* of *Aven-daffet*, (a
Maid very witty and well-bred, yet gibbous,) aged 28, fix days before this fell into a
continual burning Fever; then by the Phyfician
being purged, and let blood, from it fhe fell into a
Baftard-Tertian, pernicious, with a yellow Jaundice, and fpots like flea-bitings, which after left
marks, which difcovered the Fever to be joined
with the Scurvy. For often it happens both in
Continual, Tertian, and Quartan Fevers, as appears in *Eugaleus*. She wanted her Courfes, and
had conftipation of the Belly. I coming on the
intermitting day, gave this: ℞ *Tincture of Coral*
gr. vi. *Spec. Liberant.* ℈ß. *Manus Chrifti perlat.*
℈ii. *Lap. Bezoar.* gr. v. *with Conferve of Barberries.*
In the fame day fhe took often the Decoction of
Harts-horn, with Manus Chrifti perlat. For her
Broth I appointed thefe Herbs, *Brook-lime, Water-creffes, Borage, Cichory. May the 26th,* ℞ *Diaturb. cum Rhab.* (becaufe there was no other ready at hand) ℈iv. *It was infufed all night in Poffet-
drink, in the morning it was ftrained, and taken with
Sugar.* I being abfent, it gave four ftools without pain. Towards evening fhe expected her
unwelcom Enemy, with grief of mind. To the
Wrift I applied *Ung. Antifebrif.* to the Feet,
Wormwood, Rue. Chamomel, boyled in Water, and applied hot in bladders before the Fit came. ℞ *Spec.
Liberant.* Ʒii. *Conferv. Barbar.* ℥ii. Of this fhe
took

derived their wealth from sheep-farming in south Warwickshire. The first Isabel Fetherston gave birth to six sons and three daughters, including one set of twins, during the period from 1625 to 1641, the year of her death. John Fetherston's remarriage on 14 February 1643 made Isabel Woodward, Hall's former patient, a step-mother to the seven surviving children, aged from two to eighteen years.

The two wives had a great-grandfather in common, Richard Woodward of Butlers Marston (d. 1557), and grandfathers who were brothers. During the second Isabel's time at Packwood John Fetherston made considerable changes to the house and gardens; panelling in the hall, a study, a chamber over the little parlour and a stable wing were all added in the 1650s and '60s. Among the additions to the grounds were the yew garden, a sundial and a holly bleaching-hedge.[1]

The second Isabel Fetherston died in 1668 and is commemorated, along with her predecessor, on their husband's handsome black marble monument in Packwood church.

When Hall was called to Isabel Woodward he diagnosed a pernicious bastard tertian fever (no. 135) and yellow jaundice. Quoting Eugalenus (no. 1) he interpreted the outbreak of spots as indicating that the fever was joined with scurvy. Attending the patient on her intermitting day (when she was free from the fever fit), Hall prescribed a cordial preparation containing coral, *Manus Christi* and bezoar stone. A decoction of hartshorn was advised for the fever and the scorbutic herbs, brooklime and water-cress, with borage and chicory for the scurvy. This treatment was dated 2 May. The next treatment was prescribed on 26 May. We cannot tell from the record whether this was a relapse or a turn for the worse in an illness that had lasted over three weeks.

As 26 May was also an intermitting day, Hall prescribed a purgative made from turpethum and rhubarb 'because there was no other remedy at hand'. On the evening of the following day he recorded that 'she expected her unwelcom Enemy, with grief of mind', by which he meant the onset of the dreaded fever paroxysms. To prepare the patient for this, Hall applied an ointment composed of antifebrile drugs to the wrists, and bladders containing herbs boiled in water to the feet.

Other prescriptions were for the treatment of the jaundice and the scurvy. A plaster containing ammoniacum was applied to the area of the spleen. Used externally ammoniacum was believed to disperse swellings. An electuary of *Diacurcuma*, which was made from turmeric and saffron, was prescribed along with the scorbutics brooklime and water-cresses (scurvy-grass is noticeably absent from this regime, possibly because it was not available).

---

1. M.W. Farr, *The Fetherstons of Packwood in the Seventeenth Century*, Dugdale Society Occasional Paper no. 18, 1968.

took the quantity of a Bean often in a day, with our *Antiscobutic Water, Observ.* 26. of this Cent. For the Jaundice and Scurvy, ℞ *Ammoniac. Pul.* ℈ii. *Oxym. simpl.* ℥ii. *Aq. Agrim.* ℥i. It was repeated on the quiet day, as need required. To the Spleen was applied *Empl. de Ammon.* There was used *Elect. Diacurcum.* the quantity of a Nutmeg, after meals. Being altogether freed from the Fever, yet not the Scurvy, I prescribed the *Chalybiat Wine* (Observ. 42. *Cent.* 1.) ℥vi. *Syrup of Scurvygrass* ℥iij. *of Brook-lime and Water-cresses, each* ℥ii. Dose was six spoonfuls, with exercise. And every other day, ℞ *Pil. Stomac. Ruffi. cap. Pill.* iii. *ex* ℨß. at going to bed. And so she was cured.

Observ. LVI.

Mrs. *Hopper,* aged 24; after birth, the Afterbirth was retained and corrupted, so that it was cast forth in little stinking bits, whence a direful stink ascended to the Stomach, Heart, Liver, Diaphragma, and from thence to the Brain ; so that there was Pain of the Head, often fainting, and cold sweats ; so that there was great danger of death, yet was recovered as followeth : ℞ *Colocynthis boyled in equal parts of Water and Juyce of Rhue, with which was mixed Myrrh, the Meal of the Seeds of Line, Fenugreek, and Barly, of each a spoonful ; boyl them all together, and make a Plaster.* Which apply to the whole Belly from the Navil to the Privity. The Matrix was anointed with *Ung. Basilicon.* ℞ *Castory* gr. vi. *Myrrh, Saffron,*

L   *each*

John Trapp, schoolmaster of Stratford-upon-Avon, in 1660, aged fifty-nine

146 *Select Observations*

each gr. iij. *Mithrid.* ℈ß. *make three Pills.* Which was given at bed time. And thus in twenty four hours ſhe was delivered.

Observ. LVII.

GOod-wife *Archer* of *Stratford,* was ſuddenly taken with Convulſion of Face and Eyes, loſs of ſpeech, her Matrix carried from its proper place, and ſo caſt, as if ſhe had been the very Image of Death, ſometimes vehemently opening and caſting her Eyes hither and thither; was cured as followeth: ℞ *Caſtory* ʒi. *Juyce of Rhue a ſpoonful,* *Sage water* ʒii. *Syrup of Mugwort* ʒi. She was conſtrained to take it. To her Noſe were applied ſtinking things. Within the ſpace of few minutes ſhe both ſpake and ſtood up. The next day, ℞ *Spec. Hier. cum Agaric.* ʒß. *Pil. fætid. de Pæon.* ā ℈i. *Fæcul. Brion. Diagrid.* ā gr. vi. *f. Pil.* 5. They were taken in the morning with cuſtody. After ℞ *Briony root* ʒiii. *Sena* ʒß. *Ginger* ℈ß. *Cinamon* ʒi. *Sugar* ʒi. *infuſe them for a night in hot Whey* ℔iß. Of this Infuſion was taken ʒv for ſeveral days together. With which the Cure was perfected.

156: CECILY HOPPER OF LOXLEY

Cecily Hopper of Loxley, near Stratford, a gentlewoman, had married into a substantial south Warwickshire family. Robert Hopper was a County Treasurer responsible for the care of maimed soldiers and sailors.[1]

Cecily Hobday was born in about 1600 and on 26 February 1628 she married John Hopper at Loxley; she had at least two sons, each named William, baptised in February 1634 and March 1635, when Hall may have attended her. Both boys died aged two years. Evidence of her death has not been found.

This patient, greatly distressed by the retention of the placenta after childbirth, was reported to have recovered within twenty-four hours. Hall's treatment was a plaster over the lower part of the abdomen and a pill with castor, myrrh, saffron and mithridate. The matrix or womb was anointed with *Unguentum Basilicon*, which was composed of turpentine, pitch, olibanum (frankincense), myrrh and other resins in a base of beeswax. Named after a Greek word meaning 'royal', Basilicon ointment was attributed to Mesue but may be much older.

157: [MRS] ARCHER OF STRATFORD-UPON-AVON

Although recorded as a town dweller, Hall gave no further information (such as Christian name or age) about this patient, except in the Latin notes that she dealt in malt, Stratford's major industry before about 1700. She may have traded on her own account, as a widow or spinster, but she cannot be identified convincingly from Archer baptisms and marriages listed in the parish registers.

'Good-wife' Archer was exhibiting symptoms of hysteria resulting from a displacement of the matrix or uterus. There were facial convulsions and loss of speech but when 'stinking things' (nos 96, 127) were applied to her nose 'within a space of a few minutes she both spoke and stood up'. The three prescriptions contained the drugs used in Hall's time to deal with these symptoms. Castor, rue and paeony were regarded as having antispasmodic properties. Mugwort and bryony were both used to treat hysteria.

158: MARTHA LEWIS OF GLAMORGAN

When he treated this gentlewoman, Hall noted that she was a sister of Mr Fortescue and, like several of his other female patients, he had attended her when young in her own family (no. 41) and then later, as a married woman.

1. QSOB, I, p. 220; IV, pp. 14, 17, 20.

OBSERV. LVIII.

Mrs. *Lewes*, Sifter to Mr. *Fortefcue*, three days after Child-birth, getting cold, fell into an Ague, with torment of the Belly, was cured as followeth: She drank the *Decoction of Harts-horn*, our *Julep againft the Fever*, two fpoonfuls every fourth hour. She alfo had a Clyfter of *Milk and Sugar*. There was *Origanum* and *Marjoram* lapped up between a Linnen Cloth, and applied hot to the Belly. And fo fhe was fuddenly helped.

OBSERV. LXI.

Mrs. *Vernon* of *Hanberry*, Wife to the Minifter, aged about 30, *Auguft* 13. 1632. was afflicted with the Scurvy, joined with various Symptoms, as coldnefs in the foals of the Feet, which like a cold vapor afcending to the Stomach, made her grievous fick; after that fhe was afflicted with heat, after with a cold fweat, and all in the fpace of two hours, and then fhe was well. Further fhe was afflicted with Melancholy, trembling of the Heart, and pain of the Spleen, fo that fhe was forced to prefs it hard with her hands; fhe had cruel pains of her Teeth and Gums, Loins, Lazinefs of the whole Body, Tumor of the Feet towards evening. In the time of her Courfes fhe

L 2 was

Nicholas Fortescue (no. 173) was her father and William her eldest brother (no. 29). Martha made a good marriage in about 1630 by becoming the bride of Nicholas (b. *c.* 1610), the third son of Sir Edward Lewis, a substantial royalist, with estates across south Glamorgan. Sir Edward had built a 'fair howse' within the castle ruins of St Fagans and was said to be worth £5,000 a year.[1] Sir Edward's wealth may be judged by his will of 1623; his daughter's dowry was to be £2,000, while Nicholas received £500 in cash and half his father's clothes as well as land.[2] Martha's husband owned Carnlloyd, Llancarfan and had an income of £400 a year in 1645.[3] Sir Edward rented from the Paulets the manor of Edington (Wilts.), where he has an imposing monument (1630),[4] although in his will he declared his wish to be buried at Bedwas, north-east of Caerphilly. Although by the 1640s the Lewis family were supporters of radical non-conformity in the Llancarfan area,[5] Nicholas Lewis appeared at Middlesex Quarter Sessions as a recusant in 1640–1 and in 1642 Martha Lewis and her three servants were presented, living at Birlingham, near Evesham (Worcs.), as recusants.[6]

Martha Lewis had a daughter, also Martha, born in about 1633. Hall may have been attending her when she was visiting her family in Worcestershire, perhaps for this daughter's birth. She was suffering from an ague and an intermittent fever, accompanied by stomach pains. As this occurred just three days after childbirth, Hall's treatment was gentle and confined to a hartshorn julep, a milk and sugar enema and a herbal compress to the belly.

159: SUSANNA VERNON OF HANBURY, WORCESTERSHIRE

Susanna Vernon was the wife of John (1599–1681), Rector of Hanbury. Hanbury Hall had been purchased in 1631 by John's brother, Edward Vernon (1586–1666), an extremely successful London attorney. Their father, Richard, had held the living from 1580 to 1628 and there is a handsome monument to him in St Mary's, Hanbury. The next incumbent was John Vernon, who, after attending Balliol College, Oxford (MA in 1623),[7] was rector for the rest of his long life. Although elderly, John Vernon was one of the 1674 diocesan inspectors of parish churches; he went to four. Alone of the forty-three inspectors, John Vernon asked that another

1. Symonds, pp. 215–17.
2. PRO, Prob 11/153.
3. G.T. Clark, *Limbus Patrum Morganiae et Glamorganiae* (1886), pp. 38–52.
4. Pevsner, *Wiltshire*, p. 238.
5. Philip Jenkins, *The Making of a British Ruling Class: the Glamorgan Gentry, 1640–1790* (Cowbridge, 1983), p. 106.
6. WoQS, pp. cxcvii, 698.
7. Foster, p. 1543.

was miferably tormented, her Flux being much and inordinate, by which fhe was weakned. The Fits of the Mother often afflicted her, of which fhe was not delivered till fhe fhed tears. Sometimes fhe had filthy black fpots on her Thighs, fometimes fhe was alfo without ftools for four days. Her Urine was of various colours. ℞ *Mallowes, Mercury, Althæa*, each M i. *boyl them in fufficient quantity of Milk to* ℔i. *in the ftraining was diffolved Diaphœnic. Diacathol.* each ʒvi. *Holland pouder* ʒi. *make a Clyfter.* It gave three ftools with wind. At her going to bed fhe took ʒii of *London Treacle.* The fourteenth day, ℞ *Brook-lime, Water-creffes,* each M i. *Marygold flowers, and of Rofemary,* each p.i. *boyl them in fufficient quantity of Whey to* ℔iſſ. *To the ftraining was added* ℔ſs *of Sugar ; it was again boyled and fcummed ; after was added* ʒſs *of Saffron tyed up in a fine rag ; after a walm or two it was taken from the Fire.* Of this Decoction were taken eight fpoonfuls, *Holland pouder,* and *Cream of Tartar,* of each as much as lay upon a Six-pence, in the morning, fafting two hours after, and then taking Veal broth, altered with *Borage, Bugloſs, Brook-lime, Water-creffes,* and *Succory* ; dining at the ufual time, fupping at five. At bed time fhe took *London Treacle,* as before. For the Mother was prefcribed *Aq. Brion. compoſ.* now fo called. For the coldnefs of the Feet was applied this Plafter : ℞ *Pitch* ℔ii. *beft Rofin poudered and fifted, Frankinfence,* each ℔ii. *Sheep-fewet* ʒi. *Saffron and Mace,* each ʒii. *Labdanum* ʒiv. *Cloves* ʒi. *mix them, and boyl them for half an hour,* or more. It is to be fpread on Leather, like to a Shoo foal. This was continued for fourteen days,

or

incumbent might visit his own church, Hanbury, 'lest I should be thought partiall in my report'.[1]

Susanna was the youngest daughter of Thomas Holland, Regius Professor of Oxford, born in about 1602 and marrying in about 1627.[2] In sixteen years she had ten children, three sons and seven daughters, one of whom died as an infant in an epidemic year. Her eldest son, Richard, was baptised on 9 April 1629 and John, the next, on 23 July 1633. Hall attended Susanna Vernon on 13 August 1632, noting that she was 'religious, well-formed, beautiful'.

She was buried at Hanbury on 16 July 1681, aged about eighty, five months before her husband, in a year when death-rates in the parish almost doubled.

The observation began with a long list of symptoms, including painful gums and black spots on the thighs, which were among the positive signs of scurvy. Hall's treatment of Susanna Vernon took the form adopted in other cases of scurvy. Purgatives were administered, first in an enema and then as a decoction involving Holland powder and cream of tartar. Scorbutic drugs were prescribed but in this case, as for Isabel Woodward (no. 155), scurvy-grass, the best known of the scorbutics and one Hall regularly used, was omitted.

Other medicines were prescribed to treat specific symptoms. Compound bryony water, formerly known as *Aqua Hysterica*, was given to treat the 'Mother'; for her cold feet, a plaster which was to be spread on leather shaped like the sole of a shoe,[3] an ointment for the spleen and a nephritic plaster for the kidneys, containing red lead and opium. Although the only date given is that of Hall's first call to Susanna Vernon, the indications are that some considerable time elapsed before the patient was declared well.

159: THOMAS FERRIMAN, RECTOR OF HARVINGTON, WORCESTERSHIRE

Mr Ferriman was one of the patients mentioned only in passing as Hall recorded treating him with a preparation that had succeeded with Susanna Vernon of Hanbury, a plaster which cured an old pain in the feet.

However, the Casebook records this patient as *Generosus Feriman senior*,

---

1. Paul Morgan (ed.), *Inspections of Churches and Parsonage Houses in the Diocese of Worcester in 1674, 1676 and 1687*, Worcs. Hist. Soc., N.S.12, 1986, p. 9.

2. Nash, I, p. 548.

3. Hall in his manuscript after the prescription for the foot plaster wrote that it was to be continued *per dies 14 vel per mense vel per septimana sex.* (for fourteen days, or for a month or for six weeks). This suggests that he was giving his readers general instructions for the use of the plaster and not recording specific instructions for Susanna Vernon.

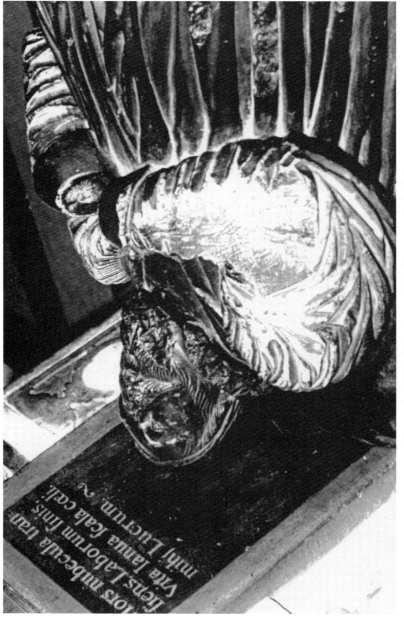

The tomb of John Thornborough in Worcester Cathedral

and in fact Hall had attended Thomas Ferriman, whose surname was noted in the 1569 Heralds' Visitation as having changed from Farmount, but retaining the original coat of arms.[1] Thomas Ferriman senior went to Queen's College, Cambridge, where he matriculated at Easter 1566.[2] In 1571 he married Magdalen Smalwait in Worcester; in 1597 he became Rector of Fladbury (Worcs.), but for nearly forty years since 1579 he had been Rector of Harvington, near Evesham. At his funeral there on 12 July 1619, the sermon was preached on the theme of Revelations 7:9 by the Reverend John Archbold DD, an old family friend, to whom Ferriman bequeathed 10s. for a bible.[3] Ferriman would undoubtedly have known Susanna Vernon and the Rector of Hanbury.

Earlier in his career, Ferriman had for four years been domestic chaplain to the Bishop of Worcester, and was present on 8 August when Queen Elizabeth I visited the bishop's palace as part of her week-long stay in 1575.[4] Ferriman made his will on 8 May 1615, leaving money to the parish poor in Worcester and Fladbury, but especially in Harvington, because it was his first preferment and 'the place where I have made my most abode'. A wealthy man, his goods were worth £389 15s. 8d., including his books (£20), plate and money (£140), leases and livestock.[5] He bequeathed £6 a year towards the education of his grandchild, Ferriman Rutter, who was later (1624–42) vicar of another Worcestershire parish, Norton-and-Lenchwick.[6]

Ferriman's son, also Thomas, succeeded him as Rector of Harvington, a desire Ferriman had expressed in his will. Thomas Ferriman junior was inducted on 30 June 1616, but died there in May 1622, aged only thirty-seven. He and his wife, Catherine, had eight children, two of whom, William and John, were apprenticed in London by 1636, when their mother died. Catherine's personal goods, mostly inherited from her husband and father-in-law, were worth £349 13s., including silver.[7]

The next incumbent of Harvington was Thomas Archbold, whose elder brother had preached at the Ferriman funeral; indeed, Thomas Ferriman senior referred in his will to the 'ancient love between our families'. However, Thomas Archbold was sequestered and died in 1654.[8]

1. *HV Worcs.*, 1569 p. 157.
2. Venn, *Alumni Cantab.*, I, part 1, II, p. 135.
3. (H)WRO, class 008.7 1619/2.
4. Nash, I, p. 577.
5. (H)WRO, class 008.7 1619/28.
6. Foster, p. 1293.
7. (H)WRO, class 008.7 1636/89.
8. Ibid., Monuments in Worcester Cathedral (typescript), p. 78.

or ſix weeks, and then removed. And for certain this Plaſter is profitable in all pain. By this Plaſter I cured Mr. *Feriman* of an old pain in the Feet. For tumor of the Spleen I uſed *Ung. Magiſt. pro Splen.* In pain of the Back was uſed our *Emplaſt. Nephritic.* As ℞ *red Lead and Wax* ℥ii. *Opium* gr. xv. *Oil of Roſes, of Water-lillies,* each ℥ii. *Juyce of Night-ſhade* ℥i. *boyl them to a Plaſter.* Spread it upon Leather. For wind of the Stomach, ℞ *Conſerve of Bugloſs* ℥ii. *Spec. Pleriſarch.* ℥ii. Doſe, the quantity of a Nutmeg. There was alſo uſed our Scorbutic Water, with Syrup of Clove Gilly-flowers. She had alſo an Antiſcorbutic Beer, and Chalybiat Wine. By the uſe of which ſhe became well.

O B S E R V. LX.

THou, O Lord, which haſt the power of Life and Death, and draweſt from the Gates of Death, I confeſs, without any Art or Counſel of Man, but only from thy Goodneſs and Clemency, thou haſt ſaved me from the bitter and deadly Symptoms of a deadly Fever, beyond the expectation of all about me, reſtoring me as it were from the very jaws of Death to former health; for which I praiſe thy Name, O moſt merciful God, and Father of our Lord Jeſus Chriſt, praying thee to give me a moſt thankful Heart for this great favour, for which I have cauſe to admire thee. About the 57*th* year of my age, *Auguſt* 27. 1632. to *Septemb.* 29. I was much debilitated with an

L 3   *immoderate*

160: DR JOHN HALL OF STRATFORD-UPON-AVON

John Hall in his manuscript frequently used the words 'Praise be to God' or 'glory to God' which indicated his deep religious conviction, as does the opening passage of this record of his own illness. His dedication as a physician is also shown here where, in spite of bleeding haemorrhoids, he rode out daily to attend his patients. Anyone who has suffered from this common affliction will fully appreciate the discomfort he must have undergone.

Hall fell victim to an epidemic fever which was proving fatal in many cases and began to treat himself using purgatives and decoction of hartshorn. He reported that the 'Disease was almost cast out by Urine', which had flowed for four days leaving him emaciated and too weak to move. For convulsions of the face and a light delirium a pigeon was cut open alive and applied to the feet to draw down the poisonous vapours. This was a variation on the use of the 'hen cut through' recommended by Dioscorides (no. 154). Later in the seventeenth century the application of a dying pigeon was a remedy reserved for patients who had little hope of survival.[1]

A point was reached where Hall could no longer deal with his own illness and his wife sent for two physicians. Preparatory to their arrival the patient was bled from the liver vein and leeches applied to the haemorrhoids. The physicians prescribed an electuary,[2] a purgative[3] and an opiate mixture.[4] An ointment was applied to the back and a plaster to the region of the heart. After another treatment with decoction of hartshorn Hall was able to eat. He then appears to have attended to his own case again and took strengthening steeled wine, scorbutics to protect against scurvy, an oil[5] for a pain in the teeth and sarsaparilla with scorbutic herbs to cure an irritation of the scrotum, 'And so I became perfectly well, praised be God'.

161: SIR THOMAS PUCKERING OF
WARWICK PRIORY

Hall had treated Sir Thomas six years earlier, in 1629 (no. 139). On this later occasion Hall prescribed a medicine named after Dr Lapworth, the Bath practitioner who had treated another patient, namely Mrs Wilson

---

1. Samuel Pepys and John Evelyn both referred to the use of pigeons for patients *in extremis*; Fernie, *Animal Simples*, pp. 402–4.

2. *Syrupus Lujula* in the electuary was syrup of wood sorrel *Oxalis acetosella*, used in fevers to allay heat and quench thirst.

3. *Electuarium Lenitivum* in the purge was one of the purgative electuaries listed in the London *Pharmacopoeia* of 1618. The list of ingredients included senna and cassia.

4. *Diacodium* in the opiate was a narcotic preparation made from poppy heads.

5. *Ol. Lig. Heraclei* refers to an oil from a wood. There is some doubt as to the meaning of *heraclei*. Quincy suggests it may be the oil of the bay-tree.

immoderate **Flux** *of the Hemorrhoids* ; yet daily was
I conſtrained to go to ſeveral places to Patients.
By riding, a hardneſs being contracted, the Flux
was ſtayed for fourteen days. After I fell into
a moſt cruel torture of my Teeth, and then into
a deadly burning Fever, which then raged very
much, killing almoſt all that it did infect, for
which I uſed the following method, which by the
help of God ſucceeded. Firſt, I purged thus :
℞ *Rubarb infuſed* ℥i. (ſurely it was infuſed in ſome
proper water, ſuppoſe ℥iii.) *Syrup. Diaſerios* ℥i.
Elect. è Succ. Roſ. ℥iii. This gave four ſtools.
After I uſed the *Decoction of Harts-horn*, and ſo
the Diſeaſe was almoſt caſt out by Urine, it flowed
very much for four days ſpace ; ſo that I was not
only much maciated, but alſo weakned, ſo
that I could not move my ſelf in my Bed without
help. I alſo had *Convulſion of the Mouth and Eyes*.
Then was a Pigeon cut open alive, and applied
to my feet, to draw down the Vapours ; for I
was often afflicted with a light Delirium. Then
my Wife ſent for two Phyſicians. I had uſed a
Clyſter with *Emollient Herbs*, and *Electu. Diacath.
& Leniti*. By the Phyſicians my Friends, was
preſcribed the following Electuary, of which I
ſwallowed the quantity of a Nutmeg twice a day.
℞ *Elect. de Gem. cal.* ℥ii. *Spec. Pleriſarch.* ℥i.
(from fear of the Scurvy.) *Manus Chriſti perlat.*
℥i. *Conſerv. Buglos. & Violar.* ã ℥ii. *Syr. Luju.* ℥i.
Syr. Viol. ℥ſſ. *Limon* ℥i. *Ol. Vitriol.* gut. vi. *f. Elect.*
The 27*th* of *Septemb.* I was thus purged : ℞ *Elect.
Lenit.* ℥iſſ. *Aq. Abſynth.* ℥iv. *Miſc.* It gave three
ſtools. At the hour of ſleep I took *Diacodium,
Syrup of red Poppies, with Diaſcordium*. For the
heat

upon Englifh Bodies. 151

heat of the Back, R *Refrig. Gal.* ℥iß. *Cerat. Santal.*
℥ß. *Succ. Sed. Acet. Vini alb.* ā coch. i. *f. Unguent.*
mol. An Emplafter for the region of the Heart,
R *Labd.* ℥vj. *Styrac. Calam.* ℥ß. *Spec. Aromat.*
Rof. ℈iv. *Mofc.* gr. iv. *Mifc.* I again was purged
thus: R *Syr. Diaferios* ℥iß. *Elect. e Succ. Rof.* ℥iii.
Aq. Cichor. q. f. It is to be obferved, before the
Phyficians came, there were drawn ℥vii of Blood
from the Liver vein, and three days after that
were the Leeches applied to the Hemorrhoids,
and thence removed ℥x. After the Decoction of
Harts-horn. Thus I was pretty well able to take
Meat. After I ufed *Chalybiat Wine,* with Juyce
of Scurvy-grafs, and *Syr. Sceletyrb. Forefti,* and
purged once a week with *Pul. fanct. Syr. Dia-*
ferios, & infuf. Rhab. For the pain of the Teeth
I ufed *Ol. Lig. Heraclei.* After I was troubled
with Itch in the *Scrotum,* which was cured with
our Decoction of *Sarfa.* with *Antifcorbutic Herbs.*
And fo I became perfectly well, praifed be God.

OBSERV. LXI.

BAronet *Puckering* of *Warwick,* aged about 44,
was cruelly vexed with pain of the Head, efpecially in the morning, and about evening; yet
when he caft himfelf upon his back, with his Head
a little declining, he felt eafe. I by the help of
God cured him as followeth: R *Pil. de Pæon.* ℥i.
de Succin. Ruffi. ā ℈i. *Cephal. Fernel.* ℈ii. *cum Aq.*
Betonic. f. Pil. N. 15. He took two at going to
bed, and three in the morning. Thefe ended,

the

the Leeches were applied to the Hemorrhoids with happy and defired event, for he was altogether freed from the Pain of his Head. After he ufed the following Opiat : ℞ *Lign. Saffafr. incif.* ʒvi. *Cinam. pul. Cal. Aromat.* ā ʒ ſ. *infund. in Aq. Buglof.* ʒxii. *per hor.* 24. *deind. coq. ad dimid. colat. adde Conferv. Flor. Cichor. Buglof.* ā ʒ ſ. *Theriac. Venet.* ʒ i. *Confeƈt. Alkerm. de Hyacinth.* ā ʒ i ſ. *Chalyb. præp.* ʒi. *Diatri. Santal. Diamb. Diamofc. dulc.* ā ɘiſ. *Lap. Bezoar.* ɘſ. *C. C. præp. Margarit. præp.* ā ɘii. *cum Syr. Confer. Citri. f. Opiat.* Dofe, the quantity of a Filbert, morning, and going to bed. Having taken cold, he fell into a Quotidian Fever in the night. I purged him thus : ℞ *Syr. Diaferios* ʒii. *Rhabar. expref.* ʒi. *Cremor. Tartar.* ɘi. *Aq. Betonic.* ʒii. *f. Hauft.* Which he retained for half an hour, and then vomited it, yet had four ftools. The next day for his Cough and Phlegm, ℞ *Syrup of Maiden-hair and Hyffop, each* ʒi. *Syrup of Scabious, Magi.* ʒſ. *make a Linƈture.* He liking it well, it was repeated, with which he caft up abundance of Phlegm. I framed him a Julep with *capillary Herbs, Snails, yellow Sanders, China, fhavings of Ivory and Harts-horn, with Syrup of Limons and Violets.* With three fpoonfuls of this Julep were taken two fpoonfuls of *Aq. Saxon. frigid.* ℞ *Magift. perlar.* ʒi. *Aq. Scabiof.* ʒiv. *Syr. Caryophil.* ʒi. *Confeƈt. Alker.* ɘi. *Mifc.* Thus he was delivered from his Fever. Afterwards for the prefervation of his Health was prefcribed the following Opiat, by Doƈtor *Lapworth* ; ℞ *Confer. Flor. Betonic. Caryophil. hortenf.* ā ʒi. *Cortic. Citri. condit.* ʒvi. *Extraƈt. Calam. Aromat.* ʒi. *Cortic. Winteran. pul.* ɘiiſ. *Sem. Pæon.*
ʒi.

(no. 176). Hall's notes show that he attended Sir Thomas on 16 September, presumably, by Puckering's age, in 1635, shortly before Hall's own death.

Sir Thomas died in March 1637 in Sussex and was buried a month later in the chancel of St Mary's, Warwick, an event noted by Dugard in his diary.[1] Puckering's exceptionally fine monument there was the work of Nicholas Stone, Wren's master-mason; it cost £200 and was erected according to the instructions of Puckering's will.[2] Sir Thomas bequeathed £10 each to six Warwickshire parishes for their poor: Kineton, Leamington Priors, Lillington, Butlers Marston, Snitterfield and Tachbrook.[3] After his death, his widow, Elizabeth (no. 109), moved back to Sussex, where she died in 1652.

Sir Thomas was again suffering from head pains and Hall recommended the cephalic pill used six years before (no. 139). Leeches were applied to the haemorrhoidal veins and an opiate prescribed. The patient then fell into a quotidian fever accompanied by a cough, which Hall treated first with a purgative followed by a linctus and a julep containing capillary herbs,[4] snails, China root, hartshorn and the cordials yellow saunders wood and ivory scrapings. The julep was to be taken with a compound water composed of cordial drugs and known as *Aqua Cordialis Frigida Saxoniae*.

On both of the recorded occasions when Hall attended Puckering he prescribed 'for the preservation of his health' a form of treatment not used elsewhere in the observations. This time he prescribed an opiate electuary composed by Dr Lapworth and a plaster to be applied to the area of the spleen.[5] He also had a fontanelle opened in the left arm as a prophylactic measure, to rid the body of acrid humours. A small cut was made in the skin and kept open for months. Samuel Jeake (1652–99) recorded in his diary that a fontanelle was opened in his neck to draw humours from his face in August 1671 but, finding it of little benefit, had it dried up the following year.[6] It is possible that the fontanelle was in place when Puckering died a short time after his treatment.

1. BL, Add. MS 23146.

2. SBTRO, DR 37, vol. 30, f.1.

3. William Cooper, *A History of Lillington* (Long Compton, 1940), p. 110.

4. 'Capillary herbs' in the julep probably refers to maiden-hair *Adianthum capillus veneris* and other species of *Adianthum*.

5. *Diachylon. comp.* in the plaster refers to *Emplastrum Diachylon Compositum* composed of mucilaginous herbs and gum resins. Also available were *Emplastrum Diachylon Simplex* and *Emplastrum Diachylon Magnum*, both containing mucilaginous herbs together with litharge or lead oxide.

6. M. Hunter and A. Gregory (eds), *An Astrological Diary of Samuel Jeake of Rye* (Oxford, 1988), p. 118.

upon Englijh Bodies. 153

Ʒi. *Ol. Cinam.* gut. iv. *cum Syr. Betonic. q. ſ. f. condit.* Of this he took the quantity of a Nutmeg, which was uſed with great ſucceſs. For his Spleen I preſcribed this : ℞ *Emp. Magiſt.* pro *Lien.* Ʒiſs. *Diachyl. comp.* Ʒvi. *Caran. in Acet. Scillitic. diſſol.* Ʒiv. *Rad. Helleb. alb.* Episdii. *Ol. Lig. Rhod.* Episdi. *Miſe. f. Empl.* It was ſpread upon Leather, and covered with ſome Sarcenet, and applied to the Spleen. By theſe he was delivered from all his Symptoms, and to prevent, had a Fontinel opened in his left Arm.

Observ. LXII.

ALderman *Tyler*, being exceedingly troubled with heat and roughneſs of his Tongue, was cured with the following : ℞ *Syr. Scabioſ. mag. Becabung. Naſturt. aquat. Succ. Cochlear. præp.* ā Ʒſs. *Syr. Tuſſilag. Liquirit. Papav. Erratic.* ā Ʒi. *Miſc.* It was taken often with a Liquoris ſtick.

Observ. LXIII.

THe Daughter of Alderman *Smith*, aged about 22, from diminution of her Courſes, and fear, fell into the Mother, with Convulſion of the Eyes, and darkneſs of ſight, it continuing all the Fit, together with diſtortion of the Neck, and palpitation of the Heart, as alſo a Fever, ſo that ſhe toſſed up and down her Bed. In the time of her

162: RICHARD TYLER, ALDERMAN OF
STRATFORD-UPON-AVON

Richard Tyler was baptised at Stratford on 28 September 1566, the second son of Alderman William Tyler (d. 1589), a town butcher.[1] In 1588 Richard Tyler married well; his bride was Susanna Woodward of Shottery Manor, whose father, Richard, was a minor gentleman with a wide kin network throughout south Warwickshire, some of whom Hall treated (nos 111, 115). In 1588, Armada year, the young Richard Tyler was reimbursed for providing arms towards the county's defence.[2]

Tyler served as a sidesman and churchwarden; he was elected a Burgess in July 1590. He lived in Sheep Street and, in Shakespeare's will, his name was removed in favour of Hamnet Sadler's as a beneficiary.[3] The reason usually cited was his self-interested behaviour as one of five inhabitants authorised to collect after the town fire in 1614.

Susanna's mother was born Frances Perrott, a Stratford heiress, whose family had been brewers in the town. After bearing eleven children in seventeen years, Susanna Tyler died in May 1611; she was omitted from her grandfather's and father's wills, although the latter bequeathed £5 to keep the young Richard at school.[4] Both men were of puritan persuasion. Richard Tyler, distinguished in the parish register by the title 'Mr' and the description 'gent', was buried on 13 December 1636 aged sixty-nine.

The alderman's sore tongue was treated locally with a lick containing the syrups of scabious, coltsfoot and wild poppy, with the three scorbutic drugs: scurvy-grass, brooklime and water-cresses.

163: MARGARET SMITH OF
STRATFORD-UPON-AVON

The most likely candidate for the alderman's daughter described in this observation is Margaret, fourth of the eleven children of Francis Smith, who had married Ursula Ainge in the town on 17 August 1592. Francis was the son of William Smith, presumed to have been Shakespeare's godfather, and lived in a house facing the High Cross; both Smiths were mercers. Hall must have treated Margaret in 1621, for she was baptised on 12 August 1599. Margaret Smith was later (1623) to marry Paul Sylvester and featured again in Hall's notes as the mother of Hester Sylvester of Burford (no. 129). Her own mother, Ursula, was buried aged forty-four on

1. Fripp, p. 890.
2. *Mins & Accts*, IV, p. 39.
3. *Life*, p. 247.
4. *VCH Warws.*, III, p. 258n.

154   *Select Observations*

her Fit I commanded to diftil into her Mouth three
fpoonfuls of *Aq. Hyfteric.* After I fumed her with
Vngula Caballina, which delivered her from her
Fit. To prevent, was given as followeth : ℞
Caftor. pul. ʒſſ. *Pil. Fætid.* ʒj. *f. Pil.* 7. *deaur.*
This purged her well, and delivered her from the
Symptoms. Laftly, ℞ *Pul. Caftor.* ʒſſ. *Extract.*
Hyfter. ʒi. *f. Pil.* N. *9.* Of thefe fhe took three
at bed-time, and two in the morning. By thefe
few Remedies fhe was perfectly cured, and never
had it after.

O B S E R. LXIV.

THe only Son of Mr. *Holy-oak* (which framed
the Dictionary) fell into a burning Fever,
pain in the Loins, and Cough, the fore-runners
of the Small-Pox, which appeared after the taking of the following Potion : ℞ *Diafcord.* ʒi.
Tinctur. Coral. Lap. Bezoar. ā gr. iii. It was given in
Fennel water. By this he was freed from pain in
his Back and Stomach, and they began to appear.
To preferve the Eyes, ℞ *Plantain water, Eye-bright*
water, and Rofe-water, each ʒi. *Camphire* ϴi. *Saf-*
fron gr. ii. *make a Collyrium.* With which the Eyes
were gently anointed often with a Feather. To
preferve the Throat and Mouth, I prefcribed that
he fhould continually gargle Milk and Plantain
water mixed, which is a moft excellent Remedy.
Syrup of Pomegranats is alfo a Secret both to defend
the Lungs, Throat, Mouth, and Breaft. Therefore I prefcribed this : ℞ *Syr. Gran. dul.* ʒii.
                                                    Peni-

6 February 1613, a few days after childbirth. Alderman Smith lived on until 1625.

Margaret Smith experienced a diminution of her courses (menstruation) and 'fear' which resulted in hysteria with convulsive fits. The hysteria was treated with prescriptions used in similar cases. *Aqua Hysterica* containing bryony root was given and the patient was made to inhale the fumes of *Ungula Caballina* or horse's hoof (no. 144).[1]

Two pills were prescribed to prevent the convulsive fits. The first was of castor with the ingredients of *Pilula Foetide* (stinking pills), which Hall directed to be gilded with gold leaf. The other was castor with extract of bryony. Hall concluded that his treatment had a satisfactory outcome.

164: THOMAS HOLYOAK OF SOUTHAM

Thomas Holyoak was born on 26 December 1616 at Stoneythorpe and was baptised at Southam on 12 January 1617. His father, Francis (1567–1653), was the county's leading Arminian minister, instituted as Rector of Southam in 1605 by Sir Clement Throckmorton. Francis Holyoak later published *A Sermon of Obedience, especially unto Authority Ecclesiastical* (Oxford, 1610) and his Latin-English dictionary (1633) was dedicated to Laud.[2]

No date is recorded for when, as a boy, he was treated for smallpox. Although Southam registers show certain years of high burial numbers, such as 1615 and 1630, there is no evidence of the cause of this greater mortality and, of course, no indication of sickness.

Thomas Holyoak was educated at Coventry and then attended Queen's College, Oxford, where he was later to be chaplain. He became Rector of Birdingbury in 1641. In the Civil War he served as a Captain of Foot in the royal army at the siege of Oxford and his loyalty was subsequently rewarded by Charles II's conferment of the degree of DD.

In 1647, when forced from his living,[3] Thomas Holyoak became a physician in Warwick, where the family continued medical practice in the next century. From 1660 to 1674 he was Rector of Whitnash. He died in 1675 and was buried in St Mary's, Warwick.[4]

An opiate was prescribed to relieve the patient in the early stages of the illness. After the pox or pustules had appeared various preparations were used to assist nursing the boy through the disease. A *collyrium* was prescribed to protect his eyes and a gargle of milk and plantain to protect the mouth and throat. Hall wanted to prescribe *Syrupus Granata* or syrup of pomegranates,

---

1. *Ungula caballina* is a possible cause for confusion as it was also used as a name for the herb coltsfoot.
2. Hughes, p. 67.
3. *Worthies*, p. 427.
4. *VCH Warws.*, VI, p. 221.

Penideor. ʒiii. *Syr. de Rof. ficc. Diamor.* ā ʒſſ. *Di-atrag. frigid. in Tab.* ʒiii. *Amyl. purif.* Əii. *f. Eclegm.* But becaufe this was not to be had, there was ufed, *Syrup of Scabious, Magiftral.* ā ʒ ſſ. *Syrup of Maiden-hair,* and *Liquoris,* each ʒi. *mix them.* This was very fuccefsful. To refrefh the Senfes, ℞ *a little Bread dipped in the Vinegar of Rofes, held to the Nofe in a fine Rag.* For Diet he ufed this Hordeat : ℞ *Hord. mund.* p. i. *Amygd. dulc.* ʒii. *f. Hordeatum* ℔i. Which was fweetned with Sugar of Violets, that the Pox might be expelled more. To the Skin was ufed a De-coction of *Liquoris, Figgs,* and *common Barly*; which was given hot. He was kept conftantly in bed, with a Fire in the Chamber. His Drink was *Ptyfan.* And thus he was cured.

Observ. LXV.

THe Lord of *Northampton*'s Gentleman had the ambulative Gout, wherein he had ex-treme pain, fometimes in one knee, fometimes in the other, fo that he could fcarce walk. There was alfo fometime a Retention of Urine, he was aged 34. He was prefently eafed by the follow-ing Medicines : ℞ *Pil. fine quib. fœtid.* ā ʒi. *ex Opopan.* Əii. *Troch Alhand.* Əi. *Sal. prunel.* gr. xv. *f. Pil. deaurat.* He took one at ten a clock at night, and four about feven a clock the next morning, and fo for three days; by which he was well purged. ℞ *Emplaft. Oxycroc. Diachyl. cum Gum.* ā ʒi. *Ol. è Laterib.* ʒi. *f. Emplaft.* Which

'a most excellent remedy', to protect the lungs and throat, but it was not available and he had to fall back on syrup of scabious and syrup of maiden-hair. This was presented in the form of an *Eclegma* which was the term used for a medicine to be licked from a liquorice stick. Bread dipped in vinegar of roses was held to the nose as a restorative, a *hordeatum*, a preparation of barley (*hordeum*), was given for a drink and a hot decoction of liquorice, figs and barley for the skin.[1] There is no reference to a local application to prevent scarring as occurred in the case of Mr Farnham (no. 78).

165: WILLIAM BEALE, LORD NORTHAMPTON'S GENTLEMAN, OF COMPTON WYNYATES

The evidence for the identity of this patient is to be found in the Compton family records; he appears in a list of household members for 1616 and also in the steward's estate account ledger for the years 1629 to 1635, when William Goodman was the agent.[2]

The equine expenses for Compton Wynyates and Castle Ashby were considerable, including stables, feed, farriery and saddlery costs, and £72,000 was apparently spent by Lord Northampton on 'great horses and rich saddles' when he inherited his father-in-law's fortune in 1610.[3] In charge of Lord Northampton's very large equestrian bills was Mr William Beale, described in March 1631 when he settled the year's accounts as 'gentleman of the horse'.[4] He had also been listed in 1616 as one of the 'Gentlemen and yeomen retayners' who formed part of the eighty-three-strong household.[5]

William Beale must have been born in the last years of the sixteenth century and was buried at Long Compton on 31 January 1640.

This patient was experiencing pain in his knees, which Hall called *Gutta ambulatina*, ambulative or moving gout. The treatment began with a purgative pill to counter the defluxion of humours which was believed to be the cause of the gout (no. 89). He was also suffering from a retention of urine and Hall included in the pill two drugs to relieve this. *Pilula foetide* was prescribed as it contained the resin opopanax, which was used to open obstructions in the body. The second item, *Sal prunellae*,[6] promoted the flow

1. The manuscript indicates that the decoction was 'for the skin' and not 'to the skin' as in Cooke's version.

2. Castle Ashby, FD 1084(5); WCRO, CR 556/274. For another patient from the Compton household, see no. 10.

3. Compton, *Comptons*, p. 54.

4. WCRO, CR 556/274.

5. Castle Ashby, FD 1084(5).

6. *Sal prunellae* was prepared by sprinkling sulphur on to melted nitre or saltpetre (potassium nitrate). This was thought to improve the properties of nitre, which was used to promote urine and relieve stranguries.

156 *Select Observations*

Which being applied to the pained part, eafed it.
The 27*th* of *Decemb.* to prevent, was given this:
Ŗ *Elect. Caryocoft.* ℥ſs. *Crem. Tart.* ℈i. *Syr. Diaſ.* ℥i.
Aq. Betonic. ℥iv. *M.* After, Ŗ *Pil. fine quib.* ℨi. *Fætid.* ℥iſs. *Troch. Alhand.* ℈i. *f. Pil.* 10. There
were given five for a Dofe, by which he was
wholly delivered.

OBSERV. LXVI.

Mrs. *Boves,* of *Kings-cotton,* aged 46, was miferably afflicted with Itch in the Fundament, and *Afcarides,* which were prefently cured as followeth: Ŗ *Pil. Hier. cum Agarick,* ℨii.
Ruffi. ℨi. *Fætid.* ℈i. *f. Pil. N* 15. Two of which
fhe took at going to bed, and three in the morning. Thefe done, I gave a drachm of the following Rotula's: Ŗ *Sem. Macedonic. Sem. Santon.* ā ℈iv. *Cortic. Granat. C. C. ufti.* ā ℨſs. *Dictam.
alb. Rhab. elect. Caryophil.* ā ℈i. *Cinam.* ℨii. *Croc.*
℈i. *Mifc. f. Pul.* with fufficient quantity of Sugar make Rotula's, weighing a drachm. There
were Suppofitories ufed fometimes of Lard,
fometime Clyfters of Milk and Sugar. She ufed
the *Rotula's* for fifteen days, by which fhe was delivered from the Itch and Worms. *Thonerus* cured a Girl of fix years old, only with thefe following: *Elect. de Tamarind. cum Fol. Sen.* ℥iii.
Magift. Jalap. gr. vi. *Mifc.* To preferve, he prefcribed *Rotul. contra Verm, Auguft. ex Fol. Sen. &c.*

OBSERV.

of urine. A plaster was applied to the painful joints. An electuary and a pill formulated as above, but excluding the *Sal prunellae,* was prescribed to prevent a relapse.

166: MARGARET BOVEY OF KING'S COUGHTON

Margaret Bovey was one of the group of patients Hall attended in this area; King's Coughton is a hamlet a quarter of a mile north of Alcester. The Bovey family had been prominent yeomen in the parish since the fifteenth century, although they were to disappear from the records by 1720.

Margaret Bovey was born about 1570, the daughter and heiress of William Harrison of Callicroft, near Drake's Broughton (Worcs.), and she married John Bovey of King's Coughton (1564–1637). John Bovey was the eldest of nine children and in 1587 inherited on the death of his father, William, whose inventory (total value £102 3s.) shows that in their house there were painted cloths, table carpets, thirty-four pieces of pewter and a joined bed. William's livestock (worth £12) included a heifer he bequeathed to John Bovey.[1]

John Bovey, a freeholder, had appeared in 1612 in the manorial court for not keeping up his 'mounds';[2] he was able to sign when witnessing another inhabitant's probate inventory. At his death he left cash bequests and money to buy *in memoriam* rings, as well as £10 to the poor of Alcester; the three sons of his deceased brother, Florizel (b. 1579), each received £20. It is clear from the will that John Bovey had no surviving children, and the main beneficiary was Margaret, who inherited King's Coughton House, land, money, jewels and plate. He was described as a gentleman in his will (20 January 1637);[3] he was buried at Alcester two months later. Hall must have treated Margaret Bovey, noted as '*Generosa*', about 1616, and he recorded, on attending Edith Stoughton (no. 175), that he had earlier used the same medication successfully for Margaret Bovey. Record of her burial has not been found.

Margaret Bovey had the parasitic roundworm *ascaris.* The first treatment was a purgative pill to act as a vermifuge to expel the worms and, in the context of Hall's beliefs, the putrescent matter from which the worms were generated (no. 40). The second prescription was for a powder which was to be mixed with sugar and formed into a rotula (no. 139). Included in this powder was *Semen santonicum* or wormseed, an efficient remedy against roundworm. In the nineteenth century a vermicidal crystalline lactone was isolated from wormseed which was named santonin and widely used as an

1. G.E. Saville, *King's Coughton* (Kineton, 1973), p. 77.
2. Ibid., p. 77.
3. (H)WRO, class 008.7 1636/30.

Observ. LXVII.

THe Lady *Brown* of *Radford*, aged 49, *Jan.* 1. 1633. having laboured of the Scurvy long confirmed, and now of a Scorbutic, continual, burning Fever, accompanied with the following Symptoms, with which she was vexed, as beating of the Heart, Wind of the Stomach and the Belly, of which she found very little ease, although she vented wind both ways. Her Mouth was continually dry, although she could content her self with a little Drink. Her Pulse was variable, weak, unequal, and often vermicular: The Heat in this Scorbutic Fever was more gentle than in an exquisit, and joined with less thirst and restlessness; or if it were much, yet it was by intervals. Her Urine was thick and red, with the like sediment, unequal, yet thirst less. She was very subject to fainting when she rose out of her Bed, with many other deadly Symptoms, yet was she helped in a few days with the few following Medicines. Having great torment in the Belly, there was injected this Clyster: ℞ *the common Decoction for a Clyster* ℥xii. *course Sugar* ℥iv. *fresh Butter* ℥ ii. *mix them.* It gave two stools. But before the Clyster was administred, she took the following Electuary: ℞ *Spec. Liberant.* ℥i. *in Conserv. Barber.* It was given an hour before the Clyster. At the hour of sleep she took five grains of *Bezoar*, and the next morning the foresaid Electuary. The Clyster was again injected,

anthelmintic until replaced by less toxic substances. Wormseed is not a seed but the unexpanded flowerheads of *Artemisia cina* and other species of *Artemisia*.

Cooke added to Hall's observation giving a short account of anthelmintic remedies recommended by Thonerus.

167: ELIZABETH, LADY BROWNE OF
RADFORD SEMELE

Hall's treatment of this case is discussed on another occasion when he treated Lady Browne for scurvy (no. 110).

168: ANNE, LADY RAINSFORD OF
CLIFFORD CHAMBERS

In about 1595 Anne Goodere, the younger daughter of Sir Henry (d. 1595) of Polesworth married Henry Rainsford of Clifford Chambers, the grandson of Charles Rainsford, who had acquired the manor in 1562.[1] Anne Goodere was born about 1571 at Coventry and had a good dowry of £1,500.[2] Sir Henry was actively anti-recusant and is known for his patronage of the Warwickshire poet, Michael Drayton (1563–1631), another of Hall's patients (no. 22). Goodere lived grandly and hospitably, with guests such as Ben Jonson and John Donne.[3] Finances must have been strained, however, for in 1632, four years after his death (his will witnessed by Drayton), £5,000 was still owed to the Rainsford in-laws.[4] When John Combe of Stratford died on 10 July 1614 he left a silver salt or £5 to Sir Henry and 40s. to Lady Rainsford to buy a commemorative ring.[5]

Lady Rainsford was one of a handful of female patients Hall greatly admired; he described her as 'modest, pious, friendly, devoted to sacred literature and conversation in the French language'. Hall treated her for renal calculi in 1633 when she was elderly; however, another patient, 'Mrs Goodyear' (no. 151), may be a relation and other Rainsfords were also attended by Hall (nos 84, 147). Anne had three sons, of whom two survived, Henry (born in 1599) and Francis (1601). Her husband, knighted in 1603, was buried on 30 January 1622, an event marked by Drayton in an elegy, 'Upon the Death of his Incomparable Friend'. There is no record of her

1. *VCH Glos.*, VI, p. 209.
2. Newdigate, *Michael Drayton*, p. 37.
3. Hughes, pp. 45, 127.
4. SBTRO, DR33/14.
5. SBTRO, Wheler's interleaved copy of *Observations*.

jected, and procured three ftools, which gave
great eafe. She often took the Gelly of Hartshorn in Broth, altered with Antifcorbutic Herbs.
At the hour of fleep fhe took this : ℞ *Aq. Cord.
frig. Sax.* ℥i. *Syr. Sceletyrb. Foreft. coch.* ii. The
third day I thus purged her : ℞ *Man.* ℥i. *Rha-
barb* ℨi. *Crem. Tartar.* ℈i. *Syr. Sceletyrb. Foreft.* ℥i.
Aq. Cichor. ℥iii. *Mifc.* This gave four ftools.
For her thirft fhe ufed the Decoction of Hartshorn. And thus fhe was cured.

Observ. LXVIII.

THe Lady *Rainsford*, aged about 62, cruelly
tormented with the Stone, Fever, Thirft,
Pain of the Back, was cured as followeth : ℞
Pul. Holland. ℨi. *Tereb. Cypr.* ℨii. *Mifc. f. Pil.*
Of which was given ℨi made in five Pills. ℞
Ol. Scorpion. ℨi. *Amygd. dulc.* ℨii. With this her
Back was anointed. ℞ *Decoct. comm. pro Clyft.*
℥xii. *Elect. Lenit. & Diaphænic.* ā ℥i. *Syr. Rof.
fol.* ℥iii. *Mifc.* This gave two ftools. Six hours
after it came away, was given another prepared
only of the faid Decoction, red Sugar ℥iv. and
Butter ℥iv. But note, every third hour fhe took
the following : ℞ *Spec. Liberant.* ℨi. *Syr. Papav.
erratic.* ℨſſ. *Hypof. q. f.* She refted quietly this
night. ℞ *Rhab. pul.* ℨii. *Aq. Fumitor.* ℥viii.
bul. ad quartam Col. adde Tart. Cryft. ℈i. *Syr.
Diaferios* ℥ii. *f. Hauft.* This gave five ftools.
The following day fhe had a Clyfter framed only
of Oil of Linfeed. At bed time fhe took this :
℞

death in the parish register. On the monument to Anne and her husband in Clifford church the space left on it to record her death is empty.

Lady Rainsford was tormented with the stone, fever, thirst and a pain in the back. Hall's treatment consisted of a regime of purgatives, enemas, an opiate,[1] a preparation containing hartshorn and a mixture of the oils of almond and scorpions applied to her back.

After administering a purgative Hall wrote that it was repeated 'six hours after it came away'. This statement appears to refer to the action of the purgative but it may have referred to a small stone or gravel voided in the urine. Except for a stone coming away in the urine or removed by a surgeon using the hazardous process of cutting for the stone, there was no remedy for calculi. It was widely believed that a stone could be dissolved and Hall noted a woman who drank over two gallons of water a day from a mineral spring in an attempt to achieve this (no. 176). The only people who benefited from this belief were the quacks, who lined their pockets with secret remedies to dissolve the stone.[2]

169: JOHN THORNBOROUGH, BISHOP OF WORCESTER

John Thornborough's earlier appointments had been as Dean of York (1589) and to the Bishoprics of Limerick (1593–1603) and of Bristol (1603–17). He was thrice married and his eldest surviving son, Edward (d. 1645), became Archdeacon of Worcester. He was a 'great adept at chemistry' and published texts on political, scientific and religious topics. A contemporary noted that he gave a dull sermon in London in 1602 on the anniversary of the Queen's accession. He was born in 1551 in Wiltshire and attended Magdalen College, Oxford,[3] where he was known for his attention to fencing, dancing, hunting and 'wooing of wenches' rather than to his books. At university, his companion-attendant was Simon Forman, later the notorious astrologer.[4] Strongly anti-recusant, Thornborough was appointed with the Earl of Pembroke's influence to Worcester on 17 February 1617.[5] Abjuring the 'superstitions of Rome' in his will, he had little sympathy with

1. *Hypocistus* used in the opiate is a drug that does not appear elsewhere in the *Observations*. It was the dried juice of the parasitic plant *Cytinus hypocistus* which grows on the root of *Cistus incanus*. It was used as a mild astringent.

2. The secret of a famous remedy for the stone sold by Mrs Joanna Stephens was bought for a large sum in 1739. It was found to consist of calcined egg shells, soap and bitters.

3. *DNB; HV Worcs.*, 1634, pp. 94–5.

4. A.L. Rowse, *The Case Books of Simon Forman* (1974), pp. 282–3.

5. John Thornborough, *The Last Will and Testament of Jesus Christ* (1630), sig. A2^v–3^r.

℞ *Spec. Liberant.* Ðii. *C. C. præp.* Ði. *Tinctur. Coral,* Ðſs. And ſo in the morning ſhe was well.

OBSERV. LXIX.

DOctor *Thornberry*, Biſhop of *Worceſter*, aged about 86, *Febr.* 1. 1663. was long tormented with a Scorbutic wandering Gout, falſly imagined by his Phyſician to be a true Gout, as appeared not only by the frequent Change of his Urine, both in colour and ſubſtance, but alſo livid ſpots in his Thighs. He had very unquiet Nights from ſalt and ſharp humors, and Vapors aſcending to his Head; and if he did ſleep, it was with terror, which happened from the ſudden ſlaughter of one in his Family, which did much terrify and perplex his Spirits, and afflicted him grievouſly with Melancholy. His Pain lay ſometimes in his Knee, otherwhiles in his Foot, without any tumor in the Foot, but about the Knee and Inſtep there was great ſwelling, and after in the Feet. I ſaid he might be eaſed, but never perfectly cured, which I effected as follows. I omitted purging, he being very weak, and having been before purged. He had a Gelly framed of Harts-horn, with Knuckles of Veal, Partridg, Raiſins, Dates, and Antiſcorbutic Herbs. It being ſtrained, there was added a little Tincture of Saffron and Alkermes, with Sugar-candy to ſweeten it. He took the Juyce of Scurvy-graſs prepared in Wine twice or thrice a day. For the Pain and
Tumor

Arminianism and was, in 1635, accused of 'laxity' by Sir Nathaniel Brent, Laud's vicar-general.[1] He ordained Thomas Dugard as a priest (1636) and both Henry Dugard (1622) and Richard Baxter (1638) as deacons.[2] Twice Thornborough clashed with the king over appointments within the diocese, on both occasions because the bishop wished to advance his own relatives.

Scandal and tragedy had struck Thornborough before he arrived at Worcester, for by April 1599 he was divorced, 'flat contrary to her Majesty's ecclesiastical laws', and remarried, claiming his second wife was not pregnant.[3] In 1612 a contemporary wrote that the eldest Thornborough son, aged twenty, had killed himself rather than face punishment for his gambling debts.[4] Three years later his second wife, Elizabeth Bales of Wilby (Suff.), was 'a suspicious person' in the murder of Sir Thomas Overbury. She was said to be intimate with the Countess of Essex and 'given to chemistry'.[5] When the divorced Countess, recently Forman's client, then married the Earl of Somerset three months after the murder, Mrs Thornborough gave an elaborate bridal-cake costing £5.[6] She was imprisoned and questioned 'as to her preparations of certain waters and powders, her procuring and delivery of poisons', for which she was apparently rewarded with land near Knaresborough (Yorks.).[7] An active magistrate,[8] Thornborough lived at Hartlebury Castle, and Hall wrote that he attended him in 1633 (1663 is a misprint), just before the bishop had granted a pew in Holy Trinity, Stratford to the Hall family, a contentious local issue.[9] Hall noted the bishop's melancholy, following his son's death in a brawl with a priest.[10]

Thornborough died in office; according to Hall's notes he would have been born in 1547, but Magdalen College recorded his age as twenty in 1571[11] and a portrait of 1630 gives his age as eighty. In his will he left bequests to all his seven children and their offspring, including £100 to one fatherless grandson, Benjamin, to assist him at university; he later became a physician. Thomas, his son, however, inherited only £5, having had 'sufficient patrimony in my lifetime' as well as a house, £30 a year and his debts paid.[12] This was the son who had married a fifteen-year-old local

1. *VCH Worcs.*, II, pp. 58–65.
2. BL, Add. MS 23146.
3. *CSPD, 1598–1601*, p. 178.
4. Chamberlain, I, p. 335.
5. *CSPD, 1611–18*, pp. 336, 338.
6. Chamberlain, I, p. 498.
7. *CSPD, 1611–18*, p. 345; ibid., *1640–1*, p. 337.
8. WoQS, pp. 234–719.
9. SBTRO, ER 78/7.
10. This dramatic incident has been impossible to trace.
11. Foster, p. 1457.
12. PRO, Prob 11/187.

Tumor was applied live-Worms, which I have often applied to others in like pains with good succefs. Afterwards I ufed the following, which removed the Tumefaction in three or four days. The Feet were bathed with this : ℞ *Brook-lime* M x. *boyl it in sufficient quantity of Beer, for a Bath* ; which was ufed morning and night. After bathing, was applied a Pultefs framed of the *Pouder of Wormwood, and Yolks of Eggs.* The firft night he flept more quietly. There were ufed alfo inwardly our *Antifcorbutic Water,* with the Juyce of Scurvy-grafs, as before, as alfo the Gelly. He alfo had an Antifcorbutic Beer. By all which he was wholly delivered from the pain and tumor in his Feet, fo that he could walk abroad.

Observ. LXX.

MR. *Simon Underhil,* aged about 40, troubled with extream Vomiting, wind of the Stomach, difficulty of breathing, conftipation of the Belly and Scurvy, was cured as followeth : ℞ *Jalap.* ℈i. *Crem. Tartar.* ℈ß. *Tereb. Cypr. q. f. f. Pil.* N. 3. which wrought well. For difficulty of breathing : ℞ *Spec. Plerifarchon.* ℨii. *Conferv. Cochlear.* ℨii. *Confeci. Alkermes* ℈i. *Mifc,* Dofe the quantity of a Nutmeg an hour before Meat. It was often repeated. There was alfo ufed *Diacurcuma* before fupper ℨii. By thefe he became much better, fo that he fent me away, and after came home to me, and faid I fhould either cure

heiress, Helen Acton of Elmley Lovett, by force in 1624, the bishop performing the ceremony; but in 1640 he refused to maintain her and four children when her husband abandoned her.[1] Thornborough's daughter, Elizabeth, Lady Willoughby, was a recusant, also separated from her husband, who subsequently quarrelled with the bishop.[2]

Thornborough had arranged for his own monument, correctly classical, (now severely damaged), to be erected in the nave of Worcester cathedral fourteen years before his death, bearing the inscription *dum spiro spero* with a number of Pythagorean symbols.[3] He was a contradictory figure, fiercely protective of his episcopal rights, remorselessly anti-Catholic, frequently in financial difficulties and with a widespread reputation for gambling and womanising. The disapproval of later generations is reflected in his extremely brief appearance in such texts as Nash's *History of Worcestershire*, although he had held the see for nearly a quarter of a century. He was buried at Worcester on 1 August 1641.

Hall disagreed with Thornborough's own physician who had attributed his symptoms of swollen and painful knees and feet to a true gout (no. 89). The state of the urine and livid spots on the thighs were seen by Hall as symptoms of scurvy and he diagnosed a scorbutic wandering gout. It was treated with a dietary jelly containing meats, hartshorn, dried fruits and antiscorbutic herbs. Other standard scorbutic remedies followed. The purges that Hall usually prescribed in cases of scurvy were omitted in deference to the patient's age and weakness. Live worms were applied to the swellings.

The observation gave more information on humoral explanations when it attributed the Bishop's 'unquiet nights' to salt and sharp humours and vapours ascending to his head. Thornborough's state of mind is discussed by Hall in a long and complex passage which Cooke clearly thought unnecessary to include.

170: SIMON UNDERHILL OF IDLICOTE

Hall treated Simon Underhill on 7 March 1629 at Idlicote, where he had been baptised on 16 November 1589 and where he lived until his death in 1664. He was the youngest brother of Sir Hercules Underhill. In the late sixteenth century the Idlicote branch of the family had suffered when William Underhill was poisoned by his eldest son, Fulk, aged eighteen, who was subsequently executed for the crime. William Underhill had owned New Place, Stratford, and sold it to William Shakespeare only two months

1. *CSPD, 1640*, pp. 130–1, 146.
2. HMC, *Var. Coll.* IV, p. 169; ibid., *6th Report*, p. 40b.
3. W. Moore-Ede, *Worcester Cathedral, its Monuments and Stories* (Worcester, 1925), pp. 132–9.

cure him perfectly, or kill him. The 7th of *March*, after his firft fleep at night, he was much troubled with Wind in his Stomach, for which was ufed this : ℞ *Pul. Pan. rub.* ℈ii. *Conferv. Flor. Viol. & Cochlear. Mifc.* He flept after that better in the morning. He had a Clyfter of a Decoction framed of *Brook-lime, Water-creffes, Scurvy-grafs,* and *Nettles,* ã ℥xii. *Holland pouder* ʒi. *Diaphœnic.* ℥i. *Spec. Diaturb. cum Rhab.* ʒiß. *mix them, and make a Clyfter.* This brought away abundance of Wind. But before the Clyfter he fwallowed this : ℞ *Conferve of Scurvy-grafs* ʒiij. *Pul. Pan. rub.* ℈i. The *9th* day, ℞ *the Juyce of Scurvy-grafs prepared* ℥viii. *Syrup of Brook-lime and Water-creffes,* each ℥ii. He ufed *Chalybiat Wine,* and *Elect. Plerifarch.* after meat, and continuing the Antifcorbutic Beer for fourteen days, he became perfectly well.

OBSERV. LXXI.

Mrs. *Swift,* (dwelling with Baronet *Brook* at *Warwick* Caftle, a Maid,) aged about 20, was miferably afflicted with the Mother, Convulfion of the Mouth, as alfo of the Arms and Hands. She had been well purged by expert Phyficians, and many other Medicines fruitlefly ufed ; yet by the affiftance of God I thus cured : ℞ *the Decoction of Briony with Uterin Herbs* ℔ß. *Spec. Hier. Picr.* ℥ii. *Holland pouder* ʒi. *make a Clyfter.* This injected, gave two ftools with fuccefs. I gave her *Aq. Hyfteric.* (now called *Aq. Brion.*) ℥i. which fhe vomiting up, I prefently exhibited the following :

M

before the murder. Fulk was succeeded as heir by Hercules, who was knighted in 1617. During the seventeenth century most of the family were Catholics.[1]

Simon Underhill married Elizabeth, the widow of Walter Savage, before 11 April 1624: she was still alive in 1638, but died before Simon Underhill. Her first husband, from Broadway (Worcs.), had died in 1621/2; she was the daughter and heiress of Richard Hall of Idlicote.[2]

At Epiphany 1632 Simon Underhill appeared before Warwickshire Quarter Sessions for not maintaining the road between Brailes and Stratford-upon-Avon.[3] He outlived all his brothers, and his will, made on 29 May 1658, suggests his marriage was childless, but his sisters and step-children were mentioned.

Underhill's distressing stomachic symptoms were treated with a pill containing jalap from the plant *Convolvulus Jalappa*, a native of South America. The name is said to have been derived from Xalapa, a town in Mexico. Jalap acts as a drastic purgative producing copious watery stools, often accompanied by griping pains. Hall recorded that it 'wrought well'. The patient felt better initially, but returned, inviting Hall either to cure him perfectly, or kill him, a comment that reflects the drastic nature of the treatments.

The second round of medication was largely devoted to treating scurvy, using scorbutic drugs taken internally and in an enema. Underhill was attended in March. There are three other observations on scurvy where the dates of treatment are given and all are in the first half of the year (no. 69, January, no. 133, February and no. 174, May). Symptoms of scurvy as a result of the winter diet were most likely to appear in the early part of the year. The belief in the need to purify the body in the spring, which resulted in giving laxatives to children (a habit that continued into the twentieth century), may have arisen from the necessity to purge away scorbutic humours which had accumulated during the winter months.

171: FULCA SWIFT OF WARWICK CASTLE

On 18 March 1617 Francis Swift, an Essex gentleman from Royden, was knighted, along with Edward Fiennes of Broughton Castle, by Charles I at Royston (Herts.).[4] The young gentlewoman Hall treated was his daughter, Fulca Elizabeth, who lived in the Warwick Castle household, unmarried

1. *VCH Warws.*, V, p. 96.
2. Morrison, *The Underhills*, p. 157.
3. QSOB, VI, p. 6.
4. Shaw, II, p. 161.

ing : ℞ *Extract. Hysteric.* ꝶi. *Fœcul. Brion.* ꝺß. *f.
Pil.* N. iii. *deaur.* Half an hour after she had taken them, she vomited them up with some Phlegm
and acid Melancholy, complaining of great heat
of her Stomach, as if it were excoriated. I presently commanded she should drink half a pint of
clear cold Water, which she presently cast up; it
was reiterated, and as soon as it was hot in her
Stomach, she cast it up again; it was again repeated, and then she contained it with ease. For her
Convulsion, ℞ *Ung. Martiat.* ℥ ß. *Ol. Sassaf. &
Succin.* ā gut. 5. *Misc.* With this was her Neck
anointed. To the Navil I applied an *Emplaster of
Caranna*, in the midst of which was put of Musk
and Civet gr. v. in Cotton-wooll. For many
days she used a Gelly of Harts-horn, with a little
Fœcul. Brion. & Aron. There was used *Sternut.
Ruland.* Being troubled with faintings, twice
in an hour there was given her the following, by
which she was wholly delivered : ℞ *Mosc.* opt.
gr. 5. *Cinam. Caryoph. Nuc. Mosch.* ā ꝶi. *cum Confect. Alkerm. f. Pil. deaur.*

Observ. LXXII.

Mrs. *Finnes*, being delivered of her third Child,
the third day fell into a burning Fever, with
thirst and great weakness, her Midwife being
with her, gave her Posset-drink made of the Juice
of Limons and of Wood-sorrel; and with her
Chickens gave her the Juice of Sorrel as Sauce. By
which her Stomach being too much cooled, she
fell

cousin to Robert, Baron Brooke (1628–47). Her mother was Elizabeth, daughter of Sir Edward Greville, and her aunt was the wife of another Hall patient, Edward Pennell (no. 101). She had one brother, Francis, and two sisters. Records of her baptism have not been found, but her monument records that she was born in 1613 and must have been treated by Hall in about 1633. He noted this patient was a virgin.

Francis Swift was involved in Castle affairs as early as 1611, when a mortgage was assigned to him in trust for Sir Fulke Greville, and for the next four decades his name appeared on various Greville property transactions, including land in Warwick and the Grevilles' manor of Admington.[1] He was one of the executors of Lord Brooke's will.[2] Fulca married a young gentleman, James Horsey, in about 1629. The Horseys were a West Country family who came to Warwickshire early in the century;[3] they made local marriages and Hannibal Horsey, James's father, bought the manor of Hunningham in 1614.[4]

Fulca had only one child, Dorothy, an infant when James Horsey died in 1630. Fulca died on 7 June 1654 and is commemorated at Hunningham, where 'she lived many years a widow, to the great comefort of neighbours, Friends, and relations, and died, infinitely lamented by all who knew her, neare the 44 year of her age'.[5] Dorothy Horsey later married Colonel George Fane, younger son of the Earl of Westmorland, whose seat was at Apethorpe (Northants.).

In the case of Fulca Swift, Hall 'with the assistance of God' matched his skill in treating hysteria against that of other 'expert' physicians. He began with an enema containing bryony, regularly used in cases of the 'Mother', as well as uterine herbs, by which we may assume he meant ones that would promote uterine evacuations, such as mugwort and ground pine. In addition to other prescriptions involving bryony, Hall used an ointment for the convulsions of the face, a plaster applied to the navel, to which was added civet[6] and musk, and a sternutatory or sneezing powder.

1. WCRO, CR 1886/2453, 2848B, BB 134, 5881–2, BB321 6767, 6769–70, BB 323 6791–2.
2. Philip Styles (ed.), 'The Genealogie, Life and Death of . . . Robert, Lord Brooke', *Miscellany I*, Dugdale Society, XXXI, 1977, p. 172.
3. *HV Warws.*, 1619, p. 195; *HV Essex*, 1624, p. 606.
4. *VCH Warws.*, VI, pp. 118, 129.
5. Dugdale, I, p. 360.
6. Civet is an aromatic substance and like musk was very costly in Hall's time. It is used in perfumery and is collected from a pouch near the genitalia of the civet cat ('Civet is of a baser birth than tar', *As You like It*, III, ii, 65).

fell into an Hydropick Tumor, with swelling of
the right Thigh and Leg, so that for the pain the
Midwife could not move it.　To which she applied a Plaster of red Lead, rolling it hard on; the
Pain and Tumor yet increasing, I was sent for,
when being come, perceiving it hard, I conceived
it to be a Scorbutic Dropsy.　She implored ear-
nestly my help, being in a very desperate condition.　She being almost suffocated with Phlegm,
I prescribed this Lincture, ℞ *Syr. Hyssop. Becabung.*
Nasturt. aquat. & Scabiof. Magistr. ā ℥ i. *Misc.*
She took of this often with a Liquoris stick, with
good event.　For a Clyster, ℞ *Mallowes, Brook-*
lime, Water-cresses, Scurvy-grass, each M i. *Roots*
of Fennel and Parfly, each ℥ii. *Tops of Elder* M ß.
boyl them in a quart of Water till it come to ℥xii. *in the*
straining dissolve course Sugar ℥iv. *Misc.* This cast in,
purged her well of Wind and Phlegm. It was reiterated the next day with good success. At bed-time
she took this : ℞ *Pal. Pan. rub.* ℨß. *C. C. præp.*
Ɔß. *Confect. Alkerm. cum Syr. Limon. f. Bol.*　That
night she was in a fine moist sweat.　It was repeated the next morning.　She was subject to
fainting upon rising, or when moved, for which
I appointed this : ℞ *Conserv. Cochl.* ℥iii. *Spec. Ple-*
rifarch. ℨß. *Misc.* She took the quantity of a Nutmeg three hours before she rose.　Multitude of
business calling me away, and hindering my return to her, she sent again to me, telling me she
had like to have been suffocated with Phlegm the
night before; for which I repeated the foresaid
Syrup, and our Antiscorbutic Water, of which
she took every morning six spoonfuls, as also at
bed-time.　By these she was recovered beyond all
　　　　M 2　　　　expecta-

164 *Select Observations*

expectation of all who gave her over for dead. She took a Clyster every other day, which was this: R *the buds of Elder* M i. *Scurvy-grass, Water cresses, and Brook-lime, each* M ß. *Nettles the whole* M i. *Roots of Parsly and Fennel, each* ʒi. *boyl them in sufficient quantity of Water to* ʒxii. *to the strained Liquor add Diacatholicon* ʒi. *Diaturb. cum Rheo.* ʒii. *mix them.* It gave three stools. To restore, she had a Restorative framed of Snails, Earth-worms, with Antiscorbutic Herbs, as also with Chicken and Partridg, with Cinamon. She also had the following Scorbutic Beer, R *the buds of Elder, Betony, Agrimony, Scabious, Wormwood, each* M i. *Carduus benedictus, Fumitory, Germander, each* M ß. *Water-cresses, Brook-lime, each* M ii. *Scurvy-grass* M iv. *Juniper berries* ℔ ß. *Shred and contuse them, and steep them in unboyled Beer, five gallons ; after boyl them to four, the following Species being in a bag are also to be boiled therein, and with the Beer hung in the Barrel, as the Seeds of Coriander and Anis, each* ʒß. *Liquoris* ʒi. *Sarsaparilla* ʒii. *Sassaphras* ʒi. *Cortic. Winteran.* ʒß. It stood fourteen days before it was drunk of, and then there was taken a draught in the morning fasting, as also before dinner and supper, and at going to bed. For the Contraction of the Leg, from the beginning, was used the following : R *Ol. Cham. Lumbric. de Castor.* ā ʒi. *Ping. Anser. Gallin.* ā ʒß. *Ung. Dialth.* ʒii. *Succ. è Fol. Cochlear. Becabung. Nastur. aquat.* ā ʒi. *Cer. q. s. f. Unguent.* This proved excellent, for in three days space she was able to go with a Staff. Every day she also took four ounces of the following : R *Scurvy-grass, Water-cresses, equal parts, Brook-lime half so much ; beat them in a stone Mortar,*

a n

and boyl them in Milk, pouring not much Liquor upon them; and drank it as before, till the Beer was ready. She took the following Clyſter twice a week : ℞ *of a Childs Urine* ʒ xii. *in which boil Leaven* ʒiſs. *Seeds of Fennel, Anis, and Dill, each* ʒiſs. *purified Honey* ʒi. *make a Clyſter.* And ſo ſhe was reſtored to her former health.

Observ. LXXIII.

MR. *Forteſcue,* (Catholick) of *Cook-hil,* aged 38, (a great Drinker, of a very good habit of Body, ſanguine, very fat,) fell into a Scorbutic Dropſy by a Surfeit, with difficulty of breathing, hard tumor of the Belly, Cods, and Feet, Wind in the Sides, the yellow Jaundice ſpread over the whole Body, and tumor of the Sides and Belly, and by all theſe was much troubled. To whom coming, I appointed what followeth, *March* 12. 1633. ℞ *Pul. Sen. Lax. Spec. Diaturb. cum Rhab.* ā ℈ii. *Syr. Cichor. cum Rheo.* ʒi. *Ser. Cereviſ. q. ſ. f. Hauſt.* It gave eight ſtools. The 13*th,* ℞ *Pil. Stomach. Ruffi, ſine quib.* ā ℈i. *f. Pil.* 5. which gave ſix ſtools. The 14*th,* a Vein was opened, and ʒvii taken. The 15th, ℞ *Polipody, Liquoris, each* ʒi. *Roots of Succory* ʒſs. *Brook-lime, Scurvy-graſs, Water-creſſes, Fumatory, Centaury, each* M iſs. *Sena* ʒiii. *Agarick ſliced* ʒvi. *Rubarb* ʒii. *Cream of Tartar* ʒi. *Flowers of Chamomel, Elder buds, each* p. ii. *Seeds of Fennel, Carrots, each* ʒiſs. *Cinamon, Cloves, Corticis Winterani, each* ʒi. *Zedoary* ʒſs. *Saffron* ℈ſs. *Raiſins of the Sun ſtoned* ʒiii.

make

172: FRANCES FIENNES OF BROUGHTON CASTLE, OXFORDSHIRE

Hall had attended the birth of Frances Fiennes's first child (no. 152) in 1632 and on this occasion was treating her after the birth of William, the second child thus christened. It is one of the few instances when Hall mentioned the presence of a midwife, who had given her a posset of the juice of lemons and the juice of the cooling drug wood-sorrel *Oxalis acetosella*. The patient then suffered a hydropic or dropsical swelling of the right thigh and leg, which the midwife also treated, using a red-lead plaster. When the pain and swelling increased, Hall was summoned and he diagnosed a scorbutic dropsy. He began a lengthy regime of treatment involving ten prescriptions, four before he was called away on a 'multitude of business' and six after he returned.

The first of the prescriptions was for a lick to relieve an accumulation of phlegm in her lungs. Eight of the preparations that followed involved scorbutic drugs. The final preparation, used twice a week, was an enema which had as its principal ingredient child's urine in which leaven (fermenting dough) was boiled. *Urina Hominis*, human urine, was one of four urines in the London *Pharmacopoeia*. The use of the urine of a child followed Dioscorides, who recommended the urine of an uncorrupted boy for laboured breathing, diseases of the eye, erysipelas and pain in the womb.[1]

173: SIR NICHOLAS FORTESCUE OF COOKHILL PRIORY, WORCESTERSHIRE

Hall was treating Nicholas Fortescue in March 1633, the year of his death and the only patient particularly noted as a 'great Drinker'. The Fortescues had acquired Cookhill Priory, in the parish of Inkberrow, in 1543 and they were one of the county's most strongly recusant families. When Nicholas inherited the estate at the death of his father, William, in 1605, their new house of courtyard plan had incorporated parts of the former monastery. Remains of the original moats are still visible.[2]

A suspected priest, caught at Rowington, was said to have been the Fortescue children's tutor[3] and it is possible that Browne, the 'Romish priest' Hall treated for fever (no. 33), was the same man. Fortescue was knighted in 1618/9, although Hall did not give him his title.[4]

His grandson, John, an active royalist leader, was obliged to compound for his estates in 1650. Nicholas Fortescue married Prudence Wheatley of

1. Gunter, *Greek Herbal*, p. 124.
2. *VCH Worcs.*, III, p. 425.
3. Joy Woodall, *From Hroca to Queen Anne* (Shirley, 1974), p. 83.
4. *HV Worcs.*, 1569, p. 57.

make an Infusion in eight pints of Water for twelve hours ; in the morning boil it till a third part be wast-ed. Dose, eight spoonfuls every day, which gave daily five Stools. The 18*th*, ℞ *Pil. Aggregativ. Stomach. Ruffi,* ā ℥ ß. *Gum. Got. præp.* gr. xiv. *f. Pil.* N. x. for two Doses, which gave five Stools, each. After meat he took this : ℞ *Diambr.* ℥ii. *Sacch. Ros.* ℥ii. *Misc.* Dose was half a spoonful. The Restorative was made as in the former Obser-vation, as also that in *Observ.* 59 of this Century ; every third day purging. For quenching thirst, instead of Beer we used the following: ℞ *the sha-vings of Saffafras, shaved Liquoris,* ā ℥ ii. *Fennel feeds* ℥ii. *Currants* ℥iß. *put them all into a Pewter pot, and pour upon them three quarts of scalding Wa-ter, after stop it very well, and set it in a cold place, till it be cold.* He used *Diacrocum* to ℥ii, every morning for five mornings, and after Meat. ℞ *Spec. Plerisarchon.* ℥ ii. *Sacch.* ℥i. Dose, half a spoonful. The 24*th* day he was purged with these Pills prescribed for the 18*th* day, which gave eight stools. After to sweat was this prepared : ℞ *Guaiacum shaved* ℔i. *Water nine pints, boil it to the half ; towards the end cast in Soldanella dried* M i. *the inner Bark of Cinamon* ℥ii. *Raisins unstoned* ℥ii. *after they are boyled enough, pour them into a Glass Vessel, in which there are three pints of White-wine.* Of which take ℥ix in the morning, and vi in the evening, covering him well that he may sweat. His Diet was drying. Every third day he had the Clyster prescribed (of Urine) in the former Ob-servation. And once a week the following Bole, ℞ *Jalap.* ℈iß. *Cream of Tartar* ℈i. *Elect. of Ta-marinds* ℥ß. *make a Bole.* It gave six Stools. By
          these

thefe the Tumor was altogether removed. But the third of *April*, by what Fate I know not, he fell into a Fever. He had two Fits, with fhaking fix hours long, three in heat. I purged him again with the forefaid Bole, which gave him five great watery Stools ; by which he was delivered from his Fever. Afterward he ufed the forefaid Antifcorbutic Beer for a month, and the following Pouder after Meat : ℞ *Pul. Pannonic. rub. Spec. Diambr. Spec. Diamofch. dulc.* ā ℥ i. *Ol. Anifi.* gut. iij. *Sacch. alb.* ℥iv. *Mifc. f. Pul.* Dofe, as much as would lie on a Six-pence. By thefe means in fix weeks time he was perfectly cured.

Observ. LXXIV.

MR. *Kimberley*, aged about 26, had laboured long of a general Laffitude, had a greater Appetite than Digeffion, a filthy yellow Jaundice, Pain in the Loins, weaknefs of the Legs, a pricking Pain of the Head, efpecially near the Ears, a frequent change of the Urine, fometimes thick, and fometimes clear like Spring water; fometimes great pain of the Legs, Tumor of the Gums, fwelling of the Fingers, with pain, Hypochondriac Winds, with many other Signs of the Scurvy confirmed, with which was joined fweating and wandring Pains. He had ufed the natural Bath without fuccefs, and had had often purging and Sudorific Decoctions, and all fruitlefs, yet he was reftored as followeth : *May* 1. ℞ *Diatartar.* ℥ii. *of which he took every day a fmall fpoonful.*

Which

168   *Select Observations*

Which gave four Stools. About three or four a clock in the morning, when his sweating usually began, and at four a clock in the afternoon, he took ℥iv of the Juyces expressed out of the following Herbs, being mixed with Sugar, and ℨi of Cinamon. ℞ *Scurvy-grass, Water-cresses,* each ℔ß. *Brook-lime* ℥ iv. *bruise them, and strain them, adding* ℨi *of Cinamon, and sufficient Sugar.* He also used this Antiscorbutic Beer: ℞ *Bark of Ash, Tamaris,* and *Capers,* each ℥ii. *Horse Radish sliced* ℥vi. *Wormwood, Fumatory, Germander, Carduus benedictus, Celendine,* each M ß. *Betony, Scabious, Ceterach, Valerian, Nettles,* each M i. *Water-cresses, Brook-lime,* each M ii. *Scurvy-grass* M iv. *let the following be put also in a bag, and boiled in the Beer, as Juniper berries bruised* ℥vi. *Cortic. Winteran.* ℥ß. *Sarsaparilla* ℥ii. *Sassafras* ℥ß. *Liquoris* ℥i. *Seeds of Anis, Carraway,* and *Coriander,* each ℥ß. *Nutmegs two. After the Beer is boiled, hang the Bag in the Vessel.* It is for four gallons of Beer. After it is barm'd, pour in of the Juyce of Pippins ℔i. *the Juyce of Scurvy-grass* ℔ii. *White wine* ℔i. After a fit time use it for ordinary Drink. For his Tumors in the Fingers were used live-Worms, as *Observ. 69.* He was purged with these Pills: ℞ *Pil. Hier. cum Agarick, Mastic. Stomac. Imperial. Ruffi,* ā ℨß. *Misc. fiat* 5 *Pil. ex* ℨi. Which was the Dose taken, and gave five Stools. May the 13th, ℞ *nine fresh Worms, and bruise them in a Mortar with two spoonfuls of White-wine; after strain them, and put it into the rest of the pint of Wine.* Of which he took three spoonfuls in the morning, noon, and evening. And every third day purged with the following: ℞ *Pil. aggregat.* ℨi.

Holkham, Norfolk;[1] they had seven children, two of whom, William and Martha, were also Hall's patients (nos 29, 41, 58). It is apparent from Hall's notes that he visited the family at Cookhill.

Hall opened the report on Nicholas Fortescue with a reference to his constitution: 'very good habit of body, sanguine and very fat'. A sanguine constitution was one where blood predominated and was marked by a ruddy complexion and a hopeful, confident disposition. Over-indulgence in drink had resulted in difficulty of breathing, with swelling of the belly, testicles and feet; a yellow jaundice was spread over the whole body. Hall diagnosed a scorbutic dropsy by surfeit.

Hall's report on his treatment during six weeks was in the form of a diary and outlined a vigorous regime to expel the morbid humours. Fortescue was purged on the first and second day and bled on the third. In the three days following he took a drink containing purgative and scorbutic drugs. Thereafter there was a medley of preparations prescribed, including restorative and sweating medicines, *Diacrocum* or saffron for the jaundice and regular administration of purgatives, one of them the drastic jalap (no. 170). Every third day the patient submitted to an enema containing urine as prescribed for Frances Fiennes in the previous observation.

Fortescue, a man in his late thirties, died in 1633, the same year that he was treated and 'perfectly cured' by Hall. Dropsy of the abdomen and lower limbs and jaundice are among the symptoms of cirrhosis of the liver, a disease of heavy drinkers.

174: GILBERT/WILLIAM KIMBERLEY OF BROMSGROVE, WORCESTERSHIRE

Noted by Hall as *Generosus*, this patient is difficult to identify; he was born in the period 1585 to 1609, but not in Stratford. He appears to be Gilbert (b. 1590) or William (b. 1592), the sons of William Kimberley, a yeoman of Bromsgrove (Worcs.). The Kimberleys were linked by marriage to the Dugards, originally a Worcestershire family from Grafton Flyford. Thomas Dugard, the Puritan, was the son of Elizabeth Kimberley, whose father was William (*c.* 1546–1612), yeoman from Whitford, near Bromsgrove.[2] Dugard referred in his diary to both an uncle and cousin (William) Kimberley,[3] and the uncle, Gilbert or William, seems to be Hall's patient.

Mr Kimberley travelled to undertake hydrotherapy, possibly to a local spa, such as Droitwich. The Dugard link is confirmed in the inventory of William Kimberley, yeoman, who had loaned 40s. to Henry Dugard, his

1. Nash, II, p. 9.
2. *HV Warws.*, 1682–3, p. 112.
3. BL, Add. MS 23146.

ʒi. *Stomac.* ʒſſ. *Gamboi. præp.* gr. xiv. *f. Pil.* 10. Dose five, which gave so many Stools. When he began to be well, he drank the foresaid Beer, an hour after which he took some of the following: ℞ *Elect. Chalyb.* ℥ iv. *Conserv. Cochlear.* ℥ii. *Misc.* Dose, the quantity of a Nutmeg. The Beer and Electuary were used for fifteen days. After meat the quantity of a Nutmeg of the following: ℞ *Conserve of Scurvy-grass* ℥i. *Bugloss* ℥ſſ. *Spec. Plerisarchont.* ℈ii. *Misc.* Every fourth or sixt days he took the following to purge: ℞ *Conserv. Violar.* ℥i. *Spec. Diatrag. frigid.* ℈iſſ. *Turbith. Gum. Mechoac. albis.* ā ℥ſſ. *Diagrid. cum Ol. Fænic. præp.* ℈ii. *Sacch. in Aq. Fænicul. dissol.* ℥ xiv. *Ol. Cinam.* gut. vi. *Ol. Anis.* gut. iv. *f. Confect. in Morsul.* Of which he took ℥vi, which gave eight Stools; it is called *Morsul. purgant. de Mechoac.* He used his Beer for three months, in which time he was delivered from those cruel intense Pains, and they did not return again. For which he returned me many thanks, and called me his Father, because he said I had delivered him from the jaws of Death, and made him perfectly well.

OBSERV. LXXV.

Mrs. *Editha Staughton,* aged 16, was miserably tormented with *Ascarides* night and day, whom I cured perfectly and speedily, as I cured Mrs. *Bove*; for which see *Observ.* 66. of this Century.

OBSERV.

son-in-law, and a further unsecured sum on account; a wealthy farmer, his goods were worth £383 6s. 8d., to part of which Hall's patient was presumably entitled.[1] Hall would have attended Gilbert in 1616 or William in 1623; as their parent had died in 1612, it is perhaps not surprising that the grateful patient called John Hall 'father'.

This is another case where the symptoms were said to confirm scurvy. Treatment with purgatives and scorbutic remedies followed a regime that lasted for three months. This observation confirms that one of Hall's favoured remedies for swellings in scorbutic illness were earthworms. He used them to treat Robert Hanslap (no. 108) and Bishop Thornborough (no. 169). In this case he applied live worms to the swollen fingers while whole worms, bruised and strained, were administered orally in white wine.

175: EDITH STOUGHTON OF ST JOHN'S, WARWICK

Edith was the eldest daughter of Anthony Stoughton (1587–1656) of St John's, Warwick. He enhanced the family's fortunes by marrying Dorothy Brett, whose father, John, originally came from Kent to settle in Warwick. St John's had been sold to the family in 1540 by Henry VIII, to whom Anthony, senior, had been Groom of the Chamber.

Anthony Stoughton, his grandson, had bought land in Warwickshire at Bulkington, Hampton-on-the-Hill and Grove Park. By 1600 'all the old People residing in the Hospital of St John's [were] dead' and by 1626 he had pulled down most of the ancient hospital and its chapel.[2] He built the 'Noble Mansion' on the outskirts of Warwick still to be seen there.

Edith was baptised at Warwick on 12 November 1616; her age in this case was not recorded in Hall's manuscript and must therefore have been Cooke's addition. He attended her on another occasion and recorded her age as seventeen (no. 180). She had a brother, Nathaniel, the heir, and three younger sisters, Mercy (baptised in 1623), Dorothy (1627–30) and another Dorothy (1630). Edith was married in 1635 to a Worcestershire gentleman, Thomas Young of Pool House, Hanley Castle, twenty-two years older than she.[3] They had a daughter and two sons, one of whom died in infancy.[4] Thomas Young was buried on 24 April 1657 aged sixty-three at St Nicholas, Warwick, alongside Edith's parents; Dugdale noted his monument.[5] Both Edith's parents had died within a month of each other,

1. (H)WRO, class 008.7 1611/178.
2. BL, Add. MS 29264.
3. SBTRO, DR 41/83.
4. *HV Worcs.*, 1682–3, p. 110.
5. Dugdale, I, p. 466.

Observ. LXXVI.

Mrs. *Wilson*, who for the recovery of her
health, took a Journey to *Bristol*, for as she
thought she was tormented with the Stone, for
which she drank of St. *Vincent's* Well too greedily,
to the quantity of eighteen pints a day, for the
expelling of the Stone; so, that thereby cooling
her Body too much, she fell into a Palsy. She
presently got her self conveyed to the Bath, where
being purged by Dr. *Lapworth*, and using the Bath,
she was restored. Returning home in rainy and
tempestuous weather, that night she was assaulted
with the Mother, with fainting, and a light Palsy
on the left side. To whom being called, by Divine assistance I helped as followeth : ℞ *Aloes lu-
cid.* ʒii. *Agaric. Troch. rec. Rhab. elect.* ā ʒi. *Cortic.
Rad. Cappar. Winteran. Tamarisc.* ā Ə i. *Faculæ
Brion. & Aron.* ā Əss. *Castor* ʒiss. *Crem. Tartar.*
ʒss. *Spir. Succini* gr. iv. *cum Syr. de Fumar. com-
pos. q. s. f. Pil.* N. 6. *ex* ʒi. Of which she took
three at a night when she went to bed, which
gave her four Stools the next day. For the wind
of her Stomach, ℞ *Spec. Diamb.* ʒi. *Ol. Salv.
Chy. Nuc. Mosch. Caryoph.* ā gut. iv. *Sacch. in Aq.
Ros. dissol.* ʒii. *f. Rotul.* To be taken after meat.
For the Palsy, ℞ *Spir. Rorismar. Ol. Succin.* ā
part. æq. With which her Neck was gently anointed. For fainting, ℞ *Spec. Plerisarch.* ʒss.
Sacch. opt. ʒii. *Misc.* Dose half a spoonful. When
she fainted, this delivered her both from her
                                              fainting,

Anthony on 13 August and Dorothy, at the age of sixty-three, on 14 September 1656.

Edith died at Warwick aged only twenty-seven and the St Nicholas register for 10 June 1644 recorded the burial of 'Yeedy the wife of Mr Thomas Young'.

Hall treated Edith Stoughton for roundworm with the same prescriptions he had used for Margaret Bovey (no. 166). He was called to this girl again a year later when she suffered a serious attack of hysteria (no. 180).

176: [MRS] WILSON

This patient has been identified as Anne, the wife of Thomas Wilson, vicar of Stratford from 1619, and mother of his seven children, born in the period 1621 to 1638. However, in Hall's notes she was recorded only as G^a and her age as thirty-four; no place of residence was given.

She therefore must have been born in the period 1577 to 1601. Her gentlewoman status does not preclude her from being the vicar's wife, for Anne Jackson of Binton (no. 154), married to a cleric, was also noted by Hall as *Generosa*. Moreover, Hall described Mrs Wilson as *religiosa*. Mrs Wilson was one of the few patients to travel for hydrotherapy to Bristol and Bath, where she was purged by Dr Lapworth, whose opiate Hall used for Sir Thomas Puckering (no. 161).

Anne Wilson, the vicar's widow, was buried in the chancel of Holy Trinity on 27 October 1642, her monument noted by Dugdale.[1] The parish register is defective for this period.

Mrs Wilson's visit to Bristol and Bath to improve her health had an effect opposite to that intended. She drank too much of the waters of St Vincent's well in an attempt to rid herself of what Hall clearly believed to have been a non-existent stone. Returning home from Bath in foul weather she had an hysterical seizure with fainting fits and a slight paralysis. Summoned to repair the damage Hall treated her first with a purgative pill containing the antihysteric drug, bryony. This was followed by a carminative to treat wind, a sweating decoction and an enema. A mixture of oil of amber and oil of rosemary (no. 93) was rubbed on her neck to treat the palsy.

To treat the fainting Hall prescribed a powder composed of *Species Pleres Archoniticon* (no. 69) mixed with sugar. He described this as a 'pouder worth Gold, which I always carry about with me'. There would have been other mixtures of powders which Hall carried in his medicine chest when he visited his patients, sometimes to be given as powders, at other times mixed

1. Dugdale, II, p. 689.

fainting, and trembling of her Heart, with which she had usually been troubled. It is a Pouder worth Gold, which I always carry about with me. She used also this Decoction : ℞ *Guaiacum* ℥viii. *Bark of the same, Rosemary, Saffaphras, Sarfaparilla, each* ℥ i. *Betony, Sage, Lavender, Germander, each* p. i. *Roots of Elicampana, Piony, Oris, Citron Pills dried, each* ℥i. *Spring water* ℔vi. *infuse them for twenty four hours in a hot place, after boyl them in a close Vessel; after straining, sweeten it with Sugar, and aromatize it with Spec. Diambr.* ℥ß. She took ℥vi of it in the morning, and sweat, and as much at four a clock in the afternoon, without sweating. She had *Clysters framed of the common Decoction, and Carminative seeds, to which was added Holland pouder.* She used also *Cyprus Terbentine* framed into Pills very often. And thus she was delivered from all these, and danger of Death.

Observ. LXXVII.

Mrs. *Wagstaff* of *Warwick,* (Widow) aged about 48, was troubled with a continual vomiting, pain of the Stomach and Head, as if pricked or stabbed with Needles and Daggers; also she had pain of her Loins, and numness of her Feet, whom I cured as followeth : ℞ *our Emetic Infusion* ℥vi. It gave her three vomits, and three Stools. For the pain of the Stomach, ℞ *new Conserve of Roses* ℥i. *Spec. Aromat. Rosar.* Ɖi. *Theriac. Lond.* ℥i. *Misc.* For two Doses. For the Back, ℞ *Oil of Scorpions* ℥ii. *Oil of sweet Almonds* ℥ii.

with honey or syrup at the patient's home to be administered as an electuary. Other remedies would have included the purgative pills he regularly prescribed at the beginning of a treatment.

177: ELIZABETH WAGSTAFFE OF WARWICK

Elizabeth Wagstaffe was a former patient of Hall, whom he had attended two years earlier for scurvy (no. 47). Her symptoms on this occasion were treated with the emetic infusion, purgatives, a carminative for the wind and an enema.[1] For her 'watching' or insomnia Hall prescribed an ointment which included laudanum to be rubbed on her temples.

178: [ALICE] COOKES OF [SNITTERFIELD]

Although Hall noted this patient's age as near forty-eight, and her status as *Generosa*, precise identification has not been possible. Families of this surname and spelling lived at Snitterfield and Luddington, of appropriate social standing, as well as another branch at Harbury. Several Stratfordians were also called Cookes, with Cox as a variant, but do not seem to be more than craftsmen and traders.

She could be Alice (d. 1629), the wife of John Cookes of Luddington, but a likelier candidate seems to be another Alice, the wife of William Cookes (d. 1617) of Snitterfield, a prosperous man, with eleven in his household in 1595.[2] Alice Cookes of Snitterfield, the mother of three sons and a daughter, was buried in the parish as a widow on 17 May 1624.

This patient's symptoms were described by Hall as the 'constant companions' of Flatus Hypochondriacus, which is a gathering of wind in the hypochondriac region of the abdomen. Hall attributed the condition to obstructions of the liver and the spleen. He countered it with a purgative, which included the resolvent and deobstructant Polypody of the oak (no. 70) and epithymum or dodder (no. 143). This was given with a syrup for the treatment of melancholy, which also contained epithymum. Culpeper was later to criticize the pharmacopoeial formulae for including Epithymum of Crete. In his opinion things growing in England were better for English bodies.[3]

Other prescriptions were used to treat individual symptoms and included a stomachic pill and carduus benedictus water 'twice distilled' to be dropped into the ear for the deafness.

1. Pellitory of the Wall *Parietaria officinalis* in the enema was used as a cooling herb and a diuretic.
2. *Mins & Accts*, III, pp. 60–1.
3. Culpeper, *A Physical Directory*, p. 124.

℥ii. *mix them.* She had a quiet night, and well eased of her pains. The next morning was cast in the following Clyster : ℞ *Althæa roots* ℥i. *Pellitory of the Wall* M ii. *Melilot, Mallows, Chamomel flowers,* each M i. *Seeds of Line, Fænugreek,* each ℥ß. of *Fennel seed* ℥ii. *boyl them in Water* ℔ii. in ℥x of the *straining was* dissolved *Cassia drawn for Clysters* ℥i. *Oil of sweet Almonds* ℥ii. *Capons or Goose grease* ℥i. *make a Clyster.* For her Side, ℞ *Ung. de Althæa* ℥ii. *Ol. Amygd. dulc.* ℥ß. *Misc.* With which her Side was anointed, and upon it put a Linnen Cloth anointed with Butter warm'd. It was done twice a day. For the wind, ℞ *Conserv. de Anthos, Bugloss,* ã ℥iß. *Conserv. Caryoph. hort.* ℥i. *Rad. Enul. Camp. condit. Zinzib. condit.* ã ℥ß. *Spec. Armat. Ros.* ℥iß. *Confect. Alkerm.* ℥ß. *cum Syr. Regis, vel Pomis, f. Elect.* Dose the quantity of a Nutmeg. After meat she took of the following Rotula's : ℞ *Spec. Diamb.* ℥ß. *Diamosc. dulc.* ℈i. *Ol. Anisi.* gut. iii. *Sacch. in Aq. Bugloss. dissol.* q. s. f. *Rot.* She purged twice a week with *Diatartar.* For watching, ℞ *Ung. Alabastr. vel Popul.* ℥ß. *Laud. Paracel. dissol. in Aq. Ros.* gr. x. with which her Temples was anointed : And so she was healed.

Observ. LXXVIII.

Mrs. *Cooks,* near 48, of a thin body, was much troubled with pain of the Stomach, darkness of the Eyes, deafness and noise in the Ears, beating of the Heart, with several other Symptoms

upon English Bodies.   173

toms, constant Companions of *Flatus Hypochon-driacus*, arising from the ill Disposition and Obstructions of the Liver and Spleen, whom I cured as followeth: First I purged the first ways with the following: ℞ *Sarsapar.* ℥ ii. *Hermodact.* ℥iß. *Guaiac. Liquor.* ā ℥i. *Sen.* ℥ii. *Polipod. Querc.* ℥ii. *Epithem.* ℥ß. *Enul. Camp.* ℥vi. *Agaric. Rhab.* ā ℥ ii. *Sem. Anis. Carui. Coriand.* ā ℥ ß. *Infuse them in a close shut Vessel in four pints of Water for twenty four hours; after boyl them, keeping the Vessel close, lest the Vapor exhale. Take of this Decoction being strained* ℔ß. *Syr. Magist. ad Melanchol.* ℥iv Dose was from ℥ii to iv. Being well purged, she took this: ℞ *Elect. Chalyb.* ℥iß. *de Tamarind.* ℥i. *Misc.* The quantity to be taken was ℥ß. to be used with exercise. Twice a week was given of the following: ℞ *Pil. Stomach. sine quib.* ā ℥ß. *de Pæon. Chamæpit.* ā ℈i. *f. Pil.* N. 12. Of which three was given at the hour of sleep. After was taken the Electuary prescribed *Observ.* 72. *Of Conserve of Scurvy grass,* ℥ii. &c. For deafness was used *Carduus benedictus* Water, twice distilled, and dropped into the Ear. By these she was perfectly cured.

OBSERV. LXXIX.

Nurse *Degle* of *Bengwort*, aged 29, troubled with spitting of blood from the Lungs, as also with the yellow Jaundice, was cured as followeth: ℞ *Oxymel simpl.* ℥iv. *Syr. Capil. Vener.* ℥ii. *Misc.* for two mornings. After she was thus purged:

purged: R *Rhab. Pul.* ʒiſſ. *Syr. Roſ. Sol.* ʒi, *Aq.
Plantag.* ʒiv. *Syr. Capil. ven.* ʒi. *Miſc.* Being
thus well purged, ſhe had a Vein opened. After
Aſtringents were uſed, as, R *Lapid. Hæmatit.
ſubtiliſ. pul. & cum Aq. Plantag. lot.* ʒi. (which
hath an admirable quality in ſtopping of Blood)
Coral. rub. Bol. Arm. ita præp. ā ʒiii. *Ter. ſigil.* ʒiſſ.
Pul. Diareos ſimp. ʒi. *f. Pul. tenuiſ.* Doſe ʒiſſ
in Barly water, in which was boiled Plantain
and Knot·graſs. It it is to be given in the morning faſting, and at the hour of ſleep, to the quantity of ʒii of *Aq. Spernol. Crol.* and ſo for many
days. Every ſecond or third day ſhe had a Clyſter,
as, R *Mallows, Althea, Beets, Mercury, each* M i.
Prunes 5. *Figs* 12. *Melon ſeed bruiſed* ʒi. *the ſeeds
of Anis and Fennel, each* ʒi. *French Barly, Rye bran,
each* p. i. *boyl them in Whey to* ʒxii. *in the ſtraining diſſolve Catholic.* ʒi. *Caſſia extracted for Clyſters*
ʒv. *courſe Sugar* ʒ ii. *make a Clyſter.* And thus
by God's help ſhe became well.

Observ. LXXX.

Mrs. *Editha Staughton*, aged 17, was miſerably
afflicted with Melancholy, her Courſes as
yet not having broken forth, as alſo with the
Mother; ſhe was very eaſily angry with her near-
eſt Friends, ſo that ſhe continually cried out
that her Parents would kill her, as alſo of all
others that came unto her. She had been purged
well by expert Phyſicians, yet her Father deſired
my counſel, whether ſhe was curable; to which

I

179: URSULA/ANNE DEACLE OF BENGEWORTH, WORCESTERSHIRE

The family of Deacle was long-established in Bengeworth, a village some few miles east of Evesham.[1] By the early years of the eighteenth century John Deacle, a prosperous London draper, had founded a school there; his fine monument (1709) survives in the parish church.

In the seventeenth century the licensing of midwives by their bishop as fit to practise was still quite widespread and three such women from Bengeworth were registered as late as the years 1710 to 1712.[2] There is no record of Hall's patient as a licensed midwife, however. She is impossible to identify precisely, but, born in the period 1582 to 1606, she seems to be either Ursula Deacle, baptised on 12 August 1582, the daughter of John, or Anne Deacle, baptised on 10 October 1589, the daughter of William, a yeoman. It seems likely that she attended the substantial gentry families in the area, where Hall had a number of patients, perhaps acting under his guidance.

The patient was spitting blood and had jaundice. Hall began treatment with a soothing linctus composed of oxymel and syrup of maiden-hair. After this she was purged and bled by opening a vein. The principal medicine was an astringent preparation composed of very finely powdered haematite or bloodstone, plantain water, Armenian bole, sealed earth and powdered orris root. These were to be mixed *f. Pul. tenuis* to make a fine powder. Plantain, used for its powers to stop bleeding, was also added to the barley water with which the powder was mixed. An enema containing the purgative *Catholicon*, a preparation designed to expel all morbid humours, was also prescribed.

180: EDITH STOUGHTON OF ST JOHN'S, WARWICK

Edith Stoughton, aged seventeen, had not menstruated. She was mentally disturbed and believed her parents and others would kill her. In this account of her illness Hall gave some indication of the relationship that was believed to exist between a patient's constitution, the illness and the measures taken to disperse and temper the malignant humour. Hall had already treated her once before (no. 175).

Edith was stated to have a melancholic constitution, which was one dominated by melancholy or black bile. A disproportionate mixture of the humours had resulted in severe melancholic symptoms of fear and delusion. Hall prescribed two enemas 'by which the Humor was rendered more

1. *VCH Worcs.*, IV, p. 207.
2. Morgan, nos 1292, 1329, 1333.

upon Engliſh Bodies.   175

I anſwered, Very hardly, being her Conſtitution was Melancholy. I adviſed there ſhould be few to trouble her, and ſo began with emollient and diſcuſſive Clyſters, as alſo ſuch as reſpected the Humor : As ℞ *of Chicken-broth (wherein was boiled Sorrel, Pimpernel, Borage, Hyſſop)* ℔ i. *common Oil* ʒiiſſ. *Salt of Tartar* ʒi. *make a Clyſter.* This was uſed two days. After ſhe was thus purged : ℞ *of the foreſaid Broth* ʒv. *Cream of Tartar* ϶iv. *Oil of Vitriol* 5 *drops, make a Potion.* By this the Humor was rendred more obſequious. After was opened a Vein on the left Arm. She was the next day after purged again. After was applied the Leeches to the Hemorrhoids. Again ſhe was purged with an Helleborated Apple, in which Apple was roſted ʒi of *Hellebore ;* afterward the Hellebore was caſt away, and the Apple given. Being well purged, we laboured to divert the Humor from the Brain by Ligatures and ſtrong Clyſters, ſtrengthning the principal parts with the following : ℞ *Conſerve of Roſes vitriolated, Borage, Bugloſs, each* ʒi. *candied Citron Pills, Conſerve of Clove Gilly-flowers, each* ʒ ſſ. *Spec. de Gem. Lætific.* ā ϶ii. *Hyacinth. præp.* ϶ i. *Confect. Alkerm.* ʒi. *Spec. Diamarg. frigid.* ā ʒiſſ. *with the ſyrup of Apples make an Electuary.* The Doſe was ʒi before meat. To diſcuſs wind, that Pouder was uſed, preſcribed *Obſerv.* 34. *Cent.* 1. As, ℞ *Coriand. præp.* ʒii. *Sem. Fænic.* &c. It was given after meat. There was alſo uſed the following Wines : ℞ *the opening Roots, each* ʒi. *Bark of Cappar roots* ʒi. *Saſſafras* ʒiſſ. *Wormwood, Groundpine, each* M i ſſ. *Ceterach, Balm, Germander, each* M i. *Flowers of Borage, Bugloſs, Scabious, each* p. i.

obsequious'. Both enemas contained tartar, chosen 'by reason of its great force in contemporating Melancholy, and Atra bilis'. Robert Burton (1577–1640) referred to differing forms of the black bile humour. Hall in using tartar was endeavouring to contemperate or synchronize two of these forms: the natural melancholy, which was cold and dry, and the atrabilious form, which was hot and dry. This hot form Burton called 'Choler adust'; others referred to it as 'burnt melancholy' (no. 77).[1]

After the humour had been tempered the patient was bled by opening a vein in the left arm. She was purged and leeches were applied to the haemorrhoidal veins. This was followed by purging with *Helleborus niger*, the drug held to be specific for treating diseases arising from black bile (no. 31). To divert black bile from the brain Hall applied ligatures (no details were given) and administered 'strong' enemas. Burton wrote that enemas draw melancholy humours from the brain and heart to the 'more ignoble parts'.[2]

This girl's mental state was such that Hall advised her father that there should be few to trouble her. Her fear and the fact that she was easily angered renders it highly probable that some of the treatment would have been forcibly applied. Later when she was more rational Hall prescribed a strengthening electuary, a laxative wine[3] and *Diacodium* to help her sleep. Hall added that 'In all Medicines we added Humectors', which may be taken to mean items reputed to moisten and soften the solid parts of the body. (Humector is a term that may also be used for an ingredient that moistens the medicine itself.)

181: JOHN TRAPP, SCHOOLMASTER OF STRATFORD-UPON-AVON

John Trapp was baptised on 7 June 1601 at Croome d'Abitot (Worcs.), where his family were yeomen. He attended the Worcester Free School before entering Christ Church College, Oxford, in 1618; he obtained an MA in 1624.[4] Hall described him as *theologus* or minister.

Trapp arrived at Stratford to be an usher at the grammar school in 1622, becoming master two years later.[5] Also in 1624 on 29 June he married Mary Gibbard; they had four children baptised in Stratford (1627 to 1636). Hall noted treating him on 11 March 1635. Later in the year, on

1. Robert Burton, *The Anatomy of Melancholy* (2nd edn, Oxford, 1624), p. 32.
2. Ibid., p. 318.
3. *Species Diamargiton frigidum* in the electuary included the four cooling seeds, pearl, coral, ambergris, musk and seventeen other ingredients. *Sem. Siler Montanum* in the wine are the seeds of hart wort.
4. Foster, p. 1503; *Worthies*, pp. 758–61.
5. Brinkworth, p. 104.

p. ii. *Broom leaves* p. i. *seeds of Fennel* ℥i. *of Carraway, and sem. Siler. Montan. of each* ℨi. *All
these were beaten, and put into a Vessel, in which was
put the shavings of Juniper, and there was poured upon them of White-wine* ℔ xxx. *And so being well
stopped, they were set in a Cellar. After they were
infused eight days, I took* 9 ℔ *of it, wherein I infused Rubarb* ℨvi. *Sena* ℥ii. *Mechoacan* ℥ß. *Dodder and Cinamon, each* ℨß. *Cloves* ℨi. And so it
was used instead of Purges. It was given every
morning two hours before dinner, with taking
some spoonfuls of Broth. After three days taking, she had that prescribed for comforting the
Brain and Heart. In all Medicines we added
Humectors. For her watching, I gave at bed-
time a spoonful of *Diacodium.* This caused rest,
and in it she sweat. There was *Tartar* often used
by reason of its great force in contemporating
Melancholy, and *Atra bilis.* And thus by the
blessing of God she was delivered from her Dis-
temper.

Observ. LXXXI.

MR. *John Trap,* (Minister, for his piety and
learning second to none) about the 33
year of his age, of a melancholy temper, and by
much Study fell into Hypochondriac Melancholy,
and pain of the Spleen, with some Scorbutic
Symptoms, *viz.* difficulty of breathing after
gentle motion of the Body, beating of the Heart,
with fainting at the rising of the Vapours, and
became

became a little better when they were difperfed.
He had a gentle Erratic Fever, fo that he was
much amaciated; after he had done preaching on
the Sabbath, he could fcarce fpeak; his Urine
changed often, his Pulfe was mutable and unequal,
and he languifhed much. Some ordinary Medicines were ufed, but not fucceeding, he defired
my help and counfel, which was readily performed by me in prefcribing the following, by which
he was reftored from the very jaws of Death, both
fafely, quickly, and pleafantly. *March* 11. 1635.
℞ *Tartar. Vitriolat.* ℈iv. *in pomo fub cineribus coct.*
With this he had two Stools, and his Urine came
in greater quantity, but like clear Spring water.
The 12th day, ℞ *Merc. dulc.* gr. xx. *Tart. Vitr.*
℈i. *Gut. Gamb. præp.* gr. iii. *Mifc.* This was
given in the Pap of an Apple; it gave him four
Stools. The 14th day he took ʒi of *Cream of
Tartar,* it gave one Stool. For his Cough and
Catarrh, in the night he held in his Mouth one of
our pectoral Rolls. The 15th he took of our
Chalybiat Wine; as ℞ *Vin. Chalyb.* ℥iv. *Syr. Sce-
letyrh. Foreft.* ℥iii. *Mifc.* The firft day he took
two fpoonfuls, the fecond day four, exercifing
two hours after. For the ftrengthning of the
Spleen, ℞ *Raifins of the Sun* ℔i. *boyl them in Sack
to the confiftence of a Pultefs, pafs it through a ftrainer,
and mix therewith Conferve of Rofemary flowers, of
Buglofs, each* ℥ß. *Spec. Lætificant. Aromat. Rofar.
Diamarg. calid. Diacinam. each* ℈ij. *Lig. Aloes ado-
rati.* ʒß. *candied Citron Pills, Cinamon, each* ʒi.
Chalyb. præp. cum Sulphur. ℥ß. *Saffron* ℈i. *mix
them.* The Dofe was the quantity of a Filbert in
the morning. The 19th, ℞ *Syr. Magift. ad Me-*
N *lanchol.*

^l^anchol. ℥ii. *Aq. Buglos.* ℥ii. *Tartar. subtilis. pul. Misc.* It gave four stools. The next day he took the Chalybiat Wine. *April* the 2. he was purged as before, with which he was cheared for three days after he took the Wine. The seventh day he purged with *Cream of Tartar* ℨi. Now he had our Antiscorbutic Beer ; and his Electuary being ended, he took six spoonfuls of the following Water : ℞ *Aq. Limacum nostr. Aq. Ranar. simpl.* ā ℥iv. *Confect. Alkermes* Əii. *Manus Christ. perl.* ℥ß. *Syr. Sceletyrb. Forest.* ℥ii. *Aq. nost. Antiscorbutic.* ℥vi. *Splenetic.* ℥ii. (both *Doncrelius*) *Misc.* This being ended, he desired his Electuary again, in which he said the greatest hope of his Cure lay, and was worth Gold. He having it, used it for eight days, purging every fourth day. But being much troubled with bitterness of his Mouth, I gave him ℨv of our *Emetic Infusion*, which removed it, and he returned to the use of his Electuary. And thus by God's blessing he was freed from all his Symptoms, and was well cured, for which he returned me hearty thanks.

OBSERV. LXXXII.

THe Earl of *Northampton*, aged about 32, being following his Hounds in a cold and rainy day, got cold, and suddenly was miserably tormented with a flatuous Pleurisy, and pain of the Belly, like to a true Pleurisy. He had a small Cough, was restless, feverish, thirsty, and the Pain was stretching. I being present when he came home,
                                          prescribed

3 October, just before his own death, Hall accompanied Trapp to Warwick on a sermon day to visit Thomas Dugard, who was schoolmaster there.[1] A year later Trapp became vicar of Weston-on-Avon, the Earl of Middlesex's living, and, from 1639, he also served Luddington, to which Lord Conway of Ragley presented.[2]

Trapp's Civil War career was eventful. He preached at Warwick Castle, acted as chaplain to the parliamentary forces and, in the summer of 1643, was captured by royalists. His publications before 1640 bore fulsome dedications to his great patrons, but, during hostilities, he seems to have rejected his former deference. When Richard Baxter refused a bishopric in 1660, Trapp's name was an alternative suggestion.[3] He retained his Worcestershire connections and dedicated his *Commentaries* to Sir Thomas Rous of Rous Lench. Trapp returned to Stratford in 1660. He was buried on 25 January 1669 at Weston-on-Avon. (For his portrait see p. 289.)

John Trapp, like Edith Stoughton in the previous observation, was of a melancholy temperament and the strain of study had brought on the condition known as Hypochondriac Melancholy (no. 29). Robert Burton devoted several pages of his treatise on melancholy to 'Love of learning or overmuch study' as a cause of illness. Quoting from one of his many sources Burton observed that other workers look to their instruments (the painter washes his brushes, the husbandman mends his plough), but only scholars neglect that instrument, their brain.[4] Burton gave perturbation of the mind as one of the causes of hypochondriac or 'windie' melancholy.

In addition, Hall also detected in his patient scorbutic symptoms and an erratic fever. Hall's claim to have restored him from the 'very jaws of Death' suggests that his patient was extremely ill at the beginning of the treatment. To strengthen the spleen, the organ associated with melancholy or black bile, Hall prescribed an electuary which the patient believed to be the 'greatest hope of his cure' and 'was worth gold'. Before this Hall administered two purgatives, both from the paracelsian school. They were *Tartarus vitriolatus* (potassium sulphate) and *Mercurius dulcis* (mercurous chloride, also known as calomel). These were given *in pomo sub cineribus coct.*, in the pap of a cooked apple. Restorative and scorbutic remedies followed. The treatment appears to have lasted about a month and at the end of this period the patient was taking the electuary and a water composed of water of snails, water of frog spawn, the cordials Alkermes and *Manus Christi* mixed with scorbutic remedies.

1. BL, Add. MS 23146.
2. Dugdale, II, p. 704.
3. Hughes, pp. 89, 151, 205, 208–9, 316, 326.
4. Burton, *Anatomy*, pp. 111–12.

prefcribed this Clyfter : R *Decoct. com. pro Clyft.* ℔i, *Diaphænic. Diacatholic.* ā ʒi. *Pul. Hol.* ℥ii. *f. Clyft.* This gave three ftools with much wind, and defired event, for the Pain was mitigated ; yet in his Breaft he felt a pricking, to remove which was this prefcribed : R *Ung. de Alth.* ℥ii. *Ol. Amygd. dulc.* ℥ſ. *diffol. & mifce ad ign. pro Ung.* With which his Breaft and Side was anointed, and upon it a double linnen Cloth fpread with Butter warm'd. By this the Pain remitted, and he had a quiet night, and fell to fleep. The day following he ufed this expectorating Syrup : R *Syr. Scabiof. Magiftral. Capil. Vener. Liquor. Hyffop.* ā ʒi. *Mifc.* He took it often upon a Liquoris ftick. In the night he held in his Mouth one of our Pectoral Rolls. In the morning he was anointed again, and fo was freed from all his pain, and he became whole.

182: SPENCER COMPTON,
SECOND EARL OF NORTHAMPTON

As this patient was born in 1601, Hall must have been treating the second earl in 1633, three years after he inherited on his father's death. Hall had attended him three years before (no. 141). As in his father's time, the estate accounts show substantial sums spent on hunting (horses, farriery, hounds, feeding bills). At Charles I's coronation, he became Master of the Leash to the king, a post formerly held by his father, presumably as a result of his interest in hunting.[1]

The earl returned from hunting with an attack of pleurisy at a time when Hall was visiting his home. A purgative enema was immediately prescribed and an ointment to be rubbed on the chest. An expectorant containing syrups of scabious, maiden-hair and hyssop was also prescribed with pectoral rolls to be held in the mouth (no. 151). Within four days the patient was said be free from pain.

1. Compton, *Comptons*, p. 61.

APPENDIX 1

JOHN HALL'S WILL[1]

The last Will and Testament nuncupative of John Hall of Stratford upon Avon in the County of Warwicke gent made & Declared the five and twentieth of November 1635.

Inp[ri]mis I give unto my wife my house in London *It[e]m* I give unto my Daughter Nash my house in Acton *It[e]m* I give unto my Daughter Nash my Meadow[2] *It[e]m* I give my goods & Moneyes unto my wife & my Daughter Nash to bee equally Divided betwixt them *It[e]m* concerning my Study of Bookes I leave them (sayd he) to you my son Nash to dispose of them as you see good As for my manuscript[es] I wold have given them unto Mr Boles[3] if hee had beene heere but forasmuch as hee is not heere at p[re]sent you may (son Nash) burne them or else doe w[th] them what you please[4]

    Witnesses heerunto   Tho: Nashe
                  Simon Trappe[5]

1. PRO, PCC, 115 Pile.
2. Three closes in Stratford, purchased by Hall and Nash about 1626.
3. Joseph Bowles of 1 Chapel Street, Stratford (now the Falcon).
4. The fate of Hall's papers (and, of course, Shakespeare's) has long intrigued scholars. Nash may have disposed of them, but, in the course of a legal wrangle, after Hall's death, over an alleged debt of £77 13s. 4d., bailiffs broke into New Place and took away 'divers books, boxes, deskes, moneyes, bills and other goods of great value'. (Frank Marcham, *William Shakespeare and his Daughter Susannah*, 1931, p. 70)
5. The curate of Holy Trinity.

APPENDIX 2

CHRONOLOGY OF JOHN HALL'S CASES

Until 1752, when the English calendar was revised to bring it into line with continental practice, the year was officially reckoned to begin on 25 March. Before that date, the year of Our Lord given by English contemporaries to events between 1 January and 24 March should be treated with circumspection. It is clear from several entries in the Casebook, however, that Hall had already adopted continental and (by then) Scottish practice and all his dating has been therefore accepted as 'new style'. He was by no means alone in this, the result of England's increasing contact with its neighbours, and this may have a bearing on the question of where Hall received his medical training. (Dates are cited or calculated.)

Year	Patients
1611	Elizabeth Boughton
1613	Joan Lane; Thomas Roberts
1614	Thomas Beaufou
1615	[Elizabeth] Gardner
1616	Anne Greene; Lady Rous; [Robert] Wilson; Margaret Bovey
1617	[Mary] Barnes; Baron Compton; Lady Beaufou; Lady Rous; Richard Wilmore; Sarah Harington; John Rogers
1618	Henry Rainsford
1619	Ferrers Randolph; George Talbot; Mary Murden; William Barnes; Thomas Fawcet
1620	Lady Northampton; Lady Rous; Dixwell Brent; Bridget Browne; Elizabeth Sheldon of Beoley
1621	John Winter; Frances Rogers; Isabel Sadler; Joyce Boughton; Margaret Smith
1622	Lady Northampton; Lord Northampton (twice); Elinor Sheffield
1623	William Fortescue; George Quiney; Elizabeth Sheldon; William Barnes (III); Sir Edward Underhill; Margaret Winter; John Emes; Martha Fortescue
1624	Elizabeth Hall; Lady Sandys; John Nason
1625	William Broad; Sir John Pakington
1626	Mary Nash; Mary Murden; Alice Collins; Mary, Countess of Northampton
1627	Julian West
1628	Mary Talbot

Year	Patients
1629	Robert Hanslap; [Robert] Butler; Lady Clark; Thomas Underhill; Katherine Sturley; Sir Thomas Puckering; Simon Underhill
1630	Christian Basse; Joan Lynes; Susanna Hall; Lady Hunks; second Earl of Northampton; Margaret Baker
1631	George Underhill; Lydia Trapp; Mary Combe; Henry Parker
1632	Katherine Combe; Frances Fiennes; Frances Finch; Susanna Vernon; Edith Stoughton; John Hall
1633	Lady Browne; Lady Underhill; second Earl of Northampton; Sir Francis Harvey; Lady Rainsford; John Thornborough; Nicholas Fortescue; Edith Stoughton; Fulca Swift; Frances Fiennes
1634	Ann Smith; Anne Hanbury; Captain Bassett; John Walker; Joan Judkin; Thomas Underhill; John Trapp
1635	Sir Thomas Puckering; Sir Simon Clark

APPENDIX 3

CONCORDANCE OF NUMBERED OBSERVATIONS

There are no discrepancies between nos 1 to 49 in Cooke's edition, Hall's manuscript and this edition.

Cooke's number	Hall's number	this edition
L	66	50
LI	50	51
LII	51	52
LIII	52	53
LIV	–	54
LV	–	55
LVI	–	56
LVII	53	57
LVIII	54	58
LIX	55	59
LX	56	60
LXI	57	61
LXII	58	62
LXIII	59	63
LXIV	60	64
LXV	61	65
LXVI	62	66
LXVII	63	67
LXVIII	64	68
LXIX	176	69
LXX	65	70
LXXI	67	71
LXXII	68	72
LXIII	69	73
LXXIV	70	74
LXXV	71	75
LXXVI	72	76
LXXVII	73	77
LXXVIII	74	78
LXXIX	75	79
LXXX	76	80
LXXXI	77	81
LXXXII	78	82
LXXXIII	79	83
LXXXIV	80	84

Cooke's number	Hall's number	this edition
LXXXV	81	85
LXXXVI	82	86
LXXXVII	83	87
LXXXVIII	84	88
LXXXIX	85	89
XC	86	90
XCI	87	91
XCII	88	92
XCIII	89	93
XCIV	90	94
XCV	91	95
XCVI	92	96
XCVII	93	97
XCVIII	94	98
XCIX	95	99
C	96	100

SECOND CENTURY

Cooke's number	Hall's number	this edition
I	97	101
II	98	102
III	99	103
IV	100	104
V	101	105
VI	102	106
VII	103	107
VIII	104	108
IX	105	109
X	106	110
XI	107	111
XII	108	112
XIII	109	113
XIV	110	114
XV	111	115
XVI	112	116
XVII	113	117
XVIII	114	118
XIX	115	119
XX	116	120
XXI	117	121
XXII	118	122

Cooke's number	Hall's number	this edition
XXIII	119	123
XXIV	120	124
XXV	121	125
XXVI	122	126
XXVII	123	127
XXVIII	124	128
XXIX	125	129
XXX	126	130
XXXI	127	131
XXXII	128	132
XXXIII	129	133
XXXIV	130	134
XXXV	131	135
XXXVI	132.	136
XXXVII	133	137
XXXVIII	134	138
XXXIX	135	139
XL	136	140
XLI	137	141
XLII	138	142
XLIII	139	143
XLIV	140	144
XLV	141	145
XLVI	141	146
XLVII	142	147
XLVIII	143	148
XLIX	144	149
L	145	150
LI	146	151
LII	147	152
LIII	148	153
LIV	149	154
LV	150	155
LVI	151	156
LVII	152	157
LVIII	153	158
LIX	154	159
LX	155	160
LXXI	156	161
LXII	157	162
LXIII	158	163
LXIV	159	164

Cooke's number	Hall's number	this edition
LXV	160	165
LXVI	161	166
LXVII	162	167
LXVIII	163	168
LXIX	164	169
LXX	165	170
LXXI	166	171
LXXII	167	172
LXXIII	168	173
LXXIV	169	174
LXXV	170	175
LXXVI	171	176
LXXVII	172	177
LXXVIII	173	178
LXXIX	174	179
LXXX	175	180
LXXXI	177	181
LXXXII	178	182

BIBLIOGRAPHY

A: HISTORY

1. Manuscript Sources

Parish registers and bishops' transcripts have been the most extensively used source for initially identifying Hall's patients and these are given a footnote reference only when in an unexpected record office.

Family papers (for the Grevilles, Throckmortons, etc.) are cited in the appropriate footnote.

Antiquarians' papers, especially of J. Harvey Bloom and R.B. Wheler, are held at the Shakespeare Birthplace Trust Records Office.

Probate material is at diocesan repositories (Worcester, Lichfield) or the Public Record Office, London.

The British Library holds Thomas Dugard's diary, Thomas Ward's notes and Hall's Casebook.

2. Printed Sources

Place of publication is London unless stated otherwise

Amphlett, John (ed.), *The Worcestershire Lay Subsidy Roll of 1603*, Worcs. Hist. Soc., 1901

Anstruther, Godfrey, *The Seminary Priests*, 4 vols, 1969–77

Atkyns, Robert, *The Ancient and Present State of Gloucestershire*, 1768

Aubrey, John, *Brief Lives*, 1972

Barnard, E.A.B., 'The Rouses of Rous Lench', *Trans Worcs. Arch. Soc.* N.S.9, 1932

——, *A Seventeenth Century Country Gentleman, Sir Francis Throckmorton, 1640–80*, Cambridge, 1944

——, *The Sheldons*, Cambridge, 1939

Beaufoy, Gwendolyn, *Leaves from a Beech Tree*, Oxford, 1930

Bossy, John, *The English Catholic Community, 1570–1850*, 1975

de Breffny, Brian, and ffolliott, Rosemary, *The Houses of Ireland*, 1984

Brinkworth, E.R.C., *Shakespeare and the Bawdy Court of Stratford*, Chichester, 1972

Buckland, Emily A., *The Rainsford Family*, Worcester, 1932

Bund, J.W. Willis (ed.), *Worcestershire County Records: Calendar of the Quarter Sessions Papers, 1591–1643*, Worcester, 1900

Burgess, H.A.C. (ed.), *Register of Admissions to the Middle Temple*, 1949

Burke, B., *Peerage and Baronetage*, 1915

Calendar of State Papers, Domestic

Chambers, E.K., *William Shakespeare, A Study of Facts and Problems*, Oxford, 1943

Clark, G.T., *Limbus Patrum Morganiae et Glamorganiae*, 1886

Cliffe, J.T., *The Puritan Gentry*, 1984 .

Clifford, D.J.H. (ed.), *The Diaries of Lady Anne Clifford*, Stroud, 1994

Colvile, F.L., *The Worthies of Warwickshire*, 1869

Compton, William, *History of the Comptons of Compton Wynyates*, 1930

Cook, Harold J., *The Decline of the Old Medical Regime in Stuart London*, Ithaca, New York, 1986

Cooper, William, *A History of Lillington*, Long Compton, 1940

——, *Wootton Wawen, Its History and Records*, Leeds, 1936

Craven, Maxwell, and Stanley, Michael, *The Derbyshire Country House*, Nottingham, 1982

Creighton, C., *A History of Epidemics in Britain*, Cambridge, 1894

Dudley, T.B., *A Complete History of Royal Leamington Spa*, Leamington Spa, 1896

Dugdale, William, *The Antiquities of Warwickshire*, 1730

Farr, M.W., *The Fetherstons of Packwood in the Seventeenth Century*, Dugdale Society Occasional Paper no. 18, 1968

Fincham, Kenneth, *Prelate as Pastor: The Episcopate of James I*, Oxford, 1990

Fletcher, Anthony, *Reform in the Provinces*, New Haven, Connecticutt, 1986

Fogg, Nicholas, *Stratford-upon-Avon, Portrait of a Town*, Chichester, 1986

Foster, Joseph (ed.), *Colonel Chester's London Marriage Licences, 1521–1869*, 1887

—— (ed.), *Alumni Oxoniensis; The Members of the University of Oxford, 1500–1714*, Oxford, 1891

Fox, Levi (ed.), *Minutes and Accounts of the Corporation of Stratford-upon-Avon*, 1593–1598, Dugdale Society, XXXV, 1990

Fripp, E.I., *Master Richard Quiney*, Oxford, 1924

——, *Shakespeare's Stratford*, Oxford, 1928

——, *Shakespeare, Man and Artist*, Oxford, 1938

Grazebrook, H. Sydney, *The Heraldry of Worcestershire*, 1873

Gunn, H.S., *Wood Bevington: a history of the old manor house of Wood Bevington*, 1912

Hamper, William (ed.), *The Life, Diary and Correspondence of Sir William Dugdale*, 1827

Harrison, Sydney E., *Sledwich, Co. Durham*, 1944

Heal, Felicity, and Holmes, Clive, *The Gentry in England and Wales, 1500–1700*, 1994

Heralds' Visitations, Harleian Society (various counties)

Hughes, Ann, *Politics, Society and Civil War in Warwickshire, 1620–1660*, Cambridge, 1987

——, 'Religion and Society in Stratford-upon-Avon, 1619–1638', *Midland History*, XIX, 1994

Humphreys, John, *Studies in Worcestershire History*, Birmingham, 1938

Hutton, W.H., *Burford Papers*, 1905

Jenkins, Philip, *The Making of a British Ruling Class: the Glamorgan Gentry, 1640–1790*, Cowbridge, 1983

Jones, Jeanne, *Family Life in Shakespeare's England: Stratford-upon-Avon 1570–1630*, forthcoming

Joseph, Harriet (ed.), *John Hall, Man and Physician*, New York, 1964

Laslett, Peter, *The World we have Lost – further explored*, 1983

Lewis, B. Roland, *The Shakespeare Documents*, Stanford, 1941

Lindley, David, *The Trials of Frances Howard*, 1993

Long, C.E. (ed.), *Diary of the Marches of the Royal Army*, Camden Society, 1st series, LXXIV, 1859

Macdonald, Mairi, 'A New Discovery about Shakespeare's Estate in Old Stratford', *Shakespeare Quarterly*, vol. 45, no. 1, Spring 1994

MacDonald, Michael, *Mystical Bedlam: madness, anxiety and healing in seventeenth-century England*, Cambridge, 1981

MacLean, John, 'The Manor and Advowson of Clifford Chambers', *Trans Bristol and Glos. Arch. Society*, XIV, part 1, 1890

McClure, N.E. (ed.), *The Letters of John Chamberlain*, Philadelphia, 1939

Miller, George, *The Parishes of the Diocese of Worcester*, 1889–90

Morgan, Paul, 'The Subscription Books of the Diocese of Worcester and Class Structure under the Later Stuarts', Univ. of Birmingham MA, 1952

———, (ed.), *Inspections of Churches and Parsonage Houses in the Diocese of Worcester in 1674, 1676 and 1687*, Worcs. Hist. Soc., N.S.12, 1986

Moore-Ede, W., *Worcester Cathedral, its Monuments and Stories*, Worcester, 1925

Morris, Henry, *Baddesley Clinton, its Manor, Church and Hall*, 1897

Morrison, J.H., *The Underhills of Warwickshire*, Cambridge, 1932

Nash, T.R., *Collections for the History of Worcestershire*, 1781–2

Newdigate, Bernard H., *Michael Drayton and his Circle*, Oxford, 1941

Nichols, John, *The History and Antiquities of the County of Leicester*, 1795–1815

Pennant, Thomas, *The Journey from Chester to London*, 1811

Pevsner, N., *The Buildings of England* (individual counties)

Phillimore, W.P.W. (ed.), *Warwickshire Parish Registers: Baptisms*, II, 1904

Poynter, F.N.L., and Bishop, W.J., *A Seventeenth-century Doctor and his Patients: John Symcotts, 1592(?)–1662*, Beds. Hist. Rec. Soc., XXXI, 1951

Prestwich, Menna, *Cranfield: Politics and Profits under the Early Stuarts*, Oxford, 1966

Raach, J.H., *A Directory of English Country Physicians, 1603–43*, 1962

Ratcliff, S.C., and Johnson, H.C. (eds), *Warwick County Records: Quarter Sessions Order Books*, Warwick, 1935–64

Rowse, A.L., *The Case Books of Simon Forman*, 1974

Ryland, J.W., *The Records of Rowington*, II, Oxford, 1922

Savage, Richard (ed.), *Minutes and Accounts of the Corporation of Stratford-upon-Avon, 1577–1592*, III, Dugdale Society; V, X (1926, 1929)

Saville, G.E., *King's Coughton*, Kineton, 1973

Schoenbaum, S., *William Shakespeare, a Documentary Life*, Oxford, 1975

Shaw, William A., *The Knights of England*, 1971

Shirt, J., 'Dame Elizabeth Puckering's Charity', *West Sussex History*, 20, 1981

Shrewsbury, J.F.D., *A History of Bubonic Plague in the British Isles*, Cambridge, 1970

Spink, Henry H., *The Gunpowder Plot and Lord Mounteagle's Letter*, 1902

Stone, Lawrence, *The Crisis of the Aristocracy, 1558–1641*, Oxford, 1967

Styles, Philip, *Studies in Seventeenth Century West Midlands History*, Kineton, 1978

——— (ed.), 'The Genealogie, Life and Death of . . . Robert, Lord Brooke', *Miscellany I*, Dugdale Society, XXXI, 1977

Surtees, Robert, *The History and Antiquities of the County Palatine of Durham*, 1840

Tennant, Philip, *Edgehill and Beyond: the People's War in the South Midlands, 1642–1645*, Stroud, 1992

Tighe, W.J., 'A Nottinghamshire Gentleman in Court and Country: The Career of Thomas Markham of Ollerton, 1530–1607', *Thoroton Society Trans.*, 90, 1986

Tyack, Geoffrey, *Warwickshire Country Houses*, Chichester, 1994

Venn, J., and J.A. (comps), *Alumni Cantabrigiensis*, part 1, Cambridge, 1922–7

Victoria County Histories

Vivian, J.L., *The Visitations of the County of Devon*, Exeter, 1895

Walpole, Horace, *Journals of Visits to Country Seats*, Walpole Society, 16, 1927–8

Ward-Boughton-Leigh, B.G.F.C., *Memorials of a Warwickshire Family*, 1906
Warriner, M., *A Prospect of Weston*, 1978
Wheler, R.B., *History and Antiquities of Stratford-upon-Avon*, Stratford, 1806
Wood, Anthony à, *Athenae Oxoniensis*, 1813–20
Woodall, Joy, *From Hroca to Queen Anne*, Shirley, 1974

B: MEDICINE

1. Books and manuscripts before 1800

Barrough, Philip, *The Method of Phisick*, 3rd edn corrected and amended, 1601
Burton, Robert, *The Anatomy of Melancholy*, 2nd edn corrected and augmented, Oxford, 1624
Culpeper, Nicholas, *A Physicall Directory or, a Translation of the London Dispensatory by the Colledge of Physicians*, 1649
——, 'A Key to Galen's Method of Physick' in *Pharmacopoeia Londinensis or, the London Dispensatory*, 6th edn, 1659
Du Chesne, Joseph (Quercetanus), *Diaeteticon Polyhistoricon*, Paris, 1606
Eugalenus, Severinus, *De scorbuto*, Bremen, 1588
Gerard, John, *The Herball or, generall historie of plantes*, 1597
——, *The Herball . . .*, very much enlarged and amended by Thomas Johnson, 1633
Hall, John, *Select Observations on English Bodies . . . now put into English for common benefit by James Cooke*, 1657
——, *Select Observations . . .*, 2nd edn 1679 and 3rd edn 1683
Lewis, William, *An Experimental History of the Materia Medica*, 2nd edn with corrections and additions, 1768
Pharmacopoeia Londinensis, in qua medicamenta antiqua et nova usitatissima, sedulo collecta, accuratissime examinata, quotidiana experientia confirmata, describuntur. 1st edn (suppressed) May 1618 and 1st edn December 1618
Pomet, Pierre, *A Compleat History of Drugs, with observations by Lemery and Tournefort*, 1712
Quincy, John, *Lexicon Physico-Medicum or, a New Medical Dictionary*, 10th edn with new improvements from the latest authors, 1787
Renou, Jean de (Renodoeus), *A Medicinal Dispensatory containing the Whole Body of Physick . . .* Englished by Richard Tomlinson, Apothecary, 1657
Riviere, Lazarus (Riverius), *The Practice of Physick*, translated by Nicholas Culpeper, Abdiah Cole and William Rowland, 1655
Turner, William, *A New Herball*, 1551
Wirtzung (Wirsung) Christoph, *Praxis Medicinae Universalis or, a generall practise of physicke . . .* translated by Jacob Mosan, 1598

2. Books after 1800

Ackerknecht, E.H., *Therapeutics*, 1973
Arano, L.C., *The Medieval Health Handbook: Tacuinum Sanitatis*, New York, 1976
Bandreth, B., *The Doctrine of Purgation*, 2nd edn, New York, 1871
Berthe, G., *Historique de la Purgation*, Paris, 1909
Brockbank, W., *Ancient Therapeutic Arts*, 1954

Bynum, W.E., and Porter, R. (eds), *Companion Encyclopedia of the History of Medicine*, 1993

Carpenter, K.J., *A History of Scurvy and Vitamin C*, Cambridge, 1988

Castiglioni, A., *A History of Medicine*, New York, 1947

Crosland, M.P., *Historical Studies in the Language of Chemistry*, 1962

Debus, A., (ed.), *Science, Medicine and Society in the Renaissance*, 1972

Estes, J.W., *Dictionary of Protopharmacology*, Canton, 1990

Fernie, W.T., *Animal Simples*, Bristol, 1899

Forsyth, J.S., *The New London Medical and Surgical Dictionary*, 1826

Garrison, F.H., *History of Medicine*, 4th edn, Philadelphia, 1929

Gray, A., *Shakespeare's Son-in-Law*, Cambridge, 1939

Gray, S.F., *A Treatise on Pharmacology*, 3rd edn, 1824

Grigson, G., *A Dictionary of English Plant Names*, 1974

Gunter, R.T. (ed.), *The Greek Herbal of Dioscorides*, Englished by J. Goodyer 1655, Oxford, 1934

Hunt, T., *Popular Medicine in Thirteenth-Century England*, Cambridge, 1990

Hunter, M., and Gregory, A., (eds), *An Astrological Diary of Samuel Jeake of Rye*, Oxford, 1988

Long, E.R., *A History of Pathology*, New York, 1965

Mann, R.D., *Modern Drug Use: An Enquiry on Historical Principles*, Lancaster, 1984

Mitchell, C.M., *The Shakespeare Circle: A Life of Dr John Hall*, Birmingham, 1947

Partington, J.R., *A History of Chemistry*, 1961

Pereira, J., *The Elements of Materia Medica and Therapeutics*, 3rd edn, 1849–50

Poynter, F.N.L. (ed.), *The Evolution of Pharmacy in Britain*, 1965

Tannahill, R., *Food in History*, 1973

Urdang, G., *Pharmacopoeia Londinensis of 1618 reproduced in facsimile with a historical introduction by George Urdang*, Madison, Wisconsin, 1944

Watson, G., *Theriac and Mithridatum: A Study in Therapeutics*, 1966

Wear, A., French, R.K., and Lonie, I.M. (eds), *The Medical Renaissance of the Sixteenth Century*, Cambridge, 1985

Wootton, A.C., *Chronicles of Pharmacy*, 1910

INDEX OF DRUGS AND PREPARATIONS

Absinthium, *see* Wormwood

Acacia, *see* Gum Arabic

Acetum, *see* Vinegar

Adeps 151n

Agaric xxxiv, 3, 35, 51, 73, 281

Agnus castus 61

Agrimony 159, 281

Alabaster ointment, *see* Ung. de Alabastro

Album Graecum, *see* Animal drugs

Alexipharmics 63

Alkekengi, *see* Winter cherry

Alkermes, *see* Kermes

Aloes 3, 85, 209, 281

Alternative medicines xxxv

Althea, *see* Mallow

Alum 27, 83, 121, 129, 161

Amber 3n, 185, 197, 281

Amber, burnt 135, 139, 255

Amber, oil of 71, 335

Amber pills, *see* Pil. Succino Crato

Ambergris, *see* Animal drugs

Ammoniacum 127, 287

Amylum, *see* Starch

Animal drugs: Album Graecum 257; Ambergris 191, 241; Bear grease 27n; Bezoar stone 59, 287; Bone marrow 27n, 189; Cantharides 91; Capon grease 235; Castor 53, 107, 291, 307; Civet 323; Cock, windpipe of 23; Crayfish 39; Dog dung, *see* Album Graecum; Duck grease 117; Earthworms 189, 209, 257, 319, 333; Earthworms, oil of 27; Earthworms, powder of 189; Eggs 11, 23, 235; Fats, animal 151; Fox lung 183; Frog 39; Frog spawn 121, 159, 227, 347; Goose dung 129; Hartshorn 15, 51, 59, 63, 75, 109, 113, 117, 137, 141, 143, 179, 197, 209, 219, 227, 245, 253, 257, 271, 293, 299, 303, 315, 319; Hartshorn, burnt 47,

111; Heartbone of a stag 227; Hen 285; Hen dung 113, 177, 269; Hen grease 117, 151; Hog grease 155, 255; Horse dung 199; Horse, hoof of 167, 265, 307; Human excrement 113; Human grease 151n; Human milk 11, 39; Human skull 209; Human urine 327, 331; Ivory 15; Leeches xxxiv, 59, 87, 251, 299, 303, 343; Mummy 55, 197; Musk 73, 191, 227, 241, 265, 323; Ox Bile 209; Peacock dung 167; Pigeon 285, 299; Pigeon dung 113n; Pike, jaw of 197; Scorpions, oil of 179, 315; Snails 13, 39, 227, 303, 347; Spiders' webs 111, 271; Swallows' nests 257; Viper flesh 75n

Aniseed 13, 235

Antimony, *see* Stibium

Antispasmodic drugs 291

Aparine, *see* Goose-grass

Apothecary weights xxxviii

Apozeme 211, 245

Aquae – waters: Aqua Bryonia Composita, *see* Aqua Hysterica; Aqua Coelestis 153; Aqua Cordialis Frigida Saxoniae 303; Aqua Dracunculus 143; Aqua Fumariae 81; Aqua Hordeata 135; Aqua Hysterica 229, 265, 295, 307; Aqua Mercurialis 267; Aqua Plantaginis 341; Aqua Portulaca 149; Aqua Vitae 19, 39, 71, 179

Aranearum telae (Spiders' webs), *see* Animal drugs

Armenian bole 11n, 61, 155, 197, 199, 341

Aromatics 141

Arsenic, red (Realgar) 105

Arsenic, yellow (Orpiment) 235

Artemesia, *see* Mugwort

Asafoedita 53, 229, 265

Assae Odorat, *see* Benzoin

Astringent 341

Astringent plaster 11

Attenuating medicines xxxv

Aurum potabile 227

Axungia gallinae (Hen grease), *see* Animal drugs

Balm 19

Balneum Maris 13

Balsams 189

Balsam of Peru 189

Barberry 209

Barley 33, 309

Barley sugar 13n, 99

Basilicon ointment, *see* Ung. Basilicon

Bath, waters of 199, 335

Bdellium gum 71n

Beccabunga, *see* Brooklime

Beers, medicated 3, 159, 267

Beets 99

Benjamin, *see* Benzoin

Benzoin 55, 79

Betony 209

Bezoar stone, *see* Animal drugs

Bistort 231

Bitters 31, 139

Black hellebore 53, 59, 63, 263, 343

Blistering plaster, *see* Vesiccatory

Bloodstone, *see* Haematite

Bole 7, 61

Boles, *see* Earths

Bole Amoniack, *see* Armenian bole

Bone marrow, *see* Animal drugs

Borage 45

Borax 23, 83

Brooklime xxxviii, 3, 127, 287

Bryony 129, 179, 229, 231, 265, 291, 295, 307, 323, 335

Bugloss 113

Burnet 99

Burnt amber, *see* Amber

Burnt argil 123

Burnt hartshorn, *see* Hartshorn

Burnt lead, *see* Lead

Calamus aromaticus 57
Calomel, *see* Mercurius dulcis
Calybs, *see* Steel
Camphor 39, 165, 175, 263
Cantharides, *see* Animal drugs
Capar 211
Capillary herb, *see* Maidenhair
Capillus veneris, *see* Maidenhair
Carabe, *see* Amber
Caranna 37, 145
Cardiacae, *see* Motherwort
Carduus benedictus 35, 141, 145, 337
Carminatives 85, 87, 161, 173, 197, 217, 233, 335
Cassia 7, 25, 61, 117, 197
Castor, *see* Animal drugs
Cataplasm 139
Catholicon, *see* Diacatholicon
Caudle 39
Celandine 93, 257
Cephalic drugs 43, 251, 265, 303
Cerrusa, *see* Lead carbonate
Chalcitis 159n
Chalk 93, 155
Chalybeate water, *see* Steeled water
Chalybiated milk, *see* Steeled milk
Chalybs praeparata, *see* Prepared steel
Chamoepith, *see* Ground pine
Chamomile 21
Chelidonium majus, *see* Celendine
Chemical remedies xxxvi
Chicory 85, 157, 179, 287
China root 51n, 129, 223, 303
Christmas rose, *see* Black hellebore
Cinnamon 57, 71
Civet, *see* Animal drugs
Claret wine 141
Clove 71, 209
Clysters, *see* Enemas
Cobweb (Spiders' webs), *see* Animal drugs
Cochlearia, *see* Scurvy-grass
Cock, windpipe of, *see* Animal drugs
Cold seeds 245, 343n
Collyrium 9, 11, 17, 71, 87, 93, 307

Colocynth 47n, 85
Coloquindita, *see* Colocynth
Coltsfoot 25, 235
Confectio Alkermes 241
Confectio Hamech 83
Conserve of barberry 209
Conserve of scurvy-grass 209
Cooling seeds, *see* Cold seeds
Copper acetate 87n
Copper sulphate 127n
Coral 51n, 83, 113, 145, 245
Coral, tincture of 59
Corallina 231
Coriander 61
Corn poppy 83, 151, 305
Cornu cervi (Hartshorn), *see* Animal drugs
Cranium humanum (Human skull), *see* Animal drugs
Crayfish, *see* Animal drugs
Cream of Tartar, *see* Tartar
Creta, *see* Chalk
Crocus martis, *see* Iron oxide
Crocus sativus, *see* Saffron
Crystal Tartar, *see* Tartar
Crystal veneris, *see* Copper sulphate
Cubebs 55, 173
Cumin 3n, 167
Cyme 3n

Dates 119
Deauro (to gild), *see* Gold leaf
Dens Ebur (Ivory), *see* Animal drugs
Dia (meaning of) 37n
Diaambra 191
Diacatholicon 37, 117, 153, 179, 341
Diacodium 299n, 343
Diacrocum, *see* Saffron
Diacubebs, *see* Cubebs
Diacurcuma 287
Diacydonium 87n
Diacymini, *see* Cumin
Diagrydium, *see* Scammony
Diamoron 135
Diamoschum 191
Dianthus, *see* Clove
Diapalm, *see* Iron sulphate
Diaphoenicon 37, 75, 179
Diaphoretics xxx
Diascordium 51n, 143, 145, 153, 197
Diatart. Quercet. 127n
Diatragacanthum 61, 99
Diatrionsantalum 261

Diatrium 261n
Dictamnus, *see* White dittany
Diuretics xxxv, 97
Dock root 157
Dodder 263, 337
Dose 115
Dragon's blood 11n

Earths 11n
Earthworms, *see* Animal drugs
Ebur (Ivory), *see* Animal drugs
Eclegma 309
Eggs, *see* Animal drugs
Elecampane 115
Electuaria – electuaries xxx, 13; Electuarium Caryocostinum 27n, 213; Elect. Chalybs. Crato 173; Elect. Gemmis Frigidi 51; Elect. Lenitivum 299
Emerald 63
Emetics xxxv
Emetic infusion 15, 43, 49, 137, 149, 179, 241, 253, 337
Emplastra – plasters: Emplastrum Ammoniacum 127; Empl. Diachalcitis 159n; Empl. Diachylon Compositum 303n; Empl. Hystericum 265; Empl. Meliloto 153n; Empl. Nephritic 295; Empl. Oxycroceum 235; Empl. pro Matrice 227; Empl. Saturn Rub., *see* Lead plasters
Enemas xxxv, 111, 241, 249, 285, 293, 343, 349
Enula campana, *see* Elecampane
Epitheme 63
Epithymum, *see* Dodder
Errhine, *see* Sternutatory
Eupatory 129
Euphasia (Eyebright) 87n

Faeces (sediment) 93n
Faecul Bryony 229
Farina, *see* Wheat starch
Ferrous sulphate, *see* Iron sulphate
Feverfew 161
Figs 309
Five opening roots, *see* Opening roots
Flower de Luce, *see* Iris

Foetida, *see* Asafoetida
Fomentation 39
Fontenelle xxxv, 303
Fox Lung, *see* Animal drugs
Frankincense, *see* Olibanum
Fraxinella, *see* White dittany
French lavender 185
Fritter 93
Frog and frog spawn, *see* Animal drugs
Frontal 17
Fuller's earth 123
Fumaria, *see* Fumitory
Fume 13, 55, 99, 105, 167, 185, 215, 265
Fumitory 29, 83, 91, 175

Galangal 55
Galbanum gum 71n
Garlic 97
Garnets 63, 101
Gemstones 63
Gilded pills 221
Gold leaf 63, 221, 227, 241, 265, 307
Golden rod 245
Goose dung, *see* Animal drugs
Goose-grass 129
Grains of Paradise 55
Grain weight, *see* Apothecary weights
Granata, *see* Pomegranate
Granats, *see* Garnets
Ground pine 71n, 265, 322
Guaiacum 17, 27, 61, 71, 123, 147, 155, 173, 185, 199, 203
Gum Arabic 11n, 197
Gypsum 61

Haematite 83, 85, 93, 341
Hand of Christ, *see* Manus Christi
Hartshorn, *see* Animal drugs
Hartwort 343n
Heira picra 31
Helleborus niger, *see* Black hellebore
Hen and hen dung, *see* Animal drugs
Henbane of Peru, *see* Tobacco
Hermodactylus 129n, 159
Hippocras 55
Hippocras bag 3n
Holland powder 37, 97, 295
Holy thistle, *see* Carduus benedictus

Hordeatum 309
Hordeum, *see* Barley
Horehound 13, 35
Horse, dung and hoof, *see* Animal drugs
Hot compress 293
Houseleek 9, 175
Human fat, milk, skull and urine, *see* Animal drugs
Humectors 343
Hyacinthus, *see* Sapphire
Hydromel 73
Hyoscyamus alba, *see* White henbane
Hypericum, *see* St John's wort
Hypocistis 315n
Hyssop 13, 25

Incising medicines xxx
Ippocras bag, *see* Hippocras bag
Iris 25
Iron oxide xxxvii, 23, 33, 93, 157, 165
Iron salts 163, 173
Iron sulphate 127, 281
Ivory, *see* Animal drugs

Jacinth 63
Jalap 257, 321, 331
Jujubs 47
Julep 13, 45
Juniper 105

Kermes 241n, 347

Labdanum 37
Lachrimae 11n
Lac mulieris (woman's milk), *see* Animal drugs
Lapis Bezoar (Bezoar stone), *see* Animal drugs
Lapis lazuli 241
Laudanum 141, 157, 241, 337
Laurel 19, 27
Lavender 179
Lead, burnt 263
Lead carbonate 83, 93, 155, 175, 263
Lead oxide 83, 263, 295, 327
Lead plasters 153n
Lead plates 197, 215, 227, 263, 267
Leeches, *see* Animal drugs
Lick 235, 305, 327
Lignum vitae, *see* Guaiacum

Lily 25
Limaces, terrestres (snails), *see* Animal drugs
Lincture, linctus 13, 25, 183
Liniment 87
Liquorice 13
Litharge, *see* Lead oxide
Lohoch e Pulmone Vulpis 183
Lohoch Sanum et Expertum 13n, 183
London *Pharmacopoeia* 1618 xxxv, xxxvi
London *Pharmacopoeia* 1746 175n
London Treacle, *see* Theriaca
Long pepper 47, 99
Lovage 161
Lozenges, *see* Trochisci
Lozenge of agaric 35n
Lozenge of Winter cherry and opium 215
Lumbrici (Earthworms), *see* Animal drugs
Lye 163

Maiden-hair 303n, 341, 349
Magistery of pearl 145
Mallow 7
Mallow poultice 159
Mandibule Lucii piscis (pike jaw), *see* Animal drugs
Mandragora 73, 277
Manna 77, 117
Manus Christi 13, 287, 347
Margarita, *see* Pearls
Marshmallow ointment, *see* Ung. Dialtheae
Mastic 101
Matrisylvia, *see* Meadowsweet
Meadowsweet 135
Medulla (marrow), *see* Animal drugs
Mechoacan 51
Medicine chest 335
Medicines, cost of xxxiii
Melita rosarum 135
Mercury herb 23, 267
Mercurial sulphate 115n
Mercurius dulcis 283, 347
Mercuris vitae 75, 149
Mercurous chloride, *see* Mercurius dulcis
Milfoil 93, 163
Mints 45
Mistletoe 209
Mithridate 19, 31, 111, 157, 191, 291

Moschata, *see* Nutmeg
Moschus (Musk), *see* Animal drugs
Morsuli 65
Motherwort 87, 93
Mugwort 107, 231, 291, 322
Mummy, *see* Animal drugs
Musk, *see* Animal drugs
Mustard 99
Mylobalans 211, 213
Myrrh 107, 291

Nasturtium Aquaticum, *see* Water-cress
Nephritic (kidney) plaster 295
Nettles 35, 161
Nightshade 93
Nuces (Nux) Moschatae, *see* Nutmeg
Nutmeg 71
Nut shells 111

Oak bark 163
Oak galls 11n, 27
Oak leaves 129
Oculi Populi 73
Odorifics 167
Olei – oils: Oil of Amber, *see* Amber; Oil of Bricks 71n; Oil of Camomile 151; Oil of Nard 179; Oil of Olives 143; Oil of Rue 37, 179; Oil of Rosemary 335; Oil of Sage 265; Oil of Scorpions, *see* Animal drugs; Oil of Spike 167; Oil of Sweet Almonds 13, 117, 151, 235, 315; Oil of Tartar, *see* Potassium carbonate; Oil of Violets 151; Oil of Vitriol 13n, 45; Oil of Wormwood, *see* Wormwood, Oil of; Oleum Amygdalum Dulcium, *see* Oil of Sweet Almonds; Oleum de Lateribus, *see* Oil of Bricks; Oleum Lignum Heraclei 299; Oleum Lumbricorum (earth-worms), *see* Animal drugs; Oleum Salviae Chymica, *see* Oil of Sage
Ointments, *see* Unguenta
Olibanum 199, 203
Onion 97
Opening roots 87n, 107n

Opiate 51, 53, 85, 99, 117, 191, 209, 241, 285, 303, 315
Opium xxxviii, 99, 121, 157n, 183, 263, 277
Opopanax 85, 309
Opthalmic water, *see* Collyrium
Orpiment, *see* Arsenic, yellow
Ox Bile, *see* Animal drugs
Oxymel 15, 35, 43, 253, 341

Paeony root 53, 65, 209, 265, 291
Panados 33
Panatella 39
Papaver erraticum, *see* Corn poppy
Parsley 97
Peacock dung, *see* Animal drugs
Pearls 51n, 63, 65, 101, 227, 241
Pearl barley 135
Pectoral drugs 35, 183
Pectoral ointment, *see* Ung. Pectorale
Pectoral rolls 279, 349
Pellitory of Spain, *see* Pyrethrum
Pellitory of the wall 337n
Penidies, *see* Barley sugar
Penny-weight 121
Pepper 71
Pharmacopoeia Londinensis, *see* London *Pharmacopoeia*
Philonium Persicum 85, 187
Philosopher's oil, *see* Oil of Bricks
Pigeon, *see* Animal drugs
Pile, jaw of, *see* Animal drugs
Pilulae – pills xxxiv, xxxviii; Pilula Aggregative 51n; Pil. Alephanginae 221n; Pil. Aureae 47n, 151; Pil. Cochiae 47n; Pil. Foetidae 85, 307, 309; Pil. Podagra 213; Pil. Ruffi 3, 85, 187, 219; Pil. Sine Quibus Esse Nolo 53, 209; Pil. Stomachicae 31, 173; Pil. Succino Crato 3, 151, 219
Piper, *see* Pepper
Pitch 55, 101
Pix (Pic) navalis, *see* Pitch
Placebo xxxix
Plantain 61, 85, 341

Plantain water, *see* Aqua Plantaginis
Plaster against worms 77, 79
Plasters, *see* Emplastra
Plerisar, *see* Species Pleres Archon.
Plumbum ustum, *see* Lead, burnt
Polypharmacy xxxv, 171, 173
Polypodium of the oak 129n
Pomegranate 11n, 63n
Poppy seed 23
Portulaca, *see* Purslane
Posset 19
Poultice 25, 185, 245, 255
Potassium carbonate 87n
Potassium sulphate 187, 347
Powders, *see* Pulveres
Prepared steel 81
Prescriptions xxxvii
Ptysan 39
Pulmo vulpis (fox lung), *see* Animal drugs
Pulveres – powders: Pulvis Rodolphi Holland, *see* Holland powder; Pulv. Sanctus 167; Pulv. Senae Montagnana 159
Purgatives xxxiv
Purslane 39, 149
Pyrethrum 71

Quince, *see* Diacydonium

Radish 59, 271, 285
Realgar, *see* Arsenic
Rear egg, *see* Animal drugs
Red lead, *see* Lead oxide
Rhodium, *see* Rose wood
Rhubarb 3, 7, 25, 85, 173, 185, 287
Rocket seed 47
Rose 9n
Rosemary 163, 167
Rose water 9n, 163
Rose wood 221n
Rotulas 251, 311
Roul 61
Royal ointment, *see* Ung. Basilicon
Rubies 63
Rue 71n, 77, 291
Rue, juice of 55, 65
Rust, *see* Steel, prepared

Sack 21, 37, 45

Saccharum tabuli, *see* Manus Christi
Saffron 15, 73, 179, 257, 287, 291, 331
Sagapenum 85
Sage 101
St John's wort 93
St Vincent's well 335
Salads xxxiii
Sal Prunellae 309
Salt of scurvy-grass 187
Salvia, *see* Sage
Sanicula 245
Santalum, *see* Saunders wood
Santonin 311
Sapphire 63
Sarcenet 203
Sarcocol 9n
Sarsaparilla 17, 43, 51, 71, 145, 185, 215, 263
Sassafras 17, 51, 71, 185, 199, 203
Saunders wood 39, 113n, 261
Savin 77
Scabious 29, 45
Scammony 27n, 75, 85, 213, 283
Scilla maritima, *see* Squill
Scorbutic beer 3, 187, 221, 267
Scurvy-grass xxxviii, 3, 87, 127, 135, 187, 191, 221
Scutum 197
Sea salt 129
Sealed Earth 61, 199, 341
Sebestens 47
Secret remedies 199
Secundum artem 9n, 57
Semen santonicum, *see* Wormseed
Sem. Siler Montanum, *see* Hartwort
Sengreen, *see* Houseleek
Senna xxxiv, 3, 47, 91, 137, 159, 161, 211, 263
Silver leaf 227
Simples xxxvi
Sinapi, *see* Mustard
Smaragdus, *see* Emerald
Smardine, *see* Emerald
Snails, *see* Animal drugs
Sneezing powder, *see* Sternutatory
Soap, medicated 87
Solanum, *see* Nightshade
Soldanella 231
Soldier's ointment, *see* Ung. Martiatum

Sorrel 61, 245
Spanish fly, *see* Cantharides
Species xxxv, 53n; Species Aromaticum Rosarum 13n; Species Confectionis Liberantis 271; Species Diamargiton Frigidium 343; Species Dianthus 167; Species Diatragacanth 61; Species Diarhodon 221n; Species Diatrion Santalon 127n; Species Diaturbith c Rhabarbo 149; Species de Gemis 53n; Species Laetificans 53, 227; Species Pleres Archonticon 127n, 239, 335
Spica, *see* Lavender
Spiders' webs, *see* Animal drugs
Spirit of wine 39
Squill 15, 25
Starch 183
Steel, prepared 81
Steeled electuary 217
Steeled milk 197
Steeled water 19, 155, 163, 281
Steeled wine 81, 87, 127, 235, 299
Sternutatory 53, 59, 99, 209, 323
Stibium 217
Stinking pills, *see* Pil. Foetidae
Stinking things 167, 229, 265, 291
Stomachic medicines 19
Styptic 165
Succinum, *see* Amber
Succory, *see* Chicory
Sudorific xxxv, 71
Sugar 23
Sulphur 27, 79, 129
Sulphuric acid, *see* Oil of Vitriol
Swallows' nests, *see* Animal drugs
Syrupi – Syrups: Syrupus Althea 97, 131; Syr. Augustanus 171; Syr. of Chicory 51n; Syr. of Chicory with Rhubarb 171; Syr. of Coltsfoot 305; Syr. Cydoniorum 203; Syr. of [five] Opening Roots

107n; Syr. Granata 307; Syr. of Hyssop 349; Syr. Laetificans 227; Syr. Lujula 299n; Syr. of Maiden-hair 85, 309, 341, 349; Syr. Magistral ad Melancholia 337; Syr. of Marshmallow, *see* Syr. Althea; Syr. of Mugwort 107, 171; Syr. of Myrtle 85; Syr. Papavere Erratico 51n, 83, 305; Syr. of Pomegranates, *see* Syr. Granata; Syr. of Poppies 45, 197; Syr. of Quince, *see* Syr. Cydoniorum; Syr. of Red Poppies, *see* Syr. Papavere Erratico; Syr. of Scabious 305, 309, 349; Syr. Sceletyrs 189; Syr. Stoechade 185; Syr. of Violets 19, 43

Tacamahacca 189
Tamarind 197, 213
Tartar, Crystal, Cream of 27n, 139, 213, 295, 343
Tartar vitriolatus, *see* Potassium sulphate
Telae Aranearum (spiders' webs), *see* Animal drugs
Terebine, *see* Turpentine
Terra Sigilatae, *see* Sealed Earth
Theriaca 19, 31
Theriaca Andromachi 71, 75
Theriaca Londinensis 19
Theriaca, Venetian 65
Tincture of Coral, *see* Coral
Tobacco 59, 235
Tormentil 77, 101, 197, 231
Tragacanth 99, 197
Tragea 217
Treacles, *see* Theriaca
Trochisci – lozenges: Trochisci Albi 263; Troch. Anhandall 47n; Troch. Alkakengi 263; Troch. Myrrha 107
Troy weights, *see* Apothecary weights
Turbith, *see* Turpethum
Turpethum 115, 287
Turmeric 287
Turpentine 7, 61, 101, 105, 215
Tussilago, *see* Coltsfoot
Tutia, Tutty, *see* Zinc oxide

Unguenta ointments: Unguentum Agrippae 179; Ung. de Alabastro 121; Ung. Album 175; Ung. Basilicon 291; Ung. Comitissae 61; Ung. Dialtheae 13, 121, 151; Ung. Martiatum 27, 71, 167, 179; Ung. de Mineo 263; Ung. Pectorale 117; Ung. Populeon 73, 111, 277; Ung. Rubrum 263; Ung. Splanchicum 127n

Ungula caballina (horse hoof), *see* Animal drugs

Urine as a remedy, *see* Animal drugs

Urethral injection 263

Uterine herbs 323

Venice Treacle, *see* Theriaca

Venice Turpentine, *see* Turpentine

Verdigris, *see* Copper acetate

Vermifuge (vermicide) 313

Vesicatory 91

Vinegar 179

Viscus, *see* Mistletoe

Vitamin C xxxviii

Vitellus ovi (egg), *see* Animal drugs

Vitriol, Oil of, *see* Oil of Vitriol

Wake-Robin root 221n

Water-cress xxxviii, 3, 127, 287

Wax 33

White copperas, *see* Zinc sulphate

White dittany 191, 231

White hellebore 121

White henbane 85, 99

White lead, *see* Lead carbonate

White ointment, *see* Ung. Album

White pitch 145

White vitriol, *see* Zinc sulphate

Wine of squill 15

Winter cherry 97, 215, 263

Woman's milk, *see* Animal drugs

Wood Sorrel 299, 327

Wormseed xxxviii, 231, 311

Wormwood 3n, 19, 25, 31, 77, 139, 255

Wormwood, Oil of, 45

Yarrow, *see* Milfoil

Zedoary 161

Zinc oxide 9n, 93

Zinc sulphate 93, 155, 165

INDEX OF MEDICAL CONDITIONS AND RELATED TERMS

After-birth, *see* Placenta

Ague, *see* Fevers, intermittent

Almonds (tonsils) 135

Amenorrhoea, *see* Courses, suppression of

Anaemia 281

Anasarca (Oedema) xxxii, 171

Apostem 25

Appetite, loss of 137, 157, 183, 203

Arthritis, *see* Gout

Ascaris (Roundworm) xxxviii, 311, 335

Asthma 13, 33, 331

Atra bilis, *see* Black bile

Back, pain in 161

Barber Surgeon 181

Bastard Tertian (fever), *see* Fevers, intermittent

Black bile xxxi, 57, 341

Bleeding from the mouth 83, 85, 165

Bleeding from the nose 121

Blood letting (venesection) xxxiv, 17, 27, 43, 53, 59, 107, 165, 175, 181, 255, 271, 285, 299, 331, 341, 343

Blood, spitting of 341

boils xxxii

Breast, pain in 33

Breathing, difficulty of, *see* Asthma

Burnt melancholy 141, 343

Cachexia 281

Cacochymia xxxii, 3, 17, 177

Calculi, *see* Stone

Camp Fever, *see* Fever, Typhus

Cancer xxxii, 155n

Canker (eroding ulcer) 155

Cardiac Passion 239

Caruncle 263

Carus 271

Catarrh 47, 221

Cephalic vein xxxiv, 53, 107, 165

Childbed Fever, *see* Fever, Puerperal

Chiragra 159

Chlorosis, *see* Green sickness

Choler, *see* Yellow bile

Cholick, *see* Colic

Cirrhosis of the liver 331

Cods (testicles), swollen 153, 261, 331

Colic 37, 161, 197

Concoction (digestion) 31, 203, 233, 251

Consent of stomach, *see* Sympathy

Constipation 249

Constitution xxxi, xxxiii, 251, 331, 341

Consumption 39, 55, 73

Convulsions of the face 69, 163, 291, 299

Coronal suture 221

Cough xxxii, 13, 73, 99, 105, 183, 235, 303

Courses (menstruation): Suppression of 71, 107, 191, 229, 265, 307, 341; Flux of 19, 93, 109, 121, 157, 161, 227

Cupping xxix, 279, 285

Cure, definition of xxxix

Deafness 337

Delirium 285, 299

Delusions 341

Dementia xxxiii

Dental abscess 123

Diarrhoea 45, 185, 203, 205, 219

Digestion, *see* Concoction

Diptheria xxi

Distillation of rheum 9
Dropsy xxxii, 49, 179, 327, 331
Dyscrasia xxxviii
Dysentery xxxii, 33, 157, 205

Empirics 217, 315
Epilepsy 53, 65, 165, 209
Eroding ulcer, *see* Canker
Erratic fever, *see* Fever, Erratic
Erysipelas xxxii, 327
Exulcerations, *see* Ulceration

Falling sickness, *see* Epilepsy
Fever xxxii, 57, 111, 153, 179, 209, 249, 285, 299, 315: Camp, *see* F. Typhus; Childbirth, *see* F. Puerperal; Erratic 51, 347; Hectic 39n; Malign, *see* F. Typhus; New, *see* F. Typhus; Puerperal 51, 113, 121n, 145, 269; Typhus 63, 123, 141; Ungaric, *see* F. Typhus
Fevers, intermittent xxxii, 293: Quotidian xxxii, 145, 163, 303; Tertian xxxii, 15, 43, 49, 121, 253; Tertian, Bastard 241, 275, 287; Quartan xxxii
Fistula 171
Flatulence 55, 119, 157, 217
Flatus hypochrondriacus 337
Flux: of belly, *see* Diarrhoea; of blood, *see* Haemorrhage; of Courses, *see* Courses
French Pox, *see* Syphilis

Gonorrhoea 145, 261
Gout 159, 213, 309, 319
Green sickness 281
Gums, swollen 123, 151, 157
Gutta, *see* Gout

Haemorrhage: menopausal 93; uterine, *see* Courses
Haemorrhoids 21, 73, 277, 299
Head, pain in 43, 47, 235, 251, 265, 303
Health, preservation of 251, 303
Hearing, dullness of 99
Heart, trembling of 191
Heartburn 31

Hectic fever, *see* Fever, Hectic
Hemiplegia 209
Horror (shivering) 51
Hot distillation, *see* Opthalmia
Humoral theory xxxi, 251, 319
Hypochondriac melancholy 49, 53, 59, 63, 87, 153, 347
Hysteria, *see* Mother

Indigestion 157, 161
Insensibility, degrees of 271n
Insomnia, *see* Watching

Jaundice 15, 179, 209, 257, 275, 287, 331, 341

Kidneys, *see* Reins
Knees, painful 309
Krasis xxxiii, 9

Leucorrhoea, *see* Whites
Lienterica 205
Ligatures 123, 343
Liver, diseases arising from 281
Liver vein xxxi, 175, 299
Loathing of meat, *see* Appetite, loss of
Lungs: Blood from 341; Rising of 279

Malign Fever, *see* Fever, Typhus
Matrix (uterus), displacement of 265, 291
Measles 123
Melancholia 57, 81, 229, 233, 319, 341, 347
Melancholy, *see* Black bile
Menopausal haemorrhage, *see* Haemorrhage
Menstruation, *see* Courses
Migraine 43
Miscarriage 47, 101
Morpheu 87, 167
Mother (hysteria) 81, 113, 167, 177, 229, 233, 265, 291, 295, 307, 323, 335

New Fever, *see* Fever, Typhus
Nocturnal emissions 197

Oedema, *see* Anasarca
Opthalmia 9, 11, 15, 87, 91
Os sacrum 101

Palsy 335
Paralysis 53, 209, 335
Phlegm xxxi
Piles, *see* Haemorrhoids
Pissing the bed 23
Placenta, retention of 291
Plague xxii, xxiii
Pleurisy 349
Podagra 159, 213
Pregnancy, treatment in 239
Puerperal Fever, *see* Fever, Puerperal
Pulmonary illness xxxii, 13, 33
Pustules 23, 81, 129, 175

Quacks, *see* Empirics
Quinsy 181, 255
Quotidian Fever, *see* Fevers, intermittent

Reins (kidneys), inflammation of 219
Rheum 9, 11, 151
Rising of the lungs, *see* Lungs
Roundworm, *see* Ascaris

Saphenous vein 107
Scab and itch, *see* Skin complaints
Scarification xxxiv, 285
Sceletyrbe 189
Scorbutic dropsy 135, 331
Scorbutic epilepsy 209
Scorbutic gout 319
Scorbutic symptoms, *see* Scurvy
Scrotum, irritation of 299
Scurvy xxxviii, 3, 87, 123, 187, 189, 191, 193, 203, 211, 219, 221, 229, 235, 239, 281, 287, 295, 319, 321, 333
Scurvy and diet 3, 321
Semen, flux of 197
Skin complaints 15, 23, 29, 81, 129, 175
Smallpox xxi, 143, 267, 307
Speech, loss of 291
Spontaneous generation (of worms) 77
Stomach complaints 19, 25, 31, 37, 45, 55, 161, 249
Stone 97, 215, 219, 315, 335
Stones (testicles), *see* Cods
Strangury 261
Surfeit: of alcohol 331; of cream 137; of herrings 197

Swellings, *see* Tumours
Sympathy 53, 173, 251
Syphilis 17, 147, 199

Teeth, painful 123, 151, 221, 299
Tenesmus 21
Tent 121
Tertian Fever, *see* Fevers, intermittent
Testicles, swollen, *see* Cods
Tongue, inflamed 305
Tonsils, *see* Almonds
Tonsillitis 139
Torticollis 69, 163
Tortua Oris, *see* Torticollis
Tuberculosis, *see* Consumption

Tumours (swellings) 27, 189, 267
Tympanites 231
Typhus Fever, *see* Fever, Typhus

Ulcer 203
Ungaric Fever, *see* Fever, Typhus
Urethra, inflammation of 7, 131, 213
Urine: blood in 213, 245; excessive (Diuresis) 299; heat of 7, 131, 213; retention of 97, 233, 309
Uterus, displacement of, *see* Matrix

Vapours 59, 75, 81, 85, 271, 285, 319
Venesection, *see* Blood letting
Vertigo 165, 195, 251

Watching (Insomnia) 121, 285, 337
Whites (Leucorrhoea) 61, 119, 199, 227, 281
Wind in the womb 223
Worms 33, 77, 79, 147, 151, 171, 209, 231, 283, 311, 335

Yard (penis) 263
Yellow bile xxxi
Yellow jaundice, *see* Jaundice

INDEX OF PERSONS

Wives and widows are indexed under both maiden and married surnames.
John Hall and James Cooke are not indexed.

Acton, Helen (Thornborough) 319
Ainge, Ursula (Smith) 231, 305, 307
Alderford, John 253; Margaret (Clark) 253
Aldersey, Ann 135, 139, 141, 157, 159, 352; Dorothy 135
Al-Razi xxxvi, 175
Andromachus 75n
Anglicus, *see* John of Gaddesden
Archbold, Catherine 247; Eleanor (Hunks) 245; Elizabeth 247; John 247, 297; Thomas 247, 297
Archer, Sir Simon 99, 251
Archer (Mrs) 291
Aristotle 77
Ashton, Elizabeth (Clopton), 205; Ralph 205
Attwood, Clare (Peers) 33, 227
Aubrey, John xiv, 193
Austin, Alice (Sheffield) xx, 81, 83, 157
Avicenna, *see* Ibn-Sina
Awry, Joan (Wilmore) 147

Bacon, Sir Francis xix, 139
Badger, Frances (Broad), 179; George 179

Baker, Daniel 233; Daniel (d. 1601) 233; Eleanor 233; Frances 267; Joan (Taylor) 233; Katherine 233, 235; Margaret xviii, xxiii, 267, 353; Peter 267; Philippa 233
Bale, Jane (Puckering) 191; Sir John 191
Bales, Elizabeth (Thornborough) 317
Ballard, Edward 277; [James] 203, 205; Margaret (Hadley) 203; William 31
Barnard, Elizabeth (Hall, Nash) xiv, xxviii, 69, 163, 221, 352; Sir John, xxviii, 69, 221
Barnes, Alice (Middlemore) 163; Elizabeth (Parry, Rainsford) 165; Elizabeth 155; Jane (Smith) 165; [Mary] 43, 109, 111, 352; Mary (d. 1615) 109, 155; Richard 155; William (I) 153, 155, 163; William (II) xix, 155, 163, 165; William (III) 109, 153, 155, 352
Barrough, Philip xxxvii
Baskerville, Thomas 63
Bassett, Sir Arthur 47, 49; Eleanor (Chichester) 47,

49; Capt Francis xix, 47, 49, 63, 353; Sir Francis 49
Basse/Bate, Christian (Judkin) 19, 75, 187, 353; Sarah (Jackson) 19; Thomas 19
Baugh, Mary 55; Mary (Nash) xix, 55, 352; Rowland 55; Rowland jun 55; Stephen 55
Baxter, Richard 145, 317, 347
Beale, William xx, 309, 311
Beaufou, Ann (Aldersey) xxii, 135, 139, 141, 157, 352; George 141; John 177; Sir Thomas (d. 1630) xvi, xviii, xix, xxvii, 123, 125, 127, 163, 183, 314; Sir Thomas (d. 1635) 137; Thomas (d. 1622) 141; Ursula (Ferrers) 177; Ursula (Hudson) 135
Beaumont, Sir Francis 275; Mary (Compton) 255, 275, 352
Bellers, Elizabeth (Emes) 23
Benlow, Andrew 227; Clare (Peers) 227
Bettes, Mrs 7, 11, 13, 43
Betts, George 13; William 43
Bilson, Dr xvii
Bird, Dr John xxix, 199n

Bishop, Anthony 115, 117; Dorothy (Corham) 117; Elinor (Farmer) 115; George 115; John 117; Richard 115; William 117

Blencowe, Isabella (Woodward) 285

Boswell, Elinor (Rainsford) 269

Boughton, Anne 43, 47; Bridget 43; Edward (d. 1589) 43; Edward (d. 1625) 131; Edward (d. inf) 43; Elizabeth (Catesby) xvi, 33, 47, 131, 133, 352; Elizabeth (b. 1620) 43, 47; Francis 43; Joyce (Combe) 43, 45, 47, 51, 352; Katherine (Combe) 33, 43, 131, 263, 353; Richard 43; Mary 43; Thomas (b. 1602) 131; Thomas (b. 1627) 43; William 239; William (d. inf) 43; William (b. 1599) 131

Bovey, John 23, 311; Florizel 311; Margaret (Harrison) 311, 313, 335, 352; William 311

Bowles, Joseph 351

Brace, Cecily (Sheldon) 113; Francis 113

Brent, Barbara (Dixwell) 171; Dixwell 171, 352; John 171; Nathaniel 9, 317

Brett, Dorothy (Stoughton) 251; John 251

Broad, Elizabeth 179; George 179, 181; Frances (Badger) 179; Frances jun 179; William xx, xxxiv, 55, 179, 181, 352

Broad, tutor to family xx, xxx, 21, 181

Brooke, Fulke, Lord xix, 323; Robert, Lord 323; Lady 247

Browne, Bridget (Throckmorton) 183, 185, 193, 352; Elizabeth xviii, xix, 3, 183, 185, 193, 195, 313, 352; Frances (Barnes) 61; George 61, 193; Sir George 185, 193; John 193; Margaret (Littleton) 193; Thomas 193; Sir William 193

Browne, a priest, xvii, 61, 63, 77, 327

Buckingham, Duke of, (George Villiers) 275

Bulkeley, Penelope (Sandys) xiv, xviii, xix, xxix, xxx, 71, 352; Sir Richard 71

Burman, Elizabeth (Richardson) xvii, xix, 223; Thomas 223

Burton, Robert 57, 343, 347

Butler, [Robert] 213, 215, 223, 352; Robert 223; William 223

Cage, Christopher 277

Cap, Anne (Ward) 277

Carryl, Cecily (Morley) 189; Elizabeth (Smith) xvii, xix, 215, 217; Mary (Dormer) 215

Catesby, Edward 131; Elizabeth (Boughton) 131, 135, 352; Sir Richard 131

Cecil, Edward, Visc Wimbledon 279; Frances (Fiennes, Sprigge) xix, xx, 279, 281, 327, 353; Sir Henry xvii, 77

Chandler, Mrs 17, 51; Elizabeth (Quiney) 17, 51; Francis 17; William 17, 33, 73

Charles I xvii, xxiii, xxv, 49, 51, 69, 99, 195, 199, 255, 321, 349

Chesne, Joseph du 59n, 127n

Chichester, Arthur 49; Edward 49; Eleanor (Bassett) 47, 49; Sir John 49

Clark, Dorothy (Hobson, Hay) xviii, xix, xxiii, 239, 241, 352; Margaret (Alderford) 231; Sir Simon xix, xxiii, 241, 243, 251, 253, 353; Thomas (b. 1617) 253

Clavell, William xx, xl, 145, 147

Clayton, Dr Thomas 255, 257

Clopton, Anne 205; Elizabeth (Ashton) 205; John 205; Margaret (Layton) 205, 209; Thomas 205; William 205

Coke, Joan (Lee) 221; Sir John 221

Colemore, William xxi, xxvii

Collier, Letitia (Kempson) 111

Collins, Alice (Greene) xxx, 229, 231, 352; Francis 127, 229; Mary 229

Combe, Constance 239; John 151, 313; Joyce (Boughton) 43, 45, 47, 51, 352; Katherine (Boughton) 33, 43, 131, 263; Mary (Lane) 33; Mary (Wagstaffe, Rous) xix, xxix, 43, 143, 239, 263; Thomas 43, 55, 229; William 43, 131; William sen 43, 229, 239, 263

Conway, Sir Edward (d. 1546) 245; Sir Edward (d. 1631) 49, 221, 245, 247, 275; Eleanor (Greville) 245; Fulke 245; Sir John 245; Katherine (Hunks) xix, 173, 245, 247, 249, 353

Cook, Philip 155

Cookes, [Alice] 337; John 337; William 337

Cooper, Mary (Martin) 85, 119; Thomas 85; Mr Thomas 25

Corham, Dorothy (Bishop) 117

Court, Alice (Morris) xv; Elizabeth 271; Frances 271; Grace (Pargetter) 269, 271; Grace 271; John xxxvii, 271; John jun 271; Revd Joseph 271; Richard 271; Susanna 271; William 271

Cowper, Anne (Gibbs) 25; Thomas 25

Cox, Hester (Sylvester) 231; Richard 231

Crew, Sir John 265; Mary (Wagstaffe) 263

Cranfield, Lord, *see* Middlesex, Earl of

Cromwell, Oliver 91

Culpeper, Nicholas xxxiv, 59, 85, 209, 337

Dampier, William 147, 149

Daston, Elizabeth (Underhill) 123, 243; Richard 243

Davenport, Sidrak xxi, xxv, xxvii, xxviii, 135
Davies, [Frances] 115; John 115
Deacle, Anne 341; John 341; Ursula 341; William 341
Delabere, Margaret (Newman) 19, 199; Richard 199, 213
Depleurs, Mr 251
Digby, Sir Kenelm 193
Dioscorides, Pedanus xxxvi, 19, 23, 81n, 111n, 113n, 189, 257, 263n, 285, 299, 327
Dixwell, Abigail (Herdson) 171; Barbara (Brent) 171; Charles 171
Donne, John 313
Dormer, Mary (Carryl) 215; Robert, 1st Lord 215
Drake, Francis 55
Draper, William 113
Drayton, Michael xiii, 41, 313
Drummond, William 41
Dudley, Edward, Lord 147
Dugard, Elizabeth (Kimberley) 331; Henry 317, 331; Thomas xviii, 111, 193, 195, 251, 303, 317, 321, 347
Dugdale, Sir William xvii, 11, 23, 37, 43, 45, 91, 93, 97, 115, 165, 183, 193, 203, 207, 217, 229, 231, 233, 257, 299, 301
Dyson, Elizabeth (Manning) 29; Francis 31; Margaret (Hanway) 29; Robert 29; Thomas sen 29; Thomas (d. 1651) 29, 31; Thomas jun 29, 31

Edley, John 31; Mary (Spearpoint) 31
Elizabeth I, 5, 137, 205, 219, 249, 255, 297
Emes, Amy 23; Elizabeth (Bellers) 23; John (d. 1655), 23; John (b. 1608), 23; John (d. 1637), 23; Joseph 23
Essex, Countess of (Frances Howard) 317
Eugalenus, Severinus 209, 287
Evelyn, John 117n

Fane, Dorothy (Horsey)323; George 323
Farman, Mr xxii, 141
Farmer, Elinor (Bishop) 115
Farnham, Thomas (b. 1563) 143, 209; [Thomas (b. 1593)] 143
Fawcet, Margaret (Sellers) 277; Thomas xix, 275, 277, 352
Fernel, Jean 43, 131
Ferrers, Edward 177; Elizabeth (Grey) 177; Ursula (Beaufou) 177
Ferriman, Catherine 297; John 297; Magdalen (Smalwait) 297, Thomas xxi, 295, 297; Thomas jun 297; William 297
Fetherston, Isabel (Woodward, d. 1641) 285, 287; Isabel (Woodward, d. 1678) 285; John 285, 287
Fiennes, Edward 321; Frances (Cecil, Sprigge) xix, xx, 279, 281, 327, 331, 353; James 279; James jun 279; John, Col 281; William, 1st Visc 297; William, 3rd Visc 279; William 279, 327
Finch, Frances (Jones) 281, 283, 353; Thomas 281
Foreest, Pieter van 87, 189
Forestus, *see* Foreest
Forman, Simon 315, 317
Fortescue, Dorothy (Throckmorton) 79; Francis 53; Sir Francis 111; Jane (Wylde) 51; Sir John of Salden 79; John 53; Sir John 51, 53, 327; Martha (Lewis) 77, 79, 291, 331, 352; Mary (Talbot) 109, 111; Nicholas xvii, 51, 77, 293, 327, 331, 353; Prudence (Wheatley) 327; William 51, 53, 77, 205, 293, 327, 331, 352
Fracastorius 51n
Freschville, Anna Charlotte 267; John, Lord 267; Sarah (Harington) xviii, xxx, 267, 352
Fuller, Elizabeth (Wagstaffe) 85, 87, 337; Nicholas 87

Gaddesden, John of 29
Galen xxxi, xxxiii, xxxv, xxxvi, 57, 65, 105, 209
Gardner, [Elizabeth] 61, 199, 352
Garrick, David xxx
Gerard, John 3, 15, 19, 151, 163, 215, 235
Gibbard, Mary (Trapp) 209, 343
Gibbs, Anne (Cowper) 25; George 25; John 23
Goodere, Anne (Rainsford) 277, 313, 353; Sir Henry 313; Mrs Goodyear 277, 313
Goodman, [Sara] 173, 247; Thomas 173; William 5, 21, 173, 309
Gradi, Matthaeus de, 107
Greene, Anne 127, 129, 352; Anne (Harvey) 261; Alice (Collins) xxx, 229, 231, 252; John 127; Letitia (Chandler) 127; Thomas jun 229; Thomas 17, 55, 127, 129, 165, 229, 233; William 127, 229
Greville, Sir Charles 175; Sir Edward 175, 323; Eleanor (Conway) 245; Elizabeth (Swift) 323; Sir Fulke 245, 323; Margaret (Pennell) 175
Grey, Elizabeth (Ferrers) 177
Griffin, Mary (Markham) 97
Grindal, Archbishop Edmund 11
Gulson, Anthony 283
Gunn, Ann (Izod) 213

Hadley, Margaret (Ballard) 203
Hall, Elizabeth (Nash, Barnard) xiv, xxviii, 69, 163, 352; Elizabeth (Savage, Underhill) 321; Richard 321; Susanna (Shakespeare) xiv–xix, xxviii, 35, 235, 239, 353; William xiv
Hanbury, Anne (Thornborough) 21, 23, 161, 353; John sen 21; John 21
Hannes, Julian (West) xix, xxx, 93, 352; William 93

Hanslap, Dorothy 187; Elizabeth 187; Margaret (Hill) 187; Nicholas 187; Robert xix, 187, 189, 193, 333, 352; Thomas 187

Hanway, Margaret (Dyson) 29

Harcourt, Valentine 53

Harington, Sir John 267; Mary (Offley) 267; Sarah (Freschville) xviii, xxx, 267, 352

Harriott, Thomas 283

Harrison, Margaret (Bovey) 311, 352; William 311

Harvey, Anne (Greene) 261; Elizabeth (Hemming) 261; Elizabeth jun 119; Francis 261; Sir Francis xviii, xl, 117, 145, 147, 261, 263, 353; Mary (Murden) 117, 119, 167, 171, 195, 261; Mary jun 119; Stephen 261; Stephen sen xix, 117, 195, 261; Stephana 117

Harvey, Dr William xiv, 263

Hay, Dorothy (Hobson, Clark) xix, xxiii, 239, 241, 352; William 241

Heath, John 31; Mary (Edley) 31, 33

Hemming, Elizabeth (Harvey) 261

Henrietta Maria, Queen 37, 267

Henry VIII 333

Henry, Prince of Wales xxii, 249

Herbert, Mrs 39; Mary (Talbot) 111; 2nd Baron Powis 111

Herdson, Abigail (Dixwell) 171

Hill, Anne (Sturley) 243; Elizabeth 187; Margaret (Hanslap) 187; Ralph 187; Richard 243

Hippocrates xxxi, 113

Hobday, Cecily (Hopper) 291

Hobson, Dorothy (Hay, Clark) xix, xxiii, 239, 241, 352; Elizabeth (Parker) 241; Thomas xxiii, 239, 241

Holland, Susanna (Vernon) xix, 293, 295, 353; Thomas 295

Holyoak, Francis xxii, 307; Thomas 187, 307, 309

Hopper, Cecily (Hobday) 291; Robert 291; William 291

Horsey, Dorothy (Fane) 323; Fulca (Swift) xviii, 321, 323, 353; Hannibal 323; James 323

Horst, Gregor 91

Horstius, *see* Horst

Hudson xx, 165, 167; Dorothy (Aldersey) 135; Ursula (Beaufou) 135; William 135

Hunks, Conway 245; Eleanor (Archbold) 245; Elizabeth 245; Francis 247; Fulke 245, 247; Henry 247, 249; Hercules 245, 247; Katherine (Conway) xviii, xix, 173, 245, 247, 353; Mary 247; Thomas 245; Thomas jun 247

Hunt, Henry 27; Mary (Russell) xxix, 27, 91; Simon 27

Ibn-Sina xxxvi, 25n

Ingilby, Francis 217; Jane (Winter) 217

Iremonger (Mrs) xx, 191

Izod, Ann (Gunn) 213; Bridget (Penny) 213; Dorothy (Randolph) 45, 213; Francis 213; Henry xix, 199, 213, 215, 223, 243; Henry sen 213; Henry jun 213; Mary 213

Jackson, Anne 279, 283, 335; John 283; Sara (Bate) 19

James I xxii, xxxv, 7, 151, 213, 245, 247, 255

Jeake, Samuel 303

Jelfes, John 15; Joseph xx, 15; Thomas 15; William 15

Jenkinson, Anne Mary (Lee) xix, 69, 109, 221; Anthony 219; Sir Robert 219, 222

Johnson, John xv

Jones, Frances (Finch) 281, 283, 353; Robert 281

Jonson, Ben 313

Judkin, Christian (Basse) 19, 75, 187; Joan (Twigge) 75, 187, 353; Robert 75; Sara 75; Thomas 19

Kempson, Edward 57; Frances (Swift) 57; George 57, 111; Leonard xix, 57, 59, 111, 149; Letitia (Collier) 111; Margaret (Sadler, Norbury) 57, 149, 151, 183; Margaret (Sheldon) 111; Richard 111; Thomas 111

Kenton, Mrs 199

Kimberley, Elizabeth (Dugard) 331; Gilbert 331, 333; William 331, 333; William sen 331, 333

Kington, Anne 83; Elizabeth (Warde) 83; John 83

Krafftheim, Crato von 3n, 37, 173

Lane, Edward 33; Joan (Whitney) xvi, 33, 37, 185, 352; John sen 37; John jun xvi, 35, 37; Margaret (Greene) 127; Mary (Combe) 33; Nicholas 33; Richard 33, 127, 185

Lapworth, Dr Thomas 299, 303, 335

Laud, Archbishop William 307, 317

Layton, Margaret (Clopton) 205, 209

Lee, Anne Mary (Jenkinson) xix, 69, 219, 221; Joan (Coke) 221; Sir Robert (d. 1637) 219, 221; Robert (d. 1605) 219, 221

Leicester, Lettice, Countess of xxi, 217

Lennox, Duke of (Esme Stuart) xxii

Lewis, Sir Edward 293; Martha (Fortescue) 77, 79, 293, 352; Martha 293; Nicholas 293

Littleton, Sir Edward 193; Margaret (Browne) 193

Lucy, Sir Thomas xv, 243

Lynes, Humphrey sen 231; Humphrey jun 231; Joan (Richardson) xx, 233, 353

Malone, Edmond xxx

Manning, Elizabeth (Dyson) 29

Mansfeldt, Count 49

Markham, Anne (Smith) 97,

215; Elizabeth (Sheldon) 97; Mary (Griffin) 97; Thomas 97
Marshall, Edward 41
Martin, Mary (Cooper) 85
Mattioli, Pietro 153n
Mayerne, Sir Theodore Turquet de xiii, xxii, 249, 251, 265n, 283
Mesue xxxvi, 25n, 185, 221, 241, 291
Mesue, junior (pseudo Mesue) 31n
Middlemore, Alice (Barnes) 163
Middlesex, Earl of (Lord Cranfield) 347
Montagnana, Bartolomeo 159
Mordaunt, Elizabeth (Throckmorton) 183; Henry 79; Lewis 79; Mary (Throckmorton) 79, 81
Morley, Elizabeth (Puckering) xviii, 189, 191; Sir John 189; Sir William 251
Morris, Alice (Court) xv; Elizabeth (Rogers) xv; John xiv; Matthew xv; Richard xiv
Murden, Mary (Woodward) 117, 143, 167, 171, 195, 352; Mary (Harvey) xviii, 117, 167, 171, 195, 261; Richard 117, 119, 167, 195
Myrepsus, Nicolaus 27n, 53, 117, 127n, 235n, 265n

Nash, Anthony 15, 55; Elizabeth (Hall) xiv, xxviii, 55, 221, 351, 352; Mary (Baugh) xix, 55, 69, 71, 352; Thomas xxviii, 25, 55, 165, 351
Nason, Elizabeth (Rogers) 129; John 129, 131, 179, 352
Newman, Margaret (Delabere) 19, 199, 203, 213
Newton, Sir Adam 191; Sir Henry 191
Norbury, John 149; Margaret (Sadler, Kempson) xix, 57, 149, 151, 183
Northampton, Elizabeth (Spencer), Countess of xix,

xx, 1, 2, 5, 13, 17, 21, 171, 173, 185, 281, 352; Henry, 1st Lord 5; James (b. 1622) 275; Mary (Beaumont) 255, 257, 275, 352; Spencer, 2nd Earl 1, 7, 255, 257, 275, 349, 353; William, Earl of xiv, xviii, xix, 1, 5, 7, 21, 37, 123, 131, 151, 157, 255, 309, 352

Offley, Mary (Harington) 267
Overbury, Sir Thomas 317

Pakington, Dorothy (Smith) 137; Sir John 137, 139, 159; Sir John (d. 1624) 137, 352
Palmer, Jane (West) 107; John 35, 107; John jun 107
Paracelsus xxxvi, 59n, 75, 115n, 141n, 187n, 217
Pargetter, Christopher 271; Grace (Court) 271
Parker, Elizabeth (Hobson) 241; [Henry] xix, 101, 105, 155, 235, 353; Sir Henry 105
Parry, Elizabeth (Rainsford, Barnes) 165; Robert 165
Paterson, William xxx
Paul of Aegina 159
Peers, Clare (Attwood) 33, 227; Clare (Benlow) xvii, 33, 227, 229; Edmund 227; Margaret (Underhill) 227; Philip 227; Robert 227; Thomas 227; William 227
Pembroke, Earl of (William Herbert) 315
Pennell, Edward xx, 175; Margaret (Greville) 175, 323
Penny, Bridget (Izod) 213
Penrice, Isabel (Simonds) 29, 91; William 91
Pepys, Samuel 299n
Pereira, Jonathon 109
Perrott, Frances (Woodward) 305
Petre, Catherine (Talbot) 185; Elizabeth (Sheldon) xix, 99; William, Lord 99
Philips, Elizabeth (Quiney) 73; William 73
Platter, Felix 213

Pliny 101
Pomet, Pierre 109
Porter, Sir Endymion 277
Potter, Lydia (Trapp) 209, 353; William, Revd 209
Powell, [Mr] 7, 15, 17
Pridgeon, Dr [William] 251
'Psamire, Mr' xx, 197
Puckering, Cecily (Carryl) 189; Cecily 191; Elizabeth (Morley) xx, 189, 191, 229, 303; Jane (Bale) 191; Sir John 249; Sir Thomas xviii, xxii, 189, 229, 249, 251, 299, 303, 335, 353

Quercetanus, *see* Chesne
Quiney, Elizabeth (Chandler) 17, 73; Elizabeth (Philips) 73; George xviii, 73, 352; Judith (Shakespeare) 35, 73; Richard 17, 73, 243; Thomas 73, 139

Rainsford, Anne (Goodere) 41, 151, 313, 315, 353; Charles 313; Eleanor (Boswell) 269; Elizabeth (Parry, Barnes) 165; Francis (b. 1601) 151, 313; Francis jun 245; Sir Henry (d. 1622) 41, 151, 153, 269, 313, 352; Henry (b. 1599) 151, 165, 269, 313; Henry (b. 1622) 269; Hercules 151, 153, 165; Hercules (b. 1625) 269; Katherine 269
Ralegh, Sir Walter 5, 17, 141n
Randolph, Dorothy (Izod) 45, 313; Edward 45; Elizabeth (Ferrers) 45, 177, 179; Elizabeth jun 45, 119, 163, 177; Ferrers 45, 119, 177, 352; Thomas 45, 119, 177
Rawlins, Edward xviii, 115; Edward sen 115
Rawson, Arthur xv
Redi, Francesco 171
Reed, Foulke 247; Francis 269
Rhazes, *see* Al-Razi
Richardson, Elizabeth (Burman) xviii, xix, 223, 227; Joan (Lynes) xx, 231, 233, 353; John 223, 231; William 223

Riland, Frances 27; Richard 27; Thomas 27

Riverius, *see* Riviere

Riviere, Lazarus 161, 283

Roberts, Thomas xx, 121, 123, 352

Rogers, Eleanor 175; Elizabeth (Morris) xv; Elizabeth (Nason) 129; Frances xx, 175, 177, 352; John xviii, xxxix, 9, 139, 352; Margaret 177; Philip 175

Rous, Esther (Temple) xvi, xviii, 143, 145, 163, 167, 352; Hester (Sandys) 143; Isabel (Woodward) 143, 195; Sir John 143, 195, 265; John 143, 265; Mary (Combe, Wagstaffe) xix, 143, 265; Mary (Savage) 143; Thomas 145; William 167

Ruland, Martin 267n

Russell, Jane (Simonds) 29, 91; Margaret (Winter) xvi, 77, 219, 352; Mary (Hunt) xxvi, 27, 91; Richard 27; Sir Thomas 219

Rutter, Ferriman 297

Sadler, Hamnet 305; Isabel (Smart) xix, 149, 181, 183, 352; John 57, 149; Margaret (Kempson, Norbury) 57, 149, 151, 183

Sandys, Sir Edwin 71; Edwin 71; Hester (Temple) 143; Martin 71; Penelope (Bulkeley) xiv, xviii, xix, xxix, xxx, 71, 73, 277, 352; Richard 71; Sir Samuel 71; Samuel 71

Savage, Anne (Sheldon) 279; Elizabeth (Hall, Underhill) 279; John 143, 279; Mary (Rous) 143, 279; Ralph 279; Mrs xxi, 277, 279

Sellers, John 277; Katherine 277; Margaret (Fawcet) 277; Thomas 277

Sennert, Daniel 209, 235

Shakespeare, Hamnet 35; Judith (Quiney) 35, 37; Susanna, *see* Hall; William xiii, xiv, xx, xxi, xxxiii, 9 and n, 11n, 19n, 27, 35n,

37, 47n, 55, 61n, 69, 73n, 111n, 127, 139, 155, 177, 223, 227, 229, 309, 319, 323n

Shaw, Ann 7; Ann (Smith) 7, 9; July 7, 9; Raph 7

Sheffield, Alice (Austin) xx, 81, 83, 157; Elinor xx, 81, 157, 161, 352; John 81, 157; Thomas 81; Thomas jun 157

Sheldon, Anne (Savage) 279; Brace 111, 113; Brace jun 113; Cecily (Brace) 115; Edward 97, 99, 257; Edward (of Douai) 101; Elizabeth (Markham) xix, 97, 99, 352; Elizabeth (Petre) xix, 99, 101, 257, 352; Francis 155; George 101; Jane 117; Margaret (Kempson) xix, 111, 113; Ralph 205, 257; Ralph (d. 1613) 99, 279; Ralph (d. 1724) 113; William (d. 1659) 99, 257; William (of Broadway) 113; William jun 101

Sheppard, James 283

Shrewsbury, Elizabeth, Countess of 255

Simonds, George 29, 91; Elizabeth 91; Isabel (Penrice) 29, 91, 93; Jane (Russell) 29, 91; Mary 91; Thomas 91

Slater, Robert 243

Smalwait, Magdalen (Ferriman) 297

Smart, Isabel (Sadler) xix, 149, 181, 352; Peter 149, 181

Smith, Anne (Markham) 97, 215; Ann (Shaw) 79, 353; Sir Charles 79, 215, 217; Dorothy (Pakington) 137; Elizabeth (Carryl) xvii, xix, 215, 217; Frances (Wilson) 161; Francis 231, 305, 307; Sir Francis 97, 215; Henry 7; Jane (Barnes) 165; John 93, 97; Margaret (Sylvester) 223, 305, 307, 352; Mary (Winter) 217, 219; Mary (Throckmorton) 79, 217; Rafe xv, 35; Ursula (Ainge) 231, 305,

307; William 305; [Mrs] 235

Somerset, Earl of (Robert Carr) 317

Somerville, Sir William 127

Spearpoint, Mary (Edley) 31

Spencer, Elizabeth (Compton) xix, 1, 3, 5, 352; Sir John 1, 5

Sprigge, Frances (Cecil, Fiennes) xix, xx, 281, 327, 352; Joshua 281

Stephens, Joanna 315

Stoker, Elizabeth xx, xxx, 101, 257, 261

Stone, Nicholas 303

Stoughton, Anthony 251, 333, 335; Anthony sen 333; Dorothy (Brett) 333; Dorothy 333, 335; Edith (Young) 311, 333, 335, 341, 343, 347, 353; Mercy 333; Nathaniel 333

Sturley, Abraham xv, 243, 245; Anne (Hill) 243; Katherine 243, 245, 353

Swift, Elizabeth (Greville) 323; Frances (Kempson) 57; Sir Francis 321, 323; Francis 323; Fulca (Horsey) xx, 321, 323, 353

Sylvester, Hester (Cox) 231, 305; Margaret (Smith) 223, 305, 352; Paul 231

Symons, John xix, 83, 85

Talbot, Catherine (Petre) 185; Francis, 11th Earl 111; George xviii, 109, 185, 352; George, 9th Earl 185; Gertrude (Winter) 77, 185, 217; Gilbert 111; Sir John 33, 77, 111, 137, 185; John, 10th Earl 109; Mary xvii, xxx, 185, 187; Mary (Fortescue) 109, 352; Mary (Herbert) 111

Taylor, Joan (Baker) 233; Dr Samuel 283

Temple, Esther (Rous) xv, xvi, 143, 145, 163, 167, 352; Peter 143; Sir Thomas 143; Lady xix

Thoner, Augustus 105, 123, 127, 161, 313

Thonerius, *see* Thoner

Thornborough, Anne

(Hanbury) 21, 33, 353; Benjamin 317; Edward 315; Elizabeth (Bales) 317; Elizabeth (Willoughby) 319; Helen (Acton) 319; Bishop John xiv, xviii, xix, xxv, 11, 247, 315, 317, 319, 333, 353; John jun 21; Thomas 317, 319
Throckmorton, Anne 79; Bridget (Browne) 183, 193, 352; Catherine 217; Clement 183, 193, 207; Clement jun 183, 193; Dorothy (Fortescue) 79; Elizabeth (Mordaunt) 183; Francis 79, 183, 193; Sir George 183; Job 183; Mary (Smith) 79, 217; Sir Robert (d. 1651) 79; Robert jun 185; Thomas 79
Tichborne, Sir Richard 193
Totnes, Earl of 41
Trapp, John xviii, xix, 73, 145, 209, 343, 347, 353; Lydia (Potter) xviii, 209, 353; Mary (Gibbard) 209, 343; Simon 9, 351
Trevor, Tudor, Lord of Hereford 165
Twigge, Henry 75; Joan (Judkin) 75, 187, 353
Twitchet, Henry 11
Tyler, Richard jun 305; Richard 223, 305; Susanna (Woodward) 305; William 305
Tyrrell, Lady (Elizabeth) xxi

Underhill, Alice (Visc. St Albans) 123; Anne (b. 1622) 211; Anne 243; Catherine (Uvedale) xix, 211, 353; Sir Edward (d. 1641) xix, 115, 211, 213, 352; Edward sen 211; Elizabeth (Daston) 123, 243; Elizabeth (Hall, Savage) 321; Francis 195; Fulk 319, 321; George xix,

195, 197, 243, 353; Sir Hercules 289, 321; Jane 211; Sir John 123; Margaret (Peers) 227; Richard 243; Simon xix, 279, 319, 321; Thomas (b. 1622) xviii, xxix, 123, 127, 353; Thomas (d. 1622) 123, 243; Thomas (d. 1669) xix, 195, 197, 243; William 319
Uvedale, Catherine (Underhill) xix, 211, 353; Sir William 211

Vernon, Edward 293; Revd John 293, 295, 297; Revd Richard 293; Richard 295; Susanna (Holland) xix, 293, 295, 297, 353

Wagstaffe, Sir Combe 263; Elizabeth (Fuller) 85, 87, 337, 353; Mary (Combe, Rous) xix, xxix, 143, 263, 265; Mary (Crew) 263, 265; Thomas 83, 263; Thomas jun 87, 263; Timothy 85, 87, 263; Timothy jun 87
Walker, Augustine 65; John 65, 209, 353; Thomas 65
Ward, Anne (Cap) 277; Anne (b. 1610) 277; Edward 277; Edward (d. 1613) 277; Frances 277
Warde, Elizabeth (Kington) 83
Webster, John 197n
Welsh, James 191
West, Jane (Palmer) 107; John 93, 107; John jun 93; Julian (Hannes) xix, xxxiv, 93, 107, 352
Westmorland, Earl of 323
Wheatley, Prudence (Fortescue) 327
Whitney, Henry 33, 185; Joan (Lane) xv, 33, 185, 352
Willoughby, Elizabeth (Thornborough) 319

Wilmore, Joan (Awry) 147; Mary 147; Richard 147; Richard (d. 1626) 147, 352; Richard (d. 1650) 147, 149; Thomas (Wilmer) 147
Wilson, Anne 11; Mrs Anne 299, 335, 337; Frances (Smith) 161; Grindal 11; Mary xl, 39; [Robert] 159, 161, 352; Robert 9; Thomas xviii, xxiii, xxv, 9, 11, 139, 335; Thomas sen 9
Wincoll, Mrs xx, xxx, 21
Winter, George 77, 217, 219; Sir George 77, 217, 219; Gertrude (Talbot) 77, 185, 217, 219; Helen 75; Jane (Ingilby) 217; John 75, 77, 79, 352; John 217, 219; Margaret (Russell) xvii, 77, 217, 219, 352; Mary (Smith) 217; Robert (d. 1606) 75, 185, 217; Robert (d. 1630) 219; Thomas 217
Wirsung, Christoph 77, 159, 175, 241
Wirtzung, see Wirsung
Woodall, John xxvii
Woodward, Frances (Perrott) 305; Isabel (Fetherston, d. 1641) 285, 287; Isabel (Fetherston) 285, 287, 295; Isabel (Rous) 143, 195; Isabella (Blencowe) 285; John (d. 1625) 285; John (d. 1665) 285; Mary (Murden) 117, 143, 167, 171, 195, 352; Richard (b. 1604) 285; Richard (d. 1557) 287; Susanna (Tyler) 305; Thomas 195
Wylde, Jane (Fortescue) 51; Sir John 51

Young, Edith (Stoughton) 311, 333, 335, 341, 343, 353; Thomas 333, 335

INDEX OF PLACES

Places are in Warwickshire unless otherwise stated.
Stratford-upon-Avon references are not indexed.

Abington, Northants. xxviii, 69

Acton, Mddx xxviii, 69, 351

Admington 323

Alcester xxix, 23, 107, 149, 311

Alderminster 195

Alveston xv, 33, 127, 185, 227

Apethorpe, Northants. 323

Ardens Grafton 57

Arrow 83, 245, 247, 249

Ashby Folville, Leics. 79

Ashby St Ledgers, Northants. 131

Aston Cantlow 93

Aston-sub-Edge, Glos. 275, 277

Atherington, Devon 47, 49

Augsburg, Germany xxxv

Avon Dassett 285

Awre, Glos. 277

Aynho, Northants. 187

Aylesbury, Bucks. 159

Badsey, Worcs. 199

Baddesley Clinton 45

Bagworth, Leics. 267

Banbury, Oxon. 5, 281

Barcheston 163, 171

Barford 251

Barnham, Sussex 193

Bath, Som. 199, 335

Beaumaris, Ang. 69

Bedwardine, Worcs. 249

Bedwas, Mon. 293

Belbroughton, Worcs. 99

Belfast, Co. Antrim 249

Bengeo, Herts. 261

Bengeworth, Worcs. 341

Beoley, Worcs. 97, 99, 257

Bidford-on-Avon 179, 253

Billesley 67, 219, 221

Bilton 131

Binton 111, 283, 335

Birdingbury 307

Birlingham, Worcs. 293

Birmingham xxiii, 119, 283

Bishops Tachbrook 87, 263, 265, 303

Bishopton xxii

Bordesley, Worcs. 179

Bradley, Worcs. 27

Brailes 115, 117, 321

Braughing, Herts. 261

Bretforton, Worcs. 271

Bristol, Som. 127, 227, 315, 335

Broadway, Worcs. 113, 117, 321

Bromsgrove, Worcs. 331

Broom 239, 243, 251, 253

Broughton, Oxon. 5, 279, 281, 327

Budbrooke 147

Bulkington 333

Burford, Oxon. 231, 305

Bushwood xxvi, xxvii

Butlers Marston 195, 303

Callicroft, Worcs. 311

Cambridge, Cambs. xiv, xv, xxiii, 239, 243, 261, 275, 297

Carlton, Beds. xiv

Carlton, Leics. 191

Castle Ashby, Northants. 1, 5, 13, 173, 275

Cawston 43, 45, 47

Charlbury, Oxon. 219, 221

Charlecote xiv, 165, 243

Cherington 257

Churchover 171

Clifford Chambers 41, 151, 153, 163, 269, 277, 313

Coleorton, Leics. 275

Combe, Hants. 269

Compton Wynyates 1, 5, 7, 275, 309

Cookhill, Worcs. xvii, 51, 53, 63, 77, 143, 279, 327, 331

Coton 171

Coughton 79, 183

Coventry xv, 195, 307, 313

Crayford, Kent 281

Croome d'Abitot, Worcs. 343

Crowle, Worcs. 29, 91

Cuddington, Bucks. 177

Denbigh, Denbs. 167

Derby, Derbys. 255

Douai, France 61, 101, 257

Doverdale, Worcs. 113

Drake's Broughton, Worcs. 311, 321

Droitwich, Worcs. 113, 137, 331

Dublin, Rep. of Ireland 165

Dumbleton, Glos. 123, 243

Dunchurch 43, 47

Edgbaston 163

Edgehill 73

Edinburgh, Scotland xxxi

Edington, Wilts. 293

Elmesthorpe, Leics. 267

Elmley Lovett, Worcs. 319

Emscote xxii, 135, 139, 143, 157, 177

Erith, Kent 191

Eton, Berks. 275

Ettington 195, 211, 227, 243

Evesham, Worcs. 139, 243

Exeter, Devon 63

Feckenham, Worcs. 145

Fladbury, Worcs. 297

Florence, Italy xxxv

Flyford Flavell, Worcs. 27

Glaseley, Salop. 51

Grafton, Worcs. xvii, 109, 111, 185, 187, 217

Grafton Flyford, Worcs. 331

Great Lever, Lancs. 205

Greenwich, Kent 191

Grendon, Northants. 279

Guilden Morden, Cambs. 241

Guy's Cliffe 135

Halnaker, Sussex 189, 251

Hampton Lovett, Worcs. 137

Hampton-on-the-Hill 333

Hanbury, Worcs. 293, 295

Hanley Castle, Worcs. 333

Harbury 337

Hardingstone, Northants. 117, 261

Harting, Sussex 189, 191

Hartlebury, Worcs. 317

Hartshill 41

Harvington, Worcs. 249, 295, 297

Haseley 183, 193

Haselor 111

Heanton Punchardon, Devon 49

Henley-in-Arden 233
Highgate, Mddx 87, 281
Holkham, Norf. 331
Honeybourne, Glos. 221
Honington 83, 93, 105, 107
Hopton Heath, Derbys. 255
Huddington, Worcs. xvii, 75,
    77, 185, 217, 219
Hunningham 323

Idlicote 319, 321
Ilmington 65, 171, 203
Inkberrow, Worcs. 29, 31, 51,
    203, 327

Kempsey, Worcs. 51
Kenilworth 253
Kineton 303
King's Coughton 311
Knaresborough, Yorks. 317
Knowle 83

Ladyholt, Sussex 189, 191
Lambcote 243
Lapworth 131
Latimers, Bucks. 143
Lawford 43, 47, 131, 239
Leamington Priors 65, 303
Ledwell Park, Oxon. 217
Leicester, Leics. 127, 141,
    143
Leigh, Worcs. 175
Lenchwick, Worcs. 269
'Libington' 31
Lillington 303
Limerick, Lim, Rep. of
    Ireland 165, 315
Lindridge, Worcs. 175
Lisburn, Co. Down 249
Lisnargarvey, Antrim 249
Llancarfan, Glam. 293
London xxii, xxvii, xxviii, 35,
    37, 41, 69, 87, 123, 249,
    267, 275, 285, 293, 297,
    315, 341, 351
Long Compton 13, 309
Long Marston 105
Loxley 123, 197, 253, 291
Luddington xxii, 31, 337, 347
Ludlow, Salop. xiv, 1, 7, 11,
    13, 15, 43

Marston St Lawrence,
    Northants. 285
Maryland, USA 227
Mathon, Worcs. 175
Melbourne, Derbys. 221

Milcote 17, 269
Milton Malsor, Northants.
    117, 261
Mitcham, Surrey 33, 185
Monkstown, Cork, Rep. of
    Ireland 247
Montpellier, France xiv
Moreton Morrell 117, 119,
    167, 195, 261
Morton Underhill, Worcs. 29

Namur, Belgium 99
Newbold-on-Avon 135
Newbold Revel 241, 253
Newnham 93
Norton-by-Lenchwick,
    Worcs. 297
Norton Curlieu 147
Nuremburg, Germany xxxv

Old Stratford 157, 161, 239
Ollerton, Notts. 97, 215
Ombersley, Worcs. xiii, xiv,
    71, 203
Oversley 83, 111
Oxford, Oxon. xv, 9, 45, 65,
    117, 177, 195, 211, 255,
    275, 293, 295, 307, 315,
    343
Oxhill 115, 117, 195, 243

Packwood 285, 287
Pavenham, Beds. xv, 243
Pebworth, Glos. 85
Pillaton, Staffs. 193
Pillerton Hersey 243
Pillerton Priors 171, 211
Polesworth 313
Pontoise, France 217
Preston on Stour 245

Quinton 27, 115
Quorndon, Leics. 141

Radbrook, Glos. 245
Radford Semele 183, 193
Ragley 221, 247
Reigate, Surrey 117
Ripley, Yorks. 217
Rous Lench, Worcs. 143,
    145, 163, 167, 195, 265,
    347
Rowington 177, 327
Royden, Essex 321
Royston, Herts. 321

Saintbury, Glos. 213

St Fagans, Glam. 293
Salden, Bucks. 79, 109
Salerno, Italy xxxi
Salford Priors 45, 105, 107,
    119, 177, 241, 253
Salisbury, Wilts. 151
Sedgeberrow, Worcs. 213
Shipston-on-Stour 61
Shottery xxii, xxiii, 223, 305
Sledwich, Durham 205
Snitterfield 303, 337
Southam 19, 75, 187, 251
Southam, Glos. xxix, 19, 199
Stanton, Glos. 45
Staveley, Derbys. 267
Stock Green, Worcs. 27
Stone, Staffs. 111
Stoneythorpe 307
Strensham, Worcs. 219
Suckley, Worcs. 21
Sutton Coldfield xv

Tachbrook Mallory 265
Talton 101, 105, 109, 121,
    155, 163
Tamworth 249
Tanworth-in-Arden 109
Tehidy, Cornw. 49
Temple Grafton 111, 113,
    137
Toddington, Glos. 213
Tredington 153
Turvey, Beds. 79
Twining, Glos. 55
Tysoe 139, 155

Umberleigh, Devon 49
Utkinton, Ches. 265

Walcot, Oxon. 219
Walton 183
Warwick xv, 5, 85, 87, 135,
    139, 141, 189, 191, 215,
    217, 229, 249, 263, 265,
    299, 303, 307, 321, 333,
    337, 341, 347
Welcombe 55, 233
Westminster, Middx 267
Weston-on-Avon 99, 175,
    257, 279, 347
Weston sub Edge, Glos. 277
Weston Underwood, Bucks.
    79
Westwood, Worcs. 137, 159
Weybridge, Surrey 29
White Ladies Aston, Worcs.
    29, 91

Whitford, Worcs. 331
Whitnash 307
Whorlton, Durham 205
Wickham, Hants. 211
Wickhamford, Worcs. 71
Wilby, Suff. 317
Wixford xvii

Wood Bevington 45, 119,
    177
Woodson, Worcs. 175
Wotton Wawen 79, 191, 215
Worcester, Worcs. xiv, xv,
    xviii, 21, 23, 35, 37, 53, 91,
    101, 135, 137, 145, 161,

175, 227, 247, 249, 297,
    317, 319, 343
Writtle, Essex 99

Yardley Hastings, Northants.
    173
York, Yorks. 255, 315